Woman Suffrage and the Origins of Liberal Feminism in the United States, 1820–1920

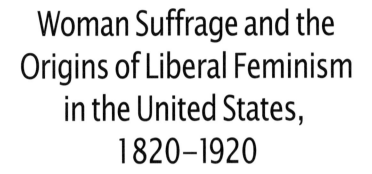

Woman Suffrage and the Origins of Liberal Feminism in the United States, 1820–1920

Suzanne M. Marilley

Harvard University Press
Cambridge, Massachusetts
London, England
1996

Text design by Joyce C. Weston

Library of Congress Cataloging-in-Publication Data

Marilley, Suzanne M.
Woman suffrage and the origins of liberal feminism in the United
States, 1820–1920 / Suzanne M. Marilley.
p. cm.
Includes bibliographical references and index.
ISBN 0-674-95465-3 (cloth : alk. paper)
1. Women—Suffrage—United States—History.
2. Feminism—United States—History. I. Title.
JK1896.M37 1996
324.6'23'0973—dc20
96-26328

For Cecilia Marilley Burke

with hope for a fuller inclusion of women

in the future American polity

Contents

Figures

Preface

Winning the Nineteenth Amendment was not easy. Before achieving the right to vote, American woman suffragists suffered many defeats and often had to rethink their strategies. This book explains why the vote mattered to the women who struggled for it. By restoring memories of women's reasons for wanting to overcome profound and pervasive opposition to their political inclusion as full citizens, perhaps women's commitment to voting can be revived and deepened.

Primary sources in my research, especially newspapers, pamphlets, and personal correspondence, helped me to reconstruct the reform networks and small-group decision making and to analyze the reformers' appeals. The minutes of the woman's rights and woman suffrage conventions in the six-volume *History of Woman Suffrage in the United States,* edited by Elizabeth C. Stanton and several other woman suffrage leaders, is the main source of basic data. The *Woman's Journal,* the *Rocky Mountain News,* and other newspapers provided substantial information about the Colorado campaigns. I have updated the spelling of words that have changed. I have also respected the nineteenth-century women's use of the terms "*woman's* rights" and "*woman* suffrage"; but I refer to them as "women."

Portions of Chapter 4 originally appeared in my article "Frances Willard and the Feminism of Fear," published in *Feminist Studies* 19, no. 1 (spring 1993) and are used here by permission. This book was aided by a summer stipend from the Institute of Scholarship in the Liberal Arts, University of Notre Dame.

Many excellent libraries, teachers, colleagues, research assistants, friends, and relatives have made this book possible. I cannot thank everyone by name here; please accept my gratitude. I received much encouragement early in this project from Martha Ackelsberg, Philip Green, Theda Skocpol, and James Q. Wilson. Portions of this book are derived from my dissertation, "Why the Vote? Woman Suffrage and the Politics of Democratic Development in the United States, 1820–1893," and I am indebted to my advisors Janet Giele, H. Douglas Price, and Sidney Verba for their wise and patient mentoring. Several conversations with the late Judith N.

Shklar during final stages of the dissertation set the course for this book. I am particularly grateful to Rogers M. Smith and Jane Jebb Mansbridge for their insightful criticisms of the book manuscript.

I appreciate the comments and criticism I received from Joan Aldous, Steve Amberg, Peri Arnold, Linda Austern, Gail Bederman, Alfons Beitzinger, Gerald Berk, Janet Boles, the late Ruth Bordin, Rebecca Bordt, Mary Ann Borrelli, D'A. Jonathan D. Boulton, Maureen Boulton, Jacqueline V. Brogan, Michael Brownstein, Peter Bruce, Mari Jo Buhle, Shelley Burtt, Carol Christy, Michael Crowe, Martha H. Davis, Jane DeHart, Georgia Duerst-Lahti, Jean Elshtain, Kenneth Finegold, Donald Fixico, faculty and students associated with Gender Studies at the University of Notre Dame, Teresa Ghilarducci, Nathan O. Hatch, Vicki Hattam, Suellen Hoy, Lynn Joy, Rita Mae Kelley, Mary Lou Kendrigan, Jeanne H. Kilde, David Klein, Donald Kommers, Dave Leege, David Levine, Alisdair MacIntyre, Ida L. Mann, William Mayer, the Reverend Richard A. McCormick, Eileen McDonagh, Nancy S. Milburn, Richard Milburn, Barbara J. Nelson, Walter T. K. Nugent, Marc O'Brien, Sharon L. O'Brien, William O'Rourke, Erskine Peters, Ava Preacher, Philip L. Quinn, L. John Roos, Penny A. Russell, Valerie L. Sayers, Kathryn Kish Sklar, Sarah Slavin, Margaret Susan Thompson, James Wagman, A. Peter Walshe, Paul Weithman, Martin H. Wolfson, and Frederick D. Wright. I accepted most, but not all, of their suggestions. I am responsible for any remaining errors in this book.

Professional staffs of the Widener and the Schlesinger libraries helped me complete my early research. I especially thank Veronica Cunningham, Rodney Dennis, Barbara Haber, and Karen Morgan. Similarly, the staffs of the State Historical Society of Colorado, the Western History Department of the Denver Public Library, the Archives of the University of Colorado at Boulder, and the manuscript collections at both the Library of Congress and the New York Public Library were gracious and patient guides to the materials in their archives. The quotations from the papers of Carrie Chapman Catt are from the Carrie Chapman Catt Papers, Rare Books and Manuscripts Division, The New York Public Library, Astor, Lenox and Tilden Foundations, and are used here by permission. James Fell, a historian, made special efforts to introduce me to the Colorado libraries. I especially thank Al Epstein for his help at the Frances E. Willard Memorial Library in Evanston, Illinois. My thanks also go to the staff of the Hesburgh Library at the University of Notre Dame, particularly Maureen Gleason, Linda K. Gregory, and G. Margaret Porter. I am grateful to Melvin L. Ankeny of the Ohio State University library for his assistance in obtaining a photograph for the figure "Waiting in Ambush." Jo Ellen Locke of the

Capital University library contributed resourceful ideas for research on electronic databases.

I appreciate the extraordinary contributions that Brian Burchett, Betsy R. Burke, Frank Colucci, Louise H. Filipic, Joni Gibley, Kathy Marko, Lisa Morgan, Crescent Muhammad, Cathy Rodrigues, Bridget Weishaar, and Kathy Welsh made in the way of editorial or research support to this project. I am indebted to Margaret M. Jasiewicz and Jennifer Morehead for the computer production of this manuscript and to my husband, Robert P. Burke, for the electronic illustrations.

I extend my gratitude to the editors at Harvard University Press, particularly Aïda Donald, Donna Bouvier, Julie Carlson, and Elizabeth Suttell, for their patience and for their rapid responses to my questions.

My family has taught me to be faithful to my work, and they have reminded me to have faith in myself. During the Progressive era, my grandfather, the late Ralph J. Marilley, and my great-aunt, the late Cornelia O'Loughlin, became firmly dedicated to higher education. In this time of weakening commitment to the study of ideas, I continue to take inspiration from their convictions. I particularly thank Joan and Richard Marilley and Marjorie and David Ransom for their generous hospitality during my research at the Library of Congress. I deeply appreciate the unconditional support that my parents, Catherine and James Marilley, have provided throughout this project. And finally, I thank Bob and our daughter, Cecilia, for their abundant love, unfailing joy, and gracious toleration during the past few years.

Introduction

*J*UST OVER seventy-five years ago the ratification of the Nineteenth Amendment to the Constitution of the United States guaranteed women the right to vote. This victory, after more than seventy years of struggle, represents one of the first peaceful transformations of a politically excluded group into an included group. Without a violent civil war, native-born, white American men vested women with equal voice in the selection of elected representatives and with the opportunity to become candidates for elective office. The story of how women won the vote reveals how a group that lacked direct political power generated a willingness among men to share this power.

Women's conversion from "second-class citizens"[1] to full members of the electorate was a profound political change: before the nineteenth century there had been no collective efforts to make women the political equals of men. The American Revolution elevated the liberal and republican ideals that eventually caused a minority of educated native-born, middle-class white women to seek political inclusion. Campaigns of native-born, propertyless white men for the vote as well as abolitionism inspired women to question whether maleness was an appropriate qualification for suffrage.[2] Eventually men who were committed to universal equal rights, such as Frederick Douglass and Henry B. Blackwell, encouraged elite women to seek political inclusion. But the idea of inherited biological differences between women and men introduced such new issues into women's quest for inclusion that the paths could not be predetermined. The assertion that women could and should be political equals was considered so radical that most women and men initially cast it aside.[3]

Some scholars portray woman suffrage as a political reform sold to the American public by elite leaders who exaggerated both its potential and its promise so that they could restore or gain a sense of belonging to the white male polity.[4] Although native-born, middle-class, white women led the struggle for woman suffrage,[5] it is important to remember that they sought a liberal goal that was perceived as radical.

The many contradictions in the suffragists' ideologies—which reveal the reformers' elitism, racism, and ethnocentric prejudices—have been thoroughly analyzed by Aileen Kraditor. Kraditor, along with William O'Neill, argued that the suffragists lost the potential to participate in radical egalitarian political and social transformations when they put self-interest first.[6] Both historians offer compelling explanations for the lack of visible and immediate change after women won the vote. But this approach measures woman suffragists' achievement by too high a standard: in reality, the suffragists had to overcome the view that women were inherently "better" than men and that voting would make them less good. Moreover, to advance their cause in political environments that treated racial segregation, white supremacy, and nativist ideologies as respectable, these leaders had to promote women's unique qualifications for the vote. Inegalitarian assumptions certainly did not vanish after women won voting rights; indeed, sexist ideas probably hindered many women from voting.[7] To expect that woman suffragists could have been the vanguard of a radical egalitarian transformation of American politics severely underestimates the ideological, organizational, and behavioral obstacles they had to overcome.

This book demonstrates that although native-born, white American woman suffragists were limited agents of radical reform because they were elites, they nevertheless encouraged liberal and egalitarian change, developed shrewd strategies to achieve it, and usually made strides as they corrected their mistakes. None of the elite women who led this movement would have denied her identity as a privileged person; indeed, to have been born to financially secure parents and raised in religious denominations that not only considered women men's equals but also encouraged their leadership provided the first American feminists with the money, self-respect, and confidence necessary for launching and sustaining radical challenges.[8]

By demanding equal rights and the vote for women, woman suffragists introduced liberal feminist dissent into a wheel that was already turning against absolute power in the forms of monarchy, "hegemonic church establishments," "near-subsistence agricultural economies," and "scholastic orthodoxies."[9] As native-born, white, mostly Protestant men struggled to prevent the rise of any public authorities with absolutist powers in the United States, women in their midst insisted that men take a critical look at the absolute powers that they themselves exercised over women. In the struggle, woman's rights reformers and woman suffragists developed three types of liberal arguments, each predominant during a different phase of the movement: the feminism of equal rights, which called for freedom through equality; the feminism of fear, which advocated putting an end to men's cruelty to women; and the feminism of personal development, which called for women's freedom through opportunities to become full persons.[10]

Generally, woman's rights reformers and woman suffragists defined their goals as liberal: they cared more about personal freedom for each woman than about making the powers of government more equally divided, increasing voter turnout, or encouraging women to agree on a comprehensive feminist reform agenda.[11] Indeed initially the reformers relied so heavily on the rationality of liberal egalitarian principles that they expected educated persons to revise both laws and personal behavior to fit such principles.[12] But their arguments were rejected, and early liberal feminists had to search for ways to counter the assumption that only men deserved full citizenship.

Their quest resulted in a clash between egalitarian "liberal" and inegalitarian "illiberal" ideas about "woman's proper place."[13] The liberal principle held that because all persons possess natural rights, all must be guaranteed political rights and stand as equal citizens. Opponents argued that natural rights could not displace naturally ordained differences between the sexes. The premise of this still popular illiberal perspective is that females possess natural talents for child-raising and men possess natural talents for protecting women and children. Illiberals argued, in short, that even if women possessed natural rights, they lacked the talents, knowledge, and informed perspective necessary to make appropriate political judgments.

During the early nineteenth century, illiberal ideas shaped women's political standing and opportunities. The social contract theorists who introduced liberal doctrines—Hobbes, Locke, and Rousseau—all excluded women from full citizenship. Hobbes and Locke each granted women some equality and an ambiguous standing in nature, but both insisted that political relations between women and men were inegalitarian.[14] Rousseau assumed from the start that women lacked natural capacities to participate in political decision-making. Carole Pateman explains that these theorists developed their visions of modern government upon the premise that natural and biological differences between the sexes require a sexual contract that predates the social contract. She defines the *sexual contract* as an unstated but logically necessary assumption that women transfer their natural rights to men in exchange for protection and that this transferal of rights makes women obedient to men.[15] After the transferal, male domination takes on a brotherly form: it allows for men's rule as equals (fraternity in the literal sense constitutes modern patriarchy). According to these modern theories of government, men's domination of women is simultaneously sexual and political; as men's political subjects, women cannot be men's political equals. The presumed inequality between men and women thus becomes a formative model for all forms of political domination.[16]

The clash of ideas over the political inclusion of women reveals the intractable character of the political problem faced by woman suffragists. Unable to deny sex differences between men and women and the part that these differences had played in the development of a division of life's labors, liberals lacked proof from reigning political theories and from social reality to support universal personal freedom. The difficulty of achieving liberal goals for women was compounded when antisuffragists refused to deny that women possessed natural rights. Following promises made by Hobbes and Locke, they affirmed women's *natural* rights but pointed to natural differences to deny *equal political* rights for women. Opponents of woman's rights justified the political exclusion of women by invoking the two major political traditions that emerged in the American colonies: an elitist republican tradition and the Americanist tradition.[17] These traditions cast doubt upon the aim of political equality and forced woman suffragists to define their goal as "inclusion," or membership—a lesser standing than full political equality would provide.

Proponents of elitist republicanism esteemed popular government; however, to create a public order based on homogeneous ideas and rules as well as protections for local control, republican leaders eschewed equal participation. Rulers should be guided by popular demands, but strong communities required each person and subgroup to contribute their particular talents to the achievement of the common good. Women were politically excluded because it was thought that they best contributed to the common good by putting their energies into domestic affairs.

The Americanist tradition was more illiberal than elitist republicanism in its attitudes toward those who did not share a native-born, white, Anglo-Saxon, Protestant male heritage. This tradition was established by the nineteenth-century descendants of the founders and the earliest colonial settlers, who believed that the special "American" mixture of liberal freedom and republican responsibility was a product of their own special, superior culture, if not biology.[18] Thus, proponents of the Americanist tradition endorsed liberal principles and republican standards for self-governance but not for groups considered different and inferior at varied points in time such as Catholics, Jews, Irish, Italians, Germans, native

American Indians, blacks, and Asians. Because this tradition celebrated the "manners and customs" by which its people had endured and prospered, Americanists fully supported the political exclusion of women. Rogers Smith observes that in the United States patriarchy's defenders have frequently resorted to Americanist discourse "by making joint appeals to traditions, customs, the common law, the 'natural order of things,' and the divine ordinance, that all define a special 'American way of life.'"[19]

The premises of the elitist republican and Americanist traditions show that opponents of woman's rights and antisuffragists were neither undemocratic nor entirely opposed to liberal advances: many republicans supported the political inclusion of Irish, Italian, Asian, and black men. Indeed, much of nineteenth-century American political history consisted of liberal republican efforts to create political equality among men—to make government more democratic by wiping away Americanist defenses of qualifications for citizenship. Defenders of the Americanist tradition could support the idea that women ought to be politically subordinated, but they made certain exceptions, especially regarding transfer of property and education, for women perceived as kin. Demands for woman's rights and woman suffrage also were justified with illiberal arguments. Some women's reformers argued quite convincingly that women deserved the vote because of the contributions they made as mothers; others argued less persuasively that America needed the votes of native-born, educated, white Protestant women.

Adapting Republican Motherhood to Liberal Feminist Aims

As Linda Kerber explains, republican motherhood emerged after the American Revolution as an ideological tradition and support structure that made wives and mothers counselors of virtue for their husbands and sons.[20] By remaining outside politics and without vested interests, women could provide objective moral guidance to their husbands and sons about voting and other political issues. Women's essential political purpose required them to remain politically excluded and was a deterrent to resistance of that exclusion. The tradition of republican motherhood defined women as essentially better than men, so full citizenship was inappropriate for and potentially damaging to women.[21]

This ideology easily shaped women's consciousness as moral authorities who were least equal to men. It also provided native-born, middle-class white women with a common moral purpose and the opportunity both to resist and to generate change despite their political exclusion.

Those who believed that virtue could thrive only if women remained detached counselors refused to challenge the political exclusion of women. Instead, they advocated *cultural feminization,* women's nonpolitical encouragement of virtue.[22] Others, particularly men and women committed to moral reform movements such as antislavery and temperance, began to argue that women's voices were needed in political decision-making and that justice required women to become moral reformers *in public.*[23]

The goals of woman's rights were inspired by the liberal and republican intellectual revolutions of the eighteenth century. Judith Sargent Murray, Mary Wollstonecraft, and Frances Wright articulated early modern liberal feminist visions of women's full political inclusion. These political ideas differed from men's tendencies to make universal claims for rights and popular sovereignty but to apply them only to men. These daring thinkers esteemed the concepts of liberal freedom and republican responsibility promoted by progressive men and looked forward to a day when such ideals would apply universally.[24]

The three dissenting political ideologies of American woman's rights reformers and woman suffragists were built upon these women's early visions. Each had distinctive themes to mobilize supporters against different forms of opposition to their cause. The feminism of equal rights was the most consistently inclusive ideology; it emerged during the Jacksonian era to counter those opposed to women's public participation in Garrisonian antislavery reform. The feminism of fear—the defense of women's right to live free from fear of violent injury or death perpetrated particularly by drunken men—flourished after the Civil War when the female-founded temperance crusade tried to stop male social drinking. By the early 1900s a new generation of suffragists articulated a feminism of personal development that aimed to secure full opportunities for women to pursue happiness.

Feminism of Equal Rights

The feminism of equal rights prevailed from the Jacksonian era until the mid-1870s. Inclusive egalitarian liberal principles, spelled out in the 1848 Seneca Falls Declaration of Sentiments, a feminist version of the 1776 Declaration of Independence, insisted that women's natural rights be recognized as no less sacred than men's. Collective support for feminist ideals of equal rights grew in the Garrisonian antislavery movement where, in the 1830s, Maria Stewart and Angelina and Sarah Grimké practiced an inclusive equality that was derived as much from the Scriptures as from the 1776 Declaration. In the 1850s, proponents of this feminism called for radical structural changes in marriage, the political system, and society; but these reformers' debates revealed a willingness to put limits on divorce rights and to portray female enfranchisement as unthreatening to the family. After the Civil War, the feminism of equal rights diminished in power but did not disappear entirely.

Elizabeth Cady Stanton, daughter of a lawyer and mother of seven, was the movement's most consistent and daring liberal thinker during the 1850s. Stanton applied the universal concept of equal rights to all aspects of women's lives and endorsed women's rights to divorce and to control the timing of pregnancies. Opposed to the Fourteenth and Fifteenth Amendments because they failed to grant women rights extended to black men, Stanton later became known for her introduction of nativist feminist arguments for woman suffrage. Stanton rapidly subordinated her convictions about the universality of natural rights and condemned the political inclusion of black and new immigrant men; she argued that the early suffragists' commitment to "equal rights for all" clashed with their Americanist identities. After 1870, mainstream woman suffragists never recovered their original commitment to equality for *all* as a natural and a political right.[25]

Feminism of Fear

During the mid-1870s, Frances Willard, the temperance leader, developed the themes of a liberal "feminism of fear." Instead of focusing on political equality for women, Willard concentrated on creating secure conditions for women's freedom. To do so, she appealed to the masses of women who organized spontaneously during the early 1870s to protest male drinking.[26] For women resistant to the idea of political equality, reluctant to join a political, nonreligious organization, or both, Willard focused on the threat of male physical abuse, particularly from drunken husbands. During the 1850s Amelia Bloomer and Stanton had used similar arguments to fortify temperance reformers in New York State. Willard's focus made suffrage expedient for prohibitionist reforms: she argued that dutiful women could guarantee physical security for themselves and their children only if they made "home protection" their primary goal and secured their ability to achieve it by winning the vote.[27]

For Willard, female enfranchisement constituted the first step in integrating the separate social and political spheres and making women authoritative moral leaders. By tapping women's fears of violent abuse and invoking religious symbolism, Willard provided traditional women with both personal reasons for seeking the vote and the moral authority to do so. In defining the vote as the chief means to achieve "home protection," her arguments were initially perceived as less threatening than the suffragists' feminism of equal rights, at least outside of the South.[28] Willard's success as a political mobilizer is shown by the steady increase in membership in the Woman's Christian Temperance Union (WCTU), from 27,000 to over 200,000, during her tenure as president.[29]

Willard made ecumenical appeals, and she aimed to mobilize black women, but her role as the leader of a "Christian" female association and her periodic criticisms of "foreign influences" limited the scope of her authority and fed nativist sentiments. In many respects, Willard, along with her suffragist cohorts, was limited by Americanist biases.

Feminism of Personal Development

The feminism of personal development was grounded in the view that because individuals generate ideas and achieve goals, no government or custom should prohibit the exercise of personal freedom. This feminism gained some momentum during the 1840s from the campaigns for married woman's property reform: educated, white, middle-class women saw opportunities to gain control of their inheritances and earnings in order to exercise choice over their investment. But after 1890 a new generation of educated, more urbane suffragists gave these themes prominence. For example, Carrie Chapman Catt and Anna Howard Shaw emphasized the personal losses that each woman suffered without the right to vote, and they concentrated on drawing attention to the basic injustice of women's political exclusion.

Catt, the major architect of a national strategy to win women the vote during the twentieth century, initially joined the WCTU but later joined the suffragists due to her unwillingness to align with the Prohibitionists. During the late 1880s and 1890s, she echoed Stanton's nativistic feminism. Catt denounced the political exclusion of qualified women in favor of unqualified men as a personal injustice suffered particularly by educated, moral, and responsible American women. In the 1890s, Catt's arguments, most of which are unpublished, were far more chauvinistic than Willard's and exemplify social Darwinism and other racialist theories adapted by suffragists. As supporters of white supremacy, southern suffragists also contributed some racist feminist arguments, but most opposed violent racial domination. Southern reformers made the movement national, which was a necessary ingredient for the passage of a federal constitutional amendment.[30]

Until 1906, the suffragists clung to a blend of nativistic sentiments and negative liberal feminist appeals against injustices to educated, middle-class, morally upstanding women. During a National American Woman Suffrage Association (NAWSA) convention that year, social reformers Florence Kelley and Jane Addams argued that nativist and racist positions failed to win support from immigrant men who shared suffragists' support for anti–child labor and municipal reform goals. They persuaded the second generation of educated, middle-class, mostly white, Protestant women that their goals for personal development depended upon secure political conditions for all Americans. In egalitarian arguments purged of nativism and racism (but flexible enough for southern progressive reformers to adapt to their more constrained agendas), Addams blended Willard's feminism of fear with a modernized conception of republican motherhood that claimed women's votes could rectify injustices in cities. College-educated and socialist women who shared Addams's arguments for inclusive equality mobilized women and built alliances across the nation with organized labor, farmers, and other progressive organizations—alliances that enabled the passage and ratification of the Nineteenth Amendment.

Political Expediency and the Necessities of Practical Politics

Many contradictions in the suffragists' ideologies derived from the reformers' practical need to appeal to diverse interests. These reformers sought liberal goals, but it was not always possible to mobilize women, male voters, or legislators with egalitarian arguments or strategies. Deep resistance to considering women as political equals sometimes forced woman suffragists to make appeals they found personally distasteful. Thus it is necessary to distinguish appeals made to circumvent opponents' arguments from those that represented reformers' basic principles.

The most formidable opposition to the political inclusion of women has been the idea that women's difference from men disqualifies them from full citizenship. In the United States four premises supported the political exclusion of women: (1) that God ordained women to serve men's desires, (2) that women consented to obey men in exchange for protection, and so, as men's natural subjects, women can never be men's equals, (3) that if women vote, put earning first, or become too educated, the family will lose its main caretaker and society will lose one of its basic structures, and (4) that because women are "good persons," they cannot be "good citizens": good citizens must sometimes engage in bad behavior.[31]

Much of the struggle for women's political inclusion was a prolonged exercise in agenda-setting by a politically powerless group.[32] From the late 1830s until Reconstruction, votes for women were considered a radical goal on a radical reform agenda. The controversy had earned a place on what political scientist John Kingdon calls the "government agenda," but it held a low priority. To pass woman suffrage legislation, its proponents had to make this issue both salient and acceptable.

Acceptability to legislators and public opinion, Kingdon argues, occurs in a softening-up process that consists mainly of reformers' attachment of compelling labels, symbols, and values to their issues. By making catchy labels, striking resonances with patriotic ideals, and linking a new and mysterious aim to traditional values, reform leaders recruit members and convert opponents. Successful softening-up and political mobilization, then, tend to depend on the effectiveness of a reform leader's *political ideology*—the platform of arguments that persuade audiences to follow that leader, join her or his organization, or support a reform goal as a nonmember.[33] To succeed, woman suffragist leaders had to develop mobilizing ideologies—arguments fashioned both to grab attention from particular groups and to overcome the strongest claims of their opponents. Once a controversial issue has been softened up, as woman suffrage eventually was, reformers can move it from the *government agenda* to the *decision agenda* of legislators and voters.

To win legislative and popular support, woman suffragists exploited those illiberal republican and Americanist ideals that clashed with liberal aims but connected with aspirations for stronger communities, religious identification, and deeper patriotism. Even with the most persuasive arguments (those least threatening to men and women dependent upon traditional roles), reformers made gains only when powerful men perceived coincidences between woman suffrage and their interests. They advanced when partisan splits among men fostered enough uncertainty legislatively and electorally to invite many new voters into the system.

Ironically, woman suffragists had to wait for men's struggles to open up opportunities for women to win the vote. Some aims—antislavery, populist, and progressive—were liberal or republican or both, whereas others, such as the aim to establish white supremacy, were Americanist or undemocratic. Woman suffragists tried to exploit them all. Reformers challenged antislavery, populist, and progressive reformers to make their egalitarian ideals more consistent with their everyday practices by including women. To the undemocratic creators of white supremacy, women called for the inclusion of all whites, arguing that "white supremacy" had actually put political power exclusively into white male hands.

In the North, liberal feminist suffragists dissented from the democratization of modern patriarchy—the effort to make all men, but only men, politically included and powerful.[34] Northern women insisted that for true democracy to exist, equal rights, the "people," and the "consent of all" had to include women. In the South after the 1890s, liberal feminist suffragists dissented from what had become an undemocratic and racist patriarchy. Although many southern suffragists had contradictory aims, their efforts to win political inclusion challenged one fundamentally illiberal element of white supremacist government: the placement of all political power in the hands of white men.

In short, the story of the southern suffragists' quest for political inclusion reveals that liberalism does not depend on democratic political structures as much as democracy depends on liberalism.[35] That is, liberal impulses can work against undemocratic political structures as well as in concert with democratic reforms. Southern suffragists faced stiffer and more complex opposition than northern suffragists, but both had to cope with institutions controlled exclusively by men: political parties, state legislatures, state and federal courts, presidencies, and governorships.

Opportunities for advancing woman suffrage on state and federal decision agendas depended upon party leaders' priorities for electoral and governing agendas, the competition within the party system, and whether woman's rights and woman suffrage were perceived as only weak threats to party leaders. Regardless of how well organized the reformers were or whether they offered compelling arguments for the right to vote, they made strides only after the inclusion of women was widely thought to be unthreatening to men in power. It was especially advantageous to woman suffrage when splits within and between political parties encouraged party leaders to mobilize new constituencies.

～✿～

Chapter 1 explains the origins of the liberal feminism of equal rights in the Garrisonian antislavery movement. Garrison targeted "the women of New England," ministers, and newspaper editors as his three main constituencies largely because he hoped to buttress his movement with moral authority. Even though controversy emerged over their public antislavery efforts, women became Garrison's most reliable constituency. When they encountered opposition to their participation in the movement, Maria Stewart, Angelina and Sarah Grimké, and Lucretia Mott justified claims for woman's rights with references to the Scriptures and natural rights doctrines. Thus these reformers used the ideology of republican motherhood to inspire collective action against the political exclusion of women as well as against slavery. Stewart and the Grimkés also promoted and practiced inclusive egalitarian standards of behavior that illuminated the limitations of an exclusively male polity. Garrison's commitment to free speech and reliance on the participation of women in his association explain his defense of the women's contributions. The mutual reciprocity between Garrison and the women who defended their own rights advanced both movements.[36]

Chapter 2 contends that despite its organizational shortcomings and small size, the 1850s woman's rights movement incubated liberal feminist reforms that included, beyond property law reform and suffrage, the establishment of egalitarian models for marriage, calls for political and social equality because of women's differences from men, and divorce reform. To sustain collective action, the reformers simply relied on shared commitments as well as the Garrisonian network; the lack of formal organization insulated woman's rights reformers from external attack and from internal power struggles. As a result, woman's rights reformers developed an autonomous agenda as well as the confidence they needed to become independent leaders after Reconstruction.[37]

Chapter 3 explains how the democratization of male suffrage altered the priorities of woman's rights reformers, transformed what had been a moral reform movement into a political movement, and put pure equal rights arguments for women's political inclusion on weaker ground. The introduction of male qualifications for suffrage, a clear advance of democratic relations among men, also demonstrates women's political subordination. When male Garrisonians decided to support the Fourteenth Amendment, they irrevocably relegated women's rights to second-class status, leaving without strong allies those who considered woman's rights equally important. Most male Garrisonians—and a few radical Republicans such as Charles Sumner—considered this action morally necessary. But these developments introduced most female Garrisonians to a painful reality of male-only politics: the issues that powerful men agree deserve action will receive attention and support before all others.[38]

During Reconstruction, when American men remained deeply divided and embittered after a shattering civil war, woman suffrage had no real chance of success. Reconstruction forced woman's rights reformers into narrower and narrower paths toward "equal rights"—rewards or benefits tailored to fit particular groups, not equal rights to all groups without regard to race, ethnicity, or sex.

During the 1870s, the newly self-christened "woman suffragists" exploited incipient reforms—such as Colorado's campaign for statehood—by attaching votes for women to state and federal legislative agendas. Such efforts deserve close attention because they reveal the strength of the opposition as well as the creative efforts reformers made to overcome it. For example, in the campaigns for woman suffrage in Colorado between

1875 and 1877, reformers often found male and female allies who, although committed to the political inclusion of women, subordinated it to winning statehood. These campaigns were among the first legislative advances that national suffragists made—in 1893 Colorado's male voters became the first state electorate to pass votes for women—so I will detail the Colorado campaigns for woman suffrage.

Chapter 4 explains how Frances Willard, the leader of the WCTU, developed a mobilizing ideology, the feminism of fear, that sustained the first independent, mass movement of American women. Willard argued that the only way women could free themselves of fear of capricious violent male behavior—associated frequently with drunkenness—was to organize, initiate programs for change, and win the vote to put real protectors of women and the home into elective office. Buttressing her arguments with symbols of motherhood, scriptural justifications, and patriotic rhetoric, Willard mobilized far more women than the suffragists.

Colorado suffragists used Willard's ideology to build a base of support among women. Albina Washburn and Mary Shields, veterans of the 1875 and 1876 campaigns, disbanded their suffrage society after the 1877 defeat and almost immediately established a state WCTU as a shadow organization from which they mobilized support for woman suffrage. The Colorado WCTU then campaigned for the vote in 1892 and 1893 after the state's People's Party gained gubernatorial and legislative control.

Chapter 5 explains why Colorado women won the vote in 1893. The feminism of fear improved the possibilities for advancing woman suffrage, but by itself this ideology was not enough to secure victories. The reformers required elections in which the entry of large numbers of new voters into the electorate was appealing to all political parties. The ascendancy of the Colorado People's Party in 1892 provided such an opportunity because the Populists' endorsement of woman suffrage forced the Republicans and Democrats to do likewise. Indeed, suffragist and former Grange member Washburn participated in both the Farmers' Alliance and the Colorado People's Party; other Colorado women mobilized support among the Knights of Labor and the radical miners, groups that shared Willard's "home protection" goal. The willingness of state and national suffragists to work together, their use of specialized ideological arguments to win support from different audiences, and the People's Party's need for votes enabled women to win the vote in Colorado in 1893. Influences of Willard's political ideology on the symbols and arguments favored by Colorado populists indicate that in some states the WCTU was a stronger shaper of populism than scholars tend to admit.

Chapter 6 argues that woman suffragists' racist and nativist arguments predominated between 1890 and 1906, and that for the reformers these inegalitarian appeals constituted points of departure, not destinations. During this period, social Darwinist theories led many people, suffragists included, to consider inherited resources, especially biology, as the fundamental shaper of destiny. Consequently, national woman suffrage leaders avoided universal claims of equality, endorsed educational qualifications for the vote, and made both racist and nativist appeals for support. Aiming to make their quest truly national, the NAWSA leaders encouraged state campaigns in the South and tolerated southern suffragists' endorsement of white supremacy. The suffragists preserved their liberal reputations, however, by refusing to endorse outright ascriptive racial qualifications for the vote. The arguments made by black American intellectuals such as Mary Church Terrell and W. E. B. Du Bois against white leaders' elitist defenses of voter qualifications reaffirmed egalitarian principles.

Still, white suffragists adopted a double standard about membership that allowed blacks to join NAWSA but not attend conventions. Because of this exclusion, black women endured a racial segregation that was more publicly humiliating than the condescending attitudes expressed by suffragists toward Catholic, Jewish, and Asian American women. The suffragists' racism and nativism reveal how their ethnocentric elitism contradicted their egalitarian aims, even while their critique of men's claim of sex-right over women—as represented by prostitution—deepened their consciousness as an oppressed group across race, ethnicity, and class boundaries. The impurities in suffragists' ideologies evidence the compromises the reformers made as they struggled to reconcile conflicts between egalitarian and Americanist ideals.[39]

Chapter 7 contends that the suffragists finally weakened their dependence upon the Americanist tradition and used egalitarian versions of the feminism of fear and the feminism of personal development to win the vote. In the early 1900s, second-generation suffragists created new, more inclusive associations to recruit members and engage allies. In 1906, dissenting from the suffragists' narrow and nativistic appeals, Harriot Stanton Blatch, Florence Kelley, and Jane Addams called for alliances with working-class, immigrant men based upon a shared support of social policies such as opposition to child labor. Addams, a key national promoter of woman suffrage during the 1912 presidential campaign, drew considerably on Willard's feminism of fear but blended it with a vision of secular, urban, and participatory republican motherhood. Suffragists in trade unions as well as leaders of NAWSA spoke on the feminism of equal rights and tailored these arguments so that they would appeal to a variety of audiences—from legislatures to organized workers. And Carrie Chapman Catt continued to decry as unjust the political exclusion of woman suffragists when new male groups were included that had not had to prove themselves capable of voting.

The reformers knit the national movement together through their "front door lobby," which put intense and effective grassroots pressure on elected officials through letter writing and personal contacts. But by choosing the federal amendment method over state-by-state campaigns, the national woman suffrage leaders conceded that elected officials were more likely than male voters to pass the measure. In passing the Nineteenth Amendment, Congress and the ratifying state legislatures again confirmed, as they had during Reconstruction, that in the United States equal rights and guarantees of liberal freedom matter more to political elites than to citizens at large. Thus, the political inclusion of women signaled more of a change in elite attitudes, standards, and behavior than in everyday popular practices. Such a partial, elite victory has left much unfinished in the struggle for women's political inclusion.

The Feminism of Equal Rights

*I*N THE United States, the organized movement for woman's rights—the crucible for woman's suffrage—emerged from the radical abolitionist reform movement led by William Lloyd Garrison. Before Garrison mobilized women and defended their rights, numerous women and some men had claimed rights for women. But Garrison was the first major male leader to seek, secure, and sustain collective action to achieve them. Although he probably never intended to open the door for women to unite and demand the vote for themselves, he certainly did so.

In 1829, women's understandings and what I call the practice of "republican motherhood" gave women the moral authority necessary for achieving nongovernmental reform—as Garrison envisioned it—through moral suasion and conversion. Garrison needed the support of native-born, middle-class white women because they represented the practice of virtue, which was then defined as the willingness to share resources and keep selfish ambitions in check.[1] Because these women proved themselves worthy members of society by educating their children and guiding their husbands with moral principles, they constituted an ideal constituency for the promotion of Garrison's vision.

Initially, Garrison did not envision women's participation in his abolitionist movement as a first step toward their winning equality. He most wanted republican mothers to promote the virtue of equality among men. Unexpectedly, however, several Garrisonian women began to present a more inclusive definition of political equality than Garrison's. By drawing upon scriptural examples of heroic women as well as scriptural commands that each person act morally, Maria Stewart, Angelina Grimké, and Sarah Grimké articulated a concept of inclusive moral equality. Female Garrisonians, in turn, began to practice this more inclusive equality in their reform organizations. They also defined and defended woman's rights as equal rights.

Garrison's recruitment of women had three implications for the feminism of the woman's rights and woman suffrage movements. First, although Garrison eventually endorsed woman's rights as an important aim of equal rights, his treatment of women primarily as respectable awakeners of conscience kept woman's rights subordinate to the antislavery goal of creating equal rights among men. For example, Garrison welcomed women's biblical references to heroic moral acts by women and men, but he himself referred only to the Bible's most general egalitarian themes. Instead he preferred the more explicitly egalitarian (but exclusive) principles of the Declaration of Independence.

Second, when the first women to assert these rights became exhausted and dispirited by the clash with opponents, the cause of woman's rights became more dependent on Garrisonian men's willingness to sustain it. In the late 1830s, Garrison defended woman's rights partly because he depended upon women's membership. Third, the people who ultimately made the woman's rights movement autonomous from Garrisonian antislavery adopted equal rights as the fundamental standard for setting goals and measuring progress. Although they did not always define expectations for achievement according to what was expected for men, the intense focus on equality oriented the first feminists toward a comparative analysis of male and female possessions—of property, opportunities, and obligations. As woman's rights defined as equal rights emerged on the political agenda, so also did conflicts about which woman's rights goals should be put first.

Liberal Religious Denominations and Noninterventionist Government

Many forms of social change under way during this period enabled the powerfully vocal minority of Garrisonian antislavery reformers to promote woman's rights. During the Second Great Awakening's "democratization of American Christianity,"[2] the ideology of republican motherhood made women more assertive about their moral responsibilities. Dissent on gender matters increased in religious denominations. It was followed by splits between those attuned to the call of the spirit (or, in the case of Quakers, to the "inner light") and those convinced that the biblical scriptures represented the most reliable and authoritative message of God.[3] During these upheavals over the nature of moral authority and appropriate forms of religious practice, a distinctive division of responsibilities evolved between national government and society: government assumed responsibility for defending and maintaining the civil order, whereas religious denominations, families, schools, and the press mediated moral conflicts.[4]

The relationship between government and society in the United States made Garrisonian antislavery reform consequential for the "liberalism of equal rights" and, thereby, for woman's rights. The government often has been characterized as weak, laissez-faire, and noninterventionist, and American society was considered pluralist, equal, and ruled by the "tyranny of the majority." This relationship between government and society emerged from a colonial civil war, and its most powerful basic consensus became a determination to protect the newly independent territory from disorder caused by invasion or violent civil conflict.[5] The framers disagreed about many issues and were deeply divided over slavery. But their shared identifications as male protector-creators of political independence, or "republican fathers," overrode their divisions on other issues. In fashioning the "three-fifths compromise," the framers prevented a split that could have made territorial unity impossible. The costs of this compromise, which at the time did not seem high, were severe limits on the national government's power to enact and enforce any consistent and comprehensive social policies that required inclusive constitutional definitions of civil rights.[6] The responsibility for resolving conflicts over civil rights was left up for grabs.

Historians of women's changing roles and responsibilities have noted that the founding fathers' (and most state governments') avoidance of responsibility for social policies left these issues to elite women, who coped with them in their roles as republican mothers.[7] As founders of benevolent societies, women informed men in power about reform projects and developed charitable enterprises.[8] Men concerned about social issues—particularly the contradictions between the ideals of liberty and equality and the realities of slavery, poverty, and the exploitation of labor—considered nongovernmental means appropriate for enacting social policy. Benevolent reformers, many of whom were women, relieved elected and appointed government officials of "charitable tasks, activities considered incompatible with the visible system of political patronage."[9]

There were even greater incentives for elected officials to avoid the slavery issue. As the first generation of citizens born in the United States began to take the reins of national power in the 1830s and 1840s, they restricted their focus to what Joel H. Silbey calls "national politics": tariffs, banking, and interstate commerce. Slavery and other "social issues" were defined as "sectional": only groups in the North, and even then primarily in Massachusetts and New York, considered slavery an issue. As Silbey states, "The simple fact was that the basic components of party differences, such issues as the bank or tariff, knew no section, and so long as they remained the central issues of the day, sectional inclinations received little hearing."[10]

Policy aims lacking concrete benefits could not be traded as political patronage; issues such as slavery that threatened to divide the government were avoided vigorously by Congress and the president. The challenge of enacting social reforms intensified during the 1830s as the leaders of national, mass-based political parties emerged and consolidated their power as an exclusive fraternal elite. This transformation made political parties the key American institution of modern patriarchy, where men rule as brothers, not fathers. Moreover, Andrew Jackson introduced a patronage system that tied electoral district leaders closely to national party leadership, and he appropriated a huge share of government maintenance jobs to exchange for favors—thereby making government's maintenance the major priority for elected officials and their appointees.[11] In short, federal officials concentrated mainly on the tasks necessary to keep electoral offices, maintain basic government services such as the post office and the port authorities, and—from their perspective—protect the sovereignty of the United States.[12]

The national government's avoidance of the slavery issue—by defining it as "sectional"—and the fact that no other national institution with a large membership (such as the Catholic Church in Brazil) promoted legislative action on it, encouraged others to become involved.[13] Committed to a nongovernmental process of antislavery reform, William Lloyd Garrison fashioned an ideology and an organization to make abolition a national issue. By introducing antislavery as a benevolent reform, he generated much controversy about the distinctions between governmental and nongovernmental reforms as well as the kind of participation appropriate for women.

For his ideology, Garrison exploited the moral authority that made liberty and equality the standards for determining unacceptable public behavior, particularly by government. His premise, starkly authoritarian, was labeled by Louis Hartz as "liberal absolutism":[14]

> What is the proposition to be discussed? It is this: whether all men are created free and equal, and have an inalienable right to liberty! I am urged to argue this with a people, who declare it to be a self-evident truth! Why, such folly belongs to Bedlam. When my countrymen shall burn their Bibles, and rescind their famous Declaration of Independence, and reduce themselves to colonial dependence upon the mother country, I will find both time and patience to reason with them on the subject of human rights. Argument is demanded—to prove what?[15]

Garrison's supporters found his frequent reminders that the principles of natural law forbid slavery riveting. Equating "natural right" with "lib-

rhetoric of Christian benevolence so that women's preeminent responsibility would be widely perceived as the practice of virtue. This rhetoric was a critical contribution to the classless, republican ideology that counterbalanced liberal ideological pressures to acquire property imposed mainly upon men: "The rhetoric of Christian benevolence suggested not only that even the most oppressed women would aspire to a higher standard of virtue than that presumably exhibited by men but women, acting together, would identify with and care for the poor and downtrodden."[27]

Ginzberg points out that these women's power in benevolent associations required camouflage: their participation had to be seen as voluntary charity; their exercise of real power and earnings had to remain hidden; and the charitable activity itself could not be politically controversial. Fanny Wright, Elizabeth Margaret Chandler, and Harriet Martineau all called women to participate in antislavery reform at around the same time as did Garrison.[28] But Garrison's invitation was special because by publicly including women as a key constituency along with the clergy and newspaper editors, he effectively asked women to deny the traditional separation of the public and domestic spheres.

When some women accepted Garrison's invitation to practice republican motherhood in public, conflict began to divide the community of benevolent women: despite their own regular petitioning and deal-making with legislators and appointed government officials, women active in less controversial pursuits condemned the activities of female Garrisonians (and temperance reformers) as "unfeminine." This opposition set the stage for a rivalry among women activists about whether women's supposedly unique resources should be dedicated to radical structural change or used to shore up the status quo.[29]

The split among benevolent women and the evolution of the woman's rights movement out of the radical abolitionist movement were unexpected. Garrison initially appealed to these elite women as a way of appropriating their moral fervor and defining the means and ends of civic virtue with a new public voice. The women who joined Garrison gained a bridge to autonomous political action, initially as Garrisonians and later for themselves. These women would have been unable to participate fully if Garrison had aimed at achieving change through exclusively male political parties and legislatures.

Garrison's Mobilization of Women

Women responded to Garrison's call. In the fall of 1831, Maria Miller W. Stewart, a free, native-born black woman, brought to Garrison her antislavery speech that aimed to mobilize her sisters to join the movement; Garrison published it in the *Liberator*. In a letter to Sarah M. Douglass of Philadelphia, a free black Quaker woman who helped to establish a "female literary association" during the spring of 1832, Garrison applauded her for embarking upon a quest for knowledge and improvement and added that "it puts a new weapon into my hands to use against southern oppressors."[30] He emphasized the important role women had in the struggle: "My hopes for the elevation of your race are mainly centered upon you and others of your sex." He also stated his hopes that women would apply benevolent skills to the reform effort:

> You cannot be ignorant of the victorious influence which you possess over the minds of men. You cannot, if you would, be passive; you must either pull down or build up, either corrupt or preserve the morals of the age. There is not a glance of your eye, not a tone of your voice—however seemingly the look of remonstrance or entreaty be disregarded, or the word of admonition or advice be slighted—but has a direct connexion with the results of masculine actions and pursuits.[31]

In response to the nervous reservations white women expressed toward participating in collective action, Garrison insisted that such false ideas and unwarranted fears be discarded: in a March 1833 letter to teenager Harriott Plummer, Garrison disputed Plummer's claim to be uninfluential. "The destiny of the slaves," he asserted, "is in the hands of the American women, and complete emancipation can never take place without their co-operation." If British women had taken steps toward ending slavery, Garrison argued, women in this country could do the same. He exhorted: "Women of New England—mothers and daughters! if I fail to awake your sympathies, and secure your aid, I may well despair of gaining the hearts and support of men."[32]

In a January 1834 letter to Helen E. Benson, the woman he later married, Garrison stated:

> I shall look to you for the formation of a Female Anti-Slavery Society in Providence. You know, or must know, that I rely upon female influence to break the shackles of the bleeding slave. Two or three days since, I was cheered beyond measure to learn that 70 females in the little village of Amesbury had organized themselves into an anti-slavery society, and that a similar organization had been made among the ladies of Portland. Let these encourage you to seek such an association in Providence.[33]

Garrison has been widely celebrated for his radical equal rights ideology and unswerving dedication to egalitarian principles, especially the right of free speech.[34] But Garrison's antislavery message also required moral character. Republican mothers provided that character; the women who accepted Garrison's invitation brought the antislavery movement rich religious symbolism and discipline. Of course, however, they eventually found themselves questioning their own political exclusion. The starkest forms of this exclusion were the common understanding that women would not speak on religious or political matters in public and coverture's denial of political will to women—their lack of rights to own property, divorce, vote, or hold office.

To mobilize women's support, Garrison put the fight against cruelty first and called for protections and security as conditions for liberty; he did not put status or equality first. Garrison frequently referred to the brutality masters exercised at will on slaves, particularly toward the female slaves in rape and beatings, as well as the emotional pain caused by selling off family members, especially infants. Without this reference to the suffering of slaves, Garrison's claims of equal rights and liberty would have had little moral appeal. Eventually Garrison trumpeted equal rights as the ideal that justified putting an end to cruelty. But he began by fixing attention on the injustice of slavery.

Some examples of female suffering in slavery that Garrison selected to ignite women's indignation and elicit their participation appear to have failed with some audiences. Despite the focus many female benevolent societies put on prostitution reform,[35] elite women may have found Garrison's detailed depiction of sexual exploitation in slavery too graphic and unseemly. In another early letter to Helen Benson, Garrison scoffed at the anger women in Providence, Rhode Island, had expressed when he tried to expose "as delicately and guardedly as possible . . . the awful situation in which a million of your sex are placed, who groan in bondage, and who have no protection whatever from the licentiousness of their tyrannical masters." To the criticisms that Helen relayed, Garrison angrily responded that these women had no "holy indignation at the conduct of those libidinous monsters who rob their victims of that which is infinitely more precious than life."[36] He encouraged Helen to persist in her organizing efforts despite these obstructions.

These messages and Garrison's open invitation to women were, however, more than adequate for mobilizing women already committed to antislavery.[37] Both the black and white women who joined Garrison's opposition to slavery had backgrounds of religious principles and rules of fairness. Maria Stewart, orphaned at age five, "was bound out in the family of a clergyman"; she later attended Methodist, Baptist, and Episcopal churches.[38] Sarah Douglass, Lucretia Mott, and the Grimké sisters were Quakers; various communities within the Society of Friends took stands against slavery in the early eighteenth century. These women were well prepared by their religion and by republican motherhood to mobilize women for Garrison.

In sum, Garrison has been accurately portrayed as the formulator of an inclusive equal rights ideology. But to mobilize women as a core constituency of active participants, he appealed to customary expectations that women act as benevolent reformers, and he emphasized the cruelties suffered by slaves. This blend of appeals to women as republican mothers and benevolent philanthropists made sense because women lacked the rights necessary to press directly for the abolition of slavery. At the time, Garrison also aimed primarily at recruiting enough women to sustain his movement and make it morally respectable. In this effort, he largely succeeded.

The Antislavery Appeals of Republican Mothers

In 1831, Maria Stewart gave her first speech rousing free black women to activate themselves in antislavery reform. She began with the expectation that women would be educators of virtue; to the males in her community she celebrated the ideals of liberty and equality. Introducing herself as a convert to Jesus, Stewart addressed African-American men as follows: "All the nations of the earth are crying out for liberty and equality. Away, away with tyranny and oppression! And shall Afric's sons be silent any longer?" Stewart also gave her sisters a wake-up call steeped in the values and symbols of republican motherhood:

> O, ye daughters of Africa, awake! Awake! Arise! No longer sleep nor slumber, but distinguish yourselves. Show forth to the world that ye are endowed with noble and exalted faculties. O, ye daughters of Africa! What have ye done to immortalize your names beyond the grave? What examples have ye set before the rising generation? What foundation have ye laid for generations yet unborn? Where are our union and love? And where is our sympathy, that weeps at another's woe, and hides the faults we see? And our daughters, where are they? Blushing in innocence and virtue? And our sons, do they bid fair to become crowns of glory to our hoary heads? [Proverbs 16:31][39]

Stewart insisted that women practice republican motherhood: "O, ye mothers, what a responsibility rests on you! You have souls committed to your charge, and God will require a strict account of you. It is you that must create in the minds of your little girls and boys a thirst for knowledge, the love of virtue, the abhorrence of vice, and the cultivation of a pure heart."[40]

In a later address to the Afric-American Female Intelligence Society of America, Stewart explained that she was speaking publicly at God's command because "religion is held in low repute among some of us"; and that her goal was racial unity because "without these efforts, we shall never be a people, nor our descendants after us." Women were the keys, Stewart argued, to the creation of this unity: "O woman, woman! Your example is powerful, your influence great; it extends over your husbands and your children, and throughout the circle of your acquaintance. Then let me exhort you to cultivate among yourselves a spirit of Christian love and unity, having charity one for another, without which all our goodness is as sounding brass, and a tinkling cymbal [1 Corinthians 13:1]."[41]

In her 1836 "Appeal to the Christian Women of the South," Angelina Grimké also invoked the images of strong women from the Bible and defined antislavery reform as a Christian obligation. "I do not believe," she wrote, "the time has yet come when *Christian women* 'will not endure sound doctrine,' even on the subject of slavery, if it is spoken to them in tenderness and love, therefore I now address *you*."[42] Most of Grimké's letter explained, in a legal and exegetical manner, why Hebrew law about servants was irrelevant and inapplicable to slavery in the United States. In her statement of true divine will about slavery and her call for immediate abolition, however, Grimké put God's will first and used many biblical images and symbols of republican motherhood. After expressing a willingness to go to jail or pay a fine for freeing a slave, Grimké asserted: "If a law commands me to *sin I will break it*; if it calls me to *suffer,* I will let it take its course *unresistingly.* The doctrine of blind obedience and unqualified submission to *any human* power, whether civil or ecclesiastical, is the doctrine of despotism, and ought to have no place among Republicans and Christians."[43] And she presented women with biblical heroines who defied illegitimate rulers and governments: "But you may say we are *women,* how can *our* hearts endure persecution? And why not? Have not *women* stood up in all the dignity and strength of moral courage to be the leaders of the people, and to bear a faithful testimony for the truth whenever the providence of God has called them to do so? Are there no *women* in that noble army of martyrs who are now singing the song of Moses and the Lamb?"[44]

Grimké eloquently cited Miriam, Deborah, Jael, Huldah the prophetess, Esther, Elizabeth, Anna the prophetess, the women who followed Jesus on the road to Calvary, Pilate's wife, and Mary Magdalene as models of women who responded faithfully to God's call in challenging, difficult circumstances. She added Roman women "burnt at the stake" and Anne Askew—a woman burned with three men on July 16, 1546, for refusing to accept the doctrine of transubstantiation—as further examples of courageous defiance of the illegitimate exercise of political authority.[45] "The *women of the South*," Grimké asserted, "*can overthrow* this horrible system of oppression and cruelty, licentiousness and wrong. Such appeals to your legislatures would be irresistible, for there is something in the heart of man which *will bend under moral suasion.* There is a swift witness for truth in his bosom, which *will respond to truth* when it is uttered with calmness and dignity."[46]

Maria Stewart and Angelina Grimké rewarded Garrison's appeal for their support with active membership and dedicated recruitment efforts. Garrison and the women portrayed biblical models of republican motherhood to enlist women in the cause of immediate abolition; each reformer urged women to exercise moral suasion to convert men away from tacitly tolerating slavery. These reform efforts succeeded handsomely: "Between 1834 and 1838," according to Keith Melder, "thousands of American women found roles to play in their own antislavery societies, later in organizations of men and women."[47] Although the largest female associations were in Boston, Philadelphia, and New York, there were some as far west as Ashtabula, Ohio. By the late 1830s women reformers had established fundraising fairs for the reform; thousands of dollars were raised including a net profit of $28,000 in Philadelphia.

Ginzberg argues that Garrison depended heavily on Maria Weston Chapman's multiple organizing talents. Chapman not only supervised the lucrative money-raising fairs, she also "edited or coedited the *National Anti-Slavery Standard,* the *Non-Resistant,* the *Liberator,* and the *Liberty Bell,* an annual gift book of abolitionist poetry and prose." She "operated the silent activities that characterized abolition as they did traditional benevolent enterprises." Although Chapman "spoke to a convention only once," she supported the Grimkés' insistence that women defend their right and responsibility to speak in public.[48] Most importantly, women were mostly responsible for the controversial petition campaigns; they demonstrated their support of antislavery by signing on. According to Melder, the number of female signatures on the petitions "vastly outnumbered" the female reform activists.[49]

The Petition Campaigns

Garrison rewarded these women with more equality and respect than they won from other male leaders. In addition to encouraging women to form female antislavery associations and publishing speeches made by Stewart and the Grimké sisters, Garrison accepted many of women's suggestions, both technical and substantive. For example, in 1833 he accepted a correction Lucretia Mott made to his draft of the "Declaration of Sentiments," a statement of organizational purpose.[50] Melder observes that Garrison's inclusion of Mott's call for transposing the phrase "We plant ourselves on the truths of Divine Revelation and on the Declaration of Independence as an Everlasting Rock" as a full-fledged amendment established "a controversial and far-reaching precedent for women's participation in the antislavery movement."[51] A male leader's public acceptance of constructive criticism from a female supporter also marks a striking change from the less visible deals that women negotiated with men through benevolent associations.

Women reformers' participation in these campaigns had two important consequences for both antislavery and woman's rights. Their mass petitioning eventually undermined trust in the voluntarist, nongovernmental vision of change. In addition, by going door-to-door for signatures, the women reformers became experienced in persuading an individual or small group to support abolition. According to Eleanor Flexner, through these petition campaigns women "secur[ed for themselves] a right which they would use later in their own interests."[52] Female antislavery reformers developed arguments for eliciting signatures that they would later use to win political inclusion for themselves.[53]

A controversy began in 1834 over women's participation in gathering petitions calling for the abolition of slavery in the District of Columbia. So many signatures were gathered that Congress's "hands off" policy on slavery was suspended temporarily. Although northern women in benevolent associations were well-practiced petitioners, their success in the antislavery cause was particularly shocking to the legislators from the South. In 1834 the House of Representatives passed the Pinckney "Gag Rule" to prevent the presentation of the petitions.[54] As fierce debate erupted about the right to petition—especially for women—and the appropriate action to take, the woman's rights issue was raised for the first time in Congress.[55]

Former president John Quincy Adams, a member of the House, dissented from the gag rule, insisting that the right of petition was basic. Subsequently, many citizens in the North demonstrated their approval of Adams's claim by signing antislavery petitions addressed to him. The women reformers' contributions were also particularly visible in the petitions sent to Adams. Flexner states that a large proportion of these came from the female antislavery societies, a fact that enraged southern representatives. Adams defended the propriety of women's signing petitions and collecting signatures.[56] As a consequence, his defense of citizens' right to petition unintentionally opened the door to a deliberation about *women's* right to petition. Although the gag rule was not overturned, Adams successfully defended women's use of this right.[57]

The petition campaigns' success also opened the door to pressure-group tactics and partisan alliances that, unlike Garrison's nonpartisan and basically nongovernmental moral suasion, aimed at influencing the state. Representative and former president John Quincy Adams argued for increased government responsibility for moral issues; by the late 1830s, according to Walter Merrill, many reformers leaned away from Garrison's plan and toward that of Adams or other more politically oriented reformers.[58] Mott, the Grimkés, Chapman, and other female Garrisonians continued to endorse nongovernmental, personal conversion as the best means for slavery's abolition. Ironically, women, a politically excluded group, contributed heavily to the development of the mass-based pressure-group politics that eventually spanned the gap between governmental and nongovernmental public responsibilities.

The strides made for woman's rights through the petition campaigns bring into focus both the catalyzing role of government in the development of woman's rights reform and the way the ambiguities in women's roles stalled the assertion of those rights. The petition campaigns boldly displayed women's political participation while they highlighted the popular concern over slavery. By collecting petitions, women proved their readiness for citizenship. Nevertheless, women's relationship with government remained ambiguous because women were not allowed to vote.[59]

Equal Rights and Woman's Rights

The authority of republican motherhood made possible women's membership in Garrison's associations, and it even protected their participation in mass petition campaigns. By defending women's rights to distribute and sign petitions, Adams and Garrison also asserted women's right to practice some form of politics in public. But two developments combined to introduce "the woman question" into the antislavery movement itself: first, Garrison's dedication to equality (principally the guarantee of free speech)[60] as the only legitimate means to govern human relationships; and second, the developing opposition to new forms of participation by women, especially speaking in public. As the challenge to female Garrisonians intensified, the defenders of "woman's rights" assailed traditional sex roles and assumptions of female inferiority.

To win support for the antislavery petitions, Garrison more evenly balanced his claims that slavery was sinful with arguments for equal political rights. For Garrison, slavery violated the close connection between natural rights and the rights of persons. By 1833 Garrison used "equal rights" and "natural rights" interchangeably in his speeches. He further claimed that the denial of equal rights was sinful. Garrison repeatedly cast good and evil, freedom and slavery, and equality and inequality as if they were conceptually synonymous dichotomies.[61] This rhetoric opened the door to arguments that the inequality of women was evil.

Garrison's definition of natural rights as equal rights in a political sense shifted the orientation of his antislavery strategy. Initially, following the Quakers' example, he had argued that moral suasion and the voluntary rejection of slavery were the only appropriate steps for abolition. In the petition campaign for the abolition of slavery in the District of Columbia, however, he began to initiate symbolic political reforms. When John Quincy Adams continued these campaigns and added a plan to pass a constitutional amendment to abolish slavery, Garrison objected only weakly. By naming equal rights the most basic democratic condition that slavery violated, Garrison allowed for a shift away from the voluntarist "giving up" of slavery and a move toward legal or legislative abolition by the mandated guarantee of equal rights for all. As much as Garrison verbally remained faithful to his original reform vision, he did not fight the shift in tide brought by reformers such as Adams or the drift toward the Civil War.[62]

Garrison's promulgation of equal rights arguments had major implications for the woman's rights movement as it took shape during the late 1830s and 1840s. First, these arguments opened the door to goals for women beyond the extension of republican motherhood into the public domain. Second, by vesting equal rights with moral character and by making slavery an equal rights issue, he made antislavery and woman's rights harder to exclude from the political agenda. Third, once the state became identified as responsible for moral issues, the exclusion of republican mothers was no longer tenable. Thus, as antislavery became more political, abolitionist women saw political rights and political power as necessary and rightfully theirs. At the same time, those who cared to maintain the original division of labor between government and society, to leave moral issues to nongovernmental institutions and remedies, and to insulate women from direct political participation resisted extending equal rights to include women. Ginzberg observes, for instance, that Juliana Tappan's abrupt, voluntary exit from antislavery reform in the late 1830s came from her unwillingness to reconcile claims for egalitarian woman's rights with her sense that woman's appropriate role was as a competent benevolent reformer who should refuse all visible positions of leadership and defer to men's judgments.[63]

Hints of egalitarian ideas appear in Maria Stewart's speeches, but they are far more pronounced in Sarah Grimké's *Letters on the Equality of the Sexes and the Condition of Woman,* written after Garrison began his vigorous promotion of equal rights. In her comparisons of the opportunities afforded to European Americans and those available to African Americans, Stewart pleaded that members of her race see themselves as worthy people who could and should imitate European Americans: "Do you ask the disposition I would have you possess? Possess the spirit of independence. The Americans do, and why should not you? Possess the spirit of men, bold and enterprising, fearless and undaunted. Sue for your rights and privileges. Know the reason that you cannot attain them. Weary them with your importunities. You can but die if you make the attempt; and we shall certainly die if you do not."[64] In a warning to European American men of impending action by African Americans, Stewart spelled out a biological basis of equality:

> We will not come out against you "with swords and staves, as against a thief" [Matthew 26:55]; but we will tell you that our souls are fired with the same love of liberty and independence with which your souls are fired. We will tell you that too much of your blood flows in our veins, too much of your color in our skins, for us not to possess your spirits. We will tell you that it is our gold that clothes you "in fine linen and purple, and causes you to fare sumptuously every day" [Luke 16:19]; and it is the blood of our fathers, and the tears of our brethren that have enriched your soils. AND WE CLAIM OUR RIGHTS.[65]

In her early moralization efforts, Angelina Grimké used similar rhetoric to broaden a claim of outright equality between the sexes, at least regarding the requirement of obedience to God's commands and the divinely endowed capacity to do the right thing in adverse circumstances: "Did the cloven tongues of fire descend upon the heads of *women* as well as men? Yes, my friends, 'it sat upon *each of them*'; Acts ii, 3. *Women* as well as men were to be living stones in the temple of grace, and therefore *their* heads were consecrated by the descent of the Holy Ghost as well as those of men."[66] Angelina Grimké also argued that neither the different human responsibilities of women and men nor their differences in political power exempted women from the moral responsibility to abolish slavery.

These passages reveal the powerful effects on Stewart and the Grimkés of a scripturally based concept of moral equality. The aim of equality led Stewart to infuse symbolism mainly from the Hebrew Scriptures into a dissident critique of racism. Likewise, Angelina Grimké put new emphasis on the inclusive presence of the New Testament's Holy Spirit in the account of Pentecost. These celebrations of inclusive equality radicalized Garrison's aims. Stewart made public the occurrence of miscegenation; Angelina Grimké insisted that men and women were equally blessed as God's messengers. Both points raised radical questions about the need for fundamental change in people's everyday lives.

The Chastisement of Women Allied with Garrison

As central participants in this first major effort to include slavery in the federal government's agenda, Garrisonian women began to bend the rules of the political game in the United States. During this confrontation those who had a vested interest in government's excluding slavery and related issues from social policy realized that the moral authority of republican motherhood had been organized and directed against them. Their response, and the response of many other male leaders (especially in the mainstream churches), was to defend the sexual contract. Traditionally, women were expected to obey men, to be silent about public affairs, and to restrict their exercise of moral authority to the household and less controversial issues. These champions of tradition brought home their message with forceful effects: under heavy criticism, Stewart and the Grimkés eventually lost heart and left the movement.

Maria Stewart probably received such criticisms after she rebuked free black men for failing to speak up about their suffering and demand rights. In a speech given in February 1833, Stewart asked, "Is it blindness of mind, or stupidity of soul, or the want of education that has caused our men who are 60 or 70 years of age, never to let their voices be heard, nor their hands be raised in behalf of their color? Or has it been for the fear of offending the whites?" Stewart urged these men to rely on "the God of Justice" and give up their fears, to speak their minds and seek rights. She warned them against spending their earnings on gambling and dancing; Stewart urged them instead to join temperance societies, raise money for their children's schools, and support antislavery reform.

Stewart also appears to have been sorely denounced for speaking in public as a woman. She defended herself eloquently, eliciting, as Angelina Grimké later did, strong biblical women in her defense:

> What if I am a woman; is not the God of ancient times the God of these modern days? Did he not raise up Deborah, to be a mother, and a judge in Israel [Judges 4:4]? Did not Queen Esther save the lives of

the Jews? And Mary Magdalen [sic] first declare the resurrection of Christ from the dead? . . . Did St. Paul but know of our wrongs and deprivations, I presume he would make no objections to our pleading in public for our rights. Again; holy women ministered unto Christ and the apostles; and women of refinement in all ages, more or less, have had a voice in moral, religious and political subjects . . . What if such women as are here described should rise among our sable race? And it is not impossible. For it is not the color of the skin that makes the man or the woman, but the principle formed in the soul.[67]

Stewart's scriptural references presented all women versed in the Scriptures with models grounded in an authority far more powerful than the ideals of liberty and equality could be at the time. Stewart echoed those who invoked similar figures during the Revolution to inspire women to raise funds for Washington's troops.[68] Despite this eloquence, Stewart's message received little support among free blacks in Boston; dispirited by the criticisms leveled at her, Stewart decided to leave the city in the fall of 1833.[69] Garrison appears not to have challenged her decision. As a sympathetic observer and friend, Garrison must have noticed her plight, but his failure to defend her suggests that he did not feel as obliged to his free black female constituents as he did to the native-born whites.[70]

The formation of female antislavery societies by Lucretia Mott and other, mostly Quaker women started just as Stewart exited Boston. In mobilizing support, these native-born white women tried to overcome racial prejudice. In Philadelphia Lucretia Mott joined like-minded Quaker women, including Sarah Douglass and other free black women Quakers, in founding the Philadelphia Female Antislavery Society. These women became the Grimké sisters' first reform community; Gerda Lerner identifies Sarah Douglass as the woman who told the Grimkés about the prejudice suffered by the free colored in the North due to fears of "amalgamation."[71]

The Grimkés were distressed by the prejudice of northern Quakers, including the Philadelphia Society of Friends, exemplified by the Quaker meetings' making free blacks sit on "colored benches."[72] By accepting free blacks as members, these Garrisonian female reformers faced anger and recrimination as the men had. In 1838, just before the second antislavery convention of American women in Philadelphia, the mayor of that city suggested that the women antislavery leaders "ask the black women to stop attending the meetings."[73] When Mott and others refused, a mob of seventeen thousand forcibly entered the newly constructed Pennsylvania Hall where the convention was to meet and burned it.[74]

Practicing egalitarian ideals by refusing to respect habits of segregation by race and sex gained these Quaker women a reputation as radical, or "ultra," reformers. Many men and women active in less controversial benevolent causes severely criticized these women for breaking the informal rules about who should participate in politics, how women should behave in public, and what should change in everyday interpersonal relations between people of different races as well as sexes. The Garrisonian women did more than simply participate and exercise power in a radical benevolent reform: they began to strip away the camouflage from women's abilities to make policy; they spoke in public to mixed audiences; and they demonstrated how organizations could practice equality. Until exhaustion overcame them, Sarah and Angelina Grimké bore the burden of justifying and defending these ideals to audiences composed primarily of native-born whites.

The Grimké sisters began what became a historic lecture tour three years after Stewart's farewell speech and just after Garrison's society formally endorsed female agents and lecturers. The two reformers initially planned to address audiences of women only; however, men who wanted to hear them found ways to attend their lectures. According to Flexner, "before anyone really knew what was happening, the Grimkés were addressing large mixed public audiences."[75] They soon faced the same kind of criticism that Stewart had encountered in her black community several years earlier. In August of 1837, the Council of Congregationalist Ministers of Massachusetts issued a pastoral letter that criticized women who chose to speak in public for "threaten[ing] the female character with wide-spread and permanent injury."[76] The Grimkés rebuked the ministers' chastisement: Angelina lectured on behalf of woman's rights, and Sarah "wrote a series of articles that were published in the *New England Spectator,* on 'The Province of Women,' which were issued as a pamphlet . . . entitled *The Equality of the Sexes and the Condition of Women,* and widely circulated."[77]

Several months earlier, Lydia Maria Child and other women leaders had decided to hold a national antislavery convention of women to celebrate their successful petition campaigns and assert woman's right to make public claims for moral reform. This convention passed a resolution stating that women's public action was necessary to fulfill the responsibilities of republican motherhood: "Resolved, that as certain rights and duties are common to all moral beings, the time has come for woman to move in that sphere which Providence has assigned her, and no longer remain satisfied in the circumscribed limits which corrupt custom and a perverted application of Scripture have encircled her."[78]

The Grimkés assumed the burden of proving why woman's rights constituted equal rights, an equation inspired partly by Garrison and partly by their determination to inform the ministers that it was inappropriate to put women in subordinate positions. In her *Letters on the Equality of the Sexes and the Condition of Woman*, Sarah Grimké explained the social changes necessary to create egalitarian relationships between men and women. She stated: "Men and women were CREATED EQUAL; they are both moral and accountable beings, and whatever is *right* for man to do is *right* for woman."[79] Men and women are both commanded by the Scriptures, she claimed, "to bring forth the fruits of the Spirit, love, meekness, gentleness, &c."[80] Sarah made explicit Angelina's earlier implicit assumption that as moral beings men and women stood equally accountable before God. She also decried as morally intolerable the inequalities caused by human institutions such as wage-setting, education, the financial dependence of women—particularly of fashionable women—and slavery.

With these arguments, the Grimké sisters enlisted their female colleagues to defend woman's rights in the North. Soon thereafter a core group of female Garrisonians used equal rights arguments to defend extending republican motherhood to the public domain and to exhort women to join the cause. In May 1838, at the second antislavery convention of American women, Angelina Grimké, Lucretia Mott, Maria Weston Chapman, and Abby Kelley each defended woman's right to participate in antislavery organizations and activities. A resolution was passed at the convention proclaiming that women had both the obligation and the right to use their intelligence in support of a moral cause such as antislavery.[81]

The Grimkés' successes within their own reform circle were not, however, matched outside of it. They continued to be the targets of severe criticism. After one year, Angelina, "who bore the brunt of public utterance . . . broke down under the strain in May 1838 and did not speak again for many years."[82] Angelina Grimké married Theodore Weld shortly thereafter, and the three resigned from public life; their exit was similar to the one that Maria Stewart had made six years earlier.

The Grimké sisters' adoption of woman's rights objectives differed from Stewart's. *Before* she was criticized for her activism, Stewart asserted woman's rights by encouraging women's participation in antislavery reform.[83] In contrast, the Grimkés claimed that reform objectives justified woman's rights only *after* the Congregationalist clergy in Massachusetts issued a letter chastising women reformers for speaking in public.[84] This difference in timing suggests that the need for women to be as politically free as men was clearer to Stewart because a free black woman's standing was less ambiguous than that of a native-born white woman. Still, Stewart and the Grimké sisters had similar conceptions of woman's rights as well as reactions to their experiences. When Sarah Grimké defined woman's rights as a claim of equal rights, she drew on a biblically based notion of moral equality. Her sister, Angelina, and Maria Stewart also asserted that women had the same obligation as men to fulfill Christian duties even if public speaking and action were necessary. Stewart and the Grimkés justified this moral equality with far more direct references to the Scriptures than Garrison made; he preferred to invoke the Scriptures' guiding principles as a whole and avoided literal references. Garrison more often referred to the ideas of political equality put forth by the Declaration of Independence, which were widely understood to apply only to men. Yet Garrison presented those more exclusive ideals of political equality as if their central premise was the moral equality that the women promoted. Stewart and the Grimkés were, in this way, equally valuable to Garrison.

Each of these bold women also decided it was personally too costly to continue her struggle for woman's rights, which indicates the virulence of early opposition to woman's rights. These women's short careers as woman's rights advocates force the question of who sustained the momentum for woman's rights reform. The answer proves that Stewart and the Grimkés had converted their male associates: Garrison and other supportive male colleagues contributed decisively to the formation of the woman's rights movement.

Garrison's Defense of Woman's Rights

During the early 1830s, the only concerted, internal opposition to women's participation in the antislavery movement came from free blacks who objected to Maria Stewart's activism. Garrison won support from elite whites with his strategy of nongovernmental, moral suasion, which drew heavily on the rhetoric of female benevolence developed by middle-class, educated women.[85] Because the initial recruitment process consisted of signing up members and distributing antislavery tracts, activities that women performed in sex-segregated associations, Garrison had no reason to make woman's rights a reform issue. Nor did the issue of woman's rights need to be raised within his organization because women of both races were accepted by their male colleagues, and Garrison especially appears to have related to them as equals. It was only after women's visible participation and defense of equality became targets of criticism that Garrison was forced to make woman's rights a major reform issue, and he defended these rights vigorously.

Although the public's rejection of Stewart went relatively unnoticed in 1833, Garrison's challenge to Congress to abolish slavery in the District of Columbia initiated institutional opposition to women's vocal and public activism. It is impossible to know whether Garrison wittingly invited this criticism; he surely knew, however, that many congressmen would see his demand as threatening the practical exclusion of slavery from the legislative agenda. Garrison's proposal and the petitions forced slavery onto the agenda. Women's efforts had enabled Garrison to pressure legislators through petition, and thereafter he relied even more on women's participation.

As the Grimkés presented their arguments for woman's rights, Garrison, the Rev. Samuel May, and fellow liberal reformers encouraged them and other women to continue their active, public participation in the antislavery movement.[86] This encouragement gave the incipient feminists a ready-made alliance with some prominent men. The alliance's composition became clear when the woman's rights issue divided segments of women and men in that society against each other.

When the Grimkés delivered their lectures to mixed audiences of men and women, antislavery societies were composed, for the most part, of members of the same sex. After the attacks on these two women, however, disputes emerged in the national male and female antislavery societies over the admission of women to traditionally male societies and over women's participation in Garrison's organization as speakers and officers. Questions multiplied about both the effects of woman leaders on the success of antislavery reform and appropriate roles for women.[87]

Followers of Garrison who opposed his support of woman's rights were worried about losing support from ministers and other community leaders who joined the Congregationalist ministers' denunciation of the Grimkés' public speaking. Melder argues that ministers throughout Massachusetts echoed the criticisms of women speaking in public leveled by the Congregationalists: "Basing their arguments on the scriptural 'appropriate sphere' of the sex, several prominent ministers published sermons denouncing public speaking by women."[88]

As Kraditor shows, the major efforts to oppose women's participation were initiated by "nonabolitionists, and the other protests and appeals before 1839 were written by clergymen who were local antislavery leaders, or on the periphery of the movement or had only recently joined."[89] Still, Garrison and some of his colleagues who supported woman's rights could not stop the denunciations of the women's activism: "the woman-question controversy," Kraditor observes, "quickly became involved in the religious and political disputes that were to tear the association apart in 1840, and its usefulness as a weapon in those other factional struggles was revealed quite early."[90]

Garrison, who by 1838 had become highly critical of clerical hierarchies and distrustful of ministers' support for antislavery, supported the Grimkés' defense of woman's rights; after 1838 he refused, despite much pressure from some associates, to remove the issue from his agenda.[91] In May 1839, a group of reformers, led by Rev. Amos Phelps and Rev. Charles T. Torrey, broke off from the American Anti-Slavery Society and formed the Massachusetts Abolition Society, with female auxiliaries. These societies included local leaders and ministers who were not officers of the Anti-Slavery Society.[92] Eventually, however, even some of those abolitionists who disagreed with, but tolerated, Garrison's defense of women's participation were persuaded that the "equality of the sexes" was "not God's will." More importantly, they insisted that the issue of women's participation impeded abolitionist gains.[93]

Ginzberg argues that including women as equals became a liability for those abolitionists who opted for political strategies over moral suasion.[94] Increasingly, voting was considered a crucial resource for antislavery activists; petitioning was disparaged as the silent expression of mere "subjects," perhaps because women passed and signed many of them. This portrayal of how some antislavery reformers became woman's rights opponents is compelling. But Ginzberg overlooks both the leadership opportunities and the boost that female Garrisonians gained from Garrison's defense of equal rights goals. In any case, the split among Garrisonians was not simply a choice between "political action" to end slavery and the inclusion of women as equals in the quest for abolition through "moral suasion." Reformers divided most sharply over the conception of women as equals to men.

When the opponents of women's participation left Garrison's organization, the woman's rights Garrisonians became even freer to campaign for their new aims and to develop skills as speakers, petitioners, and officers of antislavery organizations. But they also faced continued opposition for both their cause and their public leadership. Indeed, the threats to women's continued participation in these organizations became more intense. Between 1837 and 1840 additional conflicts over the role of women as political organizers emerged in state legislatures. The rights of women to gather petitions against both slavery and bans on racial intermarriage were challenged. Many legislators seriously doubted woman's right to articulate her own opinions.[95]

Splits followed the heated debates over the woman question and related issues, which left the antislavery movement sorely divided.[96] The women who remained active Garrisonians and supporters of woman's rights, notably Abby Kelley Foster and Lucretia Mott, struggled less visibly after the Grimkés' withdrawal, although they still disagreed among themselves. During the controversy over women's participation, Kelley suggested that the segregated female societies be abolished. Mott strongly disagreed; she told Kelley that the separate women's meetings had accomplished much "in bringing our sex forward, exercising their talents, and preparing them for united action with men, as soon as we can convince them that this is both our right and our duty."[97] Kelley did not respond directly; later she asked Garrison whether Mott, at the 1840 World Anti-Slavery Convention in London, had "sacrificed principle at the altar of peace" regarding woman's rights in the association. And plenty of Garrisonian women, such as Mary S. Parker in Boston, sided with men who claimed that the woman's rights issue weakened antislavery efforts.[98]

By 1840 most male antislavery reformers appear to have agreed that women's leadership was a liability for abolition. Only Garrison and his closest colleagues defended woman's rights reforms as appropriate and as necessary for the achievement of equal rights. Although most reformers assessed women's contributions as expendable, Garrison concluded that dismissing woman's rights would be tantamount to rejecting the movement's equal rights ideals.[99] However divided his own colleagues became on this issue, Garrison's endorsement of woman's rights goals kept the issue alive long enough to cultivate a critical mass of leadership for the woman's rights movement.

Garrison's incorporation of woman's rights into an ongoing reform effort led by a male was unprecedented in the history of woman's rights; Garrison took this bold step in spite of the divisive controversy that eventually split his organization. Besides satisfying the equal rights principles he was promoting, Garrison's defense of woman's rights also indicated his preference for women's moral authority—republican motherhood—over clerical moral authority. If, as Walter Merrill contends, Garrison's leadership positions, particularly his control of the *Liberator,* were themselves at stake during the late 1830s, then Garrison had to rely on "the women of New England's" loyalties to preserve at least one of his original constituencies. By then he had lost most of the clergy and many of the newspaper editors.[100]

Garrison's Sustained Collective Action for Woman's Rights

Garrison's decision to support woman's rights objectives, in practice as well as theory, sustained the struggle. He and a free black male colleague, Charles Remond, made the first recorded public "protest" in defense of woman's rights during the 1840 World Anti-Slavery Convention in London. When they were told that women members of the United States' delegation would not be allowed to sit at the podium, Garrison and Remond refused to join their European colleagues. They argued vigorously for the recognition of American women as contributors, leaders, and, more generally, as deserving equal rights. This unprecedented and courageous protest by Remond and Garrison signaled a key stride toward political inclusion for women.[101]

The importance of Garrison's action for the woman's rights movement should not be underestimated. After the Grimkés retired from antislavery reform, and the women in his organization as well as outside it became divided over whether woman's rights was an appropriate reform issue, Garrison's sustained defense of woman's right to speak publicly against slavery kept the idea of woman's rights alive. No less important was his continued promotion of the ideal of inclusive equality. When the opposition dealt blows damaging enough to break apart or prevent the consolidation of core female leaders for woman's rights, Garrison sustained the fledgling movement.

Garrison's repudiation of the policy of excluding women at an international antislavery convention culminated his support of woman's rights initiatives during the previous three years. He accepted responsibility for, and was determined to continue, woman's rights reform efforts. These events drew the attention of Lucretia Mott and Elizabeth Cady Stanton to woman's rights as a key issue of political representation. They imitated Garrison's leadership style and adopted his moral suasion strategy when they engineered the Seneca Falls Convention eight years later.

Two factors explain why Garrison could act so vigorously for woman's rights. The first is Garrison's leadership style; the second is the apathy of the major political parties during the 1830s toward abolition. As a leader directed by principles rather than a desire for power, Garrison was unwilling to relinquish woman's rights goals merely because they were more controversial than antislavery objectives. He insisted that the means to achieve equal rights reform such as antislavery be consistent with his vision of a society of equals because the complete abolition of slavery could not be achieved by organizations that persistently denied women full participatory rights.[102]

The detachment of the major political parties from the antislavery issue also indicates why Garrison was able to sustain his support for woman's rights. During the 1830s, the Pinckney "Gag Rule" and the controversy over the Garrisonian petition campaigns led to the exclusion of antislavery reformers' demands. Garrison then redoubled his commitments to public moral reform. In his view, the petition campaigns led by Adams and members of the clergy were dissident moral protests. Garrison demanded that Congress abolish slavery in the District of Columbia mainly to embarrass elected federal representatives. Even after moral suasion had lost its appeal for most antislavery reformers, including many loyal Garrisonians, he staunchly defended voluntary conversion as far better than coerced.[103]

Because Garrison avoided political parties, and because the parties did not try to adopt the antislavery issue, he was not constrained by imposing limitations on the participation of women. He was not accountable to constituents, nor obligated to maintain the government. If either of the major political parties had appropriated the antislavery issue during the late 1830s or the early 1840s, they would have presented Garrison and his colleagues with more formidable obstacles to their continued support of woman's rights goals. Willing bargainers for antislavery legislation from exclusively male political parties could have made the woman's rights issue expendable for Garrison and his colleagues.

~❖~

The political parties' lack of interest in antislavery reform fostered the formation of the woman's rights movement. First, party networks based upon loyalties and favors insulated legislators from antislavery reform pressure. Second, the lack of legislative attention given to antislavery reform gave Garrison and his colleagues more reason to redouble their moral reform efforts and to engage as many willing participants as possible, male and female. Third, the detachment of antislavery reform from party politics preserved the abolitionists' control of their agenda. An issue such as woman's rights could be added to that agenda without jeopardizing a "coalition." In short, if Garrison's association had cultivated ties to a particular party, the pressures to keep a single-issue focus on antislavery would probably have been intense, and woman's rights would not have been included. Nor would woman's rights have been allowed to divide the antislavery organizations as sharply. As it was, Garrison recruited women because they could provide moral authority; and as opposition to his leadership grew among editors and ministers, Garrison became increasingly dependent on women's participation. Although Garrison's identification of woman's rights as equal rights showed that he had the courage of his convictions, he also owed much to the women who supported him.

Besides staying loyal to Garrison's leadership and ideals, the women who joined his organization brought him the rhetoric and respectability of female benevolent reform. As they developed their own appeals, Maria

Stewart and the Grimké sisters introduced a theme of inclusive equality. This theme was based on both a Protestant conception of duties and a liberal interpretation of divine expectations for women in the Scriptures. By including free black women in their association, dissenting from racial segregation, and willingly assuming public leadership responsibilities, Lucretia Mott, Abby Kelley, and other Garrisonian women became radicals among radicals: they both promoted and practiced inclusive equality.

2

"Liberal Feminisms" and Political Autonomy

*B*Y THE early 1840s the Garrisonians proved themselves committed to advocating woman's rights as equal rights. Abby Kelley
Foster, Lucretia Mott, and in 1848, Lucy Stone integrated
woman's rights claims into their antislavery lectures. Garrison provided
these women a small income for speaking, space in the *Liberator* for
promoting woman's rights issues, and regular endorsements, but he
stopped short of encouraging his female antislavery colleagues to hold
their own conventions for woman's rights or start an independent journal.
By the time Elizabeth Cady Stanton, Lucretia Mott, Mary Ann McClin-
tock, Jane Hunt, and Martha Wright (Lucretia Mott's sister) planned the
Seneca Falls convention in July 1848, however, several state legislatures
had proposed property reforms for married women; women had organized
temperance reform societies; the women of the Seneca tribe had persuaded
Lucretia Mott to respect and tolerate cultural differences; massive democratic uprisings had occurred in France; and Frederick Douglass had published laments about the exploitation of women in antislavery reform.[1]
Influences beyond Garrisonian ideals pushed the five women organizers of
the first woman's rights convention. Their main constituency, however,
still consisted of Garrisonians.

Of the non-Garrisonian influences, married woman's property rights
reform inspired most of the independent claims for woman's rights. Although abolition inducted some educated, white, middle-class women into
public efforts for moral reform, various proposals for married woman's
property reform during the late 1830s and 1840s gave woman's rights
reformers new egalitarian grounds in civil law.

Many men supported this reform because it would loosen the restrictions on the exchange of inherited property during their wives' lifetimes
and would guarantee its distribution to their children and grandchildren.[2]
Some men, however—such as Ira Harris of New York State—also reflected
upon equal rights for married women beyond property ownership. As

Norma Basch shows, the debates in the New York State legislature during 1846 and early 1848 over giving married women full legal protection and independent standing in addition to property rights foreshadowed issues raised during the Seneca Falls convention of 1848. In 1846 such a major reform passed, only to be overturned by those fearful that the law would no longer "protect" marriages from impulsive exits by spouses. Ira Harris's 1846 proposal read: "*All* property of the wife, owned by her at the time of her marriage, *and that acquired by her afterwards* by gift, devise or descent, or otherwise than from her husband, shall be her *separate* property. Laws shall be passed providing for the registry of the wife's separate property, *and more clearly defining the rights of the wife thereto* as well as to property held by her with her husband."[3]

Few bolder statements of women's demands for equal rights can be found than those articulated in the 1848 Declaration of Sentiments. When its authors asserted that "all men and women are created equal" and "endowed by their Creator with certain inalienable rights," they imitated the founders' revolutionary dissent from the British crown's excessive use of coercive powers. But Jefferson and his cohorts never considered male domination of political power a problem; only the 1848 declaration questioned the legitimacy of that power. By identifying male power as absolute and dangerous to liberty, these reformers launched a rebellion against the political subordination of women. They also encouraged a reconnection of the familial sphere and civil society.

Historians studying this manifesto and the woman's rights movement of the 1850s have been struck by the sophistication and thoroughness with which reformers (especially Elizabeth Cady Stanton) used liberal ideas to call for improvements in their everyday lives. Another equally striking, but also puzzling, feature was the lack of a central organization or leadership hierarchy that might have enabled these incipient feminists to consolidate their resources, make consistent arguments, anticipate opposition, and design a unified strategy for mobilizing support. According to Ellen Carol DuBois, although Anthony, Stone, and Stanton could not have known how their male allies would betray the cause of woman's rights during Reconstruction reform, the willingness of these women to depend on Garrisonian men explains their lack of desire for organizational autonomy and why a truly independent women's movement was slow to emerge.[4]

Looking closely at the reformers' aims as well as their debates during the conventions of the 1850s reveals that despite the movement's "organizational underdevelopment,"[5] as DuBois characterizes it, the reformers invested a lot of time setting priorities and justifying woman's rights.[6] Because the reformers concentrated more on making ideological contributions than organizational strides, their movement would more accurately be described as *unevenly* developed. Given that these women possessed virtually no experience as leaders of organizations including both women and men, the male Garrisonians provided them an ideal political forum—a "free space" for developing autonomous ideas and practicing leadership.[7]

Woman's rights conventions of the 1850s served primarily as fora for consciousness-raising and supporting women's public participation as antislavery reformers. The emergence of an autonomous woman's rights movement hinged on the ideas these reformers developed to challenge authoritative views about sex roles and call for radical personal change. I consider these women leaders' continued dependence on their reputation as Garrisonians and ties to Garrison as their way of protecting—and even hiding—the momentous changes they considered and debated.

Garrisonian men sheltered and nurtured the woman's rights movement of the 1850s at least partly because its women leaders—on whom Garrison depended—demanded attention to these issues. Male Garrisonians applauded the women's initiative in taking on unprecedented responsibilities such as chairing meetings that included both men and women. The men, however, remained unobtrusive, irregular participants at the 1850s woman's rights conventions. Of all the male Garrisonians, Henry Blackwell, husband of Lucy Stone, took the most interest in woman's rights; Wendell Phillips and Thomas Wentworth Higginson participated more regularly than Garrison. Although Garrison himself participated irregularly, the reformers followed his celebration of equality and individual freedom by defining property, suffrage, and divorce rights as fundamental political liberties.

Financial and promotional dependence on Garrison's organization was neither the only nor the most important reason that the woman's rights movement remained organizationally weak. Complex issues gave the women leaders strong reasons to avoid investing their time and energy in organizational development. First, the women's approach sidestepped artificial hierarchical trappings that could threaten friendships and generate destructive power struggles. Second, their own historical account of the 1850s conventions reveals that they organized primarily as state associations—even the national convention minutes were distilled from state histories.[8] Third, these women put both family goals (such as motherhood) and antislavery ahead of woman's rights. Fourth, the vigorous opposition to woman's rights among non-Garrisonians would have made particular officers or offices easy targets for harassment. Fifth, the reformers themselves disagreed about setting priorities and justifying woman's rights. Adding factional disputes over who should control the organization and its agenda would have intensified that conflict. In short, because they had little interest in organizational development but a strong interest in articulating principled arguments for woman's rights, the reformers decided to focus on debate rather than to expand membership or develop an extensive, autonomous organization.

Deliberate Avoidance of Organizational Hierarchy

Women leaders thus agreed early on to have no other formal structure than the annual convention and the central committee. At the 1852 convention in Syracuse, New York, a majority rejected a proposal to organize a national society. A letter from Angelina Grimké Weld opposing the proposal stated that women were held together by spiritual bonds and that no artificial ties were needed: "We need no external bonds to bind us together, no cumbrous machinery to keep our minds and hearts in unity of purpose and effort; we are not the lifeless staves of a barrel which can be held together only by the iron hoops of an artificial organization."[9]

Convention members resoundingly supported Weld's statement. A few spoke devotedly for the continuation of an informal, nonhierarchical organization. Dr. Harriot Hunt "spoke as a physician in deeming spontaneity as a law of nature." Ernestine Rose, a leader of married woman's property reform initiatives, "declared organizations to be like Chinese bandages." Lucy Stone described her experience in organizations as dreadful; she said that "she had had enough of thumb-screws and soul screws ever to wish to be placed under them again." She concluded her remarks as follows: "The present duty is agitation." Samuel May agreed with these women leaders; he "deemed a system of action and co-operation all that was needed."[10]

Only two reformers, Clarina Nichols and Abram Pryne, favored creating a national woman's rights organization. Nichols argued that an organization would serve "as a means to collect and render operative the fragmentary elements now favoring the cause."[11] Nichols was unable, however, to persuade her colleagues that fragmentation was a serious problem. The reformers did accept Paulina W. Davis's resolution for the formation of state societies; they encouraged members to call yearly meetings in their states and counties. Davis's resolution confirmed woman's rights reformers' commitments to improve woman's status in all respects. Future efforts, especially conventions, would aim "to consider the principles of this reform, and devise measures for their promulgation, and thus co-operate with all throughout the nation and the world, for the elevation of woman to a proper place in the mental, moral, social, religious, and political world."[12]

The radical assertions of liberal rights for women in the 1848 declaration infused these reformers with a spirit of independence as well as vigorous respect for rights among themselves. How could they ordain a hierarchy, define tasks, and supervise each other's performance when they had just proclaimed the equality of all women?

The 1848 Declaration of Sentiments

Stanton, Mott, and their cohorts filled the 1848 Declaration of Sentiments with ideas calling for fundamental and, in many cases, more difficult democratic changes than those of its model, the Declaration of Independence. Beginning with the claim that "all men and women are created equal" was a self-evident truth, the women both introduced an inclusive definition of political equality and revealed the partiality of Jefferson and the previous social contract thinkers. By calling first for "throwing off" the government that had made women suffer and providing "new guards for future security" as well as "equal station," woman's rights founders presented a new challenge. Those who considered government limited in its powers and scope were asked to measure most traditional white, middle-class relationships between educated men and women by the standards of liberty and equality. If they did so, the reformers suggested, they could only conclude that these relationships were tyrannous.

The many women's grievances ranged from the denial of woman's rights to vote and hold office to the use of a double standard in the "code of morals for men and women" (in which women were assigned to "a sphere of action, when that belongs to her conscience and to her God") to systematic efforts to destroy women's confidence, "to lessen her self-respect, and to make her willing to lead a dependent and abject life."[13] When elected officials and voters restricted their attention to past business and set their sights on self-selected issues, these reformers informed them that new issues were now on the agenda. From women's perspectives, they pointed out, absolutist powers remained very much in place. To achieve the goals of Jefferson and his fellow revolutionaries, men must limit their control of women and be willing to govern themselves with the same moral code they expected of women.

To defend women's interests, reformers quoted a major premise of natural rights law, that "man shall pursue his own true and substantial happiness," and invoked Blackstone's claim that the obligation to obey this law supersedes "any other." Ergo, the reformers wrote, "such laws as conflict, in any way, with the true and substantial happiness of woman, are contrary to the great precept of nature and of no validity, for this is 'superior in obligation of any other.'"[14] This priority on women's happiness explicitly applied fundamental assumptions associated with the liberalism of natural rights to women without reference to innate or acquired differences from men. The principle implied that neither public policies nor particular men could legitimately continue to perpetrate the sufferings of women.

Women reformers' unqualified assertion that natural law applied to women—even though "man" was the subject for whom the claim of free pursuit was made—exemplified the use that could be made of the ambiguous conception "woman's nature." The view that "man," "mankind," or "men" included women provided access to claims of freedom as well as a "station" from which these reformers could indict laws such as coverture. In Blackstone's explication, the law of coverture made married women "civilly dead" by considering husband and wife one person. Nevertheless, here reformers displayed their belief that the principle of natural rights— even as stated by Blackstone—applied equally to men and women.

Blackstone could hardly be considered to have designed a principle extending the same protection of rights to women as to men.[15] The Seneca group's grounding of the natural rights principle, "man shall pursue his own true and substantial happiness,"[16] in natural law; their argument that freedom to pursue happiness was a gift of God; and their extension of this logic to women revolutionized traditional understandings of these authoritative "liberal" premises. Introduced by the social contract theorists and elaborated especially by Locke, the notion that happiness shall be freely pursued had been made for and guaranteed to *men*. To make an authoritative argument that the principle applied to women as well as men, the authors drew heavily on the "Adam's rib" notion that women are part of "mankind." They drew also on radical conceptions of God. Elisabeth Griffith observes that Stanton studied religious questions when she lived in Boston during the 1840s. An admirer of Theodore Parker, who "combined Unitarianism, transcendentalism, and Christian perfectionism," Stanton must have attended to his suggestion that "God was an androgynous figure." She could have decided that the Creator bequeathed women natural rights in accepting Parker's view that "each individual conscience" could "intuit God's will."[17]

The resolutions of the 1848 declaration illustrate how liberal aims for transforming the political condition of women simultaneously pointed to more radical changes.[18] The reformers' grand assertions suggest that they grasped the potential of their movement: all laws inhibiting the happiness of persons were declared invalid; all laws that prevented women from "occupying such a station in society as her conscience shall dictate, or which place her in a position inferior to that of man" were "of no force or authority"; and woman should be recognized as "man's equal" as she was made by "the Creator." The reformers advocated democratic relations between the sexes based on equality as well as a consistent application of moral codes to the "transgressions" of both.[19]

Reformers insisted that the existing public acceptance of women "on stage" as entertainers also logically entailed accepting women who addressed public audiences. To fortify this call for consistent standards of expectation and behavior, the reformers incorporated Stewart and the Grimké sisters' conceptions of participatory republican motherhood: woman should discard the limits imposed upon her in public by "corrupt customs and a perverted application of the Scriptures," and move into "the enlarged sphere which her great Creator has assigned her." They asserted, furthermore, that "the equality of human rights results necessarily from the fact of the identity of the race in capabilities and responsibilities"; and that these capacities, gifts of the Creator, required "woman, equally with man, to promote every righteous cause by every righteous means; and especially in regard to the great subjects of morals and religion."[20]

Although the reformers shared liberal aims and developed far-reaching goals, they also articulated some strongly illiberal ideas. For instance, the 1848 declaration referred to "the identity of the race" and lamented the rights distributed to "the most ignorant and degraded men—both natives and foreigners." This and other woman's rights tracts blended what Rogers Smith labels ascriptive Americanist conceptions of identity with a liberal vision of political inclusion.[21] Stanton's plea that "no woman form an alliance with any man who has been suspected even of the vice of intemperance,"[22] and her claim that the word of such a man was unreliable, fit the anti-Irish prejudices of her time. At the "Mob Convention of 1853," Dr. Harriot K. Hunt of Boston described a young man in the Boston Assessor's Office to whom she paid her taxes as "a tall, thin, weak, stupid-looking Irish boy," and she expressed her disgust that such a person could vote though she could not.[23] According to Kathleen Barry, most woman's rights reformers described Ernestine Rose's high standards for egalitarian behavior and unprejudiced attitudes as impossible to meet. Rose's candid criticisms of her colleagues' hypocrisies isolated her from other reformers.[24]

The reformers' conception of their interests as based on "the identity of the race" eventually crippled some mobilization efforts and tarnished the ultimate suffrage victory in 1920. The 1848 declaration was a radical feminist tract that envisioned far-reaching changes but also united like-minded liberal elites who did not see themselves as sharing common ground with groups different from themselves. Just as Jefferson defined the rights and standing of men in universal terms but intended them only for native-born white men, so the authors of this early feminist tract also defined woman's rights universally but meant them only for native-born white women.

The 1848 declaration stated that without legal rights and full protection guaranteed to men, women lacked the two resources required to make their freedom secure: standing in and protection from the state.[25] Throughout the 1850s the reformers continued to argue that guaranteeing equal rights to women—property, the vote, and divorce—would provide women with direct standing in the state instead of the ambiguous legal status under coverture. But initiating this quest raised new questions about what "protections" for women the state should expect from men and provide itself. The difficulties in defining "appropriate protection" for women illuminates both why it took so long for women to win the vote and why since that time women have faced deep opposition to egalitarian political aims.

The Vote as the Cornerstone of Woman's Rights

The reformers' own account documents that the claim that women should seek "their sacred right to the elective franchise" was considered controversial within the movement. Some feared that the idea of women voting "would defeat others they deemed more rational, and make the whole movement ridiculous."[26] Stanton and Frederick Douglass had to persuade the Seneca group to endorse the vote as a woman's rights goal. In a later publication supporting woman suffrage, Douglass asserted that he "dared not claim a right" which he "would not concede to women." He further explained that whether women voted was less important than the challenge to "the oppressive customs in the Old World, which so wronged woman, that they subjected her to the most laborious as well as degrading means for a livelihood." Douglass preferred "to see her elevated to an equal position with man in every relation of life."[27]

That resistance to female enfranchisement indicates that even some of the most daring challengers of male tyranny accepted modern patriarchy as a fact of life: they had difficulty even imagining women's exercise of *political* power. Although no transcript exists of the 1848 debate over woman suffrage, Amelia Bloomer, the temperance reformer and editor of the *Lily,* confirmed that she attended the Seneca Falls convention but did not sign the 1848 declaration. Bloomer was reluctant initially to support female enfranchisement mainly because she first wanted to reduce intemperance and raise women's self-esteem.[28] By 1853 Bloomer publicly supported ballots for women, but she cautioned that temperance reformers should not put the vote ahead of achieving prohibitions on the consumption of alcohol because, she implied, female enfranchisement would take a long time.[29] The reform agendas set by temperance reformers—as well as their platforms for social policy reform—deterred putting suffrage first. The general subordination of women in the United States did not deny educated, native-born, middle-class white women a capacity to promote and achieve social reform. Thus, resistance to women voting derived from these women's beliefs that making political gains depended on men's efforts to protect women as a politically powerless group.

The grievances and resolutions of the 1848 declaration hardly altered the plans of the two other major, established networks of white educated women: what I call female "feminizers" of American culture, and women active in temperance reform.[30] These groups shared with woman's rights reformers an opposition to the *idea* of female inferiority. But the feminizers and the woman's rights reformers in particular agreed on little else. The feminizers were neither liberal nor feminist, and although temperance reformers such as Amelia Bloomer celebrated equality as an ideal, most believed goals of equal rights for women put their cause at risk.

Benevolent feminizers such as Sarah Josepha Hale and Catharine Beecher called for celebrating separate spheres. By idealizing domesticity and glorifying motherhood, they contended that women's moral superiority to men more than compensated for whatever men said they lacked. Beecher and Hale agreed with Horace Bushnell that woman's rights should be home-centered, or based on improving women's standing as mothers and domestic authorities.[31] These more traditional women would probably appreciate Keith Melder's contention that they blazed a path for the creation of woman's autonomy.[32] But the woman's rights reformers would have agreed with Ann Douglas's view that the more traditional women achieved "an edge in power" but no "genuine gains in status or self-esteem."[33]

Although the feminizers' acceptance of separate spheres and celebration of domesticity probably dampened many women's fears of massive social change—and made some of them wealthy in the process—young Garrisonian women found these views intolerable. In their view, the feminizers' sentimentalization of domesticity and idealization of woman as well protected by men allowed custom to obscure how the law subjugated women. One resolution of the 1848 declaration called for women to become aware of "the laws under which they live, that they may no longer publish their degradation by declaring themselves satisfied with their present position, nor their ignorance, by asserting that they have all the rights they want."[34] The feminizers replied that most women neither needed nor desired woman's rights. To resist the idea of female inferiority, the feminizers used sentimental images of domesticity and placed women on pedestals. This acceptance of political exclusion and praise for the protections expected by middle-class women became the bedrock of traditionalism on which woman's rights opponents depended.

As stated earlier, women in the temperance movement resisted the idea of winning the vote because they feared the new, radical issue would draw attention away from proposals to improve protections for women and children from violence and poverty, problems widely considered likely consequences of alcoholism. To this argument, woman's rights reformers responded (as Stanton did to Bloomer) that with the vote and divorce rights, women would have the power to pass such legislation themselves.[35] But Bloomer insisted that woman's rights reformers "cannot consent to have woman remain silent on the Temperance question till she obtain her right of suffrage."[36] More than twenty years later, women in the temperance movement showed similar reservations about the vote even as Frances Willard powerfully linked temperance reform to female enfranchisement.[37] If political inclusion was the prerequisite for creating a viable means of self-protection, what and who would protect the women who disclaimed their "special" protections? Would enfranchised women lose protections they had had as women who could not vote?

The reformers' ambivalence surfaces in the exchange between British political theorist Harriet Taylor and the American reformers. In her celebrated article, "The Enfranchisement of Women," Taylor claimed that female enfranchisement included more rights than suffrage. She interpreted the resolutions passed at the 1850 Woman's Rights Convention in the United States as an agenda of wide-ranging, social democratic goals, not as a mandate for winning the vote.[38] According to Taylor, the enfranchisement of women entailed "their admission, in law and in fact, to equality in all rights, political, civil, and social, with the male citizens of the community."[39] She further contended that the principle of equality offered a strong foundation for claims of woman's rights. She identified the opposition to reform as the caste-based relations between the sexes:

> In all things the presumption ought to be on the side of equality. A reason must be given why anything should be permitted to one person and interdicted to another. But when that which is interdicted includes nearly everything which those to whom it is permitted most prize, and to be deprived of which they feel to be most insulting; *when not only political liberty but personal freedom of action is the pre-*

nd what is not their 'proper sphere.'" They continued, however, to
id celebrating equality. They focused instead on how political liberty
ild free women from political subjugation: "Woman, therefore, ought
hoose for herself what sphere she will fill, what education she will seek,
 what employment she will follow, and not be held bound to accept,
ibmission, the rights, the education, and the sphere which man thinks
per to allow her."[45] Thus, the American reformers insisted on a voice
women in all forms of government, not an equal share or proportion
obs, wealth, or other material resources. By calling the vote the "cor-
stone of the movement," these reformers painted their enterprise as less
ical than Taylor suggested it was.[46]

Divorce Reform as a Mobilizing Goal

pite reformers' attempts to describe woman's rights as moderate aims,
iences in the United States perceived these goals as radical threats to the
blished order. Moreover, most people believed that the claims were
ed on false premises. Take Stanton's bold arguments for divorce rights,
iments she introduced to temperance reformers in an April 1850 col-
n published in the *Lily*. Stanton referred to pending state legislation that
ild make drunkenness a ground for divorce, a ground already estab-
ed in Connecticut.[47] Stanton favored the reform as a "new door through
ch unhappy prisoners may escape from the bonds of an ill-assorted
riage." She contended that instead of barring a woman from leaving a
unkard" husband, the legislature "ought to pass laws, compelling her to
so." Later, with less exaggeration, Stanton added, "If, as at present, all
freely and *thoughtlessly* enter into the marriage state, they should be
wed to come as freely and *thoughtfully* out again."[48] This odd envision-
of the state on the one hand coercing women to abandon alcoholic
bands but on the other hand simply affording them the right to divorce
zests that Stanton aimed to achieve two goals simultaneously: the estab-
ment of an informal norm among women and divorce rights.
Blending liberal and Americanist ideologies, Stanton advocated divorce
rm to temperance reformers at the second Women's Temperance Con-
tion of the State of New York in April 1852. Appointed president of the
vention, she described divorce as a step women could take without
ting for the day when they were allowed to be professors or ministers, or
ote. Stanton added that women must oppose idleness as well as missions
onvert "the heathen across the ocean"; energies should be dedicated to
ng for children at home and building good schools to "prevent immoral-
and crime in our cities." Anthony and Bloomer also addressed this

rogative of a caste; . . . the miserable expedienci
vanced as excuses for so grossly partial a dispensat
sufficient, even if they were real, to render it oth
injustice.[40]

That fall, the participants in the Second Annual Wor
tion in Worcester, Massachusetts, took exception t
notion of "enfranchisement." Their first conventi
"That while we would not undervalue other metho
frage for Women is, in our opinion, the corner-sto
since we do not seek to protect woman, but rather to
to protect herself."[41] Taylor conceived enfranchisem
political and personal freedom, but the reformers
winning political freedom.

Although they did not fully explain their position
mainly to fortify women's abilities to protect thems
later resolutions they defined overturning "all the l
ing, and unequal laws relating to marriage and prop
goal—a goal that enfranchised woman would be
achieve. They put gaining equal access to professio
employments of society" in second place. Moreover
insisted that they were not compelled "to assert or
of the sexes, in an intellectual or any other point of v
explained why they limited their goal to woman's
enough for our argument that natural and political j
of English and American liberty, alike determine tha
taxation and representation—should be co-extensi
individual citizens, . . . have a self-evident and indi
cally the same right that men have, to a direct voic
those laws and the formation of that government."[4]

The early resolutions, summarized above, displa
reformers conceived of voting as a right that implie
quences for women's wealth or social roles. Their ca
as an escape from slavery provide further support fo
that women perceived the franchise as a means of m
sary credential for political inclusion, not as a tool fo
participation.[44] But Shklar focuses on standing or m
motivator; these reformers considered self-protectio

In later resolutions the reformers did echo Taylo
of enfranchisement by denying—just as the 1848
right of any portion of the species to decide for and

convention, with Bloomer asserting that until women could vote, "on men alone rests the responsibility of the vices and crimes of society."[49]

Stanton's support of weak restrictions on divorce and her promotion of exclusively female officers in her state temperance society brought much criticism. At its 1853 convention she defended her application of woman's rights goals to temperance issues as a means of enabling "drunkards' wives" to "escape from a wretched and degraded life."[50] Some woman's rights reformers who attended the 1853 temperance convention concurred with temperance reformers who considered Stanton's views too radical.

Although they accepted woman suffrage and the idea of equality for women in marriage, Antoinette Brown Blackwell and Clarina Nichols dissented from Stanton's defense of woman's right to divorce on the same terms as men: they argued that marriage was a sacred institution that legal divorce could never terminate.[51] After she became an ordained minister, Reverend Blackwell repeated much the same argument at the 1860 Woman's Rights Convention. Stanton used both the feminism of equal rights and the feminism of fear to justify divorce rights: no relationship should be allowed to hinder the pursuit of happiness nor to perpetuate cruelty. Reverend Blackwell countered that because "voluntary alliance[s]" created marriages, this relationship was permanent, especially due to "the possible incidents of children." Although Blackwell supported legal divorce to ensure that wives and children would obtain political protections for property, she insisted that a wife owed her husband loyalty and care. She argued that reformers should focus boys' and girls' attention on achieving before marriage a "great life purpose" that was "outside of home, outside of our family relations." Such a focus, she implied, would prevent the formation of incompatible marriages.[52]

Although Blackwell and Stanton agreed to disagree on the divorce question, the debate at the 1860 convention so distressed Wendell Phillips that he called for its excise from the minutes. His motion failed, but the reservations expressed about Stanton's divorce proposal signaled that a substantial number of woman's rights reformers were not prepared to accept as essential woman's rights her conception of property, suffrage, and divorce.[53] Their own dependence on illiberal traditions made even the most liberal woman's rights reformers uneasy.

The Nature of Ideological Opposition to Woman's Rights

The account of a woman's rights convention held in New York City in early September 1853 illustrates how threatening woman's rights were to many. The reformers retrospectively titled it "the mob convention," because many hecklers disrupted reformers' speeches and three of New York City's five newspapers derided and ridiculed woman's rights.[54]

At this convention the reformers relied on confrontational tactics and self-righteous claims of "political correctness." Garrison opened the convention with a provocative speech characterizing the opposition to woman's rights as "malignant, desperate, and satanic." He decried the "pulpit interpreters'" use of the Bible to generate hostility to the movement, and restated his basic egalitarian principle: "I have been derisively called a *'Woman's Rights Man.'* I know no such distinction. I claim to be a HUMAN RIGHTS MAN, and whenever there is a human being, I see God-given rights inherent in that being whatever may be the sex or complexion."[55]

Charles C. Burleigh, William Henry Channing, and Lucy Stone followed with speeches reinforcing Garrison's claim that women, as human beings, were entitled to basic rights. To the assumption of female inferiority, for example, Burleigh queried, "I ask, did God give woman aspirations which it is a sin for her to gratify? Abnormal! No, it is to be found everywhere."[56]

When Channing and Stone also professed women's equality, hecklers interrupted their speeches with "roars of laughter" and "hisses."[57] Hecklers hissed when Stone offered as evidence that women could be ministers Antoinette Brown's ministry before "the largest congregation assembled within the walls of my building in the city." They ridiculed Channing's claim that "[woman] should enter into politics, not to degrade herself" but to bring this enterprise "up to her own level of simple-heartedness and purity of soul." They shouted when he argued that "woman alone" had the work of elevating politics "reserved for her."[58]

The next day two opponents of woman's rights, Dr. H. K. Root and Alexander Parker, rose from the audience to speak against woman's rights on the basis of fundamentalist and literal interpretations of the Bible. To rule, Root asserted, the ladies would have to prove that they "have more intelligence, and more energy, and science than the male sex."[59] He cited three reasons why woman should not vote: (1) God commanded that man should rule because it was Eve who tempted Adam in the garden of Eden and thereby created original sin; (2) "because man's [physical] strength is greater than woman's"; and (3) because voting would bring woman into "the field of competition with man," leading "not only to domestic unhappiness, but a great many other ill feelings."[60] Parker reinforced Root's contention that because Eve caused Adam to sin, woman's judgment was untrustworthy. As Root put it, "The original cause of sin was because man gave up his judgment to woman; and it may be, if we now give up our rights to woman, some great calamity may fall upon us."[61]

Some reformers took the tactic of disputing the logic or premises of the opposition. Clarina Nichols asserted that the text stating "woman must obey her husband" gave no "reason why she should obey all the bachelors and other women's husbands in the community."[62] Ernestine Rose dissented from the law's overly precise delineation of the property entitled to widows: although the law allowed widows to receive "six spoons," it failed to distinguish between "tea or table spoons."[63]

Others ridiculed their opponents: Antoinette Brown called them "ignorant" about the "claims" made, "wrongs" condemned, and "remedy" proposed by reformers. She labeled the opponents "bigots"; Wendell Phillips summarily stated that the audience proved "that the men of New York do not understand the meaning of civil liberty and free discussion."[64] Sojourner Truth warned the men who hissed:

> Women don't get half as much rights as they ought to; we want more, and we will have it. Jesus says: "What I say to one, I say to all— watch!" I'm a-watchin'. God says: "Honor your father and your mother." Sons and daughters ought to behave themselves before their mothers, but they do not. I can see them a-laughin', and pointin' at their mothers up here on the stage. They hiss when an aged woman comes forth. If they'd been brought up proper they'd have known better than hissing like snakes and geese.[65]

The barbs exchanged at this convention between the zealous reformers and their equally hostile audience signaled the kinds of resistance that efforts to create woman's rights would meet. For instance, Root's fundamentalist interpretation of the relationship between Adam and Eve in Genesis put the reformers' use of the Scriptures into serious question. Although the reformers took pleasure in deriding their opponents, their shouting matches won them few supporters.

Woman's Rights Reformers Downplay Suffrage

One immediate consequence of the "mob convention" was that some reformers began to moderate claims for woman's rights. At the reformers' fourth national convention in Cleveland one month later, Lucretia Mott steered the reformers away from putting votes for women above other issues. After Frances Gage apologized for the announcement of the convention "which indicates simply our right to the political franchise," Mott stated: "The issuing of the call was left to the Central Committee, but it was not supposed that they would specify any particular part of the labor of the Convention, but that the broad ground of the presentation of the wrongs of woman, the assertion of her rights, and the encouragement to perseverance in individual and combined action, and the restoration of those rights, should be taken."[66]

Gage then invited woman's rights opponents to present their views during the convention so that the women could answer them. She asserted that when opponents' silence was followed by reprisals "through the newspapers," "gross misrepresentation" resulted.[67] Mott's and Gage's actions formally gave woman suffrage a lower priority than it previously had held. Although reformers, most prominently in Massachusetts and New York, continued to press for woman suffrage along with property and other rights in *state* campaigns and conventions, female enfranchisement became much less prominent at the *national* conventions after 1853.[68]

Suffrage lost prominence not because reformers considered the vote less important; after all, Anthony, Stanton, and Gage titled their multivolume history of woman's rights struggles *The History of Woman Suffrage*. But the intense resistance in the early 1850s to the idea of woman's rights, the ridicule reformers endured for wearing bloomers, and the difficulties Anthony encountered as she tried to mobilize women in New York State for temperance reform led the leaders to downplay woman suffrage as a defining goal.

By the mid-1850s a new third party had emerged to stop the expansion of slavery in the West, and woman's suffrage may have inhibited Garrisonian women's efforts to further this cause. In 1855, both Stone and Stanton indicated that protection for married woman's rights mattered most and that the vote was unnecessary to achieve this end. Just before her wedding, Lucy Stone told Antoinette Brown (later Reverend Antoinette Brown Blackwell) that although she thought that it was too early to raise "the marriage question" at the national convention, "it is clear to me, that question underlies, this whole movement . . . It is very little to me to have the right to vote, to own property &c. if I may not keep my body, and its uses, as my absolute right."[69] In late 1855 Elizabeth Cady Stanton raised the issue of woman's right to time her own pregnancies:

> Did it ever enter into the mind of man that woman too had an inalienable right to life, liberty, and the pursuit of her individual happiness? Did he ever take in the idea that to the mother of the race, and to her alone, belonged the right to say when a new being should be brought into the world? Has he, in the gratification of his blind

passions, ever paused to think whether it was with joy and gladness that she gave up ten or twenty years of the heyday of her existence to all the cares and sufferings of excessive maternity?[70]

Both the seriousness of personal rights and discomfort with the idea of women voting caused woman's rights leaders to reconsider the vote as a symbol of women's aims for autonomy rather than the predominant goal of the movement.

Democratic versus Scriptural Justifications for Rights

Knowing that many women approved of her stance on property rights, Anthony conducted petition campaigns in 1854 for both woman's property rights and suffrage. After encountering resistance to the suffrage issue in 1855, however, she concentrated on property rights reform by addressing women as a disenfranchised group and by encouraging them to persuade their husbands to vote for the reform.[71] This shift suggests that reform leaders realized the vote was hard to sell to non-Garrisonians. Stanton enthusiastically promoted property reform to legislators in Albany; she also focused on marriage reform and in particular designed arguments to justify divorce rights.[72] In 1855, Anthony strengthened her ties to Garrison and the antislavery cause, and agreed to lecture for the American Anti-Slavery Society as long as she could also promote woman's rights. According to Kathleen Barry, this arrangement assured income to the reformer, who at the time could not easily organize woman's rights meetings because "many of her friends were retiring to marriage and families."[73]

At national conventions after 1853, female leaders debated the priority that should be given to particular goals, especially suffrage and divorce. But searching for the strongest possible justifications for woman's rights consumed most of the reformers' time and energy. The leaders drew on democratic principles invoked in 1848 such as all taxpayers' right to representation and natural rights as a defense of woman's rights. Initially, most used Scripture to justify their natural rights arguments as much as or more than the democratic principle of equality.[74]

Garrison had in fact encouraged scriptural citations to justify antislavery and woman's rights in the 1830s. But when he was confronted by an opponent similar to H. K. Root at the 1854 convention, he urged that the Bible be rejected as an authority for the movement.[75] Garrison, who rarely took a stand at these conventions, asserted that "plain natural rights principles," not the established "teachings" of the Bible, constituted the authoritative base of the woman's rights movement. The convention approved Garrison's rejection of the Bible as an authority for the movement by their unanimous adoption of two resolutions:

1. That the "most determined opposition" to the woman's rights movement "is from the clergy generally, whose teachings of the Bible are intensely inimical to the equality of woman with man."
2. "That whatever any book may teach, the rights of no human being are dependent upon or modified thereby, but are equal, absolute, essential, inalienable in the person of every member of the human family, without regard to sex, race, or clime."[76]

Garrison's rejection of the Bible as the authority for woman's rights reform boosted the status of equal rights principles. Once detached from biblical arguments for the subjection of women, these principles emerged as a direct sign of God's will for human nature: equal rights became a God-given goal. The claim of an individual's experience of God's will as a valid authority for reform initiatives invited women to celebrate and use their own experience to achieve change. This personalized religious authority also encouraged men and women to identify the inequalities in their personal relationships and to use egalitarian ideals to change them.

Some reformers who dismissed the Bible as a source of justifications used democratic ideals more frequently in their arguments and focused on political action to achieve woman's rights. Stanton had depreciated the use of Scriptures as authority as early as the 1848 declaration. At the 1858 convention, Parker Pillsbury advocated that "the women . . . hold their next Convention at the ballot-box," refuse to pay taxes if they were denied the franchise, "and carry the war into the Church, . . . demand[ing] equality there as well as in the State."[77] Pillsbury even challenged women to leave unsupportive church communities: "If women had any proper self-respect, they would scorn to remain one hour in any church in which they were not considered and recognized as equals."[78]

In contrast to Stanton, Garrison, and Pillsbury, Lucy Stone appealed for more flexible, metaphoric interpretations of the Scriptures. At the 1856 national convention, for example, a theology student and woman's rights opponent named Mr. Leftwich contended that there was no "natural basis" or "universality" to woman's rights claims. Leftwich cited St. Paul's dictum that "wives obey their husbands" to undermine the claims for woman suffrage: "The claim for woman of the right to vote, inasmuch as she would of necessity vote as she pleased, and therefore sometimes contrary to her husband, involved a disobedience of her husband, which was directly antagonistic to the injunction of the Scriptures requiring wives to obey their husbands."[79]

Stone refuted Leftwich by pointing out that democratic developments of the past century had overturned Paul's other instructions: "Just as the people have outgrown the injunction of Paul in regard to a king, so have the wives his direction to submit themselves to their husbands."[80]

At the 1860 convention, two ministers, Reverend Beriah Green and Reverend Samuel Longfellow, added to the store of woman's rights arguments that rested primarily upon egalitarian ideals. Each blended the notion of equality with both the Scriptures and personal experiences of God. Green argued that mutual support was the appropriate form of interaction between the sexes.[81] Longfellow enhanced this idea by suggesting how to overcome both woman's resistance and the organized opposition to woman's rights reforms:

> The simple proposition which, it seems to me, includes the whole of this matter, is, what I should call a self-evident truth—that in all departments of life, men and women, made from the first to be co-mates and partners, should stand side by side, and work hand to hand. Not because men and women are identical, not because they are not different, but because they are different; because each has a special quality running through the whole organization of the man and the woman, which quality is needed to make a complete manhood and womanhood.[82]

Longfellow did not make this argument to defend the notion of woman's "separate sphere"; he rejected that idea outright, and he appealed to the men in the audience to respect and to create independence for women:

> If you want to know . . . , what woman's sphere is, leave her unhampered and untrammeled, and her own powers will find that sphere. She may make mistakes, and try, as man often does, to do things which she can not, but the experiment will settle the matter; and nothing can be more absurd than for man, especially *a priori*, to establish the limits which shall bound woman's sphere, or for woman, as a mere matter of speculation, to debate what her sphere shall be, since the natural laws are revealed, not to speculation, but to action.[83]

Green and Longfellow encouraged women to celebrate rather than deny or diminish their differences from men. Although the veteran reform leaders did not discuss the implications of these arguments, a support system among some clergymen for woman's rights reform appears to have emerged by 1860. The ministers' encouragement of woman's rights reform because of gender differences would later help mobilize support for woman suffrage.

When reformers stopped depending on the Scriptures to provide the authority for woman's rights reform, they no longer felt the kind of pressure to defend themselves that they had encountered in the early 1850s. By focusing on political ends and using democratic ideals to defend them, the woman's rights activists consolidated a position from which they could advocate change. But those who adopted Garrison's summary rejection of scriptural authority sharply narrowed the reformers' audience. Their new political grounding also left them ill prepared to counter post–Civil War claims that women shouldn't vote because no soldiers were women. Twenty years later, Frances Willard would follow in Stone's footsteps by invoking appeals to religious symbols of "republican motherhood": her rich, innovative interpretations of the Scriptures in defense of woman's suffrage aroused audiences less responsive to Garrisonian justifications.

～❖～

By 1861 the woman's rights reformers realized that their demands implied far-reaching changes. Stanton called for the most radical changes; Anthony and Rose usually joined her. Mott, Gage, Stone, Reverend Blackwell, and the Garrisonian males distinguished themselves as supportive of woman's rights, but they qualified their support for suffrage and divorce. Although reformers shared a commitment to the idea of woman's rights as well as a powerful liberal opposition to the male monopoly on political power, they differed over priorities. Some also designed unique ethics that guided their political practices (compare, for example, Stanton's conception of divorce as necessary to ensure each person's pursuit of happiness with Reverend Blackwell's sense of divorce as a legal tool to protect property because marriage was permanent).[84]

The fearful reactions from women outside the Garrisonian movement and the internal dissent among women reformers over divorce and suffrage suggest that woman's rights reformers could not have easily maintained a formal organizational structure during the 1850s. As historians note, the woman's rights movement more closely resembled a talkative Quaker meeting than a modern-day convention of the National Organization for Women.[85] If judged by the standards set by political organizations that have been mostly created and maintained by men, then the 1850s woman's rights movement was disorganized, even organizationally "underdeveloped," as DuBois put it.[86] But the dissension within their ranks, the opposition outside their ranks, and the reformers' own personal priorities combined to make investment in organizational maintenance risky for them. They relied on friendship instead. Friendship held the movement together despite conflicts over goals and justifications, conflicts that often generated divisive ruptures.[87]

The leaders of the woman's rights movement did not mobilize many supporters outside the Garrisonian circle of Hicksite Quakers, Unitarians, and radical abolitionists. Stanton's effort to infuse a woman's rights ideology into New York's women's temperance reform failed. Many audiences ridiculed these reformers for their innovative fashions as well as for their ideas. Although leaders tried to moderate their justifications and dilute the radical character of their goals, they could not easily dilute their claims for woman's rights. Arguing for political rights of any kind for women signaled revolutionary change and threatened most people's everyday routines.

Anthony's discovery that many women in New York State gave priority to winning property rights led her to campaign for two years on that issue. But most woman's rights reform leaders did not concentrate on property rights; instead, suffrage and divorce held the reformers' attention. The contribution Stanton and Anthony made to the campaign for married woman's property rights between 1860 and 1862 reveals that even though reformers initially wanted to win more than property reform, they willingly campaigned for what was possible to achieve at the time.

In November 1860, Stanton, Anthony, Rose, Lydia Mott, and Martha C. Wright submitted the following petition to the New York State legislature for a package of woman's rights: "We now demand the ballot, trial by jury of our peers, and an equal right to the joint earnings of the marriage co-partnership. And, until the Constitution be so changed as to give us a voice in the government, we demand that man shall make all his laws on property, marriage, and divorce, to bear equally on man and woman."[88] This merger of suffrage and divorce, with a call for property rights, displays the reformers' stubborn support of three rights they considered interdependent.

Yet at their last convention before the Civil War in early February 1861, the reformers presented a compromise proposal for conditional divorce. The proposal called for rights to divorce after desertion for three years when there were "continuous and repeated instances of cruel and inhuman treatment by either party" that impaired health or were life-threatening for a period of one year preceding application for divorce. The reformers also proposed that women should have the same right men have to divorce due to adultery.[89]

The 1861 reform, as well as Rose's and Stanton's justifications for divorce reform, derived from a feminism of fear more than a feminism of rights. Instead of calling for equal rights on the basis of natural equality, the reformers addressed the institution of marriage, in which women needed immediate personal protection. Their recommendations aimed at giving individuals property rights in marriage and (in Stanton's recommendations) a means of escape from marriages that denied basic rights. Garrisonian woman's rights reformers discovered that popular audiences found woman's rights ideals or the idea of divorce much less appealing than the opportunity to acquire property rights. Stone and Stanton concurred on the importance of women's right to time their pregnancies. By the mid-1850s, political parties exercised so strong a power over American government that many women probably didn't perceive the vote, the right to speak at meetings, or leadership skills as useful either for themselves or their husbands.

Indeed, a renewed focus on winning the vote was only made possible when the reformers discovered that in 1862 New York State legislators had passed measures diluting a mother's right to equal guardianship of her children and had repealed a law that had guaranteed a widow with minor children control of her husband's property until they came of age. The legislature took this action when the woman's rights conventions were canceled; female reformers had decided instead to work full time for the union effort and were occupied collecting petitions to abolish slavery.[90] Women's renewed interest in voting intensified when it became associated with protecting fundamental rights such as property ownership.

The debates among woman's rights reformers over goals and justifications reveal their lack of consensus on women's social roles, particularly expectations about the meaning of marriage beyond the assurance that marriage would no longer dissolve a woman's standing as a full citizen before the law. Reverend Blackwell advocated the republican ideal of citizenship as a force for firming up women's responsibilities and making women act responsibly. Stanton understood citizenship according to the liberal tradition's emphasis on securing means that would enable women to choose freely. Despite subtle differences, these reformers were willing to cooperate and compromise to advance woman's rights.

The explosive arrival of the Civil War in 1861 postponed the woman's rights debates. The war also disintegrated the protection that the Garrisonians had provided woman's rights reformers. The Republican Party's antislavery stand induced many Garrisonians to join its ranks and drop their nonpartisan alignment and practice of nonresistance, as well as to accept the failure of Garrison's moral suasion strategy. This tacit admission of failure by the Garrisonians set back for more than a century the cause of equal rights as the touchstone for the transformation of politically excluded groups into included groups. Still, the woman's rights movement of the 1850s put its leaders in a position of advantage for launching the woman suffrage movement after the war. Stanton, Anthony, Stone, and many others had the leadership skills, determination, and connections necessary to keep the woman's rights issues on the governmental agenda. Collective action for woman's rights could not be extinguished—these ideas had taken root.

3

Putting Suffrage First:
Liberal Feminist Responses to the
Reconstruction Amendments

*T*HROUGH A series of unanticipated but unavoidable collisions between competing conceptions of citizenship and political goals, the reconstruction process following the Civil War transformed the woman's rights movement into a woman suffrage movement. Before the Civil War, woman's rights reformers promoted the political integration of women without interference from major political parties because the parties were not interested in issues of citizenship, especially abolition. The Garrisonians had depended on the participation of likeminded, educated, white, middle-class women to make antislavery respectable and compelling as a nonviolent, nongovernmental social movement. Garrisonian woman's rights reformers, in turn, set an autonomous agenda that by 1861 called for equality in marriage as well as gender-neutral options for divorce. The war and Reconstruction irrevocably removed the insulation that had fostered collective action for woman's rights as voluntarist and legislatively situated in the states.

The politics of Reconstruction brought three changes for woman's rights reformers. First, the woman's rights nongovernmental social movement became a single-issue political movement for woman suffrage led by two competing organizations. Second, women reformers learned that when men agreed as *men* about what issues belonged on the government agenda, women could not stop them. Women required male allies to support and promote their cause; they also needed to exploit conflicts between men. Third, majority rule and many points of access into the power centers of the American political system encouraged woman suffragists to design multiple strategies, occasionally to eschew principle for expediency's sake, and to discover favorable entry points onto the legislative reform agenda.

Incompatible Conceptions of Citizenship

Reconstruction fundamentally altered the division of labor between decisions of the national government and nongovernmental benevolence: no longer would easy separations be made between "political" or "national" issues on the one hand and "moral" reform or "social policy" on the other. The national government assumed responsibility for preventing the reconstitution of slavery. After the Civil War and Reconstruction, defending Garrison's vision of a conscience-led social revolution also became more difficult. A prolonged, devastating war—not moral suasion or enlightened consciences—had put an end to slavery. The ideal full citizen became the soldier ready to die for his country.

The bitter history of Reconstruction reform has been told from the standpoints of key actors: radical Republicans, former black male slaves, victims, and women—especially Garrisonian woman's rights reformers.[1] As Alice Stone Blackwell observed in 1892, however, the most important force in Reconstruction was public opinion.[2] Native-born white male voters throughout the nation resisted transforming either free black men or white women into full citizens. Educated elites and radical Republicans were powerless to alter popular consciousness or awaken the consciences of the masses on behalf of inclusive equality. A grand tragedy of mutual betrayal resulted, revealing deep racial prejudice even among the Garrisonians.

Profound ideological discord followed the Civil War as perceptions of Reconstruction's purpose began to clash. After the passage of the Thirteenth Amendment, which all abolitionists cheered, radical Republicans drafted plans to guarantee citizenship rights to all black men. Woman's rights reformers dissented initially from the Fourteenth Amendment because the protections were too exclusive: to enfranchise only black men violated their vision of inclusive equality. The plan to enfranchise black men met opposition from northern and southern white men as well as from Garrisonian woman's rights reformers. Both women and men felt personally insulted by this plan: as educated, native-born whites they considered themselves better qualified to vote than former black male slaves. But when the women called for female enfranchisement as well as votes for black men, white men tended to oppose both measures. Garrisonian woman's rights reformers found themselves politically isolated and betrayed by former allies such as Wendell Phillips, Thomas Wentworth Higginson, and even Garrison himself. To their credit, the Garrisonian women's anger did not squash their commitment to equal rights reform. They prevented a major setback from destroying their quest for universal rights.

Leading and arguing, abilities that Garrisonian woman's rights reformers had developed during the 1850s, enabled these women to criticize the limitations of the Reconstruction agenda. Initially the critiques assailed lack of commitment to inclusive equality in the Fourteenth and Fifteenth amendments. As their message was ignored or rejected, the women turned to nativist Americanist ideas about the inferiority of black men and immigrants. Eventually the reformers split among themselves over whether to accept the Reconstruction amendments as steps toward equality. The split led to the easy formation of two national woman suffrage organizations, the National Woman Suffrage Association (NWSA) led by Elizabeth Cady Stanton and Susan B. Anthony, and the American Woman Suffrage Association (AWSA) led by Lucy Stone and Henry Blackwell.

Reconstruction reform's main contribution to the development of American government was the democratization of male citizenship in law: all men were declared politically equal by the Constitution of the United States. This development was revolutionary in light of the American legacy of black slavery, but educated, native-born, elite white women saw it as reactionary. As they struggled to win the vote, woman suffragist reformers learned how to build upon the democratic as well as the liberal republican precedents that Reconstruction introduced and, at the same time, how to oppose the exclusive character of an all-male government. But they also harbored much resentment for the political "elevation" of black men.

It is hard to imagine that any of the woman suffragist leaders would describe either their explicit political exclusion or the splits in their ranks that occurred during Reconstruction as advances.[3] Previously dedicated to a host of reforms, the woman's rights activists were forced to rename themselves as woman suffragists. After the Civil War, these reformers had to adjust from their standing as equal partners among the Garrisonians to a new standing as constituents holding—from the standpoint of radical Republican politicians—second-class or lesser importance. Because almost all the Garrisonian males collaborated with the radical Republicans and betrayed their original promises of support for woman's rights, the female reformers found the adjustment painful.

Nevertheless, these women had originally committed themselves to putting abolition and equal rights for slaves ahead of winning rights for themselves, claiming that the cruelty of black slavery was a far more serious moral problem than women's issues. For example, the annual woman's rights convention failed to meet in 1857 largely because Anthony had devoted her time that year to lecturing against slavery; at the outbreak of the Civil War, the woman's rights reformers postponed their conventions and legislative campaigns.

Anthony, Stanton, and Stone volunteered to recruit support for the Thirteenth Amendment in 1863. Until the amendment's passage, these women considered abolition their most pressing equal rights goal. Suffering two defeats with the introduction of the Fourteenth Amendment—the exclusion of women and the betrayal by Garrisonian men—they finally became justifiably angry at both their circumstances and their former allies.

Ironically, male Garrisonians betrayed woman's rights at least partly because democratic developments in the military set the stage for black male enfranchisement. The ascendance of the soldier-citizen ideal, its use to justify making all men politically equal, and the racist reactions against the revolutionary potential of this democratic advance freed Garrisonian men to support the Reconstruction amendments.

By framing the soldier-citizen ideal with equal rights arguments, radical Republicans carved a path for incremental civil rights reform. This strategy kept the door ajar for winning political inclusion for women. But guaranteeing voting rights only to men meant that women could no longer expect informal protections from government, as female benevolent reformers had in the 1830s. Women had to prove themselves worthy of equal rights. Thus, the establishment of a formal organization, the selection of officers, and the design of reform strategies became unavoidable.

Soldiers as Full Citizens: Ballots and Bullets

The effort to enfranchise black men sprang from the valiant service of male slaves in the Union Army as well as the affirmation by military and political leaders that soldiering was the essential manifestation of citizenship. During Reconstruction these concepts displaced the idea that political rights should reflect natural rights, particularly the female Garrisonians' view that "all men and women are created equal." At the end of the war, in desperation, even the Confederacy ordered the recruitment of black male slaves as soldiers; recruits were "to be volunteers" and to receive the "same rations, clothing and compensation . . . as other troops"; emancipation was not mentioned.[4] Union and Confederate men alike saw soldiering as the heart of citizenship. When men protected women, children, and the state by risking their lives in war, they thought they had proven their right to define the political rules of peacetime. Elevating the "soldier-citizen" ideal also strengthened the social contract tradition's placement of men as central political participants. Equating soldiering with citizenship easily excluded women, who were barred from soldiering.[5]

Black male suffrage was placed on the federal government's Reconstruction agenda because, as W. E. B. Du Bois explains, white men in power wanted to reward black men for their military service. First, the massive voluntary participation of black slave men in the Union armies helped white men see at least some black men as equals. As 200,000 black men from the Confederate states volunteered to fight against their former masters, several generals of the Union Army, grateful for this unsolicited participation, freed the slaves who joined their ranks.[6] Between 1861 and 1863, President Lincoln refused to sanction these orders; however, the generals persisted in their efforts, the volunteers became increasingly necessary for the Union's victory, and Lincoln eventually sided with the generals.[7]

Second, the petition campaign for black male suffrage initiated by the wealthy black community in New Orleans eventually won the support of President Lincoln. Lincoln urged Louisiana governor Michael Hahn to enfranchise "some of the colored," including the "very intelligent, and especially those who have fought gallantly in our ranks." Lincoln then added symbolically, "They would probably help in some trying time in the future to keep the *jewel of Liberty* in the family of freedom."[8]

Du Bois found this shift in attitudes ironic because white men did not consider black men equals until the latter volunteered to fight. He wrote that although it was "to the credit of black men, or any men, that they did not want to kill, the ability and willingness to take human life has always been, even in the minds of liberal men, a proof of manhood." Thus, it was by killing their former masters—a task that Du Bois implied required less courage than "working quietly and faithfully as a slave"—that the black men won their rights. He states, "Nothing else made Emancipation possible in the United States. Nothing else made Negro citizenship conceivable, but the record of the Negro soldier as a fighter."[9]

White male leaders' frequent analogy between the purpose of the ballot and the bullet became a central justification for the Reconstruction amendments.[10] Du Bois quotes from President Lincoln's speech to black troops after the surrender of Richmond: "Although you have been deprived of your God-given rights by your so-called masters, you are now as free as I am, and if those that claim to be your superiors do not know that you are free, take the sword and bayonet and teach them that you are."[11] After Lincoln encouraged black male enfranchisement, the Louisiana Convention of 1864 empowered former male slaves on the basis of military service, taxes paid, and intellectual fitness. Consequently, many freedmen voted in the first elections of that state's provisional government.[12]

Lincoln was not the only powerful elected official to liken ballots to bullets. Radical Republican Charles Sumner, a main advocate in the Senate of equal rights for black men, declared in early 1865 that "the cause of human rights and of the Union needed the ballots as well as the muskets of colored men."[13]

This understanding of the ballot as a weapon dates back to the roots of liberal democracy in the mid-seventeenth century.[14] This logic of arming free black men to protect themselves with ballots from laws and other acts of government that might threaten them makes it clear why these men never seriously considered extending the vote to women. Women, who were not allowed or expected to be soldiers, did not meet this implicit qualification for citizenship. Females might obtain indirect standing through their fathers, husbands, or brothers, but because it was widely assumed that women required protection by men, they could have no independent political standing.[15]

According to W. E. B. Du Bois, after Lincoln's assassination Sumner personally lobbied President Andrew Johnson for black male suffrage and reported that the new president supported the measure. But between July and December, Johnson took steps that jeopardized Sumner's and the radical Republicans' initial Reconstruction plans: he pardoned wealthy Confederates, publicly opposed black male suffrage, called for the colonization of free blacks, and even endorsed the return of former Confederate states with minimal conditions. By the end of 1865 abolitionists began to mobilize public support against Johnson's initiatives and for the radical Republicans' Reconstruction program in Congress.[16]

Multiple Perceptions of Equal Rights Ideals

Constitutional protection only for freedmen's citizenship collided with the Garrisonian doctrine of equal rights for women. After learning that the Fourteenth Amendment would establish male qualifications for the vote, woman's rights advocates quickly organized a petition campaign for woman suffrage, but they became increasingly unable to secure men's support and found themselves isolated from Reconstruction reform.[17] By late 1865 the view of soldier-citizen had already displaced the reformers' vision of inclusive political equality and had reinstated exclusive male equality as the dominant theme of discourse on citizenship.

Andrew Johnson's efforts to dilute reparations from former Confederate states closed opportunities of the reform agenda that would have granted property rights, education, and some money, in addition to full legal citizenship, to former slaves. The mass mobilization efforts that radical Republicans launched to pass the Fourteenth Amendment aimed to arrest Johnson's reactionary steps. Women, however, stood no chance of winning political inclusion.[18] The lack of support for including woman suffrage in the Fourteenth Amendment "is indicated by the almost total indifference to woman's rights arguments in the congressional debates on section two of the committee proposal. Democrats occasionally tried to make use of the movement to embarrass in debate those Republicans who considered it wholly the day of the Negro."[19] In 1892 Alice Stone Blackwell reported that when her parents presented Sumner with petitions to delete the word "male" in the Constitution, "Sumner said he had already rewritten the amendment twenty-one times in the effort to avoid the word 'male,'" but "had been unable to find any other wording which would not ensure the defeat of the amendment." The suffragists' male allies recognized that their priority was salvaging the radical Republicans' Reconstruction agenda and establishing themselves as a viable force within the two-party system.[20]

Yet woman's rights reformers still had some hope. Stone Blackwell's retrospective interpretation reveals that the Garrisonians had divided into three groups. In the first, Sumner and Phillips contended that "to unite [N]egro suffrage and woman suffrage in the same amendment would involve the certain defeat of both." The second group, including Lucy Stone and Henry Blackwell, took heart from the intra-party rift between President Johnson and the Congress over the direction of reform as well as the "general upheaval and agitation of moral issues going on at that time." They calculated that the possibility of enfranchising both women and blacks might arise from this general upheaval. The more radical strategy should thus be attempted, even though it raised the risk of defeating both measures. The third group, led by Anthony and Stanton, claimed "that if women could not be enfranchised simultaneously with the colored people, the enfranchisement of the colored people ought to be postponed indefinitely, until the women could come in with them."[21]

In 1866, as the American Equal Rights Association (AERA), the veteran Garrisonians were thus united in principle but divided in practice. Although their relationships became acrimonious, the Garrisonians kept equal rights ideals in the public eye. Woman's rights reformers were inspired by the Fourteenth Amendment in 1866, for example, not to demand woman suffrage per se, but to appeal for a suffrage law based upon the principle of *equal rights*. During the first meeting Anthony stated: "We consider no position more dignified and womanly than on an even platform with man worthy to lay the corner-stone of a republic in equality and justice."[22] Stanton asked whether it was time "to bury the black man and the woman in the citizen, and our two organizations in the broader work of reconstruction?"[23] After the formation of the AERA, Stone wrote to Abby Kelley Foster chastising her for accepting the Fourteenth Amendment and urging her to join the organization's protest against the amendment's limitations. Stone claimed that the amendment was a "poor half loaf, of justice for the Negro." In exasperation, she wrote, "As if the application of a *universal* principle to a single class, *could* suffice for the necessity of this hour!" She also admitted to feeling a poignant despair: "The tears are in my eyes, and a wail goes through my heart akin to that which I should feel, if I saw my little daughter drowning before my eyes with no power to help her."[24]

Stanton, Anthony, and Stone all initially rejected as untenable the alliance between most Garrisonian men and the radical Republicans. But the definition of black male enfranchisement by Sumner, Phillips, and Thaddeus Stevens as one step toward equal rights framed the democratization of male citizenship as a step toward a more liberal republican polity. These men, whom Stanton and Anthony eventually considered traitors, began what has become an incremental (and very slow) process for the achievement of egalitarian civil rights. Most male Garrisonians decided that the cruelty suffered by slaves and the postwar suffering of freed people in the South made black male enfranchisement morally necessary. By labeling the reform an equal rights measure, male Garrisonians presented black male enfranchisement as more than an affirmation of rule by men only—it was a step toward equality. But the Garrisonian women's resistance to this route to equality made sense under the circumstances. Why should making men equal depend on making women unequal?

As time went on, public opinion and nonradical Republicans imposed constraints on Reconstruction reform that men supportive of woman's rights could not overcome. President Lincoln's and the army generals' conceptions of African-American men changed, but the racist views held by many powerful men in the North and South did not. In the South, racist terror against blacks appeared soon after the war. Nor did the victory of the North in the Civil War foster a popular spirit for equal rights reforms among Northerners, who vigorously opposed extending the ballot to black men even before Congress passed the Fourteenth Amendment. In the fall of 1865, Connecticut voters rejected an amendment to enfranchise black men though the state "had only two thousand black citizens."[25] W. E. B. Du Bois explains that in the fall of 1867 "the South and its friends had a right to the charge that eight other Northern states refused to enfranchise a class to which they were forcing the South to give the vote."[26]

This resistance produced tensions between the Garrisonian women's strategies, tensions that first appeared in an 1867 debate between Elizabeth Cady Stanton and Abby Kelley Foster. Stanton argued that all adults should be enfranchised, but that if some were to be enfranchised before others, women should be before blacks.[27] Foster disagreed with Stanton's rejection of the Fourteenth Amendment: she contended that because blacks lacked not only rights, but also basic life necessities, the Reconstruction amendments should be supported as the first step toward equal rights. "Have we any true sense of justice?" she asked. "Are we not dead to the sentiment of humanity if we shall wish to postpone his security against present woes and future enslavement till woman shall obtain political rights?"[28]

Other reformers attending the 1867 AERA convention supported Foster's view.[29] Josephine Griffing acknowledged that she was "thankful with all my heart and soul that the people have at last consented to the enfranchisement of two millions of black men . . . I welcome the enfranchisement of the [N]egro as a step toward the enfranchisement of woman."[30] Sojourner Truth also rallied support for woman suffrage by building on reforms for black men: "I am glad to see that men are getting their rights, but I want women to get theirs, and while the water is stirring, I will step into the pool."[31]

Frances Gage and Ernestine Rose endorsed Stanton's strategy. Gage reminded the audience of women's contributions to the war and asserted that because single women must earn money to pay their bills, they were entitled to suffrage.[32] Rose denounced Congress for making the ballot an exclusive right: "Why do they get up meetings for the colored men, and call them fellow-men, brothers, and gentlemen? Because the freedman has that talisman in his hands which the politician is looking after? Don't you perceive, then, the importance of the elective franchise? Perhaps when we have the elective franchise in our hands, these great senators will condescend to inform us too of the importance of obtaining our rights."[33]

The debate between Foster and Stanton ignited the conflict that eventually split the organization. Those reformers who agreed with Abby Foster moderated their dissent against the Fourteenth Amendment by appealing for black male suffrage and woman suffrage as equal rights reforms; Anthony and Stanton intensified their demands for woman suffrage by criticizing black male suffrage. The next major conflict emerged in the 1867 Kansas campaign for both woman suffrage and black male suffrage. When Anthony and Stanton agreed to campaign in public with George Francis Train, Stone and Blackwell denounced this step as a betrayal of AERA's commitment to both black male suffrage and woman suffrage.[34]

The dispute over alliances and arguments in the Kansas campaign deepened divisions among equal rights reformers. The two pairs of leaders reacted differently to defeat, although their actual split did not occur until 1869 during debates over the newly proposed Fifteenth Amendment.

When both black male suffrage and woman suffrage suffered defeat in Kansas, the radical Republicans became scornful and unwilling to press for woman's rights. Public opinion called for drawing the line at ending slavery and opposing the enfranchisement of nonwhite males.

It seems that the two pairs of reformers considered themselves on the same path for two years after the Kansas campaign. During that time, each tacitly agreed to cultivate support for woman suffrage from varied constituencies. Anthony and Stanton sought new allies, while Stone and Blackwell sustained their argument against exclusive suffrage among former abolitionists. Henry Blackwell even assured southern Democrats that opposition to black male suffrage was no bar to the support of woman suffrage.[35]

Stone and Blackwell criticized the Republican Party for excluding women from the vote at the AERA conventions in 1868 and even during the more eventful 1869 convention. At the 1868 convention, Lucy Stone "charged the Republican [P]arty as false to principle unless it protected women as well as colored men in the exercise of their right to vote."[36] Stone thereby rejected Douglass's appeals for the Fourteenth Amendment. All of the reformers equally loyal to woman's rights and black rights refused to aid the ratification of the Fourteenth Amendment. Only after ratification in July 1868, and submittal of the Fifteenth Amendment to the states, did Stone and Blackwell modify their position on black male suffrage.

The former Confederate states reacted to the ratification of the Fourteenth Amendment in July 1868 with defiance and subversion. In Georgia, for example, the governor seated some former Confederates even though the Reconstruction acts precluded them from taking the oath of office. These men denied "the right of the black members of the legislature to hold office, arguing that the new Georgia constitution did not specifically grant Negroes that privilege."[37]

The rejection of black male suffrage in states throughout the nation undermined the continuation of *any* suffrage legislation by the Republicans between 1868 and 1869.[38] Furthermore, the subversion of the Reconstruction amendments by states such as Georgia made the radical Republicans "determined to press for" an extension of national power over the suffrage laws.[39] In the fall of 1868 conservative and radical Republicans steered through both houses an amendment that would have protected office-holding rights and voting from any kind of discrimination. Unexpectedly, however, a joint committee revised this amendment into a prohibition of the use of federal and state powers to deny the vote "on the grounds of color, race, or previous condition of servitude." The Fifteenth

Amendment that passed Congress on February 26, 1869, was radical Republicans' minimal stand against racial discrimination in government.[40] These Republicans barely achieved a legally inclusive male suffrage. They learned that even this achievement, which took on an increasingly symbolic character, met intense racial prejudice.

The introduction of male qualifications for suffrage thus submerged the cause of woman's rights.[41] Inclusive equality as pictured by the Garrisonians' liberalism of equal rights conflicted with the reality of post–Civil War political life. No men in power called on women to vote as republican mothers to protect the rights of newly free African Americans. Instead, even within the Garrison camp, some leaders saw woman's rights as radical.

Garrisonians such as Horace Greeley scrapped equal rights concepts for the soldier-citizen ideal.[42] By portraying woman's rights reformers as extremists, they distanced themselves from aims beyond reaping the "fruits of victory." The choices for female Garrisonians narrowed: they could either accept the radical Republicans' plan as limited but unavoidably necessary, or refuse to endorse the Reconstruction amendments as violations of equal rights principles. Stone and Blackwell tried to straddle these two options: they dissented from the Fourteenth and Fifteenth Amendments for their failure to enfranchise women but avoided outright opposition to ensure the consolidation of some reform.[43] Anthony and Stanton, however, ultimately decided that they had to oppose Stone and Blackwell in order to defend woman's rights as a critical rights issue.[44]

Two Woman Suffrage Organizations

In November 1868, Abby and Stephen Foster, Thomas Wentworth Higginson, and several woman's rights reformers who applauded the ratification of the Fourteenth Amendment founded the New England Woman Suffrage Association (NEWSA) "to counter political initiatives being made by Stanton and Anthony."[45] The organization welcomed abolitionists who wanted to campaign for woman suffrage. William Lloyd Garrison, George Downing, Stone and Blackwell, and Antoinette B. Blackwell all supported the NEWSA initiatives.

The NEWSA leaders aimed to preserve their alliances with the Republican Party through this new organization. It is equally likely, however, that the leaders had also decided to revise their strategy in light of the Fourteenth Amendment's passage. Formation of this society signaled an effort to revive ties with the radical Republicans and moderate dissent against the Reconstruction amendments.

At the May 1869 AERA convention, Stone and Blackwell's attempt to hold together the proponents of both black male suffrage and woman suffrage failed. A controversy emerged among the reformers that Stone and Blackwell were able to mollify only for the duration of the annual meeting. First, Stephen Foster, a militant abolitionist, called for full support of the Fifteenth Amendment from the woman suffragists, as well as an explicit repudiation of Stanton's appeals for including women. Blackwell defended Stanton and Anthony's recruitment of woman suffrage supporters who opposed black male suffrage: "We should no more exclude a person from our platform for disbelieving [N]egro suffrage than a person should be excluded from the anti-slavery platform for disbelieving woman suffrage. But I know that Miss Anthony and Mrs. Stanton believe in the right of the [N]egro to vote. We are united on that point. There is no question of principle between us."[46]

Stone then argued for accepting both Frederick Douglass's claim for black male suffrage and Stanton's demand for woman suffrage: "We are lost if we turn away from the middle principle and argue for one class."[47] But this middle course disappeared when Ernestine Rose appealed for a change of the name of the AERA to the Woman's Suffrage Association; Stone replied that she "must oppose this [change] till the colored man gained the right to vote."[48] By insisting that suffrage be secured for black men before changing the "equal rights" label to woman suffrage, Stone revealed her conversion to the idea that supporting black male suffrage was a necessary step toward equal rights. Perceiving Stone's view as a rejection of inclusive egalitarian aims, Stanton and Anthony decided they could no longer associate themselves with a nominally equal rights organization that mainly served to assure votes for black men.

Immediately after this convention, Stanton and Anthony quickly and secretly established the National Woman Suffrage Association (NWSA). The NWSA became a centralized, unitary structure, with full membership rights for women only, and its leaders focused on winning national reform. The two women established their headquarters in New York City, mobilized support among wage-earning women, and for a short time published a radical woman's rights newspaper, the *Revolution*.[49] Although they used racist appeals to win allies among Democrats, they soon demonstrated that by putting expediency ahead of principle the Garrisonians would lose a solid core of female equal rights reformers.[50] A few Democrats heartily welcomed the woman suffragists.

Stone and Blackwell considered Stanton and Anthony's creation of the NWSA in 1869 as a final rejection of their shared leadership and joined the members of the New England Woman Suffrage Association in the formation of the American Woman Suffrage Association (AWSA); its first convention met in Cleveland in November 1869. The participation of men, an equal sharing of official leadership positions among men and women, and a federalist organizational structure establishing strict membership rules distinguished the AWSA from the NWSA. Like the NWSA, the AWSA put woman suffrage above all other goals from the start. Stone and Blackwell collected enough funds to begin publication of the *Woman's Journal,* and in 1870, Boston became the center of the AWSA and the site of the journal's publication.[51]

The gradual two-year split, between Anthony and Stanton on the one hand and Stone and Blackwell on the other, resulted not only from the political necessities of the time, but also from changes in consciousness about the meaning of female enfranchisement. Between 1867 and 1869 Stanton and Anthony had detached themselves as fully as possible from the Garrisonians and radical Republicans. Their alliances with outright racists embarrassed the Garrisonians, an outcome that probably pleased Stanton and Anthony because they considered the refusal by most male Garrisonians to endorse woman suffrage as an unconscionable betrayal.[52] Stanton and Anthony also wanted women to seek the vote *as women.* Because they "shared the prejudices of their class and time," these two women stressed their standing as educated, middle-class, native-born Americans who would not tolerate being depicted as inferior to uneducated, newly freed black men.[53]

Each organization made strides for woman suffrage in the early 1870s. The centralized, woman-only NWSA kept the issue alive by protesting against institutions that denied women voting rights. For example, Susan Anthony was one of 150 women to vote illegally between 1870 and 1874. After casting her ballot during the 1872 presidential election in Rochester, New York, Anthony was arrested and prosecuted for her offense. The widely publicized trial demonstrated that women's demands for the vote were serious and likely to persist.[54] These legal challenges, combined with continuous pressure on Congress, kept the issue on the governmental agenda. By directing multiple efforts of this sort, Stanton and Anthony ensured that voters and legislators must pay attention to women's demands.

The new AWSA contributed certain organizational innovations to the movement. Although small groups made the major decisions in both the NWSA and the AWSA, Stone and Blackwell created a federalist infrastructure that encouraged formal woman suffrage associations at the local and state levels. Through the *Woman's Journal,* they also built a national communications network that later became essential for woman suffrage campaigns in the states. Through these organizational innovations, and by reviving alliances between the antislavery and woman's rights reformers, the AWSA leaders strengthened recruitment and organization-building in the woman suffrage movement.

By the first AWSA convention in November 1869, Stone and Blackwell had reconstituted most of the alliance between the antislavery and woman's rights reformers. On the "Convention Call" appeared the names of sixty-two men and fifty-three women, including those of William Lloyd Garrison, Abby Kelley Foster, Stephen Foster, Thomas W. Higginson, Samuel May, Henry Ward Beecher, and Clarina Nichols. Delegates from twenty-one states attended the first AWSA convention, a large turnout that signaled the success of Stone and Blackwell's reunification efforts. Out of ninety-three delegates to this first convention, thirty-four were males.[55] The AWSA rules mandated a general principle that "one half of the officers shall, as nearly as convenient, be men, and one half women."[56] This policy facilitated the woman suffragists' access to male voters, who alone had power to produce women's suffrage. Men's presence in the organization also made their intimate knowledge of party politics and successful legislative reform tactics readily available to the women leaders.

Stone and Blackwell decided to imitate the congressional basis of representation: each state could send as many delegates as it had congressional representatives to the AWSA conventions. The inclusion of participants from all states created a more comprehensive network for the woman suffrage movement than had existed during the 1850s, and Stone cited her commitment to this federalist structure as a chief reason against reunification with the unitary NWSA.[57] In the early 1870s, Stone and Blackwell urged the delegates to recruit support for woman suffrage in their local communities. They offered to aid any state campaigns for suffrage.[58] Moreover, by reporting their efforts in the *Woman's Journal,* local and state leaders could exchange information and support *without* appealing to the national leaders.

Racism of various sorts permeated the new suffragist movement. Stanton and Anthony had collaborated openly with the vituperative racist George Francis Train. But Stone and Blackwell also exhibited a willingness to tolerate racism before the Fifteenth Amendment was ratified. Henry Blackwell helped win support for woman suffrage from Southern Democrats by assuring audiences that they could oppose black male suffrage while supporting votes for women.[59] Lucy Stone's racism was more ambivalent. She qualified her thankfulness for the Fifteenth Amendment with reservations about black men's weak qualifications: "But I thank God for that XV Amendment, and hope that it will be adopted in every State. I will be thankful in my soul *any* body can get out of the terrible pit. But I believe that the safety of the government would be more promoted by the admission of woman as an element of restoration and harmony than the [N]egro."[60]

The split between Stanton and Anthony on the one hand and Stone and Blackwell on the other was not, therefore, a division between racists and nonracists. Except for Stephen Foster and Abby Kelley Foster, all of the woman's rights reformers at the 1868 AERA convention resisted Frederick Douglass's eloquent appeal for black male enfranchisement. In his speech Douglass reaffirmed his support for woman suffrage but insisted that votes for black men were "a most *urgent* necessity" because of the lynchings and terror perpetrated upon freed blacks in the South. He further explained, "The government of this country loves women. They are the sisters, mothers, wives and daughters of our rulers; but the [N]egro is loathed."[61]

A Feminism of "Personal Development"

Stanton's and Anthony's arguments developed into a feminism of personal development that blended with Americanist prejudices. In their rhetoric, the idea that all "men and women are equal" was supplanted with a call for human betterment, a development that required women—particularly native-born white women—to vote. This variant of liberal feminism retained only a weak egalitarianism: *All* women should have opportunities to develop their *particular* talents. By taking for granted that talents were unequal between races, classes, and ethnic groups, these women used such arguments primarily to secure opportunities for themselves. This liberal feminism blended easily with Americanist concepts of native superiority.

In her address to the National Woman Suffrage Convention in January 1869, Stanton angrily asked her audience how the women who already bore "the oppressions of their own Saxon fathers, the best orders of manhood" would endure rule by "the lower orders of foreigners now crowding our shores."[62] She asserted that the time for moral development had arrived and only women voters, not more male votes, could assure its success: "Whatever is done to lift woman to her true position will help to usher in a new day of peace and perfection for the race." Although Stanton assured her audience that she did not consider all men to be "hard, selfish and brutal," she nevertheless insisted that "woman knows the cost of life better than man does, and not with her consent would one drop of blood ever be shed, one life sacrificed in vain."[63]

A close association emerged in Stanton's thought between an incipient feminism of personal development and Americanist conceptions of supe-riority. Judith Shklar identifies freedom of personal choice and John Stuart Mill's defense of free speech as the distinctive features of the liberalism of personal development.[64] According to Stanton's understanding, wide-spread subordination denied women both free choice and free speech, which in turn stunted their full development. She denounced the practice of this injustice by liberal reformers throughout the world and asked, "While all men, everywhere, are rejoicing in new-found liberties, shall woman alone be denied the rights, privileges, and immunities of citizen-ship?"

Rather than contend only that the subordination of women consti-tuted an intolerable injustice, Stanton also condemned men for willfully repressing women's resources, especially their superior moral agencies: "The need of this hour is not territory, gold mines, railroads, or specie payments, but a new evangel of womanhood, to exalt purity, virtue, morality, true religion, to lift man up into the higher realms of thought and action." The new "aristocracy of sex" was "the most odious and unnatu-ral; invading, as it does, our homes, desecrating our family altars, dividing those whom God has joined together." She claimed, "If the civilization of the age calls for an extension of the suffrage, surely a government of the most virtuous, educated men and women would better represent the whole, and protect the interests of all than could the representation of either sex alone."[65]

Stanton's argument fit well with a rising liberalism of personal devel-opment in the country as a whole—one that emphasized choice, knowl-edge, and education. The combination led Stanton to articulate a vision of rule by an educated elite, which in 1869 would have consisted overwhelm-ingly of white Protestants.

Stone and Blackwell's reform strategy exploited the potentially close relationship between principle and expediency. When they sustained alli-ances with radical Republicans, accepted the Fourteenth and Fifteenth Amendments, and presented votes for women as the next step in equal rights reform, they rededicated themselves to equal rights ideals. At the same time, these veteran Garrisonians calculated that to win women the vote, they must first engage reliable allies. Labeling woman suffrage as the next step in equal rights reform was politically expedient. Arguing that Stone and Blackwell were more virtuous than Anthony and Stanton because they sustained the link between woman suffrage and equal rights principles would idealize their political behavior.

The NWSA and the AWSA made different and essential contributions to initiating and maintaining a national woman suffrage movement in the

United States. Lucy Stone admitted as much in a letter to Stanton in the fall of 1869. In spite of her bitter feelings toward the other two, Stone wrote, "With two societies each, in harmony with itself, each having the benefit of national names, each attracting those who naturally belong to it, we shall secure the hearty active cooperation of *all* the friends of the cause, better than either could do alone."[66] The split lasted for twenty years; after the mid-1870s it was sustained more by Stone's hard feelings toward Stanton and Anthony than by opposing campaign strategies.[67] Alice Stone Blackwell, the daughter of Henry Blackwell and Lucy Stone, is generally credited with reuniting the reform leaders in 1890.[68]

Launching the Woman Suffrage Movement in the 1870s

Woman's rights reformers had previously found it difficult to accept that most Americans of their time considered illiberal traditions such as male domination and ascriptive Americanism compelling, but liberal arguments for political inclusion and equal rights threatening. As they began campaigning for the vote, however, reformers encountered far more resistance.

As Rogers Smith explains, Chief Justice Morrison Waite strengthened the opposition to female political inclusion in the 1874 case of *Minor v. Happersett*. Although in his decision Waite admitted that women were citizens, he contended that suffrage had never been a "privilege of citizenship." He thereby reinforced the republican tradition of states' rights over electoral laws as well as the liberal view that "political participation is inessential to citizenship." In Waite's hands, therefore, Smith points out, "the status quo was confirmed rather than challenged by the discriminatory aspects of Americanism." This decision effectively eliminated any possibility of winning national woman suffrage through the courts.[69]

When they committed themselves to win the vote through legislative reform both nationally and in the states, the woman suffragists took on a challenge different from the nongovernmental aims of their forebears. Rather than simply contenting themselves with a community among antislavery reformers and in the Northeast, they chose to mobilize political support across the nation. To earn suffrage, the reformers simultaneously had to persuade a majority of men that women should vote and enlighten women about the importance of political inclusion.

Protesting disenfranchisement by voting and being arrested as Susan B. Anthony did grabbed attention, but only direct pressure on legislators could assure suffrage legislation. The creation of new territories and eventually states in the West gave reformers opportunities to lobby for their measure during state constitutional conventions. The Colorado woman suffrage campaigns of 1876 and 1877 illuminate how the former Garrisonians made headway toward their radical goal.

The Colorado Suffrage Campaigns, 1875–1877

Simple legislative passage of woman suffrage, and even the federal amendment, did not require ratification by a majority of male voters. As a result, these measures lacked weight as a democratic mandate. In contrast, the passage of votes for women by a voter referendum signaled that most men in a state were willing to share political power with women and make a commitment to the inclusion of women at all levels of government. During the suffrage movement's first forty years, 480 referendum campaigns aimed to put woman's suffrage on the ballot in the states. Of these, only seventeen referenda actually reached the ballot; in just two, Colorado and Idaho, did women eventually win the vote.[70] Although many opportunities emerged for woman suffrage reform, the institutional and ideological resistance to the measure assured its defeat. Only after reformers made the measure more appealing to both popular audiences and elected officials were they able to win campaigns.

Woman suffragists clashed with three main audiences—unpersuaded women, elected representatives, and male voters. Because in 1893 Colorado became the first state to pass suffrage reform through a voter referendum, the reformers' advances and retreats in the Colorado campaigns of 1876, 1877, and 1893 provide an optimistic early picture of reform. The decisive defeats in Colorado in 1876 and 1877 also reveal the strength of traditions excluding women in the existing electoral system.

The Contributions of Albina Washburn

Suffragists with the AWSA placed woman suffrage on the agenda of the 1876 Colorado constitutional convention. The spark for this Colorado campaign came from a Colorado woman, Albina Washburn. Her letter to the *Woman's Journal* in June 1875 describing her successful "protest vote" in two school elections convinced Stone and Blackwell of favorable opportunities in her territory.[71]

Washburn told how she had managed to vote. First, her husband agreed to submit proof of her ownership "of a few ponies" to the assessor.

She next paid a tax in her own name, "for the express purpose of introducing an entering wedge on the Suffrage question in this community, where we have never had a lecture or any public agitation on the subject." Finally she cast her first ballot in the spring of 1874; the election official was so startled that she met no resistance.[72]

When she tried to vote again in 1875, Washburn was challenged. The official in question had consulted his law books and found that school suffrage was conferred on "*citizens* who owned property and paid taxes."[73] Subsequently, both the official and Washburn searched for a definition of "citizen," not in the *Minor v. Happersett* decision of 1874 that denied women voting rights without denying them citizenship, but by consulting "Webster's" definitions of "citizen." They found two definitions: one used the words "of either sex," and the other cited "a free man." Faced with this ambiguity, the official allowed Washburn to take "the required oath" and "to drop her little ballot" into the box. Washburn thereby added to the infrequent but documented history of women voting in modern republics before formal female enfranchisement.[74]

Washburn's success as a self-made, spontaneous voter at Colorado school elections in 1874 and 1875 contrasted sharply with Anthony's and Minor's earlier failures in New York and Ohio. The local judge's neglect of federal law also indicated that men in a territory could be more open to women voting, and that the etiquette pertaining to legal standing was less rigid than in the East. Moreover, Washburn told woman suffrage reformers that their issue had not been raised in her rural district, that she was willing to struggle for the vote in that district, and that an upcoming campaign for Colorado's statehood presented a favorable opportunity to win women the vote.[75]

Washburn's news and enthusiastic appeal turned Lucy Stone's attention to Colorado. In August, Stone wrote Margaret W. Campbell, her "field-worker" colleague who was campaigning for suffrage in Iowa, about the prospects of an effort in Colorado: "Mr. Blackwell sent you a list of names of subscribers [to the *Woman's Journal*] in Colorado. I hope, as you go West, you will make the most of your opportunity in Colorado for there *is* a chance there, if we only had help enough."[76]

The ensuing correspondence between Campbell, Stone, and Blackwell reveals their campaign strategy. The leaders aimed to (1) form an alliance between the Washburns and other known supporters of woman suffrage in Colorado, (2) design and circulate petitions to put a woman suffrage amendment into the new state constitution, (3) give lectures and publish articles in the *Woman's Journal* to raise "mass support," and (4) cultivate allies through community organizations.

AWSA Appeals for Suffrage

In their petitions, articles, and speeches, Stone and Blackwell continued to rely mainly on moral suasion and emphasize equal rights. Their initial petition, presumably drafted by Stone, read as follows: "*To the Constitutional Convention of Colorado,* We, the undersigned, citizens of Colorado, of adult age, do hereby petition your honorable body in convention assembled, to so frame your Constitution—in fixing the status of voters—that *no distinction shall be made on account of sex.*" This petition set aside the question of equality between women and men; Stone's articles emphasized that a just government was based on the people's consent. She called for women's right "to an equal share with men in making the laws," thereby eschewing claims of equality due to equal moral worth.[77] Mrs. E. T. Wilkes, a Coloradan, justified her claim not as a seeker of equality but as one of many female property owners, mothers, and taxpayers:

> We have no voice in saying how these taxes are to be spent. You can bond our property to any amount to build a railroad to the moon, and we are powerless to resist. This water question is one every woman in town is interested in. Some of us have a strong preference for pure water, even if we must pay to have it. We are tired of hauling water from sixty foot wells, and would prefer our earnings should go to secure the health of our families, and relieve our over-burdened hands, rather than to be used in buying white elephants in the shape of more railroads.[78]

In her eagerness to launch a suffrage campaign, Stone did not consider whether Colorado's statehood would be controversial in the territorial legislature or the Congress. She assumed that Colorado's status as a state would be unquestioned: the Constitution is being formed, she wrote, "for Colorado when it comes into the Union as a State next July."[79] By taking Colorado's statehood for granted, Stone portrayed woman suffrage as a highly possible product of the upcoming constitutional convention. Her male allies in Colorado, however, were much less sanguine about this outcome.

Modern Patriarchy

In AWSA field-worker Margaret Campbell's first letter to Blackwell, she writes that Mr. Washburn and other male allies estimated that they could not mobilize adequate support for putting woman suffrage into the state constitution. They thought, however, that it would be possible to submit the reform "in a separate article."[80] The delegates' resistance to a clause in the new constitution was a by-product of putting statehood first: Colorado's territorial legislators wanted to control the election of the governor, and territorial governors were appointed by the president. Male proponents of woman suffrage agreed that gaining gubernatorial election power took priority over other matters. The statehood movement had been prompted by Colorado legislators' fury over "the appointment of the territorial officers from the ranks of broken down political hacks from the eastern states."[81]

As with the Fourteenth and Fifteenth Amendments to the U.S. Constitution, the woman suffragists' goal did not mesh with the agenda of the legislators who wanted Colorado's statehood. There was nothing vindictive or directly sexist in these events; the aim to make the structure of Colorado's government more directly democratic for men simply made sharing power with women less important. At the top of the legislators' list of goals were persuading the voters to agree to increased taxes and participating fully in the federal government by electing representatives and senators. Additionally, the legislators cultivated support for statehood in Congress and from President Grant.

In this latter effort, however, legislators met with difficulties. Republican Party bosses stalled Colorado's "Enabling Act" for at least six months because they considered the election of a Democratic territorial delegate a sign that once the territory became a state it might not elect Republicans.[82] The passage of the Enabling Act required promises from Colorado's Republican legislators to Grant and other party leaders that "with admission to the Union Colorado would send Republicans to the national capital."[83] Moreover, when the Enabling Act took effect, Colorado politicians had to satisfy federal officials overseeing the deliberations for statehood.

Federal oversight of Colorado's application for statehood simultaneously posed obstacles and opportunities for woman suffrage. One requirement was that the territory's constitutional convention "declare, on behalf of the people of said territory, that they adopt the Constitution of the United States" and that the constitution of the state "shall be republican in form, and make no distinction in civil or political rights on account of race or color, except Indians not taxed, and not be repugnant to the Constitution of the United States and the principles of the Declaration of Independence."[84] By requiring that Colorado's constitutional convention accept the Constitution of the United States, the Enabling Act reinforced the Fourteenth Amendment's denial of woman suffrage.

It also, however, afforded opportunities to show how the Fourteenth Amendment opposed the promise of equal rights given by the Declaration of Independence. As much as Colorado's proponents of statehood wanted to avoid complicated constitutional disputes, Stone could not afford to lose an opportunity to display these hypocrisies. But the suffragists' insistence upon a vigorous dissent from the new state constitution jeopardized the allegiance of their male allies. Some Colorado politicians must have known that the 1874 *Minor v. Happersett* decision distinguished between citizenship and the "privilege" of suffrage. These politicians would have already concluded that passing a state constitutional amendment for woman suffrage could put Colorado's statehood at risk.

Margaret Campbell informed Blackwell and Stone that resistance to woman suffrage derived from the fear that it would interfere with the achievement of statehood. She reported that the local press expressed exactly this opposition to female enfranchisement: "The newspapers so far as we have seen, are either opposed or afraid to come out boldly. The cry with them is—It will endanger the new constitution."[85]

The AWSA reformers sustained the petition campaign. Because Mr. Washburn and others encouraged Margaret Campbell to submit woman suffrage reform as a separate issue, the AWSA leaders must have concluded that they had little to lose. Through publicity, and by demanding the vote during the centennial celebrations, the AWSA leaders expected to recruit woman suffrage supporters nationally even if they lost in Colorado.

After news spread that suffrage might threaten statehood, the recruitment of reform leaders and supporters in Colorado slowed notably. Campbell sadly reported to Stone that Albina Washburn could not obtain a hearing on the issue of votes for women at the convention of the state Grange; moreover, Washburn reneged on her promise to recruit woman suffrage reformers after the convention. The women in Denver who had been interested in the campaign now gave only tenuous commitments to the cause: Campbell wrote that she discovered "a few women who would lend a hand if they had time. Dr. Alida C. Avery, and a Mrs. Richardson." Finally, Campbell requested Stone to send some copies of the *Woman's Journal* as soon as possible.[86]

Even the Washburns put winning statehood and retaining their leadership positions in the Grange ahead of votes for women.[87] Campbell remarked to Stone: "It is evident that even they put Grange business before suffrage—Mr. Washburn was elected the Grand Master of the state Grange."[88] Because the Grange did not allow the consideration of "political questions," the Washburns also had to choose between their commitments to the Grange and advocating votes for women.[89] Of course, their expression of Grange loyalty may have been a foil for their view that statehood should take priority over suffrage.

AWSA Recruitment of Radical Republicans

The Washburns' withdrawal of full support did not diminish Campbell's organizing efforts; she informed Stone that because of the couple's efforts, "a good many of the Grangers signed the petitions."[90] During December, Campbell and her husband persuaded 280 persons in Greeley to sign the suffrage petitions.[91] By consolidating gains and accepting her initial losses, Campbell sustained this Colorado effort. If she had allowed the loss of the Washburns' full support or general skepticism to weaken her efforts, there might have been no further strides toward a campaign. Instead, before the state constitutional convention, the first state woman suffrage convention met in January 1876 in Denver, where efforts by the Campbells showed results. Many of their recruits—including the Washburns—participated in the convention.

During this two-day convention, the organizational framework of a state association was created according to AWSA guidelines. Colorado suffragists designed arguments to win support from male voters, legislators, and women. Their resolutions echoed woman suffrage leaders' earlier claims: that the U.S. Constitution did not prohibit women from voting, and that the life of "Republican institutions" depended upon female enfranchisement. They also promised to demand that the legislators make laws consistent with democratic principles.[92]

After Campbell articulated familiar justifications for female enfranchisement as a *right* promised by the U.S. Constitution, state leaders shifted their argument from a call for consistency in rules to an appeal for government to represent the interests of republican motherhood. They claimed women *deserved* the vote for their distinctive contributions to society.[93] A woman minister, Reverend Wilkes, began her appeal by echoing the justifications that Campbell had used. She added, however, a list of women's unique interests as mothers, intending, presciently, to tap women's interest in temperance: "She wanted to vote because it was her right under the government; because she loved her country, had enjoyed inestimable privileges under it, and therefore had an interest in perpetuating them; because in school and kindred matters, as the mother of children, she had a direct interest in the selection of school officers; and especially on subjects of temperance—questions affecting the homes and firesides of women—they had an absorbing interest."[94]

Alida Avery, the first president of the Colorado society, blended the idea of republican motherhood with yearnings and esteem for Americanist ideals: "Here is truly virgin soil: here are wise husbandmen who will spare no pains to gather the richest ripened seed of the best harvests of older civilizations; here are honest citizens, men and women, ready and eager to plant the seed, to watch the tender growth, to guard the maturing fruit."[95] Mary F. Shields reminded the audience of woman's "gift of her sons and every needed sacrifice and service" during the Civil War.

Women such as Rev. Wilkes, Washburn, and Shields gave the national movement fresh arguments and new energy. They were prepared to appeal to men only beginning to be knotted by competitive, entrenched patronage networks—men who were more open than men in the East to women's personalized claims for the vote.[96] Albina Washburn's success in voting and the success of a few other women in other states, combined with the men's own experience of partial political inclusion as territorial citizens, helped the Colorado woman suffrage reformers. The strategy they developed was based on claims that the vote should be a reward for women's contributions to the family. These claims echoed earlier demands for consistency in laws, but sidestepped egalitarian claims with republican appeal that seemed to accept a rigid demarcation of "woman's sphere."

Consolidating Limited Gains: School Suffrage and a Referendum

In late January 1876, Colorado woman suffragists presented their petition for female enfranchisement to the Committee on Suffrage and Elections of the Constitutional Convention. H. P. H. Bromwell, a delegate to the Colorado constitutional convention and a radical Republican in the House of Representatives from 1865 to 1869, was the primary advocate of votes for women at the convention. Bromwell's prominence as a former member of Congress and leader of the Republican Party in Colorado made him an important ally.[97]

Campbell, Shields, Washburn, and Mrs. Ione Hanna each spoke to the committee. Campbell appealed to the principles of the Declaration of Independence: "By what right do men elect men to enact laws to govern women?" Campbell likened the government of women, without their consent, to "taxation without representation" and "downright tyranny." "No more states," she asserted, "should be admitted with a constitution embracing a discrimination against women." She also drew on nativist sentiments by denouncing the participation of immigrant men—"Irish, German, English, and Swede"—in framing laws "for the government of women, who are taxed without representation."[98]

Shields drew on a quid pro quo argument by informing the delegates that there were women in Colorado Springs who "paid 2/3 of the taxes" but were unable to vote on the "$250,000 bond issue" for railroad development. She also "spoke of a law under which the husband can dispose of his home and property without his wife's consent." She warned that strong support for woman suffrage in southern Colorado and especially in Colorado Springs might be enough to hinder passage of the constitution if votes for women were not included: "If you don't enfranchise us," she said, "and your Constitution is rejected by the people, don't blame us for it." She finished with moral suasion, reminding the committee that "no assembly of men ever had so fine an opportunity to distinguish themselves."[99]

Washburn appealed to past experience, speaking of a "rule of allowing women to vote in the Granges, testifying that it had worked well." Hanna assured the committee that her husband supported her endeavor.[100] These strides already made in Colorado identified an existing foundation for female enfranchisement in their own society.

The Committee on Suffrage and Elections split three to two against woman suffrage: W. W. Webster, William E. Beck, and Wilbur F. Stone opposed the measure; in favor were H. P. H. Bromwell, the former congressman, and Agapita Vigil, the only Mexican member of the convention.

Bromwell and Vigil's minority report, which denounced the exclusion of women from the polls, produced a rhetorical victory for the reformers by challenging the majority report on a number of grounds. First, they questioned the disfranchisement of "any portion of our citizens . . . except in case of crime."[101] If the main principle of government derives from the statement in Colorado's Bill of Rights, "That all government of right originates from the people," they asserted, "How then can this convention proclaim that Bill of Rights so admirably framed to set forth the true 'principles' of this government, and yet begin at the very next step by declaring that half the people are not any part of the governing power, whose will originates all government?"[102]

Bromwell and Vigil argued next that the notions of male superiority and female inferiority were false. They stated: "The practical effort of disfranchising any portion of the citizens of a republic is to create a sense of inferiority on their part, and of contempt for them on the part of the favored class."

Appealing for a rejection of the idea that men are naturally superior and women inferior, they said women had "held the scepter" in the past and were "the best governors in the school room."[103] All in all, they stated: "The truth is we are a human race; part of us are men, part of us are women—both equal—each superior and each inferior. Each is part and parcel of the same humanity."[104] This new view that disfranchisement *creates* inferiority for the excluded and superiority for the included would have lasting effects on civil rights struggles in the United States.

The two men observed that needs of urban women who were financial providers were especially neglected. "The right of suffrage," they asserted, "is part of the means of welfare of any person or class of persons. Experience has shown abundantly that the right to vote is concerned with securing food and raiment."[105] Financially needy women, they suggested, would be better protected because the politicians would have a vested interest in taking care of their needs.[106]

Bromwell and Vigil charged that "in no class of business is such discrimination allowed." Only in the "government of the commonwealth [do] we go on refusing the exercise of the plainest and most fundamental right to half the people." They said that the arguments they had heard against the vote for women were like those "used by the favored class one hundred years ago against the right of just such men as now compose this Convention." They argued that eliminating the privileges of primogeniture and entailment "dignified labor, established freedom, and in part emancipated humanity. But here we stopped half way, as if some magic worked a spell on us. We stand dazzled like the buck in the glare of the night hunter's torch, and fail to look at or perceive what is behind the prejudice which disables our intellectual eyes."[107]

The Colorado Constitutional Convention rejected Bromwell and Vigil's appeal for full female enfranchisement, but passed school suffrage for women. As in other states, the opposition to women voting in school elections was not intense, probably because supervision of school fit into the responsibilities of republican mothers. The main concern was writing a constitution that would ensure statehood, and full woman suffrage in federal or state elections could threaten the approval of Colorado as a state.[108]

The suffragists won a second-best victory, however: the legislators mandated that a full woman suffrage law would need only a plurality of votes from both the legislature and voters, as opposed to a two-thirds or three-quarters majority. This show of support signaled that the reformers' appeals had swayed numerous powerful men. The convention's subsequent decision to submit a woman suffrage law to the voters in the fall of 1877 indicates that a majority of the delegates had not taken a firm stand against full voting rights for women.[109]

The convention delegates' goal of full enfranchisement for men may have also made them more sympathetic to woman suffrage. At the time, many men in Colorado may have experienced some diminishment of standing when they moved to the territory. In their former states, most had presumably possessed full citizen rights even if they had not exercised them. The members of the convention had urged the men of Colorado to vote for statehood in order to become "a citizen of an independent sovereign State," rather than "a mere settler upon the public lands of the Territory, governed by satraps appointed and removed at pleasure."[110] Women reformers built upon the ideas and experiences encapsulated in this rhetoric.

Support for woman suffrage as an equal rights measure had spread since Reconstruction. Vigil and Bromwell were the sort of male advocates that woman suffragists depended on for every advance. Just as William Lloyd Garrison and Henry Blackwell had previously accepted responsibility and used their influence to convert men to support woman's rights and woman suffrage, Bromwell and Vigil initiated efforts to win support from Colorado legislators for female enfranchisement. The suffragists lost in the constitutional convention, but the convention's willingness to submit the measure independently in a voter referendum offset their loss.

The 1877 Referendum Campaign

When the Constitutional Convention closed its doors in 1876, women reformers had the major task of organizing for the 1877 full suffrage referendum. Albina Washburn and Alida Avery, both active in the cause, took leadership responsibilities for the 1877 campaign. In October 1876, Washburn successfully elicited financial and speaker support from the AWSA.[111]

Avery designed the reform strategy that she presented to the Colorado suffragists at their annual meeting in mid-January 1877. She reviewed the first steps taken for woman suffrage in Colorado and reminded her audience that a "voice from beyond the Great American Desert" had awakened them to reform action for woman suffrage: "The voice came from Boston, the 'hub of the Universe,' home of the Harbor Tea Party." Avery celebrated Bromwell and Vigil's minority report as "one of our most valuable campaign documents, containing as it does . . . the vital principle of all the arguments upon which we base our plea for equal rights."[112]

During the convention, Avery also proposed a moral suasion strategy for the upcoming campaign. Her two arguments were: (1) woman's responsibilities in the home both prepared and entitled her to the suffrage, and (2) votes for women would contribute to the triumph of rule by reason over rule by violence. Work for woman suffrage, Avery claimed, "must begin at home:—all good work does begin at home; husbands and wives, brothers and sisters, parents and children will discuss the question by the fireside and around the table." She urged men and women interested in the question of woman suffrage to consider the contributions that woman made in the home: "If they find that Woman's work and influence in the family are faithful and beneficent, will it be hard to infer and believe that they will continue to be faithful and beneficent when permitted to share in the government of an aggregation of families, which is a State?"[113]

Avery's focus on women's roles in the home and her aim to put rule by reason ahead of rule by violence reveal the substantial influence that the woman's temperance movement and a key leader, Frances Willard, had already exerted on woman suffragists. Barely three months earlier, Willard had presented what became a famous and powerful speech for "home protection." In this speech—which will be closely studied later—Willard encouraged mothers to seek the vote as means to protect themselves and their children from cruelties caused by drunken men.

Avery encouraged the Colorado suffragists to practice their arguments using Bromwell and Vigil's minority report as a guide. She also advocated the use of "debating societies, books, and newspapers" for discussing woman suffrage.[114] She acknowledged that there would be "some help from the East, during the latter part of the campaign," but emphasized that the distance and expense of transportation made local leadership and participation essential for success.[115]

Many prominent politicians joined the national and state leaders in the 1877 campaign. According to Joseph Brown, a committee of seventeen men was formed at a mass meeting in Denver on August 15, 1877, "to district the territory and send out speakers assigned to their respective stations."[116] A judge, a captain, a colonel, and a doctor were members of the committee; H. P. H. Bromwell, H. C. Dillon, and Gov. John Evans were speakers at the meeting. By the fall of 1877 Bromwell had become a less influential ally for the reformers. He was defeated by Thomas Patterson, a Democrat, in an election of territorial representatives to Congress just before the statehood campaign. Although Bromwell was able to rely on the respect of his peers to advocate woman suffrage at the Constitutional Convention, his loss of status probably weakened his image to voters.[117] His defeat may have been due in part to his unqualified support of woman suffrage.

Despite some major obstacles, Avery, Shields, and Washburn enthusiastically led the campaign in Colorado. They had, for example, to face the fact that in Colorado men outnumbered women. They also confronted deeply held convictions of female inferiority. According to the United States Census of 1880, Colorado males ages twenty to sixty-five outnumbered females of the same age by approximately two to one.[118] Many of these men were unmarried and lived in mining camps; they were probably uninterested in woman suffrage and would not have attended lectures in favor of the reform.[119]

Moreover, many of the women in Colorado during its early years were prostitutes, and the married and other professional women who supported suffrage were unlikely to invite prostitutes into their organization.[120] Single men headed for the mines and potential discoveries were not, for the most part, interested in starting families in Colorado, and they wanted to spend their leisure time at their will. The woman suffragists, however, *were* committed to family and its accompanying morality of monogamy, moderation in the consumption of alcohol, and civil order.

Indeed, there were even more male than female members of the Colorado Woman Suffrage Society. Of the eight vice presidents of the society, six were male; there were at least twelve male but only four female members of the executive committee.[121] Among Coloradans the clashes in this campaign occurred mainly between male supporters and opponents.

The suffrage leaders maximized their limited resources in the campaign. Mary Shields was appointed at the January convention as "the general agent" of the state suffrage association. She mobilized support and started local discussions. In April, the *Woman's Journal* reported that Shields was "prosecuting her work with marked success." The article said she "lays no claims to oratorical powers, but she has a modest and unassuming manner of presenting her subject which carries force with it." She lectured twice in Trinidad: there "several influential Spanish-speaking citizens" persuaded Shields to delay departure in order to have her appeal interpreted for the Spanish-speaking audience.[122]

Before June there are no accounts of Colorado women besides Mary Shields speaking in public for woman suffrage reform. Most prosuffrage women presumably followed President Avery's strategy of quiet persuasion in the home. In May 1877, S. Jennie Griffin, secretary of the Colorado suffrage organization, published an article in the *Woman's Journal* in which she requested additional speakers, applauded the scheduled arrival of Margaret Campbell in June, and hoped that Lucy Stone would arrive in the summer.[123]

The opposition relied upon traditional views that women should not vote. An editorial in the *Pueblo Chieftain* on January 24, 1877, caricatured the reformers who attended the convention in Denver the week before as "advanced thinkers of all varieties, long haired men and short haired women, in fact all varieties of females except those possessed of youth and beauty." Its author skeptically asked whether women were prepared to "carry muskets in the militia" and to participate in a *"posse comitatus."*

The author argued that women wouldn't want to serve as jurors and complained that women who sought to be "on an equal footing with men" would "desire to be treated with all the leniency and consideration usually extended to the sex, and at the same time to receive a man's wages without accomplishing anything like as much as a man's labor." Finally, it asked how many husbands, looking forward to "retiring to the bosoms of our families after a hard day's work in office or store, would like instead of listening to an account of home matters and the prattle of childish voices, to be obliged to discuss with our better half the electoral bill or the proceedings of the last county convention?"[124]

S. Jennie Griffin summarized the opposition's arguments as follows: (1) that women could not fight and, therefore, should not vote, (2) that "men make better laws for women than women could make for themselves," and (3) that women must prove themselves "proficient" in the "labors and occupations of men" before they would win the vote. She characterized the opposition voiced by men as substantial, and worried that Colorado lacked enough practiced suffrage supporters to confront them.

As a response to these arguments, Griffin suggested appealing to democratic ideals. To the first argument, she retorted that if "bear[ing] arms" is a condition for casting ballots, "then our government is a military and not a civil organization, approaching nearer to a despotism than a republic." She dismissed the argument that "men make better laws for women than the latter would for themselves" by asserting that this was "a man's opinion." To the claim that women must do men's work before they could vote, Griffin replied: "The founders of our republic did not think best to wait until all men showed the wisdom of statesmen, before entrusting them with the management of their own affairs. If they had, when should we ever have been free from monarchical rule?"[125]

To counter the intense resistance they met, the women leaders carefully selected speakers for particular audiences. At one point Margaret Campbell told Lucy Stone that Henry Blackwell would prove more valuable a campaigner than Lucy Stone. Campbell wrote: "I hope much from your speeches in Colorado during Sept. but for once, you will pardon me when I tell you that I hope still more from Mr. Blackwell's . . . There is a large German vote to be saved or lost in Denver, and no woman of us could make any impression on them—but Mr. Blackwell is quick to see the condition of things and is able to steer clear of making trouble with them. The temperance question must be ignored and political parties forgotten— in short, we have to be 'wise as Serpents and harmless as doves!' "[126]

The woman suffragists had thoroughly canvassed the state and made allies in almost every precinct.[127] The reformers, however, failed to convert enough male voters to endorse votes for women in Colorado; the vote was 6,612 for the measure and 14,053 against.[128] A majority of voters supported the issue in Boulder County, but by only three hundred votes. (A disproportionate number of suffragists lived in the county's utopian community of Greeley.) A near victory of 548 for and 562 against the reform was reported in Weld County—a northeastern county that bordered on Wyoming—and there was a tie in La Plata County.[129] This heavy opposition among voters contrasted sharply with the more favorable reception among the delegates to the constitutional convention and the first state legislature.

The Reasons for Defeat

Several articles in the *Woman's Journal* analyzed the failure of the campaign. To explain their defeat, Margaret Campbell and Henry Blackwell cited illegal voting, party politics, the "liquor interests," and prejudice. An important impediment to victory was the impossibility of putting women suffrage supporters at every polling place on election day; this lack of grassroots mobilizers allowed the party machinery to administrate the election without much suffragist supervision.

Blackwell further claimed that the neutral role that the party leaders had promised to play ensured defeat: "The politicians . . . quietly manipulated the printing and distribution of the tickets against Woman Suffrage. This fact alone was fatal."[130] Blackwell implied that the parties cheated by distributing fewer prosuffrage than antisuffrage ballots: "Many thousands of indifferent voters," he explained, "were induced to vote against Woman Suffrage, without even being aware of the fact, by the suppression of the tickets containing the words, 'Woman Suffrage approved,' and the substitution of other tickets, in their stead, containing 'Woman Suffrage not approved.'"[131]

Campbell claimed that woman suffragists' use of "the methods" of their opponents would have won the cause, but instead the reformers became more determined "to root out the vile system of bribery, and to cleanse the government from such corruption."[132] Campbell and Blackwell both blamed the "liquor interests" for the defeat of woman suffrage: "In the northern and middle portions of the State, the strength of our opponents consists of the liquor-selling and liquor-drinking interests, combined with the efforts of the Roman Catholic Bishop of Denver, assisted by his enthusiastic co-worker the Rev. Mr. Bliss, and their faithful organ, the *Denver Tribune*."[133] Blackwell wrote that the "liquor interest" presented very strong opposition to woman suffrage "all over the State . . . How strong this element is, in a community largely composed of unmarried men, people in Massachusetts can hardly imagine."[134]

In Blackwell's analysis, woman suffrage supporters represented the interests of marriage and civil order whereas unmarried consumers of prostitution opposed woman suffrage. The woman suffrage victory in Longmont he attributed to the absence of any "disreputable house." Blackwell wrote, "In the Fifth Ward of Denver (where no saloons exist) the vote was about a tie, while in the First Ward, where debauchery is most prevalent, the votes were three to one against us."[135] The prevalence of prostitutes led Margaret Campbell to ascribe opposition—both from the clergy and the "lowest gutter-drunkard"—as deriving from the limited "appreciation of Woman they are capable of having."[136] To Colorado's opponents of woman suffrage, woman "is a creature made for the express purpose of ministering to the requirements of their depraved natures."[137] Yet party leaders also may have opposed woman suffrage in Colorado because enfranchisement would require them to include the rich woman owners of brothels in the party machines.[138] The conflict over the rules of the political game regarding woman's behavior was accompanied by a conflict between those who wanted primarily a community of nuclear families and those who desired uncommitted sexual relations between the sexes.

Blackwell echoed Campbell's contention that "deep, old prejudices" were the chief stumbling block of the campaign: "Most men give very little thought to public questions. They glance hastily over the newspapers from day to day, and derive general impressions from what they see or hear . . . Old prejudices create a habit of mind which is a sort of instinct. To overcome this by a sudden act of independent thinking is, to most men, impossible."[139]

He also contended that the large opposition in the southern part of the state derived from a substantial Mexican population that followed the advice of Catholic priests.[140] Blackwell did not elaborate a means to cope with this problem other than a vote by fiat, under the coercion of party affiliation, as had occurred with the passage of the Reconstruction amendments.[141] The defeat in Colorado left Blackwell disenchanted with the Republican Party and prompted him to consider the formation of a third party.[142] He also suggested that victories of municipal suffrage rather than of full suffrage would be the "entering wedge" for female enfranchisement.[143]

Editorials published in Colorado papers after the 1877 campaign confirm strong antisuffrage attitudes. The editor of the *Pueblo Chieftain*

defined the reform as an "eastern issue," not an effort initiated or conducted by women in Colorado. One editorial after the election carried the
headline: "Good-bye to the Female Tramps of Boston."[144] The author
angrily told the Massachusetts "carpetbaggers" and "political hacks" to
depart, as "the people of Colorado are not at present prepared for your
advanced ideas." He also attacked the changes that the campaign brought
in women's roles such as campaigning at the polls, speaking in public, and
encouraging new thought on women's roles. Finally, the women were
charged with having "prostituted the churches" with their lectures on
Sunday evenings.[145]

Woman suffrage reformers could do little in one ten-month campaign
to displace such ideas. But the Colorado reformers did not give up their
struggle; they resourcefully searched for means to overcome this resistance
and to hold the ground that they had gained in launching their campaign.

The identification of the reform as "out of state" helped defeat it.
Indeed, national women leaders had overshadowed state leaders, even
though the latter executed much of the campaign. As early as the January
campaign, President Avery appealed as strongly as she could to the eastern
campaigners for speakers and financial support. Although Coloradan
Mary Shields was appointed as the "state suffrage agent," few additional
Colorado women seem to have campaigned for the reform outside their
local communities.[146] Albina Washburn concentrated her efforts in 1877
on winning support from the National Grange but did not succeed.[147]

The Consequences of Putting Suffrage First

The passage of the Fourteenth and Fifteenth Amendments would have
forced woman's rights reformers to make winning the vote a national
reform priority even if they had not chosen to do so. Although all these
reformers had hoped to get the vote before the Civil War, none anticipated
how the legal transformation of slavery would eventually take place. But
the conversion from slavery to freedom occurred as in many previous
struggles against tyranny: the men in the oppressed groups risked their lives
in war. The soldier-citizen ideal displaced most alternative views, especially those conjured up by natural rights or equal rights ideals. Woman's
rights reformers, who had grounded their visions of social change in the
principles of equal rights, found themselves salvaging that vision in political tides that turned abruptly and mercilessly against them.

The unambiguous political exclusion of women in American constitutional law did little to undo the ambiguity of the political condition of
educated, middle-class women. Public resistance to black male enfran-

chisement—let alone female enfranchisement—suggests that educated whites, male and female elites (or at least those who became active in politics), may have valued liberal and potentially radical egalitarian ethics more than did less educated Americans. Popular resistance first forced Republicans to pass a weaker Reconstruction plan than they preferred. The failure of woman suffragists to mobilize enough male voters to enfranchise women even in state referendum campaigns such as Colorado's in the mid-1870s made it clear that an equal rights ideology would not be enough to win the vote.

By 1870 woman's rights reformers had developed sophisticated political skills and knowledge about how to form alliances, persuade recalcitrant audiences, and set agendas effectively. The split between NWSA and AWSA signaled that women must design more than one strategy to win the vote.

By the mid-1870s the resurgence of patronage to party machines and the gutting of Reconstruction's most substantive reforms meant that Congress had left few doors open for the enfranchisement of women. The Supreme Court's decision in *Minor v. Happersett* stood as a huge obstacle to winning national citizenship. These developments made the AWSA strategy of state campaigns for the vote appear more promising than the NWSA's focus on national reform. The Garrisonians' willingness to sustain their equal rights vision through membership in the AWSA and the *Woman's Journal* enabled the design and execution of woman suffrage campaigns in the states. But it would take much time and effort to win over public opinion and create a national mood for woman suffrage.[148] Although they had organizational knowledge and leadership ability, the reformers lacked the kinds of arguments that would persuade both elected officials and voters. Soon thereafter, as president of the Woman's Christian Temperance Union (WCTU), Frances Willard offered alternative arguments that elicited a wider popular appeal than did the feminism of equal rights.[149]

4

Frances Willard and the Feminism of Fear

I N THE 1877 woman suffrage campaign in Colorado, NWSA and AWSA leaders had courageously sustained equal rights ideals and refused to allow their visions to fade. But egalitarianism proved irrelevant to many Americans in the post-Reconstruction period of adjustment and reunification. Male casualties in the war numbered over 600,000, leaving hundreds of thousands of widows and fatherless children refashioning plans for earning and family care. As veteran soldiers returned to their communities, they sought male companionship and escape from new routines by consuming alcohol. During the war women had executed far more responsibilities for earning. They willingly relinquished this extra work after the war and instead became primarily concerned with reconstituting domestic routines and assuring that men would put a high priority on familial obligations. In the early 1870s this endeavor became a public and militant struggle when female temperance reformers protested against male drinking by holding prayer meetings in saloons.

The 1870s women's temperance movement, driven by women's determination to alter men's behavior, carried new opportunities to convert women to the cause of woman suffrage. Woman suffragists recognized these opportunities, but lacked a means of linking equal suffrage to the temperance cause. In 1876, Frances Willard, a former teacher and leader new to the temperance cause, discovered a shrewd strategy to exploit this new chance for greater mobilization. Rather than proposing the vote as an effective means to achieve prohibition, Willard told audiences of traditional women that as keepers of virtue God expected them to achieve suffrage, temperance, and eventually a moral transformation of politics. Willard's arguments apparently appealed to Colorado suffragists because in 1877 they emphasized home protection as well as demands for clean water and reduced spending on railroads. By 1881 Albina Washburn and Mary Shields had folded their state suffrage society and put a state WCTU in its place.

Willard and the WCTU

Willard was the most successful political mobilizer of middle-class white women in the nineteenth century. She attracted and kept thousands of women in the WCTU, was one of the few elite white reformers who also tried to mobilize black women, and transformed the WCTU from a pretemperance organization into a major source of political power in the cause of votes for women.

The size of WCTU membership, compared with other women's organizations of the period, demonstrated Willard's ability to attract members to the union and keep them active. According to Ruth Bordin, there were 150,000 dues-paying adult members in the WCTU in 1890. This was more than one hundred times the membership of 13,000 in the National American Woman Suffrage Association.[1] As its president, Willard expanded the ranks of the WCTU. Including membership in its juvenile societies, the WCTU grew under Willard's leadership in the 1880s from 27,000 to nearly 200,000 members.[2]

Willard's reform ideology caught and held the attention of her audiences by defining goals that were meaningful to most women. Women's main goal was physical security for themselves, particularly against potentially abusive husbands. Willard also identified a concrete object of blame: the consumption of alcohol, especially by men in groups. In contrast to woman suffragists, who by the mid-1870s had become content with abstract justifications for the vote such as "consent of the governed" and "taxation requires representation," Willard boldly proclaimed that women needed the vote to protect themselves and their families against the threat of drunken men's violence.

With her "Home Protection" speech, initially presented in October 1876, Willard drew, perhaps consciously, on Bloomer's and Stanton's denunciations of the disproportionate power that state laws allowed men to exercise in the family. But instead of calling for divorce rights as Stanton had, Willard said that political activism, particularly voting, would help produce personal protection by winning temperance legislation. Although Willard imbued her ideology with Christian Protestant themes of duty, her earliest speeches lacked Stanton's blatant denunciations of foreigners. Like the suffragists' ideas, however, Willard's appeals became more racist and nativist in the late 1880s and 1890s. A creature of her time, Willard harbored ethnocentric prejudices, although she embroidered them onto a more fundamental distrust of male authority.

Stanton and Willard designed two strategies to achieve liberal democracy's aim "to secure the political conditions that are necessary for the exercise of personal freedom."[3] In contrast to Stanton's early egalitarian feminism and later feminism of personal development, Willard introduced a "feminism of fear."[4] She argued that the ballot would help women obtain the security they needed to live without fear. Willard achieved this purpose both by praising traditions that made women feel unique and by disabusing them of the reliability of male protection.

The suffragists had adopted the language of legal rights and the ideals of equality to help women obtain the same standing as men in civil society. To promote security for women, Willard and other WCTU activists adopted instead the concepts of civil order and peace. The suffragists espoused a "feminism of rights," whereas Willard promoted a "feminism of fear." Although most scholars interpret Willard's reform ideology as advocating suffrage only as a means to temperance, I argue that she designed and promoted a more complete and radical vision of the role of women. This vision put security, not autonomous rights, first.[5] Most married women's condition of financial dependence at the time limited severely the changes Willard could hope to accomplish, but her program gave middle-class women a means of coping with their relative powerlessness.

Willard's critique of the assumption of male protection, her more "republican" contention that motherhood should be the model for political leadership, and her appeals to women to protect themselves by putting direct pressure on government are the three strands of her "feminism of fear." Other notable women used motherhood to develop ideologies, but only Willard fused this with a liberal denunciation of cruelty to mobilize mass numbers of women. As Bordin observes, Willard eventually celebrated equal rights aims, which indicated that women's quest for protection was compatible with the quest for natural rights.[6] What Willard made clear, however, was that without guarantees of protection for motherhood, the legal promise of equal rights meant little to most women.

Participatory Symbols of Republican Motherhood

Willard activated women's political participation as no other leader had. She accomplished this feat by coupling temperance goals to woman suffrage and by authorizing both reforms with innovative interpretations of biblical mandates that called women to be public, moral authorities. These new interpretations challenged those who invoked the Bible to justify women's political exclusion. Willard also disputed an accepted premise of "republican motherhood": that women's teaching and practice of virtue restricted their practice of citizenship to family and church. Her famous rallying cry of "Home Protection" and her encouragement that women use the "mother-heart" to develop a responsible state aroused women's courage for politics. Additionally, Willard redesigned the WCTU into a national organization that facilitated women's political participation by making local associations the primary arena of collective action and by inviting children to join conjunctive juvenile groups.[7]

Although Willard's ideology was probably her primary contribution to women's winning the vote, the federalist organizational structure she introduced in 1874, based on strong local organizations, made possible a communications network that reached a maximum number of women. Published as a seventy-two-page pamphlet, her organizational plan, *Hints and Helps in Our Temperance Work,* centered decision-making power in "locals"—associations in villages, towns, and city neighborhoods. This grassroots focus assured the protesters control of the agenda for organized action. The choices of specific issues, strategies, tactics, and general level of militance remained largely in members' hands.[8] This network also allowed multiple goals and a range of political strategies to coexist in the same organization. Willard's plan and the leadership guidelines she published in 1883 smoothly guided the WCTU's transition from a protest organization to a conventional pressure group.[9]

Through this structure, Willard disseminated a powerful and empowering ideology. Although they differed in their reform priorities, ideologies, and strategies, Lucy Stone, Susan B. Anthony, Elizabeth Cady Stanton, and Frances Willard all aided women toward inclusion in U.S. politics. The suffragists' egalitarian ideology aimed to transform governmental assumptions, rules, and practices and to open doors for women's inclusion. Willard's protectionist ideology complemented the suffragists' more egalitarian arguments by showing women how they could fashion meaningful forms of political participation without relinquishing their distinctive identities.

Unlike most of the suffragists' appeals to reason and the ideal of equality, Willard's ideology was symbolic and sentimental; it addressed fears and aimed to calm them. Willard focused on fear because she could not assume, as could the pioneers in the Garrisonian antislavery community, a consensus in her audience that women should participate in politics. Most Americans strongly resisted the idea, as the multiple failures of referenda on woman suffrage in Colorado and elsewhere reveal.[10]

Aileen S. Kraditor observes that Willard faced an audience of women in the 1870s who had experienced the industrialization of the home and the loss of activities such as spinning cotton and churning butter. These women sought to restore the control their mothers had exercised over the nutrition and education of their children.[11] It is equally plausible to argue, as Carl Degler does, that Willard's message resonated not so much with women who felt a loss of status but rather with women who believed their roles as mothers and homemakers were much more profound and far-reaching than did their ancestors in the previous century.[12] Willard's vigorous assertions of woman's special moral authority and of the threats the saloon made to the home—as the foundation of society—also appealed to the loneliness, fears, and ambitions that Kraditor and Degler identify. Moreover, the denial of the vote to women by the Fourteenth and Fifteenth Amendments, the experience of a vicious war that created many widows, and an increase in exclusively male social drinking[13] presented middle-class white women with good reasons to organize and to exercise moral authority for their own benefit. Willard's feminism of fear addressed all of these conditions.

Willard's "Home Protection" Speech

Many white women in the 1870s and 1880s undoubtedly resisted suffrage partly because they feared men's opposition and anger. Established sex roles and psychological dispositions to defend these roles were fortified by passages from the Bible that justified political exclusion as part of widely accepted female subordination. Arguments adapted from social contract theory identified men as the free and political protectors of subordinate women and dependent children.[14] Some of these patriarchal traditions and the authority used to justify them gripped men and women alike. Willard eventually presented graphic explanations of how they had failed. But first she had to assuage her female audience's fears about challenging patriarchal traditions and the religious and political authority that supported them.

Willard recruited many religiously devoted, educated, middle-class black and white women with an ideology that invoked the Bible as its primary authority, defined motherhood as a qualification for political participation, and insisted upon political participation as the fulfillment of women's God-given roles. "Home Protection," the title of her most famous speech, became her main rallying cry—first for temperance and later for active political participation and suffrage by women. A label Willard appropriated from Letitia Yeomans, a Canadian temperance reformer who used the term during a speech in the summer of 1876, "home protection" traditionally was understood as a shorthand rationale for tariff protection of some industries. Willard made the concept relevant to women by defining home protection as the main task of motherhood. With her new label, she connected women's desires to defend and protect their families with civic duties such as patriotism and philanthropy.

Willard's "Home Protection" speech sought to inspire temperance women to seek the vote as part of their God-ordained mission to restore virtue and civilization to a society overrun by vice and immorality. Women have this mission, she claimed, because with women's instinct of mother-love "God has indicated Woman, who is the born conservator of home, to be the Nemesis of Home's arch enemy, king alcohol."[15] Willard's audience heard, as many evangelical congregations hear today, that God's mission requires them to act in spite of their fears. When she implored women to make "the surroundings of the ballot-box respectable," and to call for the rule of conscience in politics, Willard used duty to drive out fear.[16]

But Willard never adopted the literal interpretation of the biblical verses advocated by fundamentalists. She professed faith in a God who called both men and women to action.[17] She referred to God as a creator of natural multiplicity and complexity, each element of which has a divine purpose. In her view, the duty of women and men was to celebrate and preserve God's creation. She subdued fears by referring to God as *the* protector and most authoritative lawgiver. Willard urged her audience to see struggle for laws that celebrate and preserve creation as the fulfillment of spiritual duty: "All pure and Christian sentiment concerning humanity, will, sooner or later, crystallize into law . . . Thus, almost every one of the Ten Commandments, except the first which relates to love of God and man, something not susceptible of legislation, is the basis of a law in this Republic."[18]

Willard admonished her audience that the force of laws against the sale of intoxicants depended—just like laws against stealing—on the intensity of public sentiment behind them. Public sentiment ought, she argued, to harmonize with God's desires. Given that the sources of public sentiment derive from natural instincts, the challenge humans face is to bring their natural instincts into accord with God's will.

Willard thus enlisted women's ambition to fulfill God's will by showing that public sentiment should be shaped by "mother-love," not just self-interest. She asserted that women's instinct, mother-love, "sets so strongly against intoxicants, that if the liquor traffic were dependent on their patronage alone, it would collapse this night as though all the nitro-glycerine of Hell Gate reef had exploded under it."

Predicting that "Catholic women would vote with Protestant women upon this issue for the protection of their homes," Willard cast women's temperance initiatives in "the rum power's overthrow" as uniting "our thoughts as women and as patriots." Drawing together women of all denominations into the sentiment of patriotism, she quoted from Frederick Douglass's writings to illuminate the struggle between vice and virtue in society, a struggle in which vice is the aggressor that "delights in keen-edged weapons, and prefers a hand to hand conflict" and virtue is "the passive, slow to move, but ponderous and ultimately heavier power."[19] Women should recognize drinking men as a form of vice in the community, and each woman should invest her special, God-given virtues to overcome this vice in the political arena.

By tying mother-love to home protection and making this idea her rationale for women's struggle to win the vote, Willard opened public doors to the influence of mother-love. Despite women's successful resistance to alcohol, Willard contended, their weak condition relative to men's greater physical and political powers prevented them from exercising virtue and protecting the home without help from government—especially when men had been drinking.[20] Women's weakness and vulnerability to men's abuses of their power as husbands and fathers became Willard's fundamental justification for suffrage.

Like William Lloyd Garrison and leaders of the Second Great Awakening, Willard captured her audience with moral suasion—appeals to act for the greater good according to one's conscience. Her speeches and autobiography reveal, however, that Willard's strategy held more than this. The goals she stated initially were not the ones she intended or hoped that her audience would accept. Instead, Willard confronted her audience's resistance with techniques much like those of a successful magician. She initially obtained the attention of her audience by directing their focus to temperance goals and their missions as mothers. After she captured her audience, however, Willard began to link symbols of republican motherhood to voting and lobbying. To secure temperance legislation, women would have to vote. Willard thereby built a bridge from women's roles as moral authorities in the family and church communities to the more radical goal of suffrage.[21] In the process she subtly dissented from the expected roles for women and the public's frequent toleration of a moral double standard. Overcoming century-old proscriptions against women's political participation required this sort of "moral inventiveness."[22]

If traditional and working-class women thought that the vote would threaten a loss of identity or the security of their financial or psychological dependence as well as require new, more assertive behaviors, they were unlikely to support it.[23] To generate support from such women for political participation, Willard tried to convince them that their God-given motherly duties required direct pressure on government. The slogan she gave the WCTU, "For God, for Home, and Native Land," connected the authorities women served and centered them on God.[24] Sensitive to her audience's deference first to the laws of God and second to the laws of government, Willard both encouraged temperance women to set an example for less religiously interested suffragists and discouraged them from assuming limits on God's powers.[25]

Willard's emphasis on women's physical vulnerability graphically portrayed the injustices women suffered due to their unequal political condition. She described a Cincinnati bishop's amazement that women were more willing than men to sign a petition to ban the traffic in liquor, and that poor women were the most eager of all: "Many a hand was taken from the washtub to hold the pencil and affix the signature of women of this class, and many an other, which could only make the sign of the cross, did that with tears and a hearty 'God bless you.' 'That was a wonderful lesson to me,' said the good Bishop, and he has always believed since then that God will give our enemy into our hands by giving to us an ally still more powerful—Woman with the ballot against rumshops in her hand."[26] Such sentimental images grabbed attention.

Willard also conjured many pro–woman suffrage symbols. She portrayed the "small bit of white paper" used to select legislators and vote on referenda as more powerful than dynamiting selective saloons or holding localized crusades. Willard repeatedly told two evocative stories to win suffrage support. The first was the memory of her mother "gently" telling her father that laws for prohibition would pass "when women vote." When he made an incredulous retort, one that might have made many wives fearful, Willard's mother answered: "Well, I say to you as the apostle Paul said to his jailor: 'you have put us into prison. We being Romans, you must come and take us out.'" The second story recalled her feelings watching her brother leave with her father to vote in the 1856 presidential election. "Standing by the window, a girl of sixteen years—a girl of simple, homely fancies, not at all strong-minded, and altogether ignorant of the world—I looked out as they drove away, my father and my brother, and as I looked I felt a strange ache in my heart, and tears sprang to my eyes. Turning to my sister Mary, . . . I said, 'Don't you wish we could go with them when we are old enough? Don't we love the country just as well as they do?'"[27]

In the late 1870s, Willard's message about the importance of the vote was not intended to transform the WCTU into a suffrage organization but rather to consolidate and streamline the female temperance movement, which had begun as a series of protests and spontaneous crusades. Willard's success in shifting the WCTU from protest to lobbying, however, and in authorizing women's political participation—even voting—with biblical authority, made her much more than a temperance leader.

There are strong indications that Willard's primary objective, even in her earliest "Home Protection" speech, extended beyond temperance. In her rhetoric blaming men for alcohol abuse, Willard presents a picture of a zealous temperance activist, even a prohibitionist. But when we shift our focus to the object of her blame and to the action she advocated, her speeches reveal how she led female temperance reformers away from prohibitionist goals and the sometimes violent consequences of prayer protests to suffrage and social activism. She replaced risky behavior and high-cost goals with the radical but less militant aim of winning the vote. Thus, sustaining organized political action for a radical, nonviolent intermediate aim became a more immediate goal for self-protection than full prohibition.

As WCTU president, Willard praised the suffragists for struggling to win political rights but criticized them for addressing propertied women almost exclusively. The slogan "taxation without representation," Willard asserted, was "a keen perception of justice," but "the average woman, who has nothing to be taxed, declines to go forth to battle on that issue." According to Willard, the temperance crusades gave women reasons for the vote that connected with their "mother-hearts": "Not rights, but duties; not her need alone, but that of her children and her country; not the 'woman,' but the 'human' question is stirring women's hearts and breaking down their prejudice to-day."[28]

Willard also distinguished between suffragists and WCTU suffrage supporters by referring to the former as "noble women . . . who do not think as do the Temperance Unions about the deep things of religion," or yet agree about the importance of abstinence. She called on temperance reformers to overlook these differences and to concentrate on the issues the two sorts of reformers had in common: political exclusion, a desire to "Christianize," a commitment to moral choices, and peace.[29] In so doing, she dramatically broadened the base of the suffrage movement.

Moral Cruelty and Americanist Ideas

Willard's success as a political mobilizer has not overshadowed the contempt for male aggression and the ethnocentrism embedded in her ideology.[30] Shklar's concept of "moral cruelty" helps explain these flaws. Shklar argues that liberals who name physical cruelty as the worst vice or political problem often are led by their anger at that cruelty to engage in "moral cruelty," or to entrap themselves in a moralistic condemnation of oppressors. For victims of serious oppression, condemnation can grow into a condition of "deliberate and persistent humiliation, so that the victim can eventually trust neither himself nor anyone else."[31] When liberals who consider cruelty to be the worst human vice fail to distinguish damaging behavior from those who inflict the damage, and proceed, often self-righteously, to define the violent oppressor as evil, they practice moral cruelty.

Willard and other proponents of the feminism of fear made a similar sort of conflation when they asserted that most behaviors oppressive to women derived from inherent evils in men. Willard berated men for their lack of conscience, inability to resist drinking in groups, and toleration of political corruption—all behaviors that she thought resulted from men's primal instinct of self-preservation. Women, in contrast, possessed a primal instinct that was "far more high and sacred" than that of self-preservation: "the instinct of a mother's love, a wife's devotion, a sister's faithfulness, a daughter's loyalty." As a survival instinct, she asserted, a mother's love is stronger than self-preservation and is "the only antidote to vices men have created by their uncontrolled consumption of alcohol among themselves."[32] This tendency to paint women as the politically "good" and men as "bad" led Willard to assert explicitly that women would make decisions driven by conscience rather than by male motives of self-interest and desire for power. This maternalistic intolerance, voiced in elitist republican tones, often focused on "the foreign vote" and the exercise of political power by men less educated than she. As a result, Willard's legacy has been tarnished and her vision of men and women sharing power in home and government has been undermined. By borrowing so freely from the ascriptive Americanist tradition, Willard's feminism, like Stanton's after the Civil War, sullied the Garrisonian vision of inclusive equality.[33]

Willard's arguments do not meet the more inclusive and egalitarian standards of the twentieth century. In order to inspire and sustain middle-class, white women's political participation, Willard appealed to the symbols, ideas, and goals of that audience. Like Susan B. Anthony and Elizabeth Cady Stanton, Willard believed that interracial organization and struggle lacked an adequate base of public support as well as allies in the state and federal legislatures.[34]

By the 1880s and 1890s Willard was making innovative suffrage arguments undermining both the authorities that justified political exclusion and the popular conceptions men had about voting qualifications. During Reconstruction and the 1877 referendum campaign, woman suffrage opponents' basic premise was that military service was a necessary qualification for voting. As long as most men uncritically accepted the equation between "ballots and bullets," women would never win the vote. Men could simply invoke Chief Justice Waite's argument that citizenship for women could not include all forms of political participation: "the consent of the governed" was fulfilled by women's surrogate protectors—their fathers, husbands, and brothers. Because female property owners were not expected to be soldiers, their taxes did not constitute adequate entitlement to vote.

Willard's speeches splintered this view. Her principal argument was that because men's proclivity to drink alcohol prevented them from protecting women and children in the home—and actually transformed men from protectors into threats—women needed the vote to protect themselves.[35] According to this argument, women themselves became "soldiers" in the war on vice, and the ballot became their most important weapon. By calling the suffrage struggle a "great battle" to restore virtue and by depicting women as crusaders incorporating God's law into the laws of their "native land," Willard fortified virtue and duty with the obligations of patriotism. Women begin to see "that the Ten Commandments and the Sermon on the Mount are voted up or voted down upon election day; and that a military exigency requires the army of the Prince of Peace to call out its reserves."[36]

While developing this unique fusion of Americanist and republican duties, Willard extended her feminism of fear by arguing against making participation in the military a necessary qualification for citizenship. In her annual address to the WCTU in 1888, Willard asserted that suffrage opponents "now entrench themselves in 'the knock-down argument,' as I may justly call it, viz.: 'They that will not fight, neither shall they vote.' But if ever there was a last ditch, this is the one; for when in all history did any [military] controversy divide any people along sex lines? When Eve started a rebellion, Adam immediately joined it; when Ananias falsified the returns, Sapphira followed him; Deborah had her Barak, and St. Paul his plebe; men and women have 'paired off' in every great movement since the world began and always will." Willard contended that women and men share aims; they "will no more fight each other than would a pair of pet canaries."[37]

Willard reasoned that when men and women shared power in government their cooperation would assure peace. Woman's influence, she implied, would prevent the escalation of political controversies into military conflagrations. To support her argument, Willard cited the position of the renowned Episcopal preacher and author Reverend Richard Heber Newton that women would oppose war. Newton also claimed that enfranchised women would transform the state from an institution of expedient compromises into a means of moral guidance: "Woman will carry her religious nature into the State, not to establish a State religion—the last new religio-political 'fad'—but to keep alive within the body of its laws and institutions the spirit of essential religion, which will make the State the conscience of the people."[38] This utopian vision of women subduing the state hinted at the rigorous standards that feminists of fear could set: even the state would be severely limited in its power to inflict physical cruelty.[39]

Political Integration of the Sexes

Willard saw the real barrier for women as the all-male membership of political parties and legislatures. In a letter to the Massachusetts WCTU in the spring of 1884, she argued, as she did elsewhere, that the chief problem with the influx of immigrants was that they were disproportionately male. She asserted, moreover, that "men deteriorate in college, camp and court, just in proportion as the companionship of their sisters is withdrawn; that politics, the noblest science on earth, tends toward decay when men make the futile attempt to play mother to a half-orphaned world . . . Nature's law still holds, and 'two heads in council' as well as 'two beside the hearth,' is proved by experience to be the correct formula."[40] Willard proposed that domestic ideals of shared responsibilities between men and women become the model for decision-making in government: "I resolved to build my life to help make the world so homelike that women could freely go out into it everywhere, side by side with men, and also to help bring it about that men should share in larger measure than they have ever yet done the hallowed ministrations of the fireside and the cradleside, through which, as I believe, they are to reach their highest and holiest development."[41]

Willard's experience with political parties during her leadership made her progressively more critical of their politics. Initially she explained partisan conflicts and the importance of elections; she did not criticize the party *system*. By the mid-1880s, however, she betrayed some anger at the parties' leadership and processes of decision making:

> The ridiculous and childish spectacle at the State capital of Illinois, in the months past, where a hundred thousand dollars of the people's money has been expended in the art of doing nothing; the impotence of municipal government in all our cities; the outrage of the recent Presidential campaign, with the slander and virulence that have fol-

lowed it; the venality in public office, and general contempt into which professional politicians have fallen,—are the portents which accompany the close of this one-sided epoch, whose final hour is a consummation devoutly to be wished.[42]

Willard excoriated men for allowing vice to penetrate the political parties and legislatures. In the process, she conflated "exclusive control by males" and "vice." Some derision toward behavior she stereotyped as male sneaks into these passages. In her autobiography she wrote that during an 1884 WCTU presentation to a committee of the Republican Party—the party she favored from childhood—the room in which they spoke was "distasteful, almost sickening to us, by reason of the sight of the many much-used spittoons and the sight and smell of the blue cloud of smoke." Willard also described the short time limit of fifteen minutes put on her speech and the courteous but uncomfortable manner in which the committee responded. She endorsed the Prohibition Party, asserting that it would have related more favorably to the women because, unlike the exclusively male Republicans, "ladies themselves are members of and leaders" in that party.[43] Thus, Willard used women's traditional standards of respectability to drive wedges among politically powerful men.

By the late 1880s Willard extended her vision of gender integration in government to the home. She called for equal status for women, and she stressed the heavy responsibilities attached to raising children—responsibilities she thought both parents should share.[44] In her 1889 Annual WCTU Address, Willard recommended that married couples sign a pledge "of faithfulness in the common and holy task that they have undertaken which shall insure the best conditions of existence to the children."[45]

To argue, as Barbara Epstein does, that "conventional morality, and for that matter, Home Protection, implied the defense of what was in fact a male-dominated family structure" overlooks Willard's determination to revolutionize the home.[46] Willard argued that after women won the vote and participated fully in government, the state would restore the security of marriage and the family: protection would reign without male domination, thereby overturning male domination and integrating gendered domains. According to Willard, women's political inclusion—voting and holding office—would make government more likely to attend to women's needs. She asserted that besides wives' retaining their maiden names and the preference for the mother's custody of children, "the wife will have undoubted custody of herself." Confirming the importance of birth control for women, Willard predicted that "as in all the lower ranges of the animal creation, she will determine the frequency of the investiture of life with form and of love with immortality." Possibly referring to antiabortion literature, Willard lamented the proliferation of "books written by men to teach women the immeasurable iniquity of arresting development in the genesis of a new life." In a rare invocation of the ideal of equality, she quipped that "not one of these volumes contains the remotest suggestion that this responsibility should be at least equally divided between *himself* and *herself*. The untold horrors of this injustice dwarf all others out of sight, and the most hopeless feature of it is the utter unconsciousness with which it is committed."[47] She also appealed for vigorous laws against divorce to protect the interests of children.[48]

Willard did not condemn the sexual contract; she aimed to salvage it by speaking for the women and children who were victims of its violators: the fathers and husbands who abused alcohol. Her message reads as if written in the "different voice" that Carol Gilligan argues fundamentally distinguishes highly educated women from professional men: a voice that speaks from inside relationships and calls for the maintenance of relationships at the same time as it expresses women's needs.[49] Willard's voice, however, also urged female assertiveness from an Americanist position of moral superiority and purity. Gender integration, both at home and in government, required that men defer to women's moral judgments. Moral progress depended upon fundamental changes of character in men, not changes in women. Fearful of change herself, Willard denounced the willingness of women "in fine social surroundings" to allow men at their sides to "puff tobacco smoke into their faces and eyes" and called it "a survival of past savagery and debasement and of the immolation of women."[50]

Willard's feminism was full of such moralistic language. She relied upon standards of ladylike behavior: for example, ladies neither smoke nor drink in public. Moreover, Willard's esteem for presumptions that women were more virtuous than men suggested to her audiences that her vision might create female domination, not shared power between the sexes. Willard's matriarchal plan for integrating the separate spheres did not specify how women's leadership would avoid becoming overly absolute.

In her "Home Protection" speech, Willard's denunciation of the threat that drunken men posed to women and children, her call for home protection, and her use of evangelical arguments to personalize her appeals introduced the means she would use thereafter to engage attention. Although she continually told women how they could better protect themselves—through prayer, organization, and voting—she gradually swerved from her initial focus on ending men's cruelty to women. Willard encouraged women's political participation as well as a balance of power between the separate spheres, but she came to rely more heavily on illiberal symbols of Americanist rule and republican motherhood, symbols that clashed with her ultimate vision of men and women sharing power in separate but equal spheres.

Willard was nevertheless convinced that women would enter a new epoch only if leaders such as herself could discredit authoritative male traditions, integrate government, and transform the fears that maintained those authorities into a mass activism. To achieve that end, Willard pinpointed and strengthened women's traditional identities as moral authorities by fusing these identities to the human mission ordained in the Bible. As Rogers Smith observes, the liberal tradition's lack of symbols and institutions for the enhancement of ideals such as equality and liberty for women left her little choice.[51] Willard pointed out a host of new moral problems—the need to educate children, the lack of urban recreational opportunities, and widespread poverty—that traditional women could help solve. Willard's vision became especially appealing to women who were less educated, poorer, and more religiously conservative than the suffragists.[52]

Willard and Woman Suffrage in Colorado

After their disappointing defeat in 1877, Colorado suffragists Albina Washburn and Mary Shields must have found much hope in Willard's arguments. Instead of assuming women's interest in political equality, Willard first coaxed women to enter the public life. By focusing women's attention on their responsibilities to stop man's cruel threats and treating the vote as necessary for this greater end, Willard made woman suffrage and woman's rights respectable.[53] Washburn and Shields valued these direct links between political reform goals and women's everyday needs as wives and mothers.[54] As former suffragists, their intentions overlapped exactly with Willard's strategic use of "home protection" to build support for both suffrage and temperance.

Willard's influence on Albina Washburn is apparent not only in Washburn's organizational strategy but also in her arguments. In November 1876, for example, Washburn pressed for a recognition of woman's right to vote at the National Grange Convention in Chicago. Despite the Grange's inclusion of women in all its deliberations, she did not receive a warm welcome. Washburn chaired a committee of six women who considered a resolution to enfranchise women, but the five other women on the committee rejected the proposal. Washburn was left responsible for reporting the decision to the convention.

On the convention's final day, Washburn read her dissenting minority report. She began with arguments by Bromwell and national suffragists based on natural rights. Arguing that the convention should discuss the woman suffrage resolution, she asserted that only "a lack of moral courage and perhaps a thoughtless disregard of the rights of a respectable minority" prevented deliberation of the issue by the entire convention. She further insisted that principles of "universal liberty and justice" were embedded in the Constitution of the United States. The founders had not, she argued, intended the government to be "an exclusive one of one sex . . . On the contrary, there is evidently a most scrupulous avoidance of any such idea, the words 'person' and 'citizen' being used whenever practicable, and the masculine pronoun, whenever used for convenience, is always construed in law to mean also women."

Washburn also echoed Willard's arguments for "home protection"— only one month old at the time. After complaining that the Constitution taxed women and made them responsible for obeying the law just as much as men, she contended that women suffer losses that men do not: "Their children are taken from them by masculine courts, their husbands and sons are ruined by liquor sold under masculine license, their hours of labor and the wages for that labor are controlled entirely by masculine legislation. Moreover women alone are punished for social crimes in which men are equal, and generally far more guilty partners."[55]

Washburn used Willard's graphic illustrations of men's cruelty to women and children to prove that inconsistent applications of the law, both written and unwritten, generated a double standard and thus failed to deliver appropriate protective services to women. Such double standards, Washburn insisted, resulted in a manipulation of public opinion against making women full citizens: "Public opinion following the laws which men have made for their own benefit, ostracizes the weaker party, and over breaking hearts and desolated homes builds a monument to the greatest wrong of modern times."[56]

Washburn identified the complex problems that woman's ambiguous political condition presented reformers, especially characterizations of women as weak and inferior. At the height of her speech, for instance, she questioned making the "insurmountable obstacle" of sex "the test of political qualifications." Washburn thus appealed for consistent standards to judge men and women. She also added that women had *more* need of political rights than men "because of the acknowledged and inherited weakness which in all society elicits the gallantry and superficial subservience of men," that she needs "the strong weapon of the ballot to protect herself and her children from injustice."[57]

Using the presumptions of women's "weakness" to win support for woman suffrage, even when they were accompanied by a reference to male chivalry as "superficial" subservience, injected familiar inconsistencies into Washburn's Willard-inspired appeals. Willard, of course, had attached claims of woman's moral superiority to her statements about woman's physical weakness. But associating without question or qualification "inherited weakness" with women, as Washburn did, undermined the logical consistency of her earlier argument that the word "citizen" included women on equal terms with men. Despite her failure to persuade the Grange to support woman suffrage, Washburn tried to protest excluding women from offices in the Grange. When the Farmers' Alliance replaced the Grange in Colorado during the late 1880s, it opened offices to women, and Washburn was prepared to demand the full inclusion of women from the start. By then, Washburn and Shields had persuaded many Colorado women to accept woman suffrage reforms.

The Colorado WCTU: A Shadow Organization for Woman Suffrage

In 1880, together with Mary Shields, Albina Washburn established for the first time a state branch of the Woman's Christian Temperance Union. Because the WCTU was all female and centered locally, the organization gave women who had been restricted to the home and who accepted woman's "separate sphere" new opportunities to develop leadership skills without pressure to defer either to male authorities or to national woman suffrage leaders.[58] For Shields and Washburn, there was only a short distance between "woman's Christian temperance" and the goal of suffrage. In the shelter of the WCTU, Shields and Washburn could quietly show their women peers the inconsistent rules that ordered men's and women's behavior and encourage them to struggle for suffrage reform.

Colorado's women enthusiastically joined the state WCTU under their stewardship. In 1881, one year after they founded the organization, it had seven auxiliaries and no headquarters; by 1884 the Colorado WCTU had over 480 paying members; in 1888 this total had risen to 750; and in 1892 it had grown to well over 1,000 members.[59] In 1889, Mrs. C. D. H. Thompson, a WCTU member, stated in a summary of the organization's history that Willard had praised the Colorado organization for being "the first State to organize without outside help."[60]

Even with their now powerful organization, Washburn and Shields could not put woman suffrage on their state's decision agenda until the economic crisis of the early 1890s jolted the mining industry and the

Populists presented a strong third-party challenge in 1892. But when these opportunities for winning the vote emerged in the early 1890s, Coloradan suffragists were ready with a statewide membership and had articulated the arguments they needed to win.

Thus in Colorado Shields and Washburn used the WCTU to overcome women's psychological resistances to political participation, especially the idea of voting. As the low number of female participants in the 1876 and 1877 suffrage campaigns indicated, only two of eight vice presidents and only four of at least twelve executive committee members were women. Both of these steps were necessary before another campaign could be waged with any hope of success.

Because the idea of woman suffrage inevitably brought conflict into the WCTU, American temperance leaders addressed the subject with great care. Women who joined the temperance movement for moral reasons did not necessarily believe that woman was equal to man or that women should vote.[61] The WCTU encouraged activism as an extension of woman's role as mothers, and WCTU members generally joined the organization to defend the home, not to create structural change or alter woman's role in the public sphere.[62] Most middle-class white women accepted the separation of the public sphere from the private sphere, and few contended that women should exercise political power.

Within a WCTU such as Colorado's, however, where the veteran woman suffragist Mary Shields became the president for the first five years, the argument that women were both equal and different had a fertile ground for development. Before the WCTU, in the 1877 suffrage campaign, Shields and other state reform leaders had argued that woman's distinctive responsibilities and perspective justified their enfranchisement. Willard's initiation of this argument provided a strong precedent for forging links between temperance and suffrage.

As early as April 13, 1878, for instance, the *Woman's Journal* reported that at a town meeting in Longmont, Colorado, a town northeast of Denver, the licensing of alcohol sales was defeated.[63] Longmont became the site for the formation of the Colorado WCTU. In 1889, Mrs. C. D. H. Thompson recounted its start in 1880: "The first Union in the state was organized at Longmont and it was fitting it should be the birthplace of the State Union. Home Protection, Woman Suffrage and other ideas permeating our work to-day, were prominent in all the addresses of the meeting, and woman then as now, looked upon the saloon as the great adversary of God, Home and Country."[64]

Thompson's speech recognizes the overlap between the female state leaders of woman suffrage reform in Colorado in 1877 and those who became the state's WCTU leaders in 1880. Shields was elected president of the WCTU in 1880; Washburn was also reported to have attended the founding of the Colorado WCTU and the 1889 state convention.[65] Thompson remembered that the election of Shields as the first state WCTU president owed much to Shields's suffrage speeches in Longmont: "Her pleasing manner, forcible logic, and the fact that she could speak in public, decided us in inviting her to be our speaker at the Convention. The election of officers occurred the first thing, and Mrs. Shields as President displayed the wonderful executive ability, [as] you who knew her, know so well."[66]

Colorado mothers who considered themselves moral authorities easily supported temperance, especially in the agricultural communities of northeastern Colorado where many parents did not want the social culture of the mining towns or Denver to shape their children's lives. In 1877 suffragists Henry Blackwell and Margaret Campbell both had argued that the liquor interests manipulated the voters' choices against votes for women. Many of those opposed to temperance were also against woman suffrage, so the defense of temperance was linked with suffrage as well.

In fact, the shift of organized woman suffrage reformers to temperance reform in Colorado during the 1880s resulted directly from arguments antisuffragists had made in 1877. By characterizing Eastern leaders as "carpetbaggers" and their demands for women's equality as threats to the home, Colorado suffragists were forced to prove that the vote was a respectable demand for women. They also needed to illustrate more graphically than the suffragists had how political exclusion put women at risk. Willard's arguments directly countered the antisuffragists' claim. Because temperance reform had long been accepted as a woman's concern, it was safer to mobilize suffrage support under the auspices of the WCTU than as part of either suffrage organization.

The Colorado WCTU and Woman's Role

As president of the Colorado WCTU, Shields invested considerable time and energy explaining to the women members why the tasks of motherhood required public action generally and the vote in particular. Shields assured Colorado women that the WCTU was committed to a public life that maintained visible connections with "woman's role" in the home.[67] By addressing her audience as mothers, Shields encouraged them to change their views on the nature of political protection. At the 1882 Colorado WCTU convention, for example, she asserted: "The time has come when . . . mothers have determined that their children must be protected by the strong arm of the law, and that law must be backed by the strongest of all human powers—*Public Opinion.*"[68]

The forms of political participation that Shields recommended included more than voting. She advocated attending conventions and lectures, and, above all, educating men, children, and other women about the evil of "strong drink." These activities were steps in transforming society that ended with the creation of the WCTU vision of the "holy city on the hill." This vision went beyond inclusion in the existing political system to a democratic transformation of American society.[69] Colorado's WCTU reform leaders did not explicitly concentrate on changing attitudes about female inferiority, but did aim to overcome WCTU members' reluctance to participate in politics due to such assumptions.

At the 1882 Colorado WCTU convention, M. F. Gray-Pitman, a female representative from Denver, stated, "Woman is sometimes called the weaker vessel; be it so, do we not read that 'God hath chosen the weak things of the world to confound the things which are mighty,' and methinks if woman had the ballot in her hands it would not be many years before the mighty power of the liquor interest would tremble from centre to circumference."[70] Gray-Pitman added that many temperance women were "not only *willing* but anxiously waiting to use this 'home protection' weapon, this weapon that is to our *government* what the battery is to electricity or the piston to the steam engine."[71]

At the 1884 state convention, President Mary Shields boosted her audience's spirits by stating that "woman represents the conservative forces of the world, (I use the word in a preservative sense), and is therefore necessarily in antagonism to the destroying agency of alcohol." She described women's independent mobilization for temperance as the result of "ages of suffering and the sacrifice of millions of lives." Shields justified "the aggressive measures" that were "now so fiercely waged between the liquor traffic and the home" as the "outgrowth of the mysterious movement known as the 'Crusade,' divinest manifestation of God's spirit since tongues of fire sat on the Saints at Pentecost." She praised the temperance women's "sacrifice of their ideas of what was modest and womanly" as a "test of faith" that revealed to the movement's founders "a knowledge of latent power."[72] And in an 1884 petition for state temperance reform laws, the Colorado WCTU introduced the women signers as follows: "We, the undersigned, officers of the Woman's Christian Temperance Union, representing the interests of the home and family, and having no direct influence at the polls, do earnestly and respectfully petition the representatives of the Republican Party."[73]

By celebrating the radical departure from the behavior expected of middle-class white women in the 1880s, and by representing that departure as doing God's will, Shields had helped assuage any doubts about their political participation. In 1888, Colorado's WCTU president began her annual presidential address with a similar message:

> The world looks upon a strange spectacle to-day, woman in organized society, in convention, tells a story of an onward march unknown in all her past history . . . The danger to the home has driven her from its four walls for its defense and to the better interpretation of God's purpose concerning herself, and she sees in the clearer light of God's truth to which she has come, that her boy's salvation is intimately connected with the safety of the boy across the way, that society largely builds the foundation on which her home is resting, and that the people make a government which rules the nation, and so her prayers, her labors must comprehend the neighbor's boy and the interests of society, and she must strive for the government that shall make it just as easy as possible to do right, and just as hard as possible to do wrong.[74]

Temperance leaders invoked scriptural authority, both for statements of God's will and for models of daring action by women. Religious, not political, authority gave these women their sense of purpose. Willard and state leaders of the WCTU had successfully executed what could be considered the Third Great Awakening. Under Willard's leadership, such women became pioneers of a municipal reform that aimed to foster "good behavior" in all citizens. Willard's particularly white Protestant conception of the good provided alternative public standards to those put forward by political parties.

Thus the WCTU presented a strong rebuttal to the argument that women shouldn't vote because motherhood did not prepare them to choose political leaders. Colorado temperance leaders like Willard (and like abolitionists Maria Stewart and the Grimké sisters) turned that argument around in Colorado by insisting that a mother's role as a moral authority prepared her to combat the evil perpetrated both by the liquor interests and by men when they consumed "strong drink." Woman's right to vote could then be seen as a means of undoing the imbalance that had occurred in politics because of women's absence. Without women in politics, men could forget with impunity the morals that they had learned in the home.[75]

In 1888 the president of the Colorado WCTU blamed "State and Nation" for the "legalized liquor traffic" that had "set upon our homes and loved ones an enemy relentless as death, and more cruel than the grave." She also affirmed support for suffrage: "As a State for years we have declared in favor of equal suffrage. Forsooth! [W]hy should not a woman as a citizen have the means to defend life, liberty and possession and why should we not stand by the party which stands by us and promises protection to the home and loved ones?"[76]

By the middle of the 1880s, the Colorado WCTU had made woman suffrage a high priority. Both the national and the Colorado WCTU had established a franchise department encouraging WCTU members to support and work for woman suffrage. In 1885, Julia Sabine communicated her town's news about their new suffrage mobilization efforts to the *Woman's Journal*. She introduced herself as a member of a "Suffrage League in Colorado Springs," and in a show of deference to eastern leaders requested a copy of the constitution and bylaws of the Massachusetts leagues.[77] By 1889, Sabine was writing the annual report of the franchise department for the Colorado WCTU; she directed this department for at least two years.

Sabine used the *Woman's Journal* to promote suffrage among women both inside and outside Colorado. At the WCTU's state convention in 1888, she reported that she had circulated copies of the journal as well as other suffrage tracts to all local unions in the state.[78] In 1889 Sabine revealed the bargain that the editors of the *Woman's Journal* had struck with the Colorado WCTU (and presumably with other unions) to increase the pressure for suffrage levied by the temperance organization. In her words, "For every twenty-five new subscribers at $1.50 per annum, which we as a Union will send them, they will send us $20, to be used in our work. While they would prefer that it should be used in the Franchise department, they do not restrict us."[79]

Sabine's assurance that the money returned to the WCTU from personal subscriptions to the *Woman's Journal* would not be earmarked for the franchise department suggests that despite their leaders' prosuffrage statements, not all WCTU members supported votes for women. Sabine's 1888 report indicated either resistance or grave hesitation about the woman suffrage issue among her members. Although she queried "fifty unions" to find how many members voted in school elections and "how many are serving as school directors," she had received "replies from exactly six."[80] In 1889, Sabine chastised the WCTU members for their lack of enthusiasm about winning the vote: "I sometimes think my department is, of all, the most disheartening and discouraging. And this is so because our foes are of our own household. It is the apathy and selfish indifference of Christian women, who have 'all the rights they want,' that makes the suffrage work so hard for the rest of us, who can see that until we have the ballot to work with, most of our strength will be but weakness."[81] Reporting that her department had made little progress in mobilizing support, she urged the members to work for suffrage in the coming year.[82]

Although I found no direct evidence in the archives of conflicts within the Colorado WCTU, Sabine's expression of frustration suggests that some members resisted the idea of votes for women even though WCTU leaders annually made woman suffrage an organizational objective. The rank and file of the Colorado WCTU was probably less willing than its leaders to see temperance and suffrage as overlapping goals. Still, the WCTU successfully mobilized many Colorado women: in 1891 its state convention brought together 101 delegates from 21 counties and 42 locals; 35 counties were listed as lacking representation.[83]

The alliance the AWSA forged with the Colorado WCTU leaders was tentative, a potential set of ties that might become useful for launching a suffrage campaign if and when favorable circumstances emerged. The strategy of Shields, Washburn, and Sabine constituted a necessary but insufficient form of political mobilization for winning women the vote. The connections between the AWSA and the Colorado WCTU sustained the communications network necessary to design and execute a suffrage campaign similar to that of 1877, but they did not immediately make it possible to launch a new suffrage campaign. Sabine's correspondence kept Stone and Blackwell informed about suffrage's status among their closest allies, and the temperance leaders responsible for the "Franchise Department" learned about the nature of opposition and support for suffrage throughout the nation by reading the *Woman's Journal*.

Despite members' sluggish attitudes toward this issue during the 1880s, by 1892 woman suffrage reform had become the subject of the first resolution passed at the temperance organization's state convention—only a year before the state legislature finally passed woman suffrage. The first resolution in the convention gave the impression that the organization's support for woman suffrage was now solid, widespread, and based on a mix of republican and liberal principles: "RESOLVED: 1st, That in a government, whose political power inheres in the people: in a government deriving its power from the consent of the governed; in a government that has established the maxim that 'Taxation without representation is tyranny,' it is a bold contradiction and a reflection on our national intelligence and honor to deprive one half the people of the ballot."[84]

The other resolutions passed at this convention reaffirmed commitments to regulate the consumption of tobacco and alcohol, to establish homes for "incorrigible girls," and to improve the working conditions of labor. The Colorado WCTU did not endorse the Prohibition Party; in that state the WCTU followed the suffragists' nonpartisan stance. In 1890 the superintendent of the press, Elsie Chambers, had cautioned unequivocally against a close alliance with the Prohibitionists because of the unpopularity of the third party: "While personally a Prohibitionist," she asserted, "it is our policy to work on our own special lines of work in the W.C.T.U."[85]

The Colorado temperance reformers' distrust of the Prohibitionists' single-issue focus indicates the long strides Willard had made in creating a collective public agency for *women's* moral reform. Temperance women in Colorado and all over the nation busily proved they could "Do Everything": they educated the public about women's qualifications not only for the vote, but also for independent political standing. Under Willard's leadership, women proved their equality to men by directing women's unique resources toward the public good. Ultimately Willard's strategy made political equality possible for women because, as temperance reformers, they were not forced to assume roles or responsibilities for which they lacked knowledge, confidence, or both.

By 1890, the Colorado WCTU had lobbied for restrictions on the sale and consumption of alcohol, given lip service to the aim of woman suffrage, and become a social reform organization that offered shelter to the outcast and homeless as well as support to laborers who sought better working conditions. This varied agenda made Colorado WCTU reform leaders leery of tight ties with the Prohibitionists. That the Rocky Mountain temperance reformers became willing to struggle for woman suffrage proves Willard's mobilization strategy was a success. All the reformers needed now was the opportunity to campaign for the vote. Populist victories in Colorado between 1891 and 1893 gave them that opportunity.

5

An Exceptional Victory:
The Colorado Campaign of 1893

*I*N 1893 woman suffrage reformers won their first state referendum
campaign, in Colorado. Of the two major historians to cover this
campaign, Eleanor Flexner treats the victory as idiosyncratic and
Alan Grimes as the result of efforts to promote "prohibition and immigra-
tion restriction."[1] Both drew their inferences only from suffragists' accounts; neither consulted the views of temperance reformers, female
populists, or women from the labor movement. Had they done so, they
would have found substantial evidence that the effort aimed primarily to
make women citizens.

Woman suffrage reformers won their first referendum-based victory in
Colorado in 1893 because multiple political forces helped move the issue
onto the state government agenda and ensured its passage. As political
scientist John Kingdon contends, a controversial idea long perceived as a
threat becomes ripe for legislation only after (1) both elite and public
opinion are prepared for a shift and (2) a network of policy entrepreneurs
and brokers have coupled that idea to other issues important to voters and
elected officials. Ideas for policy reform, such as woman suffrage, can float
around in the "problem and policy streams" interminably; only after
leaders link such ideas to solutions for more pressing problems and assure
it will advance political careers will a reform appear on the "decision
agenda."[2]

Six major changes in the suffrage "policy stream" made the 1893
Colorado victory possible: (1) the Colorado People's Party won many seats
in the 1892 elections, (2) suffrage support was mobilized in the state WCTU
and the Grange, (3) members of Colorado's Grange and WCTU constituted
the core of the more radical Farmers' Alliance that in turn became a pillar
of the People's Party in that state, (4) by the 1890s, a larger, more educated
and urbane female population inhabited Colorado's cities, including Denver, (5) the 1890 merger of the NWSA and the AWSA into the NAWSA
ended a twenty-year divisive competition among the national reform lead-

ers, and (6) Wyoming's 1890 admission to the union as a state with women voters signaled that sentiment about female enfranchisement had softened in Congress and would no longer jeopardize statehood.

Economic Depression: Populism and Free Silver

Between 1890 and 1892 Colorado's economy nearly collapsed because prices of both silver and farm products fell catastrophically. Colorado's Democratic and Republican parties each insisted that silver be remonetized at their national conventions in 1892. But both Colorado delegations lost their bids for "free silver" when their national parties drafted equivocal positions on the issue. This loss precipitated conflict among state party leaders over electoral strategies on silver.[3]

Colorado's intraparty conflicts over silver were resolved by a fusion of Silver Democrats, and some Silver Republicans, with the burgeoning Colorado People's Party. The Colorado People's Party offered the dissidents the prosilver plank of the national Populist Party platform and a vehicle for campaigning against the traditional parties' candidates in the 1892 elections. Democratic allegiance shifted notably to the People's Party in the fall of 1892, and enough Republicans converted to clinch electoral victories for all statewide Populist candidates, including James B. Weaver, the Populist candidate for president. Although the Republican Party held on to half the seats—thirty-three of sixty-five—in the state assembly, the Democratic Party's share dwindled to five; the Populists won twenty-seven seats. This substantial victory of a third party committed to egalitarian reforms, including woman suffrage, brought strong allies for the suffragists into the state government. By recommending woman suffrage in his inaugural address, Populist governor Davis Hanson Waite advertised the presence of favorable conditions for the reform.[4]

Distraught at national leaders for their equivocation on the silver issue, Colorado's Republicans and Democrats divided among themselves, temporarily weakening the infrastructures of both parties. Then male political leaders set out against each other in search of new constituencies, opening the policy window for a successful woman suffrage reform campaign in 1893.[5]

In 1893, Colorado offered woman suffragists exceptionally favorable political circumstances. In few other states did woman suffragists, WCTU reformers, organized labor, and Populists show such unity of purpose. Each of these groups articulated its own blend of egalitarian liberal and participatory republican aims. Rather than calling primarily for the conversion of powerful wrongdoers as the Garrisonians had, these reformers insisted that in addition to casting down monopolies, American citizens must study government, treat political participation as a primary responsibility, and design political policies that would restore power to the people. In short, the mostly male Populists (whom Norman Pollack credits with undertaking a "humanitarian" quest for a "just social order") shared Willard's vision of a politically active citizenry of men and women who put respect for persons and "home protection" first.[6]

Building Suffrage Alliances via the WCTU

Frances Willard exhibited many of the qualities of a policy entrepreneur: she carefully prepared her speeches and strategies, established herself as an authoritative temperance leader early and with confidence, and persistently sought both allies and opportunities to change the political condition of women.[7] Between 1880 and 1892 Willard initiated alliances first with the Knights of Labor, applauding them for their temperance efforts, and second with the Populists. She had in mind both a transformation of the American party system and political inclusion for women. According to Ruth Bordin, these efforts brought Willard much criticism from temperance colleagues, her mother, and Lucy Stone. Willard persisted despite the criticisms, and claimed, for example, that the Knights of Labor had committed themselves to temperance, woman suffrage, and equal pay for women.[8] In her autobiography Willard explains that she decided to forge such ties as early as the 1885 WCTU national convention in Philadelphia.[9]

Whatever support she may have lost among rank-and-file members of the WCTU for reaching out to the Knights, Willard's speech at the 1885 convention aimed to mobilize maximum support among working-class men for temperance and woman's vote. "The central question of labor reform," she proclaimed, "is not so much *how to get higher wages,* as *how to turn present wages to better account.*" She urged men to recognize the needs of the home as superior to their own: "Fourteen hundred millions annually drawn, chiefly from the pockets of working men, by saloon-keepers and cigar-dealers, means less flour in the barrel, less coal in the cellar, and less clothing for the laborers' families. We grieve to see them give their money for that which is not bread, and their labor for that which satisfieth not. We suggest that if, by your request, pay day were universally changed from Saturday to Monday, this would do much to increase the capital at home."

Willard encouraged her male audience to support the public-school teaching of daily regimes for "wholesome living in respect to diet, dress, sleep, exercise and ventilation," to make a "pledge of equal chastity for man and woman," and to help "in our efforts to secure adequate protection by law for the daughters of the poor and rich alike, from the cruelty of base and brutal men." She urged the Knights to "do all in your power for the cause of prohibition" to achieve "self-mastery" and "protection and happiness in those *homes* which are the heart's true resting places!" In conclusion, Willard pleaded for woman suffrage support by promising that women would support labor's primary interests: "And that women may come to the rescue in this great emergency, also as an act of justice toward those who have the most sacred claim on your protection, we hope that you may see your way clear to cast your ballots only for such measures and such men as are pledged to the enfranchisement of women."[10]

To Willard, avoiding such a supportive constituency—as her mother and Stone advised—just because they were organized labor would have seemed a ridiculous waste of opportunity. Such gestures did not immediately or obviously reward the suffrage cause nationally, but the reform effort in Colorado benefited from Willard's brave outreach. Although a joint meeting of WCTU and Knight locals in Denver in 1890 was attended by few temperance women,[11] Populist reporter Emma Ghent Curtis credited the Knights as being major mobilizers of support for woman suffrage in the 1893 referendum.[12] In endorsing the Colorado campaign to other national leaders—an endorsement that accelerated their involvement in the campaign—Henry Blackwell singled out the presence of the Knights as reason to hope for victory.[13] And although Denver labor leaders were not particularly enthusiastic about political equality for women, they were exceptionally tolerant of religious diversity and considered the home the cornerstone of the community.[14]

Willard, Gospel Socialism, and a New Feminist Ideology

Frances Willard's embrace of the Knights helped to encourage dialogue in homes nationwide. By the mid-1880s a segment of temperance women, admittedly not a majority, caught on to Willard's radical aims and used both their homes and their participation in the Farmers' Alliance to make those aims a reality. These women fused Willard's feminism of fear with the more egalitarian feminism of rights preferred by suffrage leaders. By 1893, their new ideological conglomerate served as an authoritative justification for passing woman suffrage in Colorado.

Mari Jo Buhle contends that Willard's home protection ideology helped to foster a distinctively American gospel of socialism during the late nineteenth century. Willard admitted her conversion to socialism only just before her death. But during the 1880s, women whose political participation began in the Grange and later extended to activism in the Farmers' Alliance, populism, suffrage, and temperance built a strong, homegrown social democratic politics in the West and Midwest. Albina Washburn made strides in Colorado, while more famous Populists such as Annie Diggs and Mary E. Lease forged ties between WCTU members and Populists in rural areas across the midsection of the country. The 1890 creation of a monthly journal, *Farmer's Wife*, by women in Topeka, Kansas—followed by the establishment of the National Woman's Alliance (NWA) in September 1891—introduced a new fusion of ideas about pluralistic egalitarian reform that aimed to unite "temperance, suffrage, labor, and agrarian radicalism."[15]

The motto of the *Farmer's Wife*—"Equal Rights to All, Special Privileges to None"—and the egalitarian aims in the NWA charter renewed enthusiasm among women for political equality. In their "Declaration of Purposes" the Populists demanded recognition of the "political equality of the sexes." Refusing to blame men for the wrongs done to women, populist women assumed that populist men shared their quest for justice. Committing themselves to change their own lives and to participate in the "great social, industrial, and financial revolution now dawning upon the civilized world," populist women proclaimed their intent to study all questions about the social structure; "to carry out" the golden rule; "to aid" in the practice of "co-operation in every department of human life"; "to secure" the "utmost harmony . . . among the Sisterhood"; "to teach principles of international arbitration" in order to prevent war; and "to discourage in every way possible" the use of alcoholic beverages as well as tobacco and "other narcotics injurious to the human system."[16] These activist women also were persuaded that women's political participation was essential for securing a better protected society.

These shared purposes were professed at the annual convention of the national WCTU in Denver in late October 1892. In a presidential address that included praise for the populists, appeals to labor, calls for home protection, and endorsements of woman suffrage, Willard articulated these shared purposes in populist rhetoric that integrated multiple political traditions:

> But we all know that anything that minimizes the self-respect of any class is an offense and injury to that class. Women are never treated as if they were citizens except in bearing liabilities, paying taxes, and suffering the mischief which mismanagement brings upon the community. If we are ever to save the State, we must enfranchise the sex which at this moment has to bear the most painful burdens imposed

by nature upon humanity, and which is much more acclimatized to self-sacrifice for others than the sex which at present monopolizes the franchise. What lies at the root of everything? Give us the vote, that we may be recognized as if we were capable citizens. Give us the vote, in order that we may help in purifying politics, which at present can hardly be said to be so ideally pure that you can afford to refuse a helping hand. Give us the vote, in order that we may use it, and in using it exercise ourselves in the discharge of responsible duties, in the administration of affairs which form so large a part of the realms of most men.[17]

Here Willard's appeal fused liberal, republican, and Americanist principles. By invoking the liberal esteem for personal self-respect, she illustrated the injustice done when the state collected women's taxes but failed to provide adequate services. She also promoted the image of women as voters with republican and Americanist symbolism. In saying "If we are ever to save the State," Willard made women appear to be moral self-sacrificing saviors ready to lead the Populist effort to put purified power into the hands of the people and exercise it responsibly. The local press covered the convention; Coloradan Ellis Meredith, a reporter, wrote an article praising Willard's leadership.[18] In his address to the convention, Governor John Routt endorsed woman suffrage: "You will never be able to accomplish this grand work you have undertaken until you are allowed the ballot; and if I had it in my power, I would give every one of you the ballot before I left my present position."[19]

Although Willard's attempt to fuse the Prohibitionists, Populists, WCTU, and labor into a third party failed nationally,[20] this fragment of her vision came to life in Colorado during the 1893 woman suffrage campaign. The Colorado Populists were more tolerant of WCTU reformers' claims than their national leaders had been, and they were more willing to subordinate their prohibition goals to maximize the support they could generate for suffrage. Women in the Farmers' Alliance and those connected with the Knights of Labor believed that female enfranchisement would hasten the creation of much needed social welfare reforms.

Putting Votes for Women on Colorado's Legislative Agenda

The People's Party of Colorado included supporters of woman suffrage. Its leaders were residents of the northern agricultural counties that in 1877 had showed the most support for woman's vote. Former journalist Davis

Hanson Waite, their gubernatorial candidate, had switched from the Democratic to the Republican Party in 1856 over the issue of slavery and had ties to the Knights of Labor. Given Willard's influence with the Knights, Waite probably had come to support woman suffrage even before his nomination for the governorship. In his campaign for governor, he also invoked radical Republican ideas.[21] When the Populists proclaimed that they intended to elect a "Lincoln man" to office, they tapped the loyalties of disillusioned Republicans and revived old abolitionist ideals of individual rights and equality. These ideals allowed woman suffragists to put their issue on the reform agenda and keep it there until it passed.

Colorado Populists adopted the WCTU's rallying cry for protection of women and children in the home. Before their fusion with the Silver Democrats and Republicans in the late summer of 1892, the Populist Party in Colorado had appropriated images of "home protection" that had been part of the woman suffrage reformers' appeals in 1877 and had echoed Willard's arguments about political corruption. In October 1891, for example, the *Rocky Mountain Daily News* of Denver identified the home protection argument as a central feature of the young party's grassroots appeals. As its emblem, the "party has adopted a cut of a cottage home . . . holding that the defense of the home is its mission." They warned against voting as usual: "Don't offer them the antiquated excuse that you have always been a Democrat or Republican; don't display your unprogressiveness by such a statement. No man, in the past ten years, has been able to demonstrate the difference between them." They drove home their argument with reminders of how hard times had become:

> There is no need of convincing you that there are urgent reasons for such a movement of the people. There is not one of you but what has felt the pressure from industrial adversity in a land naturally bountiful: of low wages and no wages; of slack times and hard times; of payment due on the mortgage that stands as a vampire over the home; of the growth of the millionaire and a million of tramps; you have fought against it in labor and social organizations and have realized how helpless all was without a people united for industrial emancipation. Such has finally resulted in the formation of the People's party of the United States, which you are asked to become a part of.[22]

After the fusion of the Silver Republicans, Democrats, and the People's Party of Colorado, most candidates appealed for "free silver" and discredited the major parties' platforms. Nevertheless, in the fall of 1892 some pieces of pro-Populist propaganda were printed in the *Rocky Mountain Daily News* that repeated the theme of home protection. On September 11, the *News* published a piece in which the Arapahoe County Democratic Party justified casting their votes for the Populist candidates: "We cannot consistently with our sense of duty to country, state, homes and party, aid by our countenance and votes the elevation of anyone opposed to free silver coinage at the existing ratio to the presidential office."[23] On the same page as their declaration of changed allegiance a political cartoon appeared representing Colorado as a mother protecting her home of "Free and Unlimited Silver Coinage" against the presidential candidates, Cleveland and Harrison, who were depicted as beggars[24] (see Figure 1). The next day the *News* quoted the Populists' presidential candidate in 1892, James B. Weaver, again raising the theme of protecting home and children: "Two farmers say, 'We can no longer provide for our children as our fathers did. They sent their sons and daughters to college; but we cannot do it. There is something wrong; somebody is getting our wealth; let us talk about it.' "[25]

Colorado Populists' appeals for home protection did not propose to restore past relations. They demanded a new order, including new governmental rules preventing further concentration of power in national corporations and national political parties. In 1892 the national Populists based these demands on a combination of home protection and egalitarianism. Presidential candidate Weaver explained the need for the Populist Party as follows:

> What is the necessity of a new party? The people of this country have been voting the Democratic and the Republican tickets for more than a quarter of a century, and during all that time the majority of the voters of this country have been growing poorer, getting deeper in debt, less able to take care of their families than they ever were before, and they have read in the [D]eclaration of [I]ndependence (which is good democratic authority) the remarkable words which came from the mind and fell from the pen of Mr. Jefferson: We hold these truths to be self-evident, that all men are equal, etc.; that they are endowed by their creator with certain inalienable rights, among which are life, liberty and the pursuit of happiness.[26]

Thus the Colorado People's Party blended liberal and republican aims that resonated with both the feminism of equal rights and the feminism of fear.

A New Generation of Colorado Suffragists

In 1890 a small but shrewd and determined group of Denver suffragists organized for the South Dakota suffrage campaign. Although they initially stumbled into a nativist effort to limit immigrants' citizenship rights, these women exhibited the urbane tolerance and confident resourcefulness in building alliances that Sharon Hartman Strom first observed as distinctive of twentieth-century suffragists in Massachusetts.[27] Unlike Colorado's first generation of reformers, many of these women were earners. Rather than relying on their husbands or male allies for support, these women created independent organizations that targeted primarily female audiences. They also insisted upon claims that were either "as universal as possible or combined with specific ones for every special interest group in the state."[28] Ellis Meredith exemplified the "new suffragist"—educated, egalitarian, and entrepreneurial. In 1893 she successfully promoted a change of name from the "State Woman Suffrage Association" to the "Non-Partisan Equal Suffrage Association of Colorado" because "in the word 'equal' there is an appeal to justice which does not seem to exist in the word 'woman.'"[29] Reformers such as Meredith, Emma Ghent Curtis, and Helen Reynolds initiated alliances with many crucial male organizations both from within, as members (the Farmers' Alliance), and from the outside (the Knights of Labor).

The influence of organized, educated, middle-class Denver women had been displayed in 1889 when the national convention of the Association for the Advancement of Women (AAW) met there. The *Rocky Mountain News* reported that attendance at the convention was "one of the largest audiences ever assembled in Unity church," and that "the meeting developed the discussion of numerous subjects . . . which would have done credit to an assemblage of senators."[30] The women's speeches addressed problems such as building elementary schools with adequate open space in urban areas as well as an analysis of Hegel's "Views of Art."[31] The *Denver News,* which curiously titled its article "Female Suffrage," positively reviewed the women speakers at the convention and claimed that their discussions proved that females had intellectual abilities they could put to good use.[32]

Soon after Denver suffragists had organized themselves, Lucy Stone dispatched Louise M. Tyler to recruit more members, including WCTU suffragists and other educated and professional women.[33] In 1891, Tyler became the president of the revived state suffrage organization; in 1892 she took over as the "Superintendent of the Franchise Department" of the Colorado WCTU.[34] Tyler also chaired the executive committee of the Colorado Woman Suffrage Association for the 1893 campaign.[35] Tyler's dual leadership in both the temperance and suffrage reform struggles in the state suggests that her presence was part of national suffragists' plan to combine temperance and suffrage resources.[36]

In spite of suffragists' many allies among Colorado legislators, passage of votes for women was not easy. Although Louise Tyler and Minnie J. Reynolds lobbied in both houses,[37] several efforts failed in both the state senate and the assembly between January and April of 1893.[38] The usual sources of opposition—the organized liquor interests, sentiment for keeping women in the home, and traditional interpretations of biblical authorities—caused the repeated defeats.[39] The continuing power of this opposition casts doubt on Flexner's assumption that the 1893 victory eventually occurred because the "liquor and political machines were caught napping."[40]

On April 3, 1893, the last day of the legislature's regular session, the Colorado Senate and House passed the woman suffrage reform bill.[41] The bill promised women the same voting rights men possessed, and the referendum was set for the fall.[42] The legislature also mandated the wording of the ballots in Colorado: "The ballots were to be marked simply 'Equal Suffrage Approved' and 'Equal Suffrage Not Approved.'"[43]

The Populists provided most of the prosuffrage votes, the Democrats voted consistently against the bill, and the Republicans were divided. In the Assembly, twenty-two Populists voted for and three against the bill; eleven Republicans voted for and twenty-one against; and one Democrat voted for and three against. In the Senate, twelve Populists voted for and one against the bill; eight Republicans voted for and four against; and all five Democrats voted against.[44] The consistent support of the Populists, as opposed to the mixed results from the formerly dominant parties, allowed the passage of woman suffrage.

No account provides the details of Tyler and Reynolds's lobbying strategy. According to the movement's official chronicle, women could attend the hearings and debates.[45] Tyler and Reynolds appear to have had close access to many legislators and were able to monitor how each intended to vote.

Further, because their effort to win legislative passage of the reform had failed in 1891, these reformers may have been better acquainted with legislative procedures and internal power structures than some of the newly elected representatives. As a veteran suffragist and temperance reformer, Tyler was probably as prepared as (if not more prepared than) some of the new Populist representatives to use the legislature to advance her reform interest. When comparing the suffrage issue to other Populist measures such as a strengthened railroad commission—very few of which passed during this first legislative session—Tyler's and Reynolds's lobbying skills probably deserve much credit.[46]

To promote woman suffrage, women Populists also used pressure-group tactics. At the 1892 People's Party convention in Colorado, female delegates insisted that a quota of women be sent to the various party conventions throughout the state as well as to the Omaha convention. Emma Ghent Curtis pointed out that the delegation from the Farmers' Alliance was responsible both for converting the Knights of Labor delegation to this female participation policy and for a new rule that "empowered each county thereafter to send to the State nominating convention one delegate at large, which delegate should be a woman."

The rise of the People's Party in Colorado in 1892 presented former Granger, WCTU member, and seasoned woman suffragist Albina Washburn with new opportunities to incorporate women into government. Following the Colorado People's Party Convention in July 1892 that nominated Davis Waite for governor, Washburn wrote a detailed letter about the proceedings to the *Woman's Journal.* One of twelve female delegates elected to the convention, Washburn initiated among populist women deliberations over whether to request a suffrage plank for the party platform. The women initially rejected such a plank "since women were received as delegates without question, and the Omaha platform, in its preamble, virtually conceded the belief of the People's Party in equal political rights for all." She stated, moreover, that the women delegates at the Colorado People's Party Convention "were actually and practically voting on equal terms with men." Washburn recounted that she had drafted and read the following resolution during the closing session of the convention: "*Resolved,* That we, the People's Party of Colorado, composed of men and women who desire the restoration of the people's rights, hereby declare our allegiance to the principle of political equality for all American citizens without regard to sex."[47]

Regarding the principle of equal rights, the male leaders of Colorado's People's Party practiced what they preached.[48] Women were elected delegates to all of the party's conventions, and when Albina Washburn raised the issue of woman suffrage, she did not face the severe opposition she had fifteen years before at the National Grange Convention. Although the Omaha platform of 1892 had disappointed Willard with its overly general resolution to establish "equal rights and equal privileges for all the men and women of this country,"[49] many county conventions of the Colorado party (as well as Republican county conventions) took the step she wanted: they included an equal suffrage plank in their platforms.[50]

Women in the Colorado Farmers' Alliance continued their campaign for suffrage both outside and inside the People's Party. In December 1892, after the People's Party victory, three women were elected officers of the Colorado Alliance. These women had close contact with "three members of the new Legislature" who were also alliance officers. These three, Curtis said, "pledged themselves to do all in their power to get a suffrage bill safely through the coming session of the Legislature; and they kept their promises. We watched them, and therefore know." Curtis also reported cooperation between the alliance and the Knights to enfranchise women: "the State Alliance appointed a committee to act in conjunction with a similar committee appointed by the Knights of Labor, the duty of this double committee to be the careful watching of legislation and the spurring up of such legislators as were inclined to lag. This committee was instructed to look after the suffrage matter, and it proved faithful."[51]

Combining Curtis's explanation with that of the suffragist historians, we can reconstruct the leadership network responsible for the reform. Women inside the Populist Party pressured the male members to pass it, while WCTU and woman suffrage leaders lobbied the state legislature from outside. As former abolitionist Governor Waite encouraged passage from above, elected representatives, especially Populists, faced demands for female enfranchisement from all sides.

From State to Nation to Precinct

Mobilizing voters to ratify woman suffrage in the Colorado referendum was more complex than the legislative struggle. To achieve ratification, a state campaign had to appeal to male voters of all groups, including some Democrats and Republicans as well as Populists. Most importantly, money was a huge obstacle: the woman suffragists "entered the campaign with only twenty-eight members and $25.00 in the treasury."[52]

After its legislative passage, the woman suffrage bill also needed speakers and activists who could appeal to men and women with loyalties to causes other than temperance and populism. The woman suffrage leaders in Colorado recognized their problem early. Soon after their legislative victory the name of their suffrage organization was changed to the "Non-Partisan Equal Suffrage Association of Colorado," and they elected a new slate of officers to execute the campaign.[53] Tyler became the chairman of the executive committee, a low-profile position; Martha Pease, who was not connected to any other organization, was elected president; and Ellis Meredith became vice president.[54]

These leaders quickly took two steps to raise financial and popular support. First, they nominated a woman, Mrs. Ione Hanna, for the Denver school board and brought enough women to the polls to elect her.[55] Second, they sought financial aid and lecturers from NAWSA as well as money and moral support from advertisements in the *Woman's Journal*.

The *Woman's Journal* had reported the passage of the woman suffrage amendment by the Colorado legislature in its April 15, 1893, issue.[56] One week later the journal announced that Susan B. Anthony had promised to raise $20,000 for campaigns in Kansas, Colorado, and New York.[57] It remained to be answered how much money and how many speakers the NAWSA would actually contribute to Colorado.

Through extensive correspondence, Lucy Stone, Henry Blackwell, Ellis Meredith, Carrie Chapman, and Susan B. Anthony built a leadership network and shaped the strategy for the ratification campaign. All the national leaders' appraisals of campaign possibilities display both a primary concern for victory and a careful calculation about how to invest scarce resources. Remembering the 1877 defeat, most of the national leaders were skeptical about the impending Colorado campaign. For example, Anthony's response to Meredith's initial request for assistance was to ask, "Are all those Mexicans dead?"[58] And although Blackwell was enthusiastic, Lucy Stone was not.

The suffragists' policy emerged from debate among leaders, not from a single leader. By letter, Blackwell urged Stone, who preferred Kansas over Colorado as a site, to approve Colorado's campaign, and he outlined a strategy linking the two campaigns:[59]

> I wish that you & Alice would call Laura Johns & Mrs. Carrie Lane Chapman into a *Council of War*. If I understand aright Colorado votes *first* on the Woman Suffrage Constitutional Amendment. It is *very important* to carry Colorado & if that be impossible (of which I am not at all sure) then it is very important to get the largest possible vote . . . I suggest that Mrs. Johns & Mrs. Chapman confer with Mrs. Louise Tyler of Denver & work up Colorado *first of all*. Not merely by meetings, but by a quiet move on the newspaper press and the Labor Unions & Knights of Labor. If we can get 1. The Republican machine of Colorado 2. the Labor Organizations & 3. The newspapers—and push the *Enrollment* which can use the same books as Kansas (I have 500 printed)—we can get a *committee of men at each voting precinct* of Colorado and that will carry the State. Dont try to enlist the W.C.T.U. Let the Temperance question *quietly alone. You four people* can plan it all out at Chicago.[60]

Blackwell failed to convince Stone to support the Colorado effort. Yet his campaign strategy—the vision of a small group directing a quiet campaign by winning over labor and the newspapers and by leaving the WCTU to act independently—foreshadowed the major elements of the plan that

Chapman later presented to Meredith: a quiet campaign, led by a small group that relied upon party politicians to convert voters.[61]

During June, Ellis Meredith persuaded the national women leaders that Colorado's 1893 campaign was worthwhile,[62] in part by describing how the requirement of a mere plurality of votes in the fall referendum would make victory possible.[63] Besides emphasizing the advantages brought by the Populists' new power, Governor Waite's endorsement, and women's recent increased participation in school elections, she pointed both to the low 51 percent threshold needed for a referendum victory and to the advantages of the "Australian ballot system"—ballots that allowed voters to select candidates rather than vote for a party slate. In an ironic twist on the idea that these ballots enlarged voter preferences, Meredith observed that the new ballots could favor the suffragists because voters formerly trained to select the party ticket would still be "prone . . . to put [their] cross under the device and never cross names at all." Moreover, Meredith insisted (without explanation) that when a voter failed to mark his ticket, "every ballot of that kind counts as one for us."[64] She also reported that the statewide "post card survey poll" of newspapers by the Colorado Equal Suffrage Association (CESA) found only eleven papers opposed to suffrage and thirty-three supporting it. Of the eleven opposed, only five expressed "bitter opposition."[65]

To Chapman's belief in the better opportunity for victory in Kansas, Meredith replied: "We feel that we have twice as much show as Kansas to get suffrage, and I'll tell you why. There is not a single particle of organized opposition in the state. In Kansas there is already opposition which will be strengthened by all the opponents of the measure as time goes on."[66] The fact that this woman suffrage "amendment" required only a majority rather than a two-thirds vote for passage won the eastern reformer over; Chapman admitted that she had been unaware of this advantageous rule, observed that a large vote in Colorado would boost the Kansas effort, and offered to participate in the campaign.[67]

Chapman's quiet campaign used a central committee composed of a few women and a male representative of each party rather than a large association. In the eight campaigns that had failed, she also believed that the political parties' control of voters' choices was the chief stumbling block. Probably because she wanted to avoid acrimonious confrontations with the liquor interests, Chapman deduced that concerted subtle pressure would be better than a highly visible effort.

Chapman explicitly instructed Meredith that to mobilize voter support the committee should first promote woman suffrage resolutions at the state party conventions; second, engage senators from Wyoming as advocates;

and third, coordinate mobilization efforts with the state's WCTU. To obtain party endorsements, Chapman insisted that the members of the campaign's central committee should not be "simply suffragists. They must know politics and how to work a campaign." For example, they should quietly "see that in every precinct in the State a trusty *man* is found who will work to secure the nomination of delegates to the State Conventions . . . Then get a resolution through each convention in favor of the amendment." She warned against making any public speeches "unless at picnics, celebrations etc. until after conventions in the fall. Then have a short, sharp campaign of two or three weeks only."[68]

For the short campaign, Chapman recommended that Wyoming senators promote woman suffrage to the Colorado male voters. Respected speakers among each group—Republicans, Populists, miners, and conservatives—should be engaged to speak for the cause; for each group Chapman listed names, and she mentioned that the radicals were skilled in coping with "other classes." Above all, Chapman encouraged the enlistment of men because "committees of women . . . cannot do the political wirepulling necessary."

Chapman recommended that the Colorado suffragists encourage the participation of WCTU members, "but always as *women* and not prohibitionists." The word "prohibition" had to be kept out of the campaign: "It is like a red flag flashed in the face of a bull." Still, Chapman encouraged Meredith to elicit funds from the local WCTUs as well as from prominent politicians.[69] According to statistics collected by the WCTU national office, in 1892 the Colorado WCTU had $1,591.70 in its state treasury and its locals had raised $12,072.95. Colorado's WCTU locals ranked among the top ten state temperance fundraisers in the nation. How much money they shared with the suffragists in the 1893 campaign remains unknown.[70] But in September, when Colorado's WCTU state convention appointed two state lecturers for suffrage, Mrs. M. J. Telford of Grand Junction and Rev. Ella F. Leonard of Denver, they probably also committed some funds to the effort.[71]

Meredith and Anthony concurred with the major elements of Chapman's strategy.[72] Meredith, however, rejected Chapman's suggestion to send delegates to all of the party conventions in the state; to carry out that plan would have required "not 3 trustworthy men, but 156."[73] Anthony modified Chapman's suggestion of a quiet noneducational campaign to a quiet educational campaign; she insisted that an educational campaign be executed to win male allies. Although the women were imprecise about the difference between an "educational" and a "noneducational" campaign, it appears that Anthony supported some open meetings and public speeches, whereas Chapman preferred informal contacts and closed meetings. Anthony further suggested that each convention of males that met in Colorado before the election be asked to adopt a resolution favoring woman suffrage because "such resolutions will help create sentiment on our side [illegible] faster than anything we can do in our separate meetings."[74]

The suffrage leaders' correspondence reveals a consensus to advance the cause with leadership in small groups, to make suffrage a single issue, and to appeal to state party leaders' needs for more voters. Describing themselves as nonpartisan and excluded, the reformers could suggest that women had not yet committed themselves to a party. In a letter to Meredith, Anthony urged an issue-based campaign: "Don't be Democrats, nor Republicans, nor Populists—don't be Prohibitionists nor Saloonists. Don't be religionist or agnostic—just be nothing but *woman and her disenfranchised.*" She especially emphasized the importance of nonpartisan appeals: "Our *one aim* must be to get the *right for* women to have their opinions, on every question counted at the ballot box—no matter what those opinions are—the bad ones as well as the good ones—the demand shall be counted!!"[75]

Meredith assured Anthony that Colorado suffragists would adhere to nonpartisanship and make arguments only for suffrage: "We entirely agree with you, and are pushing our claims for suffrage simply and solely on the grounds of right and justice." Meredith also reassured Anthony that although the Populists had been "trying to get us to come out for them, . . . we will not hear of it; individually many of us are with them, but the association is and will remain strictly non-partisan."[76] To win votes from all sectors, the woman suffrage supporters had to represent all political parties. The single-issue focus on winning women was also strategic: it helped avoid conflict among woman suffrage supporters on other issues.

Their agreement that the campaign be quiet, led by small committees of men and women, and nonpartisan consolidated the strong leadership of Chapman, Meredith, and Anthony. Their alliance to form a strategy for the campaign effectively bridged the two eras of suffrage reform, but the younger leaders took full responsibility for executing the campaign and did so without mishap. The women's thorough exchange of information and candid views about strategic options made for a smooth transfer of power.[77]

The leadership network that emerged (see diagram, p. 140) was based on informal ties; as far as we know, no meeting ever occurred among all the leaders to discuss strategy, choose officers, or establish any formal ties. This informal network had a national as well as a state component. Henry Blackwell monitored the campaign from Boston and published the reports

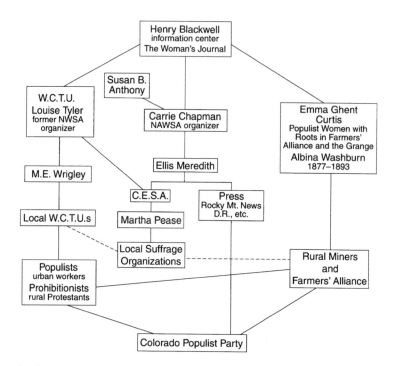

Leadership Network, Colorado Woman Suffrage Reform, 1893

of the suffragists, temperance reformers, and Populist women each week in the *Woman's Journal*. Ellis Meredith mediated when necessary between Chapman and the Colorado reform leaders. As a reporter for the *Rocky Mountain Daily News,* she also maintained an important connection with the press.

One problem not quickly solved, however, was the Colorado organization's lack of money. In late June, Meredith told Anthony, Stone, and Chapman that they had a critical need for funds: "Try and understand that money was never as tight in the history of the country as it is now. Every mine and Smelter in the state is shut down, practically."[78] Even though Blackwell and Stone donated three hundred dollars to Chapman for the campaign, the money problem persisted. In early July, Chapman told Meredith, "I do fear that these panicky times will make it difficult to get financial help."[79] The 1893 depression was intense enough nationally to make fundraising difficult everywhere.

Chapman temporarily resolved the money crisis by creating a credit system for the reformers. She instructed Meredith to have "pledge books" made for collecting donations, and she arranged to have her own salary paid from the funds gathered at her lectures.[80] During the August meeting of the NAWSA Congress in Chicago, the financial state of the Colorado campaign improved somewhat. At the congress, Henry Blackwell appealed successfully for Carrie Chapman's commission to Colorado; he raised forty dollars for her travel "on the spot."[81] Later, Helen Reynolds reported that the state Republican and Populist parties had given the suffragists money.[82]

The reform leaders' plans for this campaign reveal a day-to-day focus on politically expedient maneuvering within the existing political system. Still, when read in full, this correspondence reveals unyielding convictions that the enfranchisement of women and justice were one and the same. The suffragists refused to accept any male-created vision of justice or any male-controlled plan for its enactment, including any plan from the populists. They had learned caution from repeatedly experiencing the willingness of male equal-rights reformers to sacrifice women's aims for other parts of their program.

Practical Politics

According to Aileen Kraditor, Anthony's and Meredith's single-issue arguments signaled a shift in suffragist ideology. The ballot was no longer a means to an end; it had become an end in itself.[83] By focusing on the ballot as their singular objective, however, Anthony and Meredith did not neglect its potential for justice. Instead, they restricted their appeal to suffrage in order to make the issue more accessible to different constituencies, regardless of party. This was a realistic perspective given that reformers needed a majority of votes from enfranchised men. The single-issue focus relieved them from appealing for suffrage only for the educated or becoming too dependent upon any other overly narrow group of voters. As Anthony wrote to Meredith, Chapman's aim was "not . . . to direct but to get into support with the best men and women there all parties and classes and cooperate with them in settling upon the best plan of action and the best means to execute it."[84] What Kraditor laments as a loss of principle, Kingdon would applaud as necessary to place a controversial issue of justice on a government agenda.

As in many cases, the suffragists' appeals could be effective only if they linked their cause to the goals of each political party and class. Thus, making the vote an end in itself was a means of winning necessary support from male voters and from women, group by group. It did not entail rejecting the purposeful use of the ballot. Without the plan of engaging party leaders to campaign for female enfranchisement within each particular group, the reformers could easily have become marginalized outside the dominant arena of party politics. The nonpartisan stance and single-issue focus gave the Colorado reformers and later campaigns a way of consolidating a majority of voters in favor of woman suffrage from all parties, classes, ethnic groups, regions, and religious affiliations.

To win the campaign, reform leaders initiated three separate but related mobilization processes. First, women members of the Farmers' Alliance, Populist Party, and related groups collected petitions and campaigned in mining and farming counties.[85] Second, leaders with overlapping loyalties to the WCTU and the CESA reached the urban working class as well as the rural, middle-class, "dry" Protestants through the *Colorado Temperance Bulletin* and the *Woman's Journal*.[86] Third, the CESA, the most public of the organizations, executed a quiet educational effort aimed at winning support from members of the professions and the middle class.

Woman suffragists in the People's Party started to mobilize for the 1893 election early that summer. In a June letter written to the *Woman's Journal*, Albina Washburn expressed strong hope for victory. She admitted "that power once seated, no matter how unjustly, gives way but inch by inch to the demands of a subject class, however unlawfully subject." She noted, however, a visible shift in public opinion favoring woman's rights and woman suffrage: "One thing is certain, suffrage sentiment has grown much of late, and seldom have we a public meeting here that is not more or less tinged with the spirit looking toward woman's enfranchisement. At our Farmers' Institutes women take part, and in reading their papers usually manage to mention the ballot. If not, the very fact that they are there and there to stay, among voters and debaters for public welfare, presents an object-lesson which forces conviction on the unthinking." Washburn also reported that several women had won election or reelection to the local school boards, victories that testified to women's full participation as enfranchised citizens in school politics.[87] As Kingdon would put it, a new "mood" had emerged in the state.

By mid-August many accounts appear of the Colorado Populists campaigning for woman suffrage. Mrs. James B. Weaver, the wife of the Populists' 1892 national presidential candidate, spoke in Denver in early August for woman suffrage.[88] The Populist Party's success and support of the reform also stimulated the two traditional parties to recognize the extensive organization and participation of the suffrage reformers. By late September, most county conventions of the three political parties had endorsed woman suffrage.[89]

On August 5, one week before plans were finalized for Chapman's trip to Colorado, the CESA held a "Woman's Day" meeting at the Chautauqua on Colorado's Palmer Lake where a state senator, Charles Hartzell, was the principal speaker. In his speech, Hartzell compared the suffrage reformers to Christopher Columbus, who also "was reviled and jeered at, as a visionary and dangerous dreamer." Hartzell proclaimed that the first days of jeering were over and that support for woman suffrage had replaced opposition: "So certain as this old earth of ours shall continue to revolve, and the sun of reason shall continue to shine, so certainly will the day come which will witness the grand success, which will crown the efforts of those who labor for liberty and the equality of all."[90] Hartzell's proclamation of support at a major state festival signaled that the state reform leaders had hurdled the biggest obstacle—they had won advocates among the politically powerful men of their state without the direct help of national leaders.

Evidence of state leaders' strides appeared in Chapman's first report from Colorado to the *Woman's Journal*.[91] Writing that she was "amazed at the hopefulness of the outlook" for the campaign, Chapman continued, "There is positively no expressed opposition in Denver. It seems this is the best organized trade union city in the United States, and everyone has declared for us. Last evening we had a meeting attended by about fifteen hundred people, and with more men in it than in any meeting I have ever addressed. It was enthusiastic, and the press is cordial this morning, except one paper. So I think there is a fair prospect that we may win."[92]

Now a full convert to Colorado's cause, Chapman confirmed the state's financial distress; soon after her arrival she implored the readers of the *Woman's Journal* "to give to a suffrage campaign *with a real live hope in it* . . . at once."[93] She enthusiastically relayed that she had made the acquaintance of "Judge Belford . . . , who will speak for us and is a brilliant man, [who] was converted by Mrs. Stone many years ago. So the seed grows and bears its fruit."[94]

Chapman was especially impressed by the Populists. She reported that the silver issue had displaced most other party concerns and that the Colorado People's Party had a majority of the votes "in many localities." She noted that the liquor interests were "making a still-hunt to drum up votes against the Amendment," but that the Populists insisted that such efforts would fail.[95] In two short weeks, Chapman had decided to trust the Populists; her praise reveals that she now considered nonpartisanship as no bar to celebrating this innovative political party.

Chapman did not correspond extensively about her experience in Colorado. She appears to have followed the lecture schedule that the state leaders gave her, and they applauded her contributions after the November victory.[96] According to her biographer, Jacqueline Van Voris, she "covered over a thousand miles throughout the Rockies during the next two months. She visited twenty-nine of Colorado's sixty-three counties, speaking in two or three places in many of them." After she missed the train for one meeting, Chapman agreed to ride down a mountain on a handcar, and wrote a hair-raising account of her trip.[97]

The WCTU woman-suffrage tracts reveal interesting blends of the feminism of fear with the feminism of equal rights. Appeals used to attract attention for the cause stressed the justice of the demand, making equity a dominant theme. Such appeals lacked the confrontational, high-pressure selling language used late in the campaign—language that made Willard's feminism of fear the predominant theme. The expedient use of ideals suggests that the suffragists had learned to adapt ideals to the varied tasks of mobilization.

To kick off the woman suffrage referendum campaign, a letter published in the *Colorado Temperance Bulletin* on June 1, 1893, celebrated the state legislature's passage of the woman suffrage law and called upon all women's organizations of the state "[to make] common cause with the most progressive minds of the state, who favor suffrage as resting upon fundamental principles of justice and right." The letter advocated participation in the campaign by the "distribution of literature, by house to house visitation and enthusiastic public meetings." Admitting that the liquor interests loomed as "strenuous" opponents, the letter also reported that the support of labor organizations already had been "proclaimed."[98] This letter suggested that ties already existed between the WCTU and labor; the appearance of the same announcement in the *Woman's Journal* two days later indicates that from the start temperance leaders were heavily involved in the Colorado campaign.[99]

Woman suffrage was reported to be "one of the principal features" of the Colorado WCTU's September convention.[100] In late September, the *Woman's Journal* published mobilization guidelines by Mrs. M. E. Wrigley, the Colorado WCTU's franchise superintendent:

> Now, in working for our enfranchisement, dear sisters, don't let us say anything about purifying politics, don't say the ballot given to women will destroy the liquor traffic, don't say that when we vote we shall be eligible to office, don't say the least unkind or uncomplimentary word about the men, don't antagonize anybody, not even women who say 'woman's sphere is the home,' etc. While we do believe that woman's ballot will make the wheels of government go round with less friction and added force, yet we need not say much about it just

now. But let us urge by voice and pen the truth (denied by no sane person) that father and mother, brother and sister, according to Genesis 1:26, have equal rights to record their sentiments at the ballot box.[101]

Wrigley's guidelines showed more sensitivity to the Populists' egalitarian participatory aims than Willard had demonstrated in the fall of 1892. Avoiding talk about "purifying politics," men's weaknesses, "destroying the liquor traffic," and freeing women from the home signaled a conciliatory approach that fit the state's political mood and struck the Populist theme. This consensual vision fused the bedrock premise of universal equal rights in the Declaration of Independence with the scriptural authority of Genesis 1:26: "Then God said, 'Let us make man in *our* image and likeness to rule!'"[102] This Genesis passage, along with the very next phrase—"and let *them* have dominion"—had come to serve as evidence that God was both male and female and that the authority for rule by "fathers," or men as potential fathers, was ambiguous at best. Although Kraditor contends that suffragists such as the Colorado reformers detached the goal of votes for women from the goal of social change that originally inspired their quest for enfranchisement, Wrigley's candid advice makes it clear that some suffrage leaders thought a modicum of expediency necessary to win.[103] Once achieved, the ballot could be put to purposeful use.

It was easy for the Colorado WCTU to adopt the single-issue, nonpartisan strategy for woman suffrage because the organization had made the reform a high priority from its inception. Mary Shields, its first president, had been the leading state lecturer on woman suffrage during the 1877 campaign. For Shields and the leaders who followed her example, the WCTU helped cultivate commitment to winning women the vote. Through the WCTU the disappointed suffragists also had built up members' confidence and self-respect, and had encouraged women to invest their special management and educational skills in the public sphere. The Colorado WCTU had fostered women's campaigns for political equality by identifying women as partial citizens *and* as wives and mothers.

Late in the campaign, the CESA's appeals blended the feminism of fear with an egalitarian feminism that emphasized home protection and women's vulnerability without the vote. A one-page leaflet, entitled "A Few Leading Questions," asked and answered sardonically fifteen confrontational questions about woman's lack of political rights in the family and as citizens: "Shall men and women, who obey the laws, have a right to make them? No, only men. Who shall make the laws that concern women only? Men . . . May not married women have a voice in making the laws that determine what share of the property acquired by labor of both wife and husband during marriage they shall have? They may not . . . When a husband brutally assaults his wife, who shall make the laws to punish him? Men only."[104] Another tract, addressed "To the Women of Colorado," challenged women with the question: "Are you willing to be classed politically with idiots, criminals and [the] insane, when your own enfranchisement is offered you?"[105]

There was no ambiguity about women's role in this propaganda; the suffragists defined political exclusion as unjustified subjection. They targeted men and women as independent audiences. Compelling questions urged women readers to support votes for women and become politically active: "Does not your heart swell with patriotism as you see the best interests of Colorado struck down and our fair state lying prostrate under the blow? . . . Are you not interested in politics when in spite of the strictest economy want creeps into the household, when the mother is forced to pinch and save and deny her children; when the self-supporting woman sees her wages reduced, and when on every side arises a long, low undertone of sorrow, the cry of the suffering poor?" To relieve economic suffering, the suffragists asserted, women must participate in politics and promote legal reforms: "Charity can never do it. Philanthropy can never do it. Only right laws, rightly executed, can reform social conditions. The ballot is the greatest power and protection of this day and age."[106]

The women who wrote these tracts used moral suasion to arouse women's anger and compel them to act. They also echoed inclusive egalitarian appeals made for woman's rights reforms during the 1850s. One pamphlet asserted that just government was based on "the consent of the governed," that "the right of suffrage is one of the inalienable rights meant to be secured by the [C]onstitution," and that "taxation without representation is tyranny." Although these reminders about the meaning of liberal republican principles were the most reliable, consistent, and fundamental for woman's rights and woman suffrage reformers, the addition of specific information about women's suffering in that state made the Colorado appeals distinctive. For example, one leaflet informed men that "16,000 women" in Colorado were self-supporting and that "hard times for men are doubly hard for women."[107] Instead of criticizing woman's separate sphere or men as oppressors as the earlier reformers had, these Colorado suffragists assailed the political system for denying women the vote and making women and children suffer. Like Willard and the strongest male populist thinkers, they linked injustice to women with the problems faced by labor.

Some pamphlets directly linked the Populists' silver issue and women's demand for the vote: woman suffrage, they argued, would add 50,000 voters to the ranks of silver supporters. The suffragists also tied the silver issue to "home needs," a theme the Populists had adopted. This appeal suggested that the government had trespassed on home privacy; because woman's sphere was no longer separate, women had to vote to defend themselves: "It is said that woman's sphere is home. But the money question has power to reach into the most sheltered home and bring want and desolation. Many working women are without employment; many more are working longer hours at reduced salaries. Women have not invaded politics, politics have invaded the homes. What are you going to do about it?"[108]

Other such appeals smartly overturned the argument that women should not vote because they belonged only in the home. It is easy to imagine how, in a deeply depressed economy, these appeals might have converted men who valued "home" as the place to ensure the protection of women and children.

Colorado's WCTU leaders may not have written these particular pamphlets. But the influence of Willard's feminism of fear throughout the Colorado campaign and especially on the CESA pamphlets is unmistakable. Even the battery of questions with repeated pointed responses reflects Willard's argumentative style.[109]

Newspaper editorials and speeches from the clergy reinforced these pamphlets. One editorial in the *Denver Republican* replied to one criticism—that the enfranchisement of women would bring "the vicious classes of the sex" to the polls while the "decent women" would "stay away"—by stating that women voters would be far less likely than men to compose the "bought-and-delivered vote." Women voters, the editorial argued, would check, not enhance, the patronage element of the electoral system: "How many women, Professional Ward-Workers, can you drive as unthinking cattle to vote, when good women shall teach them they must vote to give their children—the little baby in their arms—better opportunities than they themselves have had?"[110]

Most of the clergy in Colorado supported woman suffrage in 1893. A Loveland Presbyterian minister's speech for the measure so impressed Albina Washburn that she reported it to the *Woman's Journal.*[111] Another clergyman, a Roman Catholic priest in Denver, spoke in favor of the reform immediately before the election, reminding his audience that women had served as deaconesses in the early church and that women were important advisers to ministers.[112] The Rev. Myron Reed, a Congregationalist minister in Denver, spoke in favor of woman suffrage in mid-October. Beginning with a quote from Walt Whitman—"I have claimed nothing to myself which I have not carefully claimed for others on the same terms"—Reed encouraged men to support woman suffrage as an act of unselfishness.[113]

The referendum vote for woman suffrage in Colorado on November 7, 1893, was tallied as 35,798 in favor and 29,551 opposed. The reform passed with a 55 percent majority.[114] Only thirteen out of fifty-six counties opposed the measure. Eight of these counties were in the southern part of the state, and five bordered New Mexico. The opposition vote ranged from a 52 percent rejection in Custer County to 84 percent in Costilla County.

In two of the opposing nonsouthern counties, a breathtaking one vote in Douglas County and two votes in Park caused the loss. In more of these nonsouthern counties, Lincoln and Grand, the total vote was less than 150, suggesting that the reformers may have sidestepped these counties to campaign harder in more populated areas.[115] Although there was a 55 percent majority for the reform statewide, several regions presented much higher support. The nine northwestern and west central mining counties produced majorities ranging from 58 percent to 78 percent in favor of votes for women. The voters in the most northeastern counties also showed heavy support for the reform: in these eight counties, the returns ranged from 53 percent approval in Arapahoe County to 70 percent in Morgan County (see table).

Powerful Populist allies, as well as the successful recruitment strategies of the state WCTU and suffrage leaders, explain the victory better than do demographic changes. According to the U.S. Census of 1890, males constituted 59 percent of the Colorado population; this percentage reveals a substantial increase in the female population since 1880 when males outnumbered females by three to one.[116] Yet in 1890, males still composed between 61 percent and 66 percent of Colorado's voting-age population—those people between twenty and sixty years of age. Faced with such a disproportionately male population, the woman suffrage reformers would have been unable to recruit enough male supporters without the aid of many men in the political parties. Chapman later laughingly commented that the heavy male population made victory possible in Colorado whereas the disproportionately female population in Massachusetts precluded serious consideration of the issue.[117] Colorado men knew that they would not lose control of their state government if they gave women the vote.

After the ratification of woman suffrage, the Colorado Populists accepted credit for winning it and quickly tried to consolidate women's support for their candidates and program. According to the Populists, "thirty Populist counties gave majorities for equal suffrage," with only one opposed. By comparison, only "ten Republican counties provided majori-

Election results, 1893 Colorado woman suffrage referendum
by region, county, and party

Region	County	Party[a]	Pro–woman suffrage vote (%)
Northwest	Eagle	Populist	62
	Garfield	Populist	59
	Rio Blanco	Populist	58
	Routt	Democratic	62
North Central	Boulder	Populist	72
	Clear Creek	Populist	64
	Gilpin	Populist	57
	Grand	Republican	41
	Larimer	Populist	67
	Summit	Populist	58
Northeast	Arapahoe	Republican	53
	Logan	Republican	64
	Morgan	Republican	70
	Phillips	Republican	67
	Sedgwick	Populist	65
	Washington	Republican	63
	Weld	Populist	69
	Yuma	Populist	61
West Central	Delta	Populist	71
	Gunnison	Populist	58
	Mesa	Populist	78
	Montrose	Populist	66
	Pitkin	Populist	62
Central	Chaffee	Populist	62
	Douglas	Republican	50
	El Paso	Republican	60
	Fremont	Populist	56
	Jefferson	Republican	62
	Lake	Republican	48
	Park	Populist	50
East Central	Cheyenne	Republican	68
	Elbert	Democratic	52
	Kiowa	Republican	68
	Kit Carson	Populist	65
	Lincoln	Republican	44

Election results, 1893 Colorado woman suffrage referendum
(*continued*)

Region	County	Party[a]	Pro–woman suffrage vote (%)
Southwest	Archuleta	Republican	45
	Dolores	Populist	66
	Hinsdale	Populist	73
	La Plata	Republican	36
	Mineral	Populist	66
	Montezuma	Populist	71
	Ouray	Populist	59
	San Juan	Populist	60
	San Miguel	Populist	52
South Central	Conejos	Republican	35
	Costilla	Republican	16
	Custer	Republican	48
	Huerfano	Republican	28
	Pueblo	Republican	43
	Rio Grande	Populist	68
	Saguache	Populist	57
Southeast	Baca	Democratic	56
	Bent	Populist	72
	Las Animas	Democratic	26
	Otero	Populist	64
	Prowers	Republican	67

Source: "To the Women of Colorado: The Record of the Parties on the Equal Suffrage Amendment," November 1893. State Archives, Office of the Secretary of State, State of Colorado.
   a. The party that had carried the previous year's elections.

ties for woman suffrage and eleven Republican counties voted against it." The Democrats contributed "two counties with majorities for woman suffrage and two counties opposed."[118]

If the Populist Party accurately analyzed these outcomes, then their support explains the heavy approval of woman suffrage in the northwest and west-central sections of the state. (The table includes the Populists' list of the counties "controlled" by each party.) Even though their analysis holds Republican southern counties responsible for the opposition to the reform, it does not explain why so many northeast and east-central Republican counties approved it. Some credit must also be given to the WCTU, the CESA reformers, and even the state's weakened Republican machine for promoting a measure that the Republican state convention had endorsed.[119]

Although the CESA and the WCTU campaigned separately for woman suffrage, the reformers' retrospective analyses reveal the strong links between the two groups. All those who campaigned for woman suffrage credited the outcome to the Populist Party's support of equal suffrage and to the extensive reform network in Colorado. From Boston, Henry Blackwell attributed victory to votes from the mining towns, to the support of "the plain people," to the Populists, and to the "unselfish energy, eloquence, and organizing ability of Mrs. Carrie Lane Chapman."[120]

Helen Reynolds, the corresponding secretary of the CESA, concurred with Blackwell's citation of Chapman and the Populists, but also observed that the generally positive attitude taken by the newspapers in the state made an "immense" contribution to the cause. Reynolds also credited Louise Tyler with having organized "auxiliary leagues that were responsible for working at the polls on election day," a step that Reynolds assessed as decisive for the victory. She praised the donation of an office by a wealthy Denver woman, Mrs. Elizabeth B. Tabor. Finally, Reynolds revealed that the CESA had sent a circular letter to all of the county conventions requesting that the political parties pass a set of suffrage resolutions. This effort succeeded in its purpose. According to Reynolds, "Out of 180 sets of resolutions, over two-thirds were [e]ndorsed, the convention in most cases putting a woman suffrage plank into its platform."[121]

There were some crucial differences between the failure of 1877 and this success of 1893. In 1877, woman suffrage reformers had tried to "buttonhole" or "jawbone" voters *at* the polls. Two conditions prevented their success: (1) there were separate ballots for supporters and opponents of the reform, and (2) the party leaders distributed the ballots. Local Republican and Democratic party leaders could see (if not control) which ballot a voter took and probably could punish the voter in some small ways afterward.

In 1893, in contrast, Colorado voters used the Australian ballot. The new ballot made it impossible for party leaders or party employees to dictate voter choices. Moreover, to guarantee that supporters would mark their ballots correctly, the CESA printed voting instructions for its workers to pass out at the polls. Reynolds emphasized that this step was necessary because voters otherwise might not bother with the amendments at the bottom of the ballot.[122] Reynolds believed that the distribution of these instructions had increased the votes for woman suffrage: "Wherever this was done, the vote was quite heavy and our majorities larger. In one ward in Denver where we failed to find women workers, we were sharply criticized by both voters and judges of election because there was no one there with the leaflets."[123]

Chapman reinforced Reynolds's claims about the importance of the Australian ballot, instructions at the polls, and small group leadership. In her campaign summary, delivered as an address to sympathetic Bostonians in December 1893, she explained that the suffragists had created cooperative committees of seven men and women (in threes and fours of each sex) in each of the most populated counties. In Chapman's view, the willingness of Colorado women "to have the men take the lead in the campaign" helped assure victory. She also emphasized that an organized interest of antis named "remonstrants" did more harm than good when they circulated tracts that "quoted the pernicious influence of woman suffrage in Wyoming." So many Colorado residents had resided previously in Wyoming that their response to this claim was to state, "Why this is an abominable lie." Chapman credited "the fine condition of organized labor" as well as the Farmers' Alliance and Populists, but downplayed the WCTU's role. In her words, the "brewers and saloon-keepers" constituted the reform's chief opponents even though "there never has been any very extensive temperance movement in Colorado."[124]

The activists made special efforts to reach both the wealthy and the working class. Martha Pease, president of the CESA during the 1893 campaign, described their approach to wealthy voters: "To reach the very elite who would not attend a promiscuous assembly, we held parlor meetings." The CESA, Pease wrote, sent to these meetings "our most eloquent speakers armed with their very sweetest smiles, their most honeyed words and their best clothes."[125]

Emma Ghent Curtis, editor of the Populist newspaper the *Royal Gorge* and delegate to the 1892 Populist Party Convention, sent an article to the *Woman's Journal* that corrected previously published accounts by crediting organized labor's contributions to the victory. Curtis reported that between January and April the Farmers' Alliance and the Knights of Labor pressured for and monitored the measure's legislative passage. During the fall campaign, women union members carried out much of the house-to-house campaigning for suffrage in the mining towns surrounding Canon City.[126] Curtis also noted that previous accounts had overlooked the services of Lenora Barry-Lake, who canvassed for woman suffrage "under the auspices of the Knights of Labor."[127]

Ella Beecher Gittings, corresponding secretary of the Colorado WCTU, took strong exception to Chapman's speech, which had suggested that temperance women had played a minimal role. Gittings reminded readers that the Colorado State Equal Suffrage League (CSESL) had existed for only two years, whereas the WCTU had "been organized more than fourteen years (local unions existed in 1875)." Gittings pointed out that the WCTU's "franchise department" had persistently advocated suffrage: "In the recent campaign the whole energy of the seventy local unions of Colorado was focused upon the equal suffrage movement. Local meetings were held, lecturers kept afield, money was spent for literature, and a weight of personal influence brought to bear which no one can estimate." Gittings took particular exception to Chapman's assumption that the organized opposition of the liquor interests must have been "instinctive" because temperance forces appeared weak. She quipped that if that were so, the WCTU "has indeed been a failure." She listed numerous temperance achievements, including the local option—residential restrictions on the consumption and purchase of alcohol—and Sunday closing laws. Gittings's final remarks admitted how bitter WCTU reformers had felt when their suffragist allies failed to recognize their contributions: "We have no desire to be hypercritical, but we think it scarcely fair that the equal suffrage leagues who, with fresh steeds and burnished trappings, rode gallantly 'in at the death,' should seek to wrest all the honors from the toiling 'beaters of the bush.' But, beyond and above all this, we are unwilling that the blot of 'never any extensive temperance movement' should rest upon Colorado's fair name."[128]

Julia A. Sabine, a former superintendent of the franchise department in Colorado's WCTU, later reinforced Gittings's claims. She explained that when she organized a woman suffrage league in Colorado Springs in 1885, its members were "composed almost wholly of WCTU women" who eventually decided that "work could be better done in connection" with the temperance organization "and the separate organization was dropped." Voting mattered to Colorado temperance women: "The work of electing women to the place of School Directors, and of arousing the women of Colorado to vote at school elections, was begun by the WCTU, and was one of their most treasured projects." She observed that Mary Jewett Telford, editor of the *Challenge,* a Colorado temperance journal, made it, from the first issue, a "suffrage paper." Although she conceded that no one could know "how much of the final triumph is due to this quiet educational work, carried on so long in face of discouragements," she lashed out at Chapman and the editors of the *Woman's Journal* for their "satirical accusation" of "coming forward now with the assurance that we have worked a long time for the cause."[129]

Without WCTU support for the vote in Colorado throughout the 1880s, as well as during the rise of the Populist Party, the CESA would have lacked the strong local organizations necessary to mobilize suffrage support. As chairman of the executive committee of the CESA, former superintendent of the franchise department in the state WCTU, and past president of the state's suffrage association, Louise Tyler was an essential campaign policymaker. Her overlapping affiliations in the CESA and WCTU as well as her leadership experience made Tyler the equivalent of a twentieth-century corporate trustee whose interlocking positions in diverse enterprises facilitate the flow of information and the achievement of shared goals.[130]

Unfortunately, the Colorado WCTU's deliberate suppression of their prohibitionist sentiments during the campaign meant that after victory they could not take easy credit for their contributions. The efforts of Colorado's WCTU remain ambiguous even today. Although temperance clearly did not hurt the cause—voter support for suffrage was above the state average in twenty of the twenty-six counties that had WCTUs in 1893—at least eighteen of twenty-seven counties that lacked WCTU locals also showed above-average support.[131] If Chapman had evaluated only this evidence, it is not surprising that she had not grasped the importance of the WCTU's input. What mattered in Colorado was that the state temperance leaders employed the WCTU as the double agency Willard's ideology had enabled it to be: a means by which women could play traditional roles but act radically to improve their political conditions. Willard's arguments had to have dampened the virulent opposition that had defeated the measure in 1877.

In addition, state leaders exercised more control over the leadership and execution of the 1893 campaign than they had in the 1877 effort. The Colorado leaders achieved legislative passage without any support from the NAWSA, and they sustained their mobilization efforts in the summer of 1893 with no promise of aid from national leaders. Moreover, three different organizations, with female leaders in each, pressed for suffrage from inside the state: the WCTU, the Populists, and the CESA. The commitment of these leaders to winning the vote in turn can be attributed to the momentum that Mary Shields, Albina Washburn, and other suffrage leaders from the 1877 campaign sustained in the sixteen-year interim between these attempts.

Although support from individual Populist legislators and the party as a whole was necessary for the reform to pass, it was the initial victory of the Populist Party that introduced favorable conditions for the passage of woman suffrage. The party's victory disrupted the control that the Republicans had exercised over elections and allowed women to become an unaligned, potential constituency for each of the parties. By the fall of 1893, it was the competition between the three parties that had made organized opposition to the reform risky; suffragists were prepared to take advantage of unstable parties seeking voters.

Finally, the suffragist leaders' adoption of a nonpartisan, single-issue strategy protected them from becoming isolated or labeled as a "special interest." The reformers kept a safe distance from each of the parties, but appealed to the values of each constituency to win support for female enfranchisement.

~·❖·~

The 1892 Populist Party victory in Colorado did for woman suffrage reform what antislavery reform did for woman's rights in the 1830s: it provided a context that prepared and enabled white men to see the political exclusion of women as unjust. Populists in Colorado stressed the injustice of the economic depression that afflicted industries and workers in the state in 1893. They also stressed the unfairness of their own political exclusion by the dominant national parties. The men in the state who had campaigned vigorously for the remonetization of silver but had experienced the rejection of their demand for economic relief also began to see the injustice of women's political exclusion.

Just as Garrison had argued that the principle of equality gave woman the right to participate as speakers in antislavery reform, so did the Colorado Populists claim that the ideals of equality and fairness dictated that women should vote. The Populist victory in Colorado in 1892 led many male voters to rally around a party that was demanding egalitarian political reforms.

The nonpartisan, single-issue strategy that leaders of woman suffrage reform adopted in Colorado prepared them to take advantage of both the Populist victory and this party's egalitarian ideals without making a long-term commitment to the party itself. After the referendum victory, as we have seen, the Populists claimed that their support clinched the victory. They then tried to convert women to their party by reminding them that eastern Republicans had refused to accept votes for women and in most states had vigorously opposed it. If Colorado women wanted to ensure the passage of woman suffrage in other states, the party urged, they should become Populists.[132]

The Colorado women, however, did not answer the Populists' call. In 1894 the Populists were voted out of office, and the Republican Party regained power. According to the suffragists' official history, the state Democratic Party's women's branch constituted a major force for reuniting the disintegrated political organization in 1894.[133]

The relationship between the woman suffrage reformers and the Populist Party in 1893 and 1894 resembles the relationship between woman's rights reformers and the radical Republicans during Reconstruction. In

Colorado the woman suffragists were able to take advantage of the power that the Populists earned in 1892 without repaying them, just as twenty years earlier the radical Republicans had taken advantage of women's efforts in the antislavery movement but did not include votes for women in their package of constitutional amendments. In both these reform efforts, deep bitterness followed the disintegration of the alliances. Just as woman's rights reformers expressed deep anger at the betrayal of their antislavery allies, Colorado Populist Governor Waite expressed profound resentment when the newly enfranchised women in Colorado refused to vote his party back into power in 1894.[134]

Given the adoption and execution of a nonpartisan strategy to win woman suffrage in Colorado, it is perhaps not surprising that women were hesitant to join the Populist Party after the suffrage victory. As we have seen, many Colorado women had already identified with a political party by 1893. These women shared the disillusionment of their fellow men at the corruption and narrowness of the Republican and Democratic parties' national leaders, but by the 1894 election, the Populist Party too had been widely criticized for its halfhearted commitments to fair labor legislation and its failure to achieve goals beyond the electoral reforms that liberal Republicans also supported. Waite was a radical Populist who dropped the crucial silver issue from his platform; as a result, he lost support from those who had bolted from the two major parties and elected him in 1892.[135]

Once enfranchised, Colorado women joined political parties as independent citizens: each chose the party most compatible with her agenda of public priorities. In all the parties, most women accepted the fact that men exercised decision-making power; their new task became coping with "the long series of internal dissensions, of factions within factions and the repeated divisions in every organization bearing a party name."[136] Colorado women, like the already enfranchised men, had to learn to work around internal party disputes to achieve their goals.

After their enfranchisement, women once again formed associations outside the parties and adopted nonpartisan lobbying strategies to fight the corruption that party patronage produced.[137] Their experience of political exclusion taught women to preserve their independent networks for just such emergencies. Both the nonpartisan strategy and the organizations that the women had used to gain political inclusion thus unexpectedly became a crucial ongoing political asset as well as an agency for promoting women voters' issues.

Enfranchised women in Colorado thus sustained their independent, critical perspective on the government. They also helped make citizen interest groups an institution of political accountability that differed from pressure groups seeking to aggrandize or protect their own power. For example, Colorado women organized many of the first "progressive" citizen reform groups in their state during the early twentieth century.[138] Joseph Brown cites the women's formation of the Civic Federation of Denver, led by women from three political parties, as an instance of women's continued use of the nonpartisan reform strategy. And in 1912, Martha Wentworth Suffren quoted Denver progressive reformer Judge Ben Lindsey's assertion that "the entire Citizens' ticket [was] won by [a] ten thousand majority over the bi-partisan machine candidates, and the result is due largely to the fact that women vote in Denver. I do not believe such a victory would have been possible had it not been for this fact."[139]

Organized women voters of Colorado also contributed heavily to state legislative achievements. Colorado Representative Edward Taylor, speaking in the House of Representatives on April 24, 1912, testified that Rocky Mountain women had achieved much political reform. In his words, "It would require fully one-third of the last 10 volumes of our Colorado session laws to fully describe the laws that have been enacted as a direct result of the influence and energy of the women in the State." Taylor particularly noted the effectiveness of the Colorado Federation of Women's Clubs and the Women's Clubs of Denver in gaining educational, health, and related welfare legislation.[140]

The national reform leaders' knowledge of the high thresholds set by most states' electoral laws and understanding of the deeper resistance that public opinion elsewhere posed to winning women the vote prevented them from making the Colorado campaign a blueprint for future efforts. Still, the Colorado victory provided a powerful symbol of hope for reformers. Progressive Coloradans such as Judge Ben Lindsey regularly praised Colorado women for their dedication to social policy reform.[141] Articles and letters from Colorado suffragists appeared regularly in the *Woman's Journal* both as appeals and, more importantly, as examples of how women were voting.[142] In her 1909 book *Equal Suffrage*, Helen Sumner devoted a section to the Colorado campaign and the consequences of the reform. She reported that in 1906, when women made up 47.4 percent of the population, they constituted 41.5 percent of the registered voters and 37.3 percent of voters overall.[143] Sumner observed that because machine rule in Colorado exemplified "a typical corporation, machine-politician-ruled state, with the addition, perhaps of a degree of wild Western recklessness and contempt for law," its "experiment in equal suffrage, . . . except for the sparse population of the state, is a fair trial under nearly normal conditions in an approximately representative community."[144]

The 1893 woman suffrage victory in Colorado did not stimulate immediate gains in other states or from the national government. The Kansas campaign of 1894 failed. Anthony and Blackwell attributed the defeat to the overly partisan alliances of state suffrage leaders—Kansas women had municipal suffrage—and the unexpected opposition of the Republican party.[145] Official suffrage historians reported that the Kansas Democrats had claimed: "We oppose woman suffrage as tending to destroy the home and family, the true basis of political safety."[146] Moreover, Kansas already had a state constitutional amendment for Prohibition; thus, the WCTU could not have executed a quiet campaign in that state.

The belief that the political inclusion of women threatened the family thus continued to pose a formidable obstacle even after the Colorado victory. The victory did, however, set an important precedent for future change. The nonpartisanship and cooperation between the suffragists and temperance reformers showed how this issue could be moved onto the agenda and the vote could be won.

During the second decade of the twentieth century, more opportunities arose for winning women the vote, and the suffragists made much use of nonpartisanship. In the meantime, a national electoral realignment was under way that introduced persistent divisions along regional and party lines. This electoral realignment enabled the Southern Democrats to create a one-party system that became a mainstay of white supremacy. Moreover, the return of stable two-party (as opposed to three-party) competition throughout the nation dried up favorable opportunities for woman suffrage reform. As a result, national suffrage leaders decided to rely more heavily upon nativism and racism between 1896 and 1906.

6

Airs of Respectability: Racism and Nativism in the Woman Suffrage Movement

*B*ETWEEN 1885 and 1900 the American woman suffrage movement changed from the radical cause of former Garrisonians into a quest for citizenship by diverse groups of women. Although elite white leaders succumbed to racist and nativist sentiments, such sentiments never fully eclipsed their egalitarian aims. Muted egalitarian themes emerged because (1) suffragists were ambivalent about their racism and nativism, (2) feminisms of personal development cropped up that encouraged white elites to exploit their privileged education and wealth but also stimulated positive self-conceptions among oppressed black and working-class women, (3) victims of the reformers' racism and nativism informed elite leaders that such views were hypocritical and unjust, and (4) those who opposed votes for women continued to portray the measure as radically egalitarian.

In the United States during the late nineteenth century, "intellectually respectable" social Darwinism and racialist theories overshadowed egalitarianism. As many scholars have observed, these inegalitarian theories oriented suffragists toward portraying their cause as traditional.[1] The quiet alliances fashioned by Anthony, Stone, and Blackwell with Willard and the WCTU; the merger of the radical NWSA with the conservative AWSA; the adoption of nonpartisanship; the treatment of votes for women as a single issue; the assertion that women's moral superiority entitled them to the vote; and numerous appeals to nativist and racist sentiments obscured the egalitarian nature and potential of woman suffrage.[2] At the same time, radical themes in Willard's feminism of fear suggest that by 1890 a number of "respectable" women had decided to buck tradition. Egalitarian-minded suffragists faced a dilemma: how, if at all, should white women—many of whom were southern, from Christian evangelical denominations, and ambivalent about equality—be incorporated as suffragists?

The turn toward toleration and away from a primary allegiance to equality for women was a change that Anthony struggled for, even against Stanton. In the mid-1880s, Stanton urged Anthony to avoid making the movement more respectable lest it disintegrate the movement's commitment to overthrow male domination in the home, church, workplace, and government.[3] Anthony disagreed, arguing that the traditional women Willard mobilized should be welcomed and would help in the pursuit of a federal constitutional amendment.

To address Stanton's worries about losing commitment to equality, Anthony urged that the movement become open to all potential members. Anthony correctly anticipated that refusing to accept members who were southern, Christian, temperance reformers, Catholic, atheist, or agnostic would have been foolhardy. Stanton eventually conceded, but without entirely relinquishing her egalitarianism.[4] Putting toleration first encouraged "respectable" prosuffrage women from the WCTU or women's clubs to join. Courting these "respectable" members led suffragists to use nativist and racist themes that denounced the easy political inclusion of new male immigrants, supported educational qualifications for the vote, and defended southern white supremacy. In short, the decision to welcome respectable white women was accompanied by disdain for growing numbers of black and working-class suffragists.

The new generation of leaders also fostered the "feminism of personal development" that had emerged during Reconstruction. Young leaders defined the vote less as a symbol of political equality and more as a political benefit for each woman to exercise as she pleased. Judith Shklar accurately depicts this major change:

> Social Darwinism, health and hygiene-oriented reform, and the Social Gospel were notably undemocratic paths to progress, and the women's movement became a part of this intellectual mainstream. Liberalism had also altered, moving from civic freedom to a concern for self-development and the nurture of the individual personality. For women interested in the suffrage, voting increasingly was just one step toward the fulfillment of these immensely personal ends.[5]

Although some scholars might dispute Shklar's depiction of "health and hygiene-oriented reform, and the Social Gospel" as "notably *undemocratic* paths to progress," her portrayal of the aims of late-nineteenth and early twentieth century suffragists as highly personalized captures their distinctive emphases. As progressive reformers, the mostly native-born Protestants decided that their Anglo-Saxon ancestry and education provided the best qualifications for political inclusion. Following the lead of powerful men, they became less tolerant of the lack of preparedness for political participation by immigrants and newly freed blacks.

Despite cold responses from white leaders, currents of support for suffrage strengthened among black and working women who cultivated egalitarian principles and kept sight of possibilities for radical change. As second-generation white reform leaders showed "respect" for personal choice and varied aims by their nativistic appeals and willingness to include southern white supremacist suffragists in their organization, black women pointed out the contradictions in such policies and called for a more integrated movement. Black female reformers such as Ida B. Wells, Anna Julia Cooper, and Mary Church Terrell kept egalitarian principles alive in their speeches by occasionally embarrassing white leaders with requests for inclusion and by defying their efforts to segregate members.[6] Black suffragists refused to bow to white supremacist attitudes; instead, they envisioned how they would use the vote to foster personal development for blacks. The strides black women made while white women united across region and class were truly exceptional acts of courage.[7]

From the late 1880s until the ratification of the Nineteenth Amendment, suffragists made many racist and nativist arguments for the vote. Adopting Henry Blackwell's "statistical argument," they promised that women's votes would reduce the influence of the black male voters in the South. In an 1867 letter entitled "What the South Can Do," Blackwell proposed that the southern legislatures make reunification possible by accepting the Reconstruction amendments on their face, but then moving immediately to enfranchise women in order to ensure white supremacy. In the early 1890s, native-born white male legislators in Arkansas and Mississippi introduced the idea that the votes of educated, property-holding women could buttress the exclusive system of white supremacy.[8] Although the legislatures in these states rejected votes for women, suffragists often invoked white supremacy and Blackwell's strategy to recruit support in the South. The leading southern white suffragists "believed that in their time white political supremacy was a necessity."[9]

While campaigning in the Midwest and Plains states, Carrie Chapman Catt established common ground with her audiences through nativist remarks about Native American Indians and immigrants. Elizabeth Cady Stanton metamorphosed from the most consistent and daring of liberal thinkers into an outraged Americanist decrying the rights of men she considered less educated, less prepared to think through political problems, and less qualified to assure responsible government than she.[10] In 1909 the WCTU "passed a resolution that the right to vote should be based upon intelligence, not upon sex."[11] Eschewing equality as moral reason for enfranchisement, they concentrated instead on promoting their own reference group's standards as evidence both for their inclusion and for the establishment of these standards for all Americans.

Henry Brown Blackwell's Statistical Argument

Woman suffragists assumed that blacks and most new immigrants were inferior. They also aimed to secure the domination of native-born, white, Protestant ideas and habits in American culture. It would be wrong, however, to consider the reformers' racism and nativism as thematically unambiguous. Their speeches and open letters display both strong convictions and an uncomfortable ambivalence about what they were saying. Instead of bald racism and nativism, these tracts usually show a complex set of conflicting ideas and dispositions, especially over the meaning of racial and ethnic inferiority. As they appealed to racist and nativist views, suffragists often added that not all blacks and immigrants were either inherently inferior or likely to remain unqualified if the state supplied them with adequate education.

In "What the South Can Do," Blackwell used rhetoric to distance his own more egalitarian views from those he proposed. In his letter, Blackwell assessed the "southern problem" *as if* he were making decisions as a southern legislator: "Consider the result from the Southern standpoint. *Your* 4,000,000 of Southern white women will counter balance *your* 4,000,000 of Negro men and women, thus the political supremacy of *your* white race will remain unchanged."[12]

Blackwell's separation of his views from his conception of how southern legislators would think suggests that he may have concocted this argument as much to put woman suffrage on the political agenda as to promote black disenfranchisement. As Marjorie Spruill Wheeler points out, Blackwell did not think about the distribution of the black population in the South. He overlooked the fact that in the black belts there were more blacks than whites; this strategy would never have made black men a minority in these districts.[13]

That Blackwell, a participant in Garrisonian abolitionism, could have written this letter reveals how desires for rapid reunification fed a growing racism. Early in the letter, Blackwell warned white southerners that the "problem of the negro" caused the anguish of war, and he encouraged them to see that they could no longer fight the North: "Wise men try to see things as they are, uncolored by opinion or preference. The interest of both North and South, since they must live together, is peace, harmony, and real fraternity. No adjustment can fully succeed unless it is acceptable to both sections. Therefore the statesman and patriot must find a common ground as a basis of permanent reconciliation."[14] His invocation of "peace, harmony, and real fraternity" suggests that Blackwell so wanted to promote nonviolent reconstruction that he adopted a racist argument. At the time, the southern white founders of the Ku Klux Klan and Knights of the White Camellia had initiated the terror against the freedmen that played a central role in the creation of southern white supremacy.[15]

Blackwell thought he had discovered a way to persuade the southern legislatures to accept the principle of political inclusion for both newly free African Americans and women. If southerners perceived the Reconstruction amendments as principles only—principles that actual patterns of political participation would prevent from leading to the political domination of blacks over whites—then they would be willing to abolish the legalized exclusion of ascriptive groups. He thus painted a vision that would insulate white control: "If you are to share the future government of your States with a race you deem naturally and hopelessly inferior, avert the social chaos, which seems to you so imminent, by utilizing the intelligence and patriotism of the wives and daughters of the South." He even encouraged the South to lead on the question of inclusion so that "the negro question would be forever removed from the political arena." According to Blackwell, full political inclusion would restore the agenda to issues of interest to all citizens; sectional conflict would diminish; and the civic bonds of the nation would be restored. "Capital and population would flow, like the Mississippi, toward the Gulf. The black race would gravitate by the law of nature toward the tropics."[16]

Blackwell's strategy backfired: southern legislatures designed elaborate means to disenfranchise all black and many poor white men. But by the mid-1880s he had hardly modified his appeal in urging southern suffragists to seek the vote for educated women. His rationale, however misguided, appealed to them, perhaps because elite southern women tended to oppose outright political exclusion and extreme violence against blacks, such as lynching.[17] In any case, by the early 1890s white southern woman suffragists were exploring whether white supremacy would be gender inclusive.

After the emergence of, first, a southern suffrage movement whose leaders advocated the enfranchisement of only white women, and second, criticism of "lily-white" suffragists by black intellectuals, Blackwell clarified his principles. Although he admitted supporting an educational suffrage, he emphatically opposed restrictions based on ascriptive characteristics. In December 1904, Blackwell applauded the news that the New Orleans *Times-Democrat* would endorse the proposal to extend "the right to vote in municipal elections to unmarried property-owning women." But he refused to support restrictions that would exclude voters on the basis of race or sex: "One thing is certain—insurmountable qualifications of property, nativity, celibacy, race, sex, or religious opinions are wrong in principle and unjust in practice." Blackwell appealed instead for strong educational qualifications: "The mere ability to read and write seems insufficient. We have that qualification here in Boston now, yet two-thirds of our legal voters are poll-tax defaulters, and two convicts actually serving their time in prison have just been elected as Alderman and Representative."[18]

By supporting educational qualifications for suffrage, elite white leaders such as Blackwell, Stanton, and Carrie Chapman Catt pursued political inequality and equality simultaneously. Literacy tests and other "merit" examinations masked the reconstitution of repressive white domination. But like John Stuart Mill and other suffrage reformers in England, these elites desired measures that would nurture an intelligent, informed, and independently minded electorate.[19] Beginning with educational qualifications, many white reform leaders invoked the relatively egalitarian principle that all educated citizens could eventually become voters regardless of their race, ethnicity, or gender, although they preferred government controlled by educated, native-born white Protestants. Ideas such as Blackwell's "Southern strategy" reduced egalitarian principles to rights of simple inclusion—rights that conveyed no power.

Carrie Chapman Catt

After the turn of the century, Catt became the most ubiquitous and shrewd entrepreneurial leader of the woman suffrage movement. Catt joined the Iowa WCTU during the late 1880s and edited "the temperance column in the *Charles City Intelligencer*."[20] Although she admired Willard as a leader, by 1890 Catt had left the WCTU because she insisted suffrage be separated from prohibition. Participating in the 1893 Colorado suffrage victory made her the national leader most experienced in carrying out a successful state campaign. NAWSA adopted her suggestions for organizational innovations in the mid-1890s, selected her as its president from 1900 to 1904, and chose her again in 1915. In addition to representing NAWSA in the Colorado victory, Catt helped to establish the International Woman Suffrage Alliance in 1902; this international experience prepared her for interactions with many different people and organizations.[21] She is best known for a "winning plan" that secured the passage and ratification of the federal amendment between 1915 and 1920.[22]

Long celebrated for her organizational genius, Catt also contributed an ideology for mobilizing traditional women that began as nativist feminism but evolved into a more tolerant feminism of personal development. Originally, she isolated educated, middle-class, native-born white women and addressed them as an independent, ill-treated, but qualified constituency of potential citizens. To deny the vote to intelligent, loyal American women, she argued, was an insult.[23]

Discouraged by an 1892 congressional committee's inattention to this "natural rights" argument, Catt decided to design appeals that powerful men would take seriously.[24] Arguments that relied on the grand ideals of equality and justice, she decided, only allowed other issues to take precedence in the minds of male voters. Similarly, during the 1890 South Dakota referendum she had spied local party machine leaders paying voters to defeat woman suffrage. Jacqueline Van Voris argues that after such incidents Catt "always kept her broad vision of equal rights" but focused on building a stronger national organization and winning increased attention for the cause. Her strategic motto became: "In matters of principle go against the current, but in matters of custom go with it."[25]

Catt's motto manifests the turn toward pragmatic tactics that distinguishes second-generation woman suffragists. She decided that mobilizing only wealthy elite women could put the suffrage effort on a more solid footing. To this end, Catt marshaled her argument for female moral superiority and Americanist race superiority.

In two early unpublished speeches, "Subject and Sovereign" and "The American Sovereign," Catt portrays as a major injustice extending political rights to Negroes, Native American Indians, and new immigrants while denying these rights to native-born white women. In "Subject and Sovereign," Catt argued that by offering the vote (as well as "government blankets" and other goods) to Sioux Indians west of the Missouri River in the Dakotas, the national government created "new sovereigns" and left disfranchised American women as "subjects." To intensify feelings of unfairness in her audience, Catt presented a litany of cruelties including tortures and brutal murders that she alleged the Sioux perpetrated against Americans. She also asserted that whereas women had demanded the vote, the Indians had neither asked for nor wanted it. "Gentlemen, I ask you," she declared dramatically, "where is there a principle of government, of economics, of common sense or justice which should have established that inconsistency?"[26]

In "The American Sovereign," Catt forged a similar nativistic argument about both ethnic-led urban political machines and new immigrants from southern and eastern Europe. Making majority rule sovereign, she posited, was the "underlying principle of the far-famed American liberties . . . Take away that sovereign and what kind of government do we possess? Only usurpations of power, despotism, or anarchy." Americans' liberties were endangered, Catt said, because "the political boss has donned the imperial robe." Also threatening liberty were the new immigrant groups that bolstered the party machines and their bosses: "Today there has arisen in America a class of men not intelligent, not patriotic, not moral, nor yet not pedigreed. In caucuses and conventions, it is they who nominate officials, at the polls through corrupt means, it is they who elect them and by bribery, it is they who secure the passage of many a legislative measure."

Catt especially discredited newly arriving immigrants from southern and eastern Europe as less wealthy, less intelligent, and less resourceful than those born in central and northern Europe. There are, she observed, "fewer Germans and Englishmen and more Hungarians and Italians. Fewer Swedes and Danes and more Russian and Polish Jews." She barely qualified her nativist sentiments on this score: these were "men and women whom America gladly welcomes. She still has need of every honest brain and honest muscle; but the fact remains that every year we are receiving fewer good people and more of the slum element." Catt also suggested that rule by party machines exacerbated associated problems: "Does ignorance and poverty cause political corruption, or does political dishonesty cause poverty and crime?"

Women's enfranchisement, Catt argued, would "purify politics" and enable the "perpetuation of the American republic." She unequivocally supported imposing native-born American standards for evaluating personal behavior in school, the workplace, and social life, and Catt depicted American women as the potential voters who could achieve this end. "It is plain," she asserted, "that the ballot in the hands of women means an element a much greater proportion of which has been born upon our soil, educated in our public schools, familiar with our institutions."

Finally, Catt insisted that the new immigrants were the "gravest problem ever presented to the American people." She predicted, as Blackwell had, that adding the votes of loyal native-born American women could outnumber the votes of these immigrants. The "census of 1890 proves that women hold the solution in their hands . . . Expediency demands it as the policy which alone can lift our nation from disgrace. I do not ask the ballot for women as a privilege, nor a favor. I ask it as the highest duty which citizens owe to the nation whose best interests they are pledged to defend."[27] Although we have no evidence on this subject, Catt may have used these very speeches in the victorious Colorado campaign of 1893.

In her two early speeches, Catt was thoroughly nativistic. But she also wrote two Fourth of July speeches, one as early as 1889, that celebrated freedom for all in the inclusive language of an assimilationist. Here Catt stated, "We have met to-day in commemoration of that victory [of the forefathers]. We have come not as Catholics or Protestants, not as Jews or Gentiles, not as Democrats or Republicans, not as friends or enemies, but simply and solely as American citizens, rejoicing that the victories of Bunker Hill, Valley Forge, and Provincetown rendered it possible for us to enjoy the protection of so liberal a government and the possession of such beneficent institutions."[28]

Although Blackwell and Catt were willing to exploit nativistic and racist sentiments, they avoided endorsing these ideas as principles. Most white southern suffragists concurred with this judgment.

Woman Suffrage and White Supremacy in the South, 1890–1904

As Anthony became firmly committed to winning the vote by federal amendment, she must have realized that it would require two-thirds support in both the House and the Senate. Because woman's vote needed ratification by three-quarters of the states, or thirty-six of forty-eight, national woman suffrage leaders could not avoid organizing southern campaigns.[29] As members of the WCTU, many southern women had already converted to suffrage. By 1890, wealthy, educated, and prominent women such as Laura Clay of Kentucky, Caroline Merrick of New Orleans, and Belle Kearney of Mississippi had persuasively appealed for national attention and support of their interest in woman suffrage.[30]

As Wheeler explains, southern white women of the planter classes who wanted the vote initially thought that white supremacy—and after 1896, the one-party system—offered them better opportunities for political inclusion than had the two-party system imposed during Reconstruction. This assessment may have been partly correct. According to historian William A. Link, poor and illiterate white and black men in the South particularly opposed woman suffrage.[31] Their disenfranchisement probably signaled to politically interested elite white women, most of whom lived in cities, that a strong source of opposition had been removed.[32] Unable to see the formidable opposition that men of their class (as well as many women) would present to their demands, these women organized suffrage campaigns throughout the South.

White southern suffragists' campaigns emerged just as educated African Americans were forming lasting national organizations and articulating a vision of civil rights reform. To avoid overt clashes between the two groups, NAWSA leaders refused to admit that they excluded African-American women from membership in NAWSA. Although national leaders stopped short of approving campaigns that would enfranchise only white women, they never seriously considered subverting the informal rules that sustained segregated cultures. Infrequently, white leaders developed cordial friendships with prominent black women, which facilitated communication across racial divides.[33] But these personal relationships paled against the NAWSA's official approval of white southerners' preference for winning the vote as a states' rights issue. Both Shaw and Catt made every effort to prevent black woman suffragists from attending national conventions or joining white reformers as equals in major public events. African-American suffragists were even asked to march separately as "the colored delegation" in the 1913 parade that greeted Woodrow Wilson.

Although some white leaders protested the appropriateness of white supremacy, all agreed at the outset that southern white women would strengthen and reinforce the white supremacist system "without taking the vote away from those already enfranchised."[34] In 1891, the year NAWSA decided to "do suffrage work in the South,"[35] the Populist movement still had momentum, and white supremacy lacked formal legal supports. Stanton-minded egalitarians could easily have seen a southern woman suffrage movement as a militating force against the most violent defenders of "the lost cause." In her 1891 NAWSA convention speech, "The Degradation of Disfranchisement," Stanton invoked skeletal memories of the struggle for equal rights: "We can not make men see that women feel the humiliation of their petty distinctions of sex precisely as the black man feels those of color. It is no palliation of our wrongs to say that we are not socially ostracized as he is, so long as we are politically ostracized as he is not. That all orders of foreigners also rank politically above the most intelligent, highly-educated women—native-born American—is indeed the most bitter drop in the cup of our grief."[36]

Reconciled to incorporating traditional women, Stanton asserted, "Let us henceforth meet conservatives on their own ground and admit that suffrage for woman does mean political, religious, industrial and social freedom—a new and a higher civilization."[37] White national leaders applauded the formation of southern woman suffrage associations as well as the headway that states such as Louisiana made in winning women taxpayers the right to vote on tax matters. By 1894 northern suffragists felt the southern women's efforts had created some of the best opportunities for winning state campaigns; their 1895 convention was set for Atlanta.

Southern woman suffragists justified their political inclusion with reasons that were little different from those of reformers in other regions. In January and February 1895, just before the Atlanta convention, the *Woman's Journal* published a two-week column entitled "Why Southern Women Desire the Ballot" that included answers from forty-two southern women. The reasons published ranged from principles of equal rights and natural rights to means of protecting and improving oneself, overcoming dominance by foreigners, winning child custody, raising the age of consent, and establishing cooperation between the sexes. Only one writer admitted support for white supremacy, which she equated with "intelligent supremacy." Another called for "a 16th Amendment which will set the female slaves free and give them the ballot to protect themselves, as it has protected the male slaves in their pursuit of life, liberty, and happiness."[38] Written just before the political realignment of 1896 and the subsequent legalization of white supremacy, these letters confirm that southern white women cared most about winning political rights for themselves. In fact, these women's distrust of white men's monopoly of power strongly suggests that southern white men would have perceived such criticisms as radical and threatening. In this context, the advent of legalized white supremacy during the years immediately after the open mobilization for female enfranchisement—the "reactionary revolution"—appears as a backlash against ideas such as woman suffrage as well as against improvements for black middle-class and skilled laborers.[39]

In their own states, white southern suffragists were usually thought of as a respectable group making radical demands. They also brought traditionalism into NAWSA, which was mostly welcomed. Before their 1895 convention in Atlanta, Susan B. Anthony and Carrie Chapman Catt campaigned for six weeks throughout the South, displaying their support for a well-developed regional movement led by white women. At the Atlanta convention, NAWSA created an organizational committee chaired by Catt to formulate a national reform strategy. Drawing on her experience in the 1893 Colorado campaign and victory, Catt argued that

> the suffrage association had been agitating for forty years but had failed to organize the sentiment it created. Three things should be provided at once: correlation of national, state and local branches; a program of concrete aims; a finance committee that would finance. The plan called for a standing committee on organization, to map out the national work and put organizers in the field. The organizers were to travel in pairs, a speaker and a business manager, to raise money . . . for the account of the Organization Committee. It recommended four regional conferences of states, North, South, East and

West, midway between national conventions . . . Investigation of laws affecting women and children was recommended with support of improved legislation.[40]

National political parties continued to rely on decentralized power structures—coalitions of city, county, and state bosses united by their vote-getting and job-distributing machines. Woman suffragists could not hope to win without a plan that put similar sustained pressure on local officials throughout the nation.[41] Catt's singular focus on organization also deflected conflicts among suffragists over ideology, party identification, racism, nativism, and appropriate priorities for women.

In 1895, NAWSA's organization committee, on which Catt served with southerner Laura Clay and Populist Annie L. Diggs, also drafted a carefully guarded "plan of work." The committee recommended that demands for state constitutional amendments be avoided until after party endorsements were obtained, that local unions lead in campaigning for school and municipal suffrage, and that NAWSA mobilize nationally but invest extra resources in the West and South where there were few suffragists. Their emphasis on building strong local organizations, making incremental gains, and obtaining party endorsements helped leaders establish the grassroots base for a federal amendment campaign as well as for state efforts.

Amending state constitutions required overcoming different ratification procedures in each state. For example, in Massachusetts, a state constitutional amendment needed two-thirds of the vote of two successive legislatures plus approval by a voter referendum. As Sharon Hartman Strom contends, such rules gave suffragists little hope that the state-by-state path alone would win women the vote.[42] Accordingly, once they had enough state victories and had established enough organizations in every state to garner a base of support in Congress, the reformers shifted their attention to winning a Constitutional amendment. In 1895 no one knew which states would pass the measure or where suffrage organizations would grow. Led by "respectable women" who would gain a hearing for their views no matter how radical, southern women appeared as likely as most others to win favor for the reform. And mobilization of a southern base could help dampen opposition to a federal amendment.[43]

Initiating campaigns for woman suffrage in the South was tactically both daring and damaging. It took courage to challenge the authority of men responsible for terror and laws such as Jim Crow, poll taxes, and literacy tests.[44] Southern chivalry protected respectable white women from retribution by physical violence, but not from threats by innuendo or ridicule. White suffragists presented white southern Democratic men with an unanticipated but serious challenge from within. To counter this threat, elected male officials in the South accused the suffragists of "unfeminine behavior." Although reformers quickly responded that such accusations were "unchivalrous," they found themselves repeatedly treated as radical privileged white women who did not appreciate the protections of men. The suffragists won less popular support in the South than in any other part of the nation. Indeed, most southern WCTU locals initially evaded pressures to endorse votes for women, and many southern women opposed the measure.[45] Southern suffragists' toleration of white supremacy gave NAWSA conservative members, but in their home states these women were perceived as threatening the southern way of life.

During slavery most native-born, white southern women had religiously dedicated themselves to developing strong families and maintaining stable ties between masters and slaves. These women, whose diaries often reveal profound piety and self-effacement, were less preoccupied than their male relatives with subordinating free blacks.[46]

According to historian Anne Firor Scott, by 1870 a few white southern women had asserted their support for woman suffrage and even joined one of the national suffrage associations. During the 1880s, southern white women's participation in both social justice issues and the suffrage cause escalated after Frances Willard's WCTU recruitment efforts.[47] The white southern women who endorsed suffrage at any time between 1870 and the ratification of the federal amendment in 1920, however, were considered by most white southerners as supporters of a "radical cause."[48]

As they began their reform efforts in the 1890s, most of these suffragists accepted white supremacy as part of what had nationally become segregated cultures. But southern white supremacy was multifaceted, not monolithic. The southern suffragists whom Wheeler studied range from the "Negrophobic" Gordon sisters in Louisiana to Mary Johnston of Virginia, whose private communications reveal her opposition to white supremacy and hopes for social democracy in the United States. Southern suffragists opposed using violence to enforce white domination and aligned themselves with male southern progressives who committed themselves to rule by law. In the 1890s, southern white woman suffragists argued that women's moral influence would ensure that law and persuasion, rather than terror and violence, would be used to shore up white supremacy.[49] Most also subscribed to the idea that education and fair treatment would "elevate" African Americans and prepare them for full citizenship.

Seen retrospectively, the rejection by both the South and the North of even minimal Reconstruction policies set back the liberal agenda for the whole nation. The white, male, Democratic political monopoly defensively established a southern bulwark under the ideal of states' rights against Republican and other northern influences. This process accentuated the North's urban ethnic balkanization and made segregation by race more pronounced. By turning in on itself, the South repudiated equal rights aims, consistent penal laws, social welfare benefits, and the like.[50] Northerners did little to oppose this development.

Northern and southern progressive thinkers supported both rigorous meritocratic standards for governance and increased spending for education. They believed these policies would encourage each person to develop and contribute to society his or her unique skills and talents. These concerns came together when, in the mid-1880s, Carrie Chapman joined Henry B. Blackwell in promoting both educational qualifications for suffrage and female enfranchisement. By arguing that southern blacks and new immigrants needed education before voting, nativist and racist arguments became respectable.

Still, the reactionary turn of the South slowed the suffragists' progress. Undeniably, the deaths of Susan B. Anthony, Elizabeth Cady Stanton, and Henry B. Blackwell forced a new generation of leaders to make independent decisions and strategies. But the northern national leaders were educated, professional women who were able to make their own way. Their crisis was small and surmountable, whereas the South's stubborn assertion of regional political autonomy, its new one-party system, and its unflinching dedication to white supremacy posed resilient barriers to reformers' inclusive aims.

Despite the national suffragists' endorsements of segregation, they did not completely blind themselves to ethical problems posed by collaboration with white supremacists. The minutes of NAWSA's 1903 Annual Convention in New Orleans display definite ambivalence from northern leaders about the views of the southern reformers. At this convention, President Anna Howard Shaw placed a "question box" on the convention floor for anonymous queries that she would answer extemporaneously. According to the published minutes of the meeting, the "color question" kept coming up. "Finally Dr. Shaw said: 'Here is a query that has been dropped in the box again and again and now I am asked if I am afraid to answer it: "Will not woman suffrage make the black woman the political equal of the white woman and does not political equality mean social equality?"'" Shaw answered, "'If it does, then the men by keeping both white and black women dis[en]franchised have already established social equality!' The question was not asked again."[51]

At this convention, Mississippian Belle Kearney drew on the Americanist tradition to make vigorous racist assertions about the implications of female enfranchisement in the South:

> The civilization of the North is threatened by the influx of foreigners . . . ; by the greed of monopolistic wealth . . . ; by the strength of the liquor traffic and encroachments upon religious belief. Some day the North will be compelled to look to the South for redemption from those evils on account of the purity of its Anglo-Saxon blood . . . Just as surely as the North will be forced to turn to the South for the nation's salvation, just so surely will the South be compelled to look to its Anglo-Saxon women as the medium through which to retain the supremacy of the white race over the African.

To Kearney's claims of regional purity and racial supremacy, Catt responded with guarded but distinct criticism. She asserted that recognizing states' rights meant that "Louisiana has the right to regulate the membership of its own association, but it has not the right to regulate that of Massachusetts or vice versa." As for platitudes about "Anglo-Saxon" blood, Catt reminded her audience that at one time "the ancestors of the Anglo-Saxons were regarded as so low and embruted that the Romans refused to have them for slaves. The Anglo-Saxon is the dominant race today but things may change. The race that will be dominant through the ages will be the one that proves itself the most worthy." Catt also pleaded for mutual respect instead of competitive regional defensiveness: "Let us try to get nearer together and to understand each other's ideas on the race question and solve it together."[52] These words suggest that Catt considered collaboration with the southern campaigns to be a step toward national reconciliation and perhaps an opportunity to encourage racial toleration in the South.

Catt's objections to the celebration of Anglo-Saxon blood strikingly contradict her previous use of such symbols in her nativist appeals. Whether she objected to Kearney's assertion of southern cultural superiority or had decided that such bald nativistic and racist appeals were not what this audience wanted to hear, Catt's response to Kearney reveals some ambivalence about ethnocentric, racist appeals and the southern strategy.

African-American suffragists often dissented from NAWSA's racism and segregationist policies. They remembered that Sojourner Truth, Mary Ann Cary, and Frances Ellen Harper had considered themselves full partners with the movement's founders. But given the far greater power of the white women, these protests had to be extremely subtle. At the 1903 convention, for example, Susan B. Anthony, Alice Stone Blackwell, and Elizabeth Miller accompanied author "Dorothy Dix" (Mrs. Elizabeth M. Gilmer)[53] to a meeting of the Phyllis Wheatley Club. This African-American women's literary club also "maintained a training school for nurses, a kindergarten and a night school." The convention minutes reveal that the club honored Anthony with a bouquet of flowers and the following tribute: "When women like you, Miss Anthony, come to see us and speak to us it helps us to believe in the Fatherhood of God and the Brotherhood of Man, and at least for the time being in the sympathy of woman."[54] The phrase "for the time being" may not have been lost on their white visitors.

The failure of even one southern woman suffragist campaign to progress very far in a southern legislature between 1896 and 1906 taught all these reformers that respectability alone would not win women political rights in an undemocratic, racist system. Nevertheless, the southern suffragists' support of white supremacy did not stop them from radically criticizing male rule in the North: they insisted that men did not adequately protect women, that men's exclusive rule threatened civilization's future, and that social policy reforms such as prohibition could control men's licentious behavior.[55]

Southern woman suffragists proved that some southern whites had concerns other than white supremacy. Wheeler presents evidence supporting Scott's insistence that southern suffragists always were more interested in what women would do with the vote than in the political standing of blacks.[56] In the 1890s they "sought basic legal rights: the right of married women to own and dispose of property; to conduct business transactions with all the privileges of single women; and to claim their own wages." In 1895 Tennessee suffragists asserted "that married women wanted to own their own clothes and their own earnings and to have equal partnership in their children. Virginia suffragists also worked for a mother's rights bill, permission for women to serve on school boards, and the admission of women to the state bar." Throughout the South, suffragists aimed to win women admission to the best colleges and universities, which were reserved for men.[57]

Elected officials and antisuffragist southern women opposed reformers' claims with all the arguments made in the North—voting will make women unfeminine, divorces will proliferate, Scripture prohibits it, men provide adequate protection for women, and not enough women demand the vote. They added, however, the unique southern argument: female enfranchisement will make it hard to bar free black women from the polls.[58] Southern woman suffragists' support of white supremacy did not matter; opponents perceived the measure as a threat to white domination largely because they thought that they would face more difficulties preventing black women from voting than black men.

The fear that free black women could not be prevented from voting as easily as black men reveals that political white supremacy in the South went beyond matters of race. As Jacquelyn Dowd Hall observes in her dissection of lynching as a policy of social domination, the system made white men far more powerful than all other groups, especially in the practice of sexual freedom. The threat of violent retribution to black men for stepping out of line warned white women to avoid interracial sexual relationships while white men preserved their sexual access to black women.[59]

Southern antisuffrage arguments reveal a mixture of ridicule and discomfort at the implications woman suffrage would have for white supremacy. In her study of antisuffragists in North Carolina, Elna Green points to state senator Willie M. Person's sardonic protest that woman suffrage "would enable every colored woman in the State, who could read and write, to vote. Why my cook would vote, while my wife would not." But Governor Thomas W. Bickett, in 1917, took the issue more seriously, declaring that a "negro man could be controlled but nothing could frighten a negro woman."[60]

Although there has been little study of the "sexual contract" that emerged in the South during the suffrage campaign, Hall reports how the former Texas suffragist Jesse Daniel Ames, who initially tolerated white supremacy, came to disavow and oppose it. In the 1930s Ames organized the Association of Southern Women for the Prevention of Lynching (ASWPL). Ames's ASWPL built on southern associations for interracial cooperation as well as the legacy of southern campaigns for woman suffrage and temperance.[61]

The failure of the first woman suffrage campaigns precipitated traces of skepticism about the white supremacist strategy among southern suffragists as well as deliberate reconsideration by northern suffragists. Although the southern reformers remained loyal to white supremacy as a system, they eventually disagreed about including race as a qualification for voting. Between 1905 and 1907 a few southern suffragists initiated campaigns to enfranchise only "white women," which caused divisive debates between northern and southern suffragists; southern leaders also disagreed among themselves about whether to pursue a blatantly racist strategy. None of these campaigns was successful, and the divisions they created signaled that southern suffragist leaders could no longer assume a consensus about the nature and purpose of white supremacy.[62]

The strides made toward an organized articulation of black intellectual views in the North between 1901 and 1910 undoubtedly put a brake on suffragists' endorsement of white supremacist southern campaigns. While southern legislatures consolidated their Democratic monopolistic party system, northern black and white liberal intellectuals were dissenting from these exclusionary southern practices, particularly the disenfranchisement of black men. Few Americans had listened seriously to Ida Wells's condemnation of lynching during the early 1890s, but northern suffragists must have noticed the *Atlantic Monthly*'s publication in 1901 of the critical reflections of W. E. B. Du Bois, Archibald Grimké, William Garrott Brown, and others on southern political developments. The debate between W. E. B. Du Bois and Booker T. Washington over the African-American reform agenda, the formation of the Niagara movement, and incidents such as the Atlanta race riot of 1906 must have gained some attention from woman suffragists with Garrisonian roots.

In 1904 Mary Church Terrell, the leader of black women's clubs, addressed the NAWSA annual convention in Baltimore. She spoke just after members had "endorsed the bill before Congress for a national board of child and animal protection." Terrell challenged the white suffragists to defend American black people as well as children and animals:

> A resolution asks you to stand up for children and animals; I want you to stand up not only for children and animals but also for negroes. You will never get suffrage until the sense of justice has been so developed in men that they will give fair play to the colored race. Much has been said about the purchasability of the negro vote. They never sold their votes till they found that it made no difference how they cast them. Then, being poor and ignorant and human, they began to sell them, but soon after the Civil War I knew many efforts to tempt them to do so which were not successful. My sisters of the dominant race, stand up not only for the oppressed sex but also for the oppressed race![63]

Terrell's speeches, including "A Plea for the White South by a Colored Woman," decried deepening political inequality and injustices suffered by her race. She also pleaded especially that white mothers help form policies for educating African-American children.[64] These newly emerging egalitarian liberal critiques warned the suffragists about the dangers of their entanglement in racist southern politics.

By 1905, northern suffragists were obviously uncomfortable with the southern women's white supremacist campaigns. Blackwell explained that although he endorsed educational qualifications for the vote, he was opposed to explicit qualifications based on race or sex. NAWSA refused to endorse "blatantly racist campaigns in 1906 and 1907."[65] And President Anna Howard Shaw explained to Laura Clay that the national association could not endorse suffrage for white but not black women, because even though most reformers nationwide supported white supremacy in the South, taking such a stand nationally would imply that reformers had forsaken suffrage for the securing of white racial domination.[66]

To the leaders of the 1907 Mississippi campaign to enfranchise "white women only," Blackwell disavowed personal belief in a "white man's government," but mentioned that "he knew Southerners did" have such belief. In a letter written to Laura Clay of Kentucky in the fall of 1907, Alice Stone Blackwell confirmed the widespread toleration among suffragists nationally for southern white supremacy as a check against "political corruption." She rejected, however, the idea that NAWSA would ever endorse explicitly racist suffrage reforms by saying that inclusion based solely on ascriptive characteristics without regard to education or character was "intolerable" and "wrong."[67]

Henry Blackwell also began emphasizing that the suffrage aim should be connected to other political reform efforts in the South. In August 1904 he urged "Georgia suffragists to couple with their demand for political equality an effort to secure legislation against child labor in factories, and to reform or abolish the cruel and demoralizing chain-gang system. To remove such relics of barbarism may well signalize the advent of women in politics. By rescuing others from oppression, women will commend to public approval the demand for their own enfranchisement."[68]

After many defeats between 1890 and 1910, white woman suffragists in the South became even more convinced that they wanted to win the vote. As a result, many felt less threatened as southerners in a national movement and more comfortable following the national leaders' strategies. NAWSA's efforts to limit black suffragists' participation certainly also helped to keep southern white reformers involved.

After 1910 some white southern suffragists disagreed over whether to pursue a states' rights approach to winning the vote or to try for a federal constitutional amendment. As both sides became increasingly opposed to how men governed in the South, most of the southern suffragists argued that female enfranchisement would bring better social policies and more humane government, albeit a white government. After 1910 the southern suffragists' advocacy of social policy reforms overshadowed their testimonials of loyalty to white supremacy. At the same time, those suffragists defending a states' rights approach became a minority throughout the South.[69] By 1912 NAWSA had a national organization of native-born, educated, white, middle-class women poised to launch a federal amendment campaign.

NAWSA leaders never altered their practice of racial segregation, however.[70] When various groups of African-American suffragists petitioned for delegate status at national conventions, their requests were relentlessly denied. The national leaders feared the loss of their white southern contingent more than the anger of African-American women. But as historian Mary Martha Thomas puts it, "By the 1890s blacks tended to support a political philosophy of universal suffrage, whereas white women advocated a limited, educated suffrage."[71]

Always a loyal supporter of woman suffrage, in 1911 W. E. B. Du Bois sharply pointed out in the *Crisis* that the movement had become exclusively focused on winning the vote for white women.[72] Black reformers refused to view themselves as inferior; in her 1912 article, "The Justice of Woman Suffrage," Terrell urged all blacks to support votes for women. In an angry attack on politically powerful white men, she asserted, "To prove that it is unjust to withhold from one-half of the human race rights and privileges freely accorded the other half, which is neither more deserving nor more capable of exercising them, seems almost like a reflection upon the intelligence of those to whom they are presented."[73] Ida Wells-Barnett protested segregation at the 1913 march in Washington by leaving the scene until the parade started and then entering it with the white delegation from Chicago.[74] Suffragists in some northern cities such as Chicago and New York appear to have included African-American women in their organizations. Catt probably urged a double standard on membership as part of a calculation that the southern states were too numerous to write off at any point, even in the federal amendment campaign. But this exclusionary policy left a bitter legacy for any future women's movement.

Suffragist Nativism against Jews and Catholics

Catt's fearful warnings about new immigrants in "The American Sovereign" applied to both Catholic and Jewish immigrants from southern and eastern Europe. After 1906 Florence Kelley's and Jane Addams's dissent from this nativism led to new appeals and less offensive language, but Jewish and Catholic women undoubtedly felt distrust toward the suffragists. In 1890, led by Matilda Joslyn Gage, some suffragists displayed their distrust of Christianity and Catholic immigrants by establishing the Woman's National Liberal Union, which overtly denounced Catholics.[75]

Additionally, despite Frances Willard's deliberate efforts to appeal to all women, the fact that the WCTU was a Christian organization made it unlikely that any Jewish women would either try to join or be accepted. In an 1888 speech to the International Council of Women, temperance suffragist Anna Howard Shaw disparaged Jewish beliefs in her interpretation of the conversion of St. Paul: "To this Jew, bound by the prejudices of past generations, weighed down by the bigotry of human creeds, . . . struggling through the darkness and gloom which surrounded him, when as a persecutor he sought to annihilate the disciples of a new faith, . . . there dawned the electric light of a great truth." Encouraging her audience to consider themselves imitators of Paul who must suffer rejection, she used the stereotype of Jews as betrayers of Christians: "This is the penalty paid by good people who sacrifice themselves for others. They must live without sympathy; their feelings will be misunderstood; their efforts will be uncomprehended. Like Paul, they will be betrayed by friends; like Christ in the agony of Gethsemane, they must bear their struggle alone."[76]

Nor is it likely that Catholic women would have felt welcome. In the late nineteenth century most Catholics probably considered "Christian" organizations to be almost entirely Protestant. Anna Howard Shaw, president of NAWSA from 1904 to 1914 and an ordained Protestant minister, did not mince words in preferring Protestants to Catholics. In one speech, Shaw criticized the British prime minister William Gladstone for minimizing "the spread of Roman Catholicism in England" with his statement "It is chiefly among women." Shaw jumped on this canard, calling "all too common" the habit of writing about women as if they "have neither discernment nor judgment." Women, she argued, "should refuse to submit to being referred to as unthinking, irrational and hysterical beings, petty and uncontrolled by reason and common sense." Earlier in the speech she referred to "the influx of hordes of foreigners, untrained, and not always of a desirable class."[77]

In order to discredit male authority, the pioneer leaders sometimes referred to papal influences as undesirable features of American life. Catholic clergy, in turn, regularly warned of the deleterious consequences of votes for women. By the early twentieth century Roman Catholics were themselves disagreeing on the prudence of woman suffrage. In a list of "eminent advocates of woman suffrage" published in 1902, suffragists topped the roll of clergymen with Archbishop John Ireland of Saint Paul, Minnesota.[78] Fearful of more intense nativist discrimination, other Catholic priests and bishops continued to bolster the opposition.[79] For example, throughout the movement's final decade, the editors of the Catholic intellectual magazine *America,* although open to the question, opposed the measure.[80]

Henry Blackwell and Alice Stone Blackwell explicitly courted Catholics' support and aimed to dispel the view that all Catholics think alike. In one editorial, Alice Stone Blackwell explained that the pope's recent statement of opposition to woman suffrage did not mean that its Catholic supporters "will now feel obliged to oppose it." She reminded her audience that many American priests and bishops publicly dissented from the pope's views when "a former Pope censured the methods used in the campaign for Home Rule in Ireland." This dissent was accepted, she wrote, on the grounds that "the Pope was infallible only on questions of theology, and that in politics he was liable to error, like other men." Blackwell added that, according to one Catholic antisuffragist, even "Monsignor Satolli, . . . the Pope's official representative," admitted when asked that woman suffrage "was not a doctrine of theology, but a secular question upon which all Catholics were free to think as they chose." She listed, among others, Archbishop Ireland and Cardinal Archbishop Vaughn as supporters of woman suffrage.[81]

Although less blatantly negative messages were directed at Catholic and Jewish immigrants than at black suffragists, who were formally excluded from NAWSA, the NAWSA remained predominantly the province of native-born, educated, white Protestant women. Only after they realized that they could not achieve suffrage victories without the votes of non-Protestant males did the suffragists dilute their nativistic symbolism. The disproportionately small number of blacks in most northern cities provided little incentive for suffragists to temper or hide their racism.[82]

Nativist Maternalism and the Story of Li Po Ton

The nativism leveled at Asian women by American woman suffragists shows more profound ambiguities. Although Asian women did not become visible in the movement until after 1905, the sex trade in Asian women played a central role in "A True Story," a narrative written by Carrie Chapman Catt and first published in 1891. "A True Story" portrayed the sale of a young woman, Li Po Ton, into international prostitution and described her sufferings after she arrived in San Francisco. Written to recruit woman suffrage support, this story graphically depicted how political exclusion prevented educated, white, Protestant women from overthrowing the worst forms of female victimization, particularly prostitution. This story's importance to the suffrage movement is shown by its frequent publication—three times in the *Woman's Journal,* once in the *Woman Voter,* and once as a suffrage pamphlet. It appeared in print most frequently after 1910.[83]

In this story Catt's nativism is ambiguous because she blended the real problems of some Asian women with exaggerated conceptions of the power and powerlessness of her Asian characters. Certainly some young

Asian women—many were only girls—were sold into prostitution or entered the trade because they saw no better option. But Catt's portrayal also contributed to negative stereotypes about the Chinese. Li Po Ton is rendered as defenseless, weak, and dependent on the protection of native-born, white, educated Protestant women. The Chinese men in the story— Chin Wah, Li Po Ton's grandfather who sells Li Po Ton into the sex trade, and Wah Lee, the pimp in San Francisco—appear as ruthlessly cruel patriarchs.[84]

In this narrative Li Po's life begins as a twin sister of her patriarchal grandfather's only male heir and namesake, Chin Wah. Although she enjoys many hours playing with her brother, Li Po is denied the means of living an independent life: she is not allowed to learn to read, her feet are bound, and her grandfather refuses to show her love or affection of any kind. "Yet there was another grief which sometimes sent a quick, sharp pain through her little child-heart; for she had not been slow to notice that her grandfather, the great Chin Wah, had plenty of caresses and words of affection for her twin brother, but paid no more attention to her than if she had been one of the cabbages in his garden."

The oppression of Li Po Ton deepens when her brother assumes airs of superiority and arrogantly scorns her. "'Oh, ho!' he exclaimed. 'I can't play with you any more. I have just had my first lesson in reading, and a man is coming every day to teach me more. I am going to be a great man, like grandfather, and ride in a palanquin; but you can't learn to read. Grandfather said so. You are a girl.'" After this encounter, Chin Wah begins to dress in elegant clothes of many colors; Li Po senses that an insurmountable barrier has arisen between them. As he learns to read, she must occupy herself with lessons from her mother in sewing and embroidery.

When Li Po Ton turns twelve, her grandfather sells her into the sex trade. Catt renders the progression of Li Po's sale in terrifying, vivid terms. Standing before her grandfather and a strange man, Li Po is "filled with terror" at the sight of "his fierce black eyes. Cold chills ran up and down her back as he tapped her on the head, examined her feet, felt of her arms, shoulders and legs." As the two men negotiate the price, she runs to her mother who, powerless to stop the transaction, gently tells Li Po "what she feared it might mean, and together they wept." The pathos of this scene is heightened when the child sees her grandfather receive payment: "With her heart filled with terror, Li Po Ton flew back to her mother, and fell at her feet in a spasm of agonized weeping." But when told she must leave with the strange man, she practices the "filial respect and obedience" taught to "children of both sexes." Catt remarked that "Li Po Ton had no thought to question whither she was going or why."

Catt may have taken pains to tell her readers about the respect of Chinese children for their elders to suggest that an American-raised child might have questioned this behavior or tried to run away. But her primary concern is to show that Li Po Ton had no choice regarding her sale into the sex trade.

Catt describes Li Po Ton's transport from her home to "a great city," to "a boat," and finally to "the biggest ship she had ever seen," as if it were the process of slow death. Li Po travels "with a dull, heavy pain in her heart," she "sat still as a mouse, speaking not a word," and at night she "quietly cried herself to sleep."

Catt conveys the evolution of Li Po's psychological death as a sequence of emotional responses to her sale that send her more and more deeply inside herself. Struck initially by physical terror at the audacity of the sale itself, but unable to defy it, she meekly complies. Turning inward, carrying the dull ache in her heart along with constant fear, she travels from her home to the boat. Although she tries to imagine what lies ahead of her, she wonders in vain: "Had she known how to pray, she would have prayed for death. As it was, she looked through the round port-hole windows at the rolling, foam-capped waves, and longed to bury all her sorrows beneath them forever. Well might she make this wish, for Li Po Ton was a slave."

Arriving in San Francisco, Li Po finds her anguished journey turn into a nightmare in which her senses of mystery at "the strange language" and the "interesting but terrifying" streetcars culminate in her being driven "down a dark alley." Once inside "a long, low room," Li Po encounters her purchaser, "Wah Lee," who pays $300 for her; then, taking her to "a little tumble-down, dark-looking building, . . . thrust her inside, locking the door after her."

Allowed only one full meal and one night's rest in the small room where six women lived, Li Po shares her experiences with her new female friends. Eventually these "women acquainted the new-comer with her fate. They told her she would not be permitted to rest another night." When Li Po Ton asks whether they might escape, she is told that the "door was always locked," and that "the master told us once of a woman who ran away, and when they found her they boiled her alive in hot lard." Uprooted from home, disconnected from parental ties, and forced to obey the master Wah Lee, Li Po finally becomes willing to try an escape from this trap. The experience of slavery constituted a lesson in how to achieve freedom.

All day the little maid sat stupefied with horror. Li Po Ton was one of the twelve hundred Chinese women slaves in the city of San

Francisco. After supper that night, Wah Lee bade her go to bed again, and she climbed up to her berth. Soon he returned, bringing with him a group of men. One placed a piece of money in his hand, and was bidden to climb up to her berth. When he had gone, another came, and then another, until the poor girl had fainted. Night after night the experience was repeated. Sometimes she screamed; but Wah Lee only bound her mouth, and gave her no breakfast. And this was in the land that boasts liberty to be the inalienable right of every individual.

In this deft use of the feminism of fear, Catt depicted a cruelty that she expected her readers to understand was suffered by many girls and women forced to become prostitutes. But two components of the Americanist stereotype of Chinese males are present here: the cold-blooded, misogynistic, patriarchal grandfather as portrayed by Chin Wah, and the merciless, capitalistic pimp as depicted by Wah Lee.[85] The first cruelty came when Li Po's grandfather denied her the right of personal development; the second, when she was forced to provide continuous sexual services to Wah Lee's clients.

Catt uses the final section of her story to raise her readers' consciousness about how American men use the legal system to threaten rather than protect women. The section begins with Li Po Ton's late-night escape, a last-gasp attempt for freedom and survival. As she searches for a hiding place, Li Po longs for "some little dark corner, some forgotten spot, where no human being would ever look . . . To starve in peace was the boon she craved." She stumbles on such a spot near a garbage dump. In the morning municipal workers find her; Li Po had fainted, but later she awakes in a room in the "Home for the Friendless" and is greeted by Mrs. Miller, a social worker. At this point, Catt depicted Li Po Ton as "afraid of Americans. She suffered so cruelly in their land, she thought they must all be wicked." Li Po initially refuses to eat, but eventually she tells her story to an interpreter. The social worker assures Li Po Ton of care and protection from Wah Lee.

Unfortunately, Mrs. Miller lacks the support of the law for her promise.

Somehow, a knowledge of her presence there leaked out. The Chinese master heard the rumor, and speedily a writ of *habeas corpus* was issued to command Mrs. Miller to produce her charge in court the next morning. Here was a dilemma. A lawyer was consulted, but he could offer little consolation. Wah Lee, he said, would probably bring Chinese friends enough to prove that the girl was his wife, and the court would give her back to him.

Mrs. Miller tries to explain the complexities of American law, including its uncertain outcome, to Li Po Ton, but Li Po refuses to believe that Wah Lee will not retake her and commits suicide with a penknife.[86] Catt's moral message was that female social workers lacked the standing they needed to intervene successfully in cases of sexual slavery that included child abuse. The ultimate villain lay in the American court system, which denied female social workers and their evaluations of social crises equal standing with that of men in the roles of husbands, fathers, or bosses/owners.

Li Po Ton as an Emblematic Figure

The Li Po Ton story reveals Catt's projection onto Chinese men of the worst elements of patriarchal decision-making and attitudes about women. The exotic Chinese setting diverted attention from her audience's own painful family and community experiences. Theodore Dreiser's *Sister Carrie* and *An American Tragedy* give us the experience of native-born white American girls not unlike that of Li Po Ton. Still, Li Po Ton's story undoubtedly represented the experience of many female Chinese immigrants to California before 1880. Early Chinese immigrants did not arrive here in families. The men came by themselves as "forced laborers" for building railroads, and many of the first female Chinese immigrants were prostitutes.

Historian Lucie Cheng Hirata observes that in 1852 there were 11,794 Chinese in California. Of these, only seven were women—two of whom were independent prostitutes, and two others of whom worked for one of the famous entrepreneurial prostitutes, Ah-choi. Only three of the seven were not engaged in the sex trade. In 1870, among the 3,536 adult Chinese women in California, 2,157 listed their occupation as prostitutes. Of these, 67 percent were in San Francisco. By 1880 the number had declined: only 759 of the 3,171 Chinese women in California were listed as prostitutes.

Hirata explains that prostitution was a survival response to the severe poverty in China. Poor families regularly sold their daughters into the sex trade; when more well-off families faced a financial crisis, such as paying the bride price for a son, a daughter might be sold into prostitution. According to Hirata, "a number of prostitutes in San Francisco were originally orphans who were sold into brothels by their relatives." If they could not obtain their quota of females to trade, agents would go into the countryside to lure or kidnap girls. The procurers used enticements such as promises of marriage, jobs, or education.

Hirata described the typical "compartments" prostitutes lived in as follows: "Most of the lower-grade prostitutes lived in the street-level compartments usually not larger than 4 x 6 feet and facing some dim alley. There were a few articles of furniture—a bamboo chair or two, a wash-bowl, and hard bunks or shelves covered with matting. The door usually held the only window in the room, and it was always covered with bars or a heavy screen, behind which the women, dressed in cotton tunics and trousers, could stand and call to passersby."[87]

Catt portrayed Li Po Ton's quarters in a comparable way: "The room was low and narrow. Bunks rested against the wall on one side. There was just room for three bunks from floor to ceiling, and just room for two tiers, placed end to end. There were six bunks and six women. Between the bunks and the opposite wall was a space about three feet in width. The only furniture was six blue-painted wooden stools. There was a door, and one tiny square window, securely cross-barred with iron, like the windows of a penitentiary."[88] The similarities in these accounts suggest that Catt visited the neighborhood where Chinese prostitutes lived or that she gleaned her information from a direct description by a newspaper or police reporter.

Hirata also tells us that kidnappings were often "carried out by force, and the victims were frequently daughters of relatively well-to-do families. On an official visit to the United States in 1888, Chinese envoy Fu Yun-lung composed a memorial that was inscribed on the gravestone of a Cantonese woman who had committed suicide after being kidnapped and sold into prostitution in San Francisco."[89] Catt may have picked up this hint, embroidering it into her story of Li Po Ton.

This marks Catt's first turning point away from a thorough-going nativism. The Li Po Ton story was nativist in its stereotypes of Chinese fathers as authoritarian patriarchs and procurers of prostitutes, but its eventual villain was the male dominance in the American state as embodied in its court system. Male control, not immigrants, deserved the blame for injustice to women.

Still, Catt pointed to the female social worker, white and Anglo-Saxon, as the maternal "ideal citizen" whose disfranchisement prevented her from ensuring that girls and women obtained full protection from the state. Women already mobilized by Willard would have found this maternal ideal citizen appealing. And most such women would also have applauded the view that women have a fundamental right to refuse men's requests for sexual services or pleasure. Lucy Stone and Elizabeth Cady Stanton had made similar assertions in the 1850s. In the early twentieth century the opposition to prostitution would unite suffragists across region, race, and ethnicity.

But in forging these bonds, reformers often spoke in maternalistic voices with tones of Americanist cultural superiority. Mrs. Miller takes care of Li Po Ton; the Chinese girl's suffering, debilitation, and fear define her as a weak immigrant who needs the help of the strong, native-born white woman. After the turn of the century, suffragists often labeled prostitution as the "ancient evil," or as "white slavery." The label "white slavery" undoubtedly was both a euphemism that elite white women used to refer to the "unrespectable" sex trade and a blinder about the disproportionate number of black prostitutes.

~✦~

The suffragists' racist and nativist appeals left a legacy of injustice, deepened stereotypes, and divided political action that ironically undermined their own project of generating solidarity among women *as women*. In struggling to win political inclusion for all women, these elite women presented themselves as not only respectable, but also culturally dominant leaders of foreign women. Representing themselves to black and immigrant women as potential protectors who would be more trustworthy than any men, they simultaneously asserted their dominance as white, native-born women in a racist and xenophobic society.

The Lady of the House—Go away, I will give you no more help. In the last eight years you have stolen more than $40,000,000 worth of silverware that belonged to the folks in this house. If you are let in you will do it again. No, don't explain. It's the same old story. If you once get in, then silver goes. Get away; if you don't I'll set the dog on you. He looks quiet enough now, but if he's once aroused he'll tear you to pieces. So get.

1. *"The Lady of the House,"* Rocky Mountain News, *September 11, 1892. This cartoonist blended themes of home protection and republican motherhood by depicting the woman, Colorado, and her dog, Silver, protecting their home state from beggar presidential candidates Grover Cleveland and Benjamin Harrison. (Colorado Historical Society)*

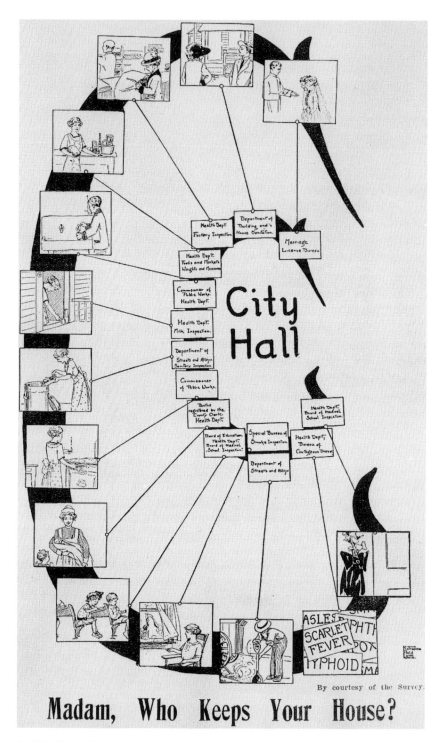

By courtesy of the Survey.

Madam, Who Keeps Your House?

2. *"Madam, Who Keeps Your House?"* The Woman's Journal, *June 1, 1912. By illustrating in this poster the direct links between domestic tasks and municipal departments, the prosuffrage Woman's Civic Club of Chicago induced women to participate actively in municipal politics. (The Schlesinger Library, Radcliffe College)*

TO THE WOMAN IN THE HOME

HOW CAN A MOTHER REST CONTENT WITH THIS— WHEN SUCH CONDITIONS EXIST AS THIS?

There are thousands of children working in tenements like the one in the picture. There are thousands of children working in mines and mills and factories. Thousands more are being wronged and cheated by society in countless ways. Is not this your business? Intelligent citizens who cared could change all this—provided always, of course, that they had the power of the ballot. Do you care? Mothers are responsible for the welfare of children—all children. Do your duty as a mother and demand Votes for Women.

3. *"To the Woman in the Home,"* The Woman's Journal, *July 27, 1912. A sharp contrast between the homes of the rich and the poor became this political cartoonist's argument for women's votes to stop child labor. (The Schlesinger Library, Radcliffe College)*

4. *Three prizewinning antisuffrage cartoons: "The Three Sexes" by W. Bowles;
"To the Rescue" by E. Braverman; "In Peril" by H. W. White.* The New York
Times, *February 5, 1911. With themes that were both unchanging and distinctive
of the Progressive era, these cartoonists displayed multiple antisuffrage ideas. "The
Three Sexes" depicted the model suffragist as an odd object of ridicule, not desire,
for handsome and intelligent men. "To the Rescue" associated suffragists' demands
with the cries of babies who were unable to carry or even understand the burdens
of government hauled by Uncle Sam. "In Peril" portrays woman suffrage as the
last in a series of modern reforms—office positions, school board representation,
and trade unions—and the one that most threatened the home.*

THE ANTI SUFFRAGE QUARTETTE

The repertoire of this admirable combination includes all the familiar sophistical melodies: "Protect the Home," "Sweet Woman's Sphere's the Home," "Keep Your Dear Mother Out of Politics," "Oh, Leave Things As they Be," "Let the Woman Mind the Baby," "Let 'Em Use Their Influence," etc., etc., etc.

5. "*The Anti Suffrage Quartette,*" The Woman's Journal, *March 23, 1912. Here, four representative opponents of votes for women—the white slaver, the female "anti," the Big Biz leader, and the liquor lobbyist—are depicted as singers in unison of a verse so well memorized that they can sing it with their eyes closed. (The Schlesinger Library, Radcliffe College)*

Facing page, top: 6. "To the Male Citizen," The Woman's Journal, *July 27, 1912. This cartoonist promotes the idea that if scrubbing the floors of public buildings is considered womanly, then women also should have the opportunity to supervise street cleaning. (The Schlesinger Library, Radcliffe College)*

Facing page, bottom: 7. "The Blind Goddess: Can This Be Justice?" The Woman's Journal, *June 19, 1909. Notice how prejudice divided urban electorates in the Progressive era: this cartoonist derisively pictured a poor male immigrant voting as ordered by party bosses while "The Law" barred educated, tax-paying white women from the ballot box. (Sophia Smith Collection, Smith College)*

TO THE MALE CITIZEN

IF THIS IS WOMANLY—   WHY NOT THIS?

Housekeeping is woman's work—no man denies that. Government is public housekeeping—practically everybody agrees to that. Isn't it foolish then to keep out of government the very people who have had most training for a large part of its function?.

Men have never regarded it as unwomanly for women to do the scrubbing and cleaning indoors—even in public places like office buildings. Why, then, should they think it unwomanly for women to keep the streets clean?

Be logical and insist that women should no longer shirk their duty as housekeepers. You need their help. Demand Votes for Women.

THE BLIND GODDESS!   CAN THIS BE JUSTICE?

THE BOARD OF STRATEGY

—Courtesy The Philadelphia North American

8. *"The Board of Strategy,"* The Woman's Journal, *April 11, 1914. This caricature of meetings between corporate bosses and a female antisuffragist ridiculed the alliance between Miss C. E. Markeson, an antisuffragist, and the Montana Liquor Dealers' Protective Association. After 1910 this sort of suffragist cartoon began to displace the nativist images portrayed in figure 7. (Sophia Smith Collection, Smith College)*

Facing page, top: 9. "The 'heathen Chinee!'" The Woman's Journal, *August 31, 1912. This cartoonist celebrated the passage of woman suffrage in a Chinese province by caricaturing the shocked reactions of American ladies. (The Schlesinger Library, Radcliffe College)*

Facing page, bottom: 10. "Waiting in Ambush," The Woman's Journal, *February 7, 1914. This cartoonist portrayed a woman suffragist who, with enlightened public opinion as her guardian, was on the verge of doing battle with forces supporting female antisuffragists: white slavers, the liquor interests, corrupt politicians, child-labor exploiters, and food dopers. (The William Oxley Thompson Memorial Library, The Ohio State University)*

The "heathen Chinee!"

Cleveland Plain Dealer.

WAITING IN AMBUSH

JUSTICE HANDICAPPED

11. *"Justice Handicapped,"* The Woman's Journal, *January 23, 1915. Here woman suffragists are caricatured in a direct battle to make justice prevail over the profits white slavers made by selling young women into prostitution. (Sophia Smith Collection, Smith College)*

7

The Feminism of Personal Development and the Drive for a Federal Amendment

*M*ANY FACTORS pushed national woman suffrage leaders to take new directions in the early twentieth century. Nativistic and racist appeals were a threefold failure: none had led to any victories after 1894, changed many antisuffragists' minds, or engendered a unified commitment for the vote across race, class, or region. On the positive side, woman suffragists had been heartened by social policy reforms such as mothers' pensions, child labor reform, and antiprostitution efforts. These changes had been promoted by women in nonsuffragist organizations such as the General Federation of Women's Clubs, black women's clubs, and the Socialist Party.

By 1900, so many women had joined an organized interest that the suffragists faced multiple constituencies whose ideals and political priorities were often at odds. Although inflammatory nativist statements aroused some white, middle-class Protestants, they alienated Jewish and Catholic immigrants. On the other hand, appeals to natural rights and equal rights as principled reasons for the political inclusion of women attracted little support from white elites. In 1890, at NAWSA's inaugural convention, Stanton's effort to revive the feminism of equal rights fell on deaf ears.[1] Elected representatives on the House Judiciary Committee hardly listened to Catt's natural rights appeals in 1892.[2] Elite white suffragists clung instead to the themes of self-reliance, personal responsibility, and individual citizenship that Stanton struck in her famous 1892 speech, "The Solitude of Self."[3]

The language of equal rights did not disappear in the last phase of the struggle, however. Egalitarian appeals were published in the *Woman's Journal;* Alice Paul militantly promoted votes for women as democratic; black suffragists called for inclusive egalitarian standards; and socialists sustained the association between female enfranchisement and the quest for equality. But egalitarianism lost out to the popularity of racialist theories and liberals' inclination to think that only educated voters could achieve political equality.[4]

Between 1900 and 1915 the American woman suffrage movement became a mass movement. Despite white elitism, racism, and nativism, support for woman suffrage spread among female socialists, trade unionists, temperance reformers, black women's clubs, and the settlement movement. Each proposed different purposes for women's votes. Because most suffragists identified themselves first as southern or northern, white or black, or working-class or socialist, national leaders needed to develop overlapping commitments and avoid divisive clashes between groups. Fragile coalitions emerged slowly as various leaders' efforts to unify many different women eventually succeeded just enough to win the vote.

The key was making votes for women a compelling goal without diminishing the primary aims of diverse constituencies. Leaders such as Harriot Stanton Blatch, Florence Kelley, Jane Addams, Carrie Chapman Catt, and Alice Paul fashioned and encouraged an inclusive feminism of what I call "personal development." This feminism justified the vote as a political right that women deserved and needed. Groups' criteria for good citizenship and personhood often conflicted, but they shared the then radical premise that women should have the right to vote.

Feminisms of personal development varied widely because each subculture of women possessed a distinctive political identity and its own conception of political self-interest. For example, Carrie Chapman Catt's reliance on the argument that it was unfair to enfranchise new immigrant males but not women contrasted sharply with Mary Church Terrell's insistence in 1915 that if black men valued their right to vote they should not hesitate to support votes for women. Eager to obtain the best jobs, safety in the workplace, child care, and fair wages, working-class women emphasized how, as earners, they had already assumed their rightful place in the public sphere.

Despite these tensions, group leaders employed feminisms of personal development to cultivate collective confidence among members. Leaders such as Addams, Blatch, Kelley, and Terrell, who mobilized new suffragists among wage earners, immigrants, and blacks, injected these feminisms with egalitarian themes. But white leaders such as Anna Howard Shaw and Carrie Chapman Catt steered away from equality and depicted votes for women as the justice of simple inclusion. Thus divided leadership made the mass suffrage movement multifaceted, but united by a shared conviction about women's qualifications for the vote. All leaders faced the challenges of recruiting members, maintaining cordial communications across multiple divides, and encouraging men of their group to support votes for women.

White, Protestant, middle-class suffragists accepted the Americanist tradition insofar as they assumed that educated white Protestants should set the rules of the game, control power, and determine appropriate political behavior. But the suffragists differed from strict Americanists—most of whom were antisuffrage—by disagreeing that women should remain in the home, consider themselves inferior to men, and accepted exclusion from political power. The later generation of suffragists realized that many men and women would never either accept the idea that women are equal to men or be willing to state openly such a belief. Instead of trying to win support for political equality, they appealed to educational qualifications, maternal knowledge, and the justice of simple inclusion.

Carrie Chapman Catt, Harriot Stanton Blatch, Maud Wood Park, Alice Paul, and numerous other reformers considered the groups' differences as personal matters that should not interfere with putting woman suffrage on government agendas. As the leader of the "old guard," only Anna Howard Shaw preserved explicit religious symbols and rhetoric. To mobilize support within the United States, Blatch, Kelley, and Addams labeled the reform a progressive evolutionary step that would help solve the problems of prostitution, illiteracy, poor sanitation, child labor, and danger in the workplace. To build a strong international movement, Catt compared progress within the United States to the progress of nations. Although Blatch opposed Catt's heavy reliance on "organization and education," and Catt became wary of street demonstrations, both women concentrated on designing and using tactics that would advance their cause among voters and legislatures. A common goal became overcoming the obstacles posed by local party machines in major cities such as New York.

Sharon Hartman Strom observes that the nativist proclivities of the first generation and their high-minded views about women's special abilities to clean up "boss rule" tied the suffrage cause to anti-Catholic organizations and the regionally unpopular WCTU.[5] Around the turn of the century, more college-educated leaders such as Pauline Agassiz Shaw, Mary Hutcheson Page, and Maud Wood Park emerged. These reformers eschewed the nativist sentiments and straitlaced styles of the first generation for more urban populist perspectives and tolerance for diversity. In 1903 they established the College Equal Suffrage League, and began promoting votes for women through organizations of teachers, women's clubs, and public events such as fairs. Like Coloradans Ellis Meredith and Helen Reynolds, they also formed alliances with organized labor, consumers, and ethnic groups; of these, the alliance between suffragists and the Women's Trade Union League (WTUL) and other unions strengthened the grassroots power of the suffragists in Massachusetts. As Meredith Tax and Nancy Schrom Dye demonstrate, working-class women considered the improvement of wages and working conditions as their top priority and perceived alliances with second-generation suffragists as sensible.[6]

Harriot Stanton Blatch

In 1894, Harriot Stanton Blatch challenged and rejected Stanton's defense of an educational qualification for suffrage. A Fabian Socialist, Blatch assailed her mother for attaching herself to the "read and write fetich" and for falsely accusing educated foreign men of ignorance when all they lacked was the ability to communicate in English. She sardonically posited that if Stanton were to "land in Germany," she would "be the most intelligent voter in the whole Empire on women's questions."

Blatch further argued that Stanton wrongly neglected the suffrage needs of the working class, whose opinions were "more valuable than any other class, upon such a question, for example, as the housing of the poor." She reminded readers that during slavery "the whole southern section of the United States was ruled by its men who could 'read and write.' They had it all their own way, and what did they do with their power? No, no, we are ever vainly trying to get morals and character out of intellect, but they grow on quite other soil." Government, Blatch asserted, "is not the end of man, but merely a method of expressing collective thought, and achieving concerted action." And, putting "thought" ahead of John Stuart Mill's valued "opinion," Blatch reminded Stanton of the liberal principle of inclusion: "Thought is not collective if any human being capable of thought is excluded. We cannot escape the law that society is never stronger than its weakest link."[7]

When she leveled this challenge, Blatch lived in Britain. At NAWSA's 1898 convention, she urged suffragists to accept the public's demand for "proved worth," and to realize that "it is the paid worker who has brought to the public mind conviction of woman's worth."[8] After moving to the United States in 1902, she joined her local branch of the WTUL and united women in New York City across class and race. Two years later she established the Equality League of Self-Supporting Women, "a suffrage organization that emphasized female 'self-support'" and encouraged the militant activist style of trade unionist politics that Blatch admired in her working-class colleagues Leonora O'Reilly and Rose Schneiderman.

Although Blatch's "perspectives and associations" remained "fundamentally elite," her arguments were more tolerant, consistently liberal, and positive about women earners than those of previous suffragists.[9] In a 1912 letter to the *New York Times,* she stated: "In truth the demand for votes for women is a result, not a cause of the great economic revolution in women's lives. Economic conditions create a political right for wage-earning women and the entrance of the State into the home, touching as it does education, sanitation, &c., creates a political duty for wife and mother. Is it beyond the range of possibility that political power might be used by women in the future to make home life possible for all?"[10]

By calling attention to the advantages of the cross-class alliances that militant British suffragists created, Blatch enriched the international character of this movement and turned attention away from nativism.[11] By 1911 her range of activities included organizing the first street campaigns, including major parades that blended poor and rich women; focusing blame for suffrage resistance on "political conservatism"; demanding that suffragists oppose candidates against female enfranchisement; increasing lobbying legislators in Albany for the vote; and chiding the press for its inadequate coverage of woman suffrage.[12] Her publicity efforts paid off: newspapers that previously had covered the reform effort only occasionally now began to give it regular attention.

Florence Kelley and Jane Addams

Child labor reformer Florence Kelley made a firmer commitment to socialists' causes than to their principles. In search of allies, she attended NAWSA's fiftieth anniversary convention in 1898, where in support of working women's need for the ballot she said, "No disfranchised class of workers can permanently hold its own in competition with enfranchised rivals." Kelley observed that even though the Federation of Labor now enrolled "as many women as possible," wage-earning women's standing without the vote left them vulnerable to arbitrary treatment. In the United States, she asserted, where women thus far were not "treated as a class apart" but forced instead to "abide by that universal freedom of contract which characterizes labor in the United States," lacking the vote left women powerless to defend their interests at the centrally important polls.[13]

Subtle signs that Blatch's and Kelley's ideas as well as the tactics preferred by CESA members might generate different strategies for reform appeared at the 1904 NAWSA convention. Previously, issues such as women's property rights, child custody, child labor, and government regulation of vice in the Philippines had been secondary concerns. This convention, however, gave more attention to social policy issues. Maud Nathan read a report by Florence Kelley that graphically summarized the child labor problem, applauded women's strides in stopping it without the vote, and urged the suffragists to join her campaign. Nathan also called for attention to "the condition of women wage-earners"; she suggested that "some of the evils from which they suffer would not exist if the women had the right to place their votes in the ballot-box." In addition, Mary Church Terrell appealed for more attention to the suffering of black people, Dr. Samuel J. Barrows reported on prison reform, and Lucia Ames Mead spoke about the peace movement.[14]

Thus, an active minority of reformers dissented from the elitism of what formerly had been an egalitarian movement. By 1904 some suffragists had even joined the burgeoning Socialist Party. Socialists objected vigorously to national suffrage leaders' disdain for immigrants. But as Mari Jo Buhle points out, many socialist women became suffragists first, and these women refused to relinquish their dedication to winning the vote, their conviction that the aim was fundamentally egalitarian, or their insistence that by campaigning for suffrage as an egalitarian aim, the Socialist Party could expand its membership. Although male leaders of the Socialist Party never made woman suffrage one of their highest priorities—and so lost an opportunity to root the party more securely in the United States—their endorsement facilitated substantial grassroots campaigning by socialist women who wanted to win the vote. Socialist suffragists renewed egalitarianism within the suffragist movement and mobilized substantial working-class support.[15]

NAWSA's 1906 convention marks a turning point toward social policy and away from suffrage as a single issue. Kelley and Addams dissented from nativist sentiments, which they felt had tarnished the movement's reputation and stalled its progress. Their arguments made the movement more tolerant and egalitarian as a whole but more conflicted internally. Florence Kelley celebrated women's use of the petition to create child labor laws and other industrial reforms across the nation. Appealing to maternal instincts, she reported that some industries still required employees to bring children to work as assistants and that children might be employed all night in factories. "The present occupants of Tammany," Kelley claimed, "dare not, as a political measure, reveal the extent to which they are failing to provide for the children, letting them slave their childhood away in the cellars and garrets of the most terribly crowded tenement houses in the world."

Kelley encouraged disenfranchised women to unite with immigrant fathers of such children and struggle together for both the vote and laws for compulsory education. Supporting this issue, she predicted, would encourage immigrant men to back woman suffrage. Kelley also harshly criticized suffragists' nativist claims: "I have rarely heard a ringing suffrage speech which did not refer to the 'ignorant and degraded' men, or the 'ignorant immigrants' as our masters. This is habitually spoken with more or less bitterness. But this is what the workingmen are used to hear applied to themselves by their enemies in times of strike. Rather should we recognize that, while for the moment they have power which we need, they have the same interest in the rising generation of citizens, so largely the children of working people."[16] She plainly stated that suffragists' claims echoed bosses' prejudices against working-class male voters. Women would not win support from these voters as long as the latter sensed that such a reform would strengthen the power of business owners and managers.

At this same convention Jane Addams presented her famous speech "The Modern City and the Municipal Franchise for Women." Although this speech introduced her much-celebrated idea that civic housekeeping justified woman suffrage, Addams also took great pains to show why bearing arms should not be a qualification for citizenship. She suggested that although the medieval city served as a citadel to protect the lives of its citizens and often depended upon warfare for survival, the modern city aimed to establish internal stability. "There was a certain logic," she argued, "in giving the franchise only to grown men, when the existence and stability of the city depended upon their defence, and when the ultimate value of the elector could be reduced to his ability to perform military duty. It was fair that only those who were liable to a sudden call to arms should be selected to decide as to the relations which the city bore to rival cities, and that the vote for war should be cast by the same men who bore the brunt of battle and the burden of protection."

But in the modern city, she explained, which aimed to produce and distribute the products of industry and supply its inhabitants with social welfare, the ability to bear arms and the tendency to resolve conflicts by warfare had become increasingly irrelevant. The new cities' enemies were not external but internal: "unsanitary housing, poisonous sewage, contaminated water, infant mortality, the spread of contagion, adulterated food, impure milk, smoke-laden air, ill-ventilated factories, dangerous occupations, juvenile crime, unwholesome crowding, prostitution and drunkenness."

Addams's call for woman suffrage to combat poverty—and to ensure that women's special nurturing capacities would not remain wasted—echoed Willard's view that women could provide protections against cruelty better than men. Addams contended that a city largely consists of "enlarged housekeeping" and that "most of the departments in a modern city can be traced to woman's traditional activity; but, in spite of this, so soon as these old affairs were turned over to the care of the city, they slipped from woman's hands, apparently because they then became matters for collective action and implied the use of the franchise." In June 1912, the *Woman's*

Journal published a chart, "Madam, Who Keeps Your House?" similar to one Addams might have used to illustrate this point (see Figure 2).

Addams suggested further that when the city initiated garbage collection and street cleaning, women simply gave up their authority on "housekeeping" because many did not consider voting "ladylike." She urged women to overcome this traditional view and accept their responsibilities for the legal "regulation of industrial conditions, Americanizing of immigrants who live in cities,"[17] and supervision of the procedures and operations of juvenile courts. Addams rejected nativist appeals and instead appealed to women's sense of motherly obligation: "The problems of race-antagonisms and economic adjustments, must be settled by a more searching and genuine method than mere prowess can possibly afford." Following Willard's logic, she assumed that women could develop such solutions better than men.

Addams strikingly claimed that women should seek the vote unselfishly as an obligation rather than as a right: "Perhaps we can forecast the career of woman, the citizen, . . . she would bear her share of civic responsibility, not because she clamors for her rights, but because she is essential to the normal development of the city of the future." Another illustration in the *Woman's Journal,* "To the Woman in the Home," graphically portrayed Addams's sense of public mothers' chief concerns (see Figure 3).

Kelley's and Addams's appeals renewed the suffrage movement with more egalitarian ideology and inclusive mobilization strategies. By 1906 many middle-class white women had identified maternal interests, including social reforms, that they pursued without the vote. As Theda Skocpol asserts, these women did not need the vote to create substantial policy reforms such as protective legislation and the Children's Bureau.[18] But the suffragists had to demonstrate why the vote could help women achieve social policy reforms.

These new strategies clashed most sharply with Shaw's. In 1910 Florence Kelley resigned from NAWSA's national executive board largely because Shaw and other women refused to adopt her innovative tactics.[19] As expedient as cross-cultural alliances may have been, many suffragists refused to relinquish their nativism, and class conflict continued. Such conflicts did not disintegrate the movement because the reformers concentrated on winning the vote.

Carrie Chapman Catt

International ties prompted NAWSA leaders to speak about votes for women in more inclusive language. The first meeting of the International

Woman Suffrage Alliance (IWSA) coincided with NAWSA's 1902 annual convention in Washington, D.C. Anna Howard Shaw, president of NAWSA, greeted the foreign delegates by saying, "You will show us that those who speak English are not the only ones whose hearts are alive to the great flame of liberty."[20] IWSA president Catt promised that "It will be the proud duty of the new International Alliance, if one shall be formed, to extend its helping hand to the women of every nation and every people and its completed duty will not have been performed until the last vestige of the old obedience of one human being to another shall have been destroyed."[21] Although appeals for suffrage qualified by education or tax-paying continued, Catt's role launching the IWSA led her away from Americanist and nativist appeals and toward a more inclusive perspective. Her call for the 1906 IWSA meetings in Copenhagen, Denmark, stated, "Individuals of whatever race, nativity or creed, who believe in the right of the woman citizen to protect her interests in society by the ballot, are invited to be present."[22]

As IWSA president, Catt slowly realized the limits of her earlier nativist sentiments. In her 1908 speech to the International Woman Suffrage Convention, she defended votes for women as an evolving international democratic reform that was finding "paths of least resistance" and praised Norway for enfranchising women in 1907. Although the United States had led the creation of "man suffrage," she viewed its problem of illiteracy (particularly among blacks and men of "foreign parentage") as having generated "poverty, insanity, and criminality." These problems, Catt said, "had made our State governments conservative." But she expressed optimism that woman suffrage would pass eventually because of "irresistible forces which make for human liberty, and against which kings and armies struggle in vain."

Catt called for the development of an international "spirit" that is "lofty, pure, and inspirational to women across borders." Although she refused to endorse outright the militant tactics the British suffragettes had just introduced, Catt praised their controversial efforts:

> I conscientiously believe that these English women of the twentieth century, suffragists and suffragettes, are striking a tremendously effective blow in behalf of the political liberty of the women of all the nations. Let those who will, criticize. English women are making history today, and coming generations will pronounce it nobly made. When they have won their cause, all women should understand that their proper relation to these plucky, self-sacrificing English women is not that of critic, but of debtor.

Blending Willard's rhetoric with Stanton's aims, she promised, "The time is not far distant when the women of the world shall enter into their own kingdom of individual freedom. In home, church, and state."

By referring to the Scandinavians as "in the lead" for this effort, Catt provoked a competitive attitude toward winning the reform. Blending inclusion with competition, she announced that woman suffrage associations had formed in Bulgaria and South Africa as well as in all the nations of western Europe.[23] Foreign quests for female enfranchisement led to at least one major unexpected outcome—women voting and holding elective office in a Chinese province long before many American women could vote.

Between 1910 and 1912 Catt undertook another global organizing mission, the high point of which was a visit to China, where political upheavals had led to the liberal revolution of Sun Yat-sen. In 1912 in the province of Canton, a small band of radicals called the Tung Ming Hui opened the polls to all adult males and females and slotted ten seats in the provincial government for women. Catt delightedly observed the women legislators at work, and she lamented Sun's denial of the vote and elective office to women, which had made the Tung Ming Hui's effort a one-year experiment. According to Jacqueline Van Voris, this experience inspired Catt to do her utmost to enfranchise women in the United States. After witnessing this temporary but unexpected suffrage victory, Catt also admitted her bigotry: "Once I was a regular jingo but that was before I had visited other countries. I had thought America had a monopoly on all that stands for progress, but I had a sad awakening."[24] Catt continued to decry the easy enfranchisement of new immigrant men, but she stopped making blatant nativist remarks.

The Unchanging Nature of the Opposition's Claims

Despite Catt's new perspective and the suffragists' more inclusive arguments, the antisuffragists continued to find receptive audiences for their arguments that woman's vote was a threat to the home, to God's will, and to government stability. Although the mass movement for woman suffrage indicated change in woman's consciousness, their opponents remained stubborn.

The antis conveyed their message in political cartoons as well as speeches. Three "Prize-Winning Anti-Suffrage Cartoons," published on February 5, 1911, in the *New York Times,* focused attention on an idealized conception of women. "The Three Sexes" ridiculed woman suffragists as uninterested in sex and as objects of ridicule for handsome and intelligent men. "To the Rescue" built upon this ridicule by associating suffragists' demands with the cries of babies and by depicting the reformers as un-fulfilled or underdeveloped mothers. "In Peril" categorizes woman suffrage as the last of four reforms—the first three of which, "office positions," "school board representation," and "trade unions"—overshadowed and threatened the structure of the home (see Figure 4). These cartoons display the ideological presumptions of the sexual contract: that women's main tasks should be providing the domestic services of sexual pleasure, child care, and home maintenance.

In 1912, Senator Franklin W. Collins of Nebraska testified against woman suffrage before the U.S. Senate Woman Suffrage Committee. Collins mainly urged the senators not to threaten men's expectations of what women should provide as housewives. "Can she add," he asked, "to her responsibilities without materially subtracting from her efficiency in the home, the church, and society?" If woman obtained the ballot, he queried, would "she not be in honor bound to fight by the side of man—to accept the consequences of her own exercise of political power?" Collins asserted that because women had not cleaned up political parties in the states that already enfranchised them, they could do little to improve or transform the power structure as it was. In explicitly Americanist terms Collins stated his opposition to votes for women as a quest for "a renaissance of the American family" where children "shall be trained in their own homes by their own mothers," a quest he claimed exhibited "those exalted ideals following which man and woman have struggled upward together from the depths of barbarism to the loftiest plane of civilization and progress the world has ever known."[25]

Few suffragists desired the kind of society that Collins feared, but his projections illuminate how dependent many men felt on women's domestic service and lack of independence. In response to such arguments, the suffragists offered some caricatures in the *Woman's Journal*, such as "The Anti Suffrage Quartette," that portrayed antis as uniform and unbending (see Figure 5).

Women's lukewarm interest in the vote outside of college-educated, eastern communities must have continually confounded the suffragists. Although membership in the NAWSA grew steadily after 1900, the movement's activists continued to be mainly white, educated, elite women. Southern male antisuffragists did not need to organize themselves because antisuffrage women in the South presented a determined opposition.[26] Even after ratification of the Nineteenth Amendment, most women chose not to vote. Realizing that most women cared far less about political inclusion than they did, reform leaders emphasized the symbolic importance of this right, particularly for mothers.[27]

The suffragists also lacked unambivalent male allies. Still popular was the view that men's unique service as soldiers commanded the full rights of citizenship. During the Progressive era, women's second-class standing was strengthened. By blending Americanist ideas about "customs and manners" and republican ideals of "states' rights and homogeneous communities," Supreme Court justices protected male domination from Reconstruction through the New Deal. To maintain separate spheres, powerful men repeatedly denied women equal access to jobs and provided woman suffragists with few opportunities to build lasting coalitions or commitments to the achievement of political inclusion.[28] Suffrage leaders were forced to promote their cause as unthreatening to men and often as something less than full equality.

The Erosion of Party Opposition

After 1904, the achievements of civil-service reformers and other Progressives weakened the political machine. Until civil-service reformer Theodore Roosevelt became president in 1901, presidents had timed the enactment of post-Reconstruction civil-service reform to blanket in their own patronage appointees and so reduce the jobs available for distribution by the incoming party's president. To preserve electoral bonds based on friendship, presidents since Grant had deliberately stunted the development of the civil service.[29] Roosevelt's commitment to the permanent creation of a merit-based civil service gave women powerful Progressive allies among Republicans; later, Woodrow Wilson became a similar Democratic ally. Suffragists demonstrated that women's citizenship could be helpful for their causes.

Celebrating merit as the central qualification for holding office, male civil-service reformers undermined the idea that maleness mattered most for the exercise of political power. Educated white women among the suffragists stood to benefit immediately from merit standards. Of course, merit standards never displaced the male friendship networks of the political party machines, but the promise of employment to *qualified* candidates created a new "free space" for alliances between suffragists and civil-service reformers.[30] The illustration "To the Male Citizen" portrays how the reformers exploited the view that gender should no longer disqualify women from such employment (see Figure 6).

Some urban party machines also became more flexible during the Progressive era. Historian John D. Buenker argues that the posture of city political machines (the Tammany machine in particular) toward reforms such as woman suffrage was highly variable: "In actuality, the machine proved itself a highly dynamic instrument, ready and willing to support changes in the governmental structure when the exigencies of practical politics so dictated, even if this meant a complete about face from a previous stand."

Buenker discovered that the party machines made an "about face" on woman suffrage. The introduction of proimmigrant ideas by the settlement workers, and the broadened appeal of the suffragists, gradually encouraged the machines to support votes for women and other reforms: "Once it became apparent that the idea was politically popular, that its impact upon the machine's methods of operation would not be catastrophic, and above all, that its enactment might actually add significantly to the growing power of the urban vote, most city politicians ceased their opposition and became open, if not avid, advocates of female voting."[31]

Building on Blatch's pressure tactics, in March 1909 Florence Kelley, whose father was a state legislator, gave the members of the Equal Suffrage League in New York City advice about how to convert elected officials: (1) learn the names of legislators; (2) call at the homes of "the New York men," (3) send them letters by special delivery or by registered mail, (4) do not send "stereotyped letters"—instead, send "letters from organizations or many from individuals," (5) "learn the procedures for action on bills under consideration that may have been pushed aside," (6) "learn the names of Senators and Congressmen," and (7) "write to Congressmen and Senators in New York State and ask them to vote to have the suffrage bill discharged since the committee that has jurisdiction over it has not acted."[32]

As Ronald Schaffer observes, Catt's 1910 organizational plan for the Woman Suffrage Party in New York City and Kelley's mobilization model closely imitated the structure and administrative behaviors of the Tammany political machine. Each district would have a captain that would "form a committee . . . to canvass the district thoroughly by such means as seem possible." Canvassers would "list all voters and women as for, against, or indifferent." Supporters would be invited to join the suffrage party and sign the "National Petition to Congress"; those who expressed indifference would receive literature and encouragement to plan for further discussion.[33]

According to Schaffer, reformers "throughout the nation" imitated the organizational model developed by the Woman Suffrage Party in New York City.[34] Historians of woman suffrage campaigns in various states confirm the presence of a new generation of suffragists who often organized into an "equality league" for suffrage and directly pursued alliances with organized interests as well as public support. Although the leaders concentrated their mobilization efforts in the cities, their adoption of open air meetings, impromptu street corner speeches, protest tactics—and their use of the automobile to cover entire states—raised the profile of suffrage in rural areas, especially in the South.[35]

By transforming their reputation among political machines and parties from enemy into valuable ally, woman suffragists won the vote. This transformation occurred as suffragists diluted nativist and Americanist feminist arguments and began to articulate more inclusive feminisms of personal development.

A Progressive Woman Suffrage Movement

By 1910 important woman suffrage leaders, particularly in New York City, noticed how prejudices divided urban electorates and signaled an opposition to nativism as well as racism. We can map this change by comparing cartoon illustrations in the *Woman's Journal* before and after 1910. In June 1909, a cartoon entitled "The *Blind* Goddess! Can *This* Be Justice?" derisively pictures a poor male immigrant voting while a police officer bars a mother, a female taxpayer, and a woman college graduate from the ballot box. The male political machine with its dependence on immigrants stands as the hidden target of criticism here; the voter appears as a puppet (see Figure 7). After 1910 these diminutive images of immigrants disappear and are replaced with caricatures of meetings between corporate bosses of all kinds and female antisuffragists (see Figure 8).

Local leaders adopted more inclusive strategies. Under its "State Correspondence" section for New York, the February 5, 1910, edition of the *Woman's Journal* announced "a colored woman suffrage mass meeting" at the "Mount Olivet Baptist Church" for that same day, which was to be attended by the noted white elite suffragist Mrs. Belmont and Mrs. Ella Hawley Crosset.[36] As Ellen DuBois also points out, in New York City elite women built several alliances with working-class women for suffrage reform.[37]

Chinese women entered the struggle after 1910. In its April 11, 1912, edition, the *New York Times* reported that a suffrage meeting had been held for Chinese women "in the Peking restaurant at Seventh Avenue."[38] Three days later a long article appeared describing Chinese women's plans to march in an upcoming suffrage parade.[39] American woman suffragists applauded the steps taken by the Tung Ming Hui. On March 30, 1912, the *Woman's Journal* published a front-page illustration that celebrated votes for Chinese women; on August 31, 1912, they reprinted a similar cartoon from the *Cleveland Plain Dealer* (see Figure 9).

In the Midwest, Illinois suffrage leader and sometime author Catherine Waugh McCulloch produced a suffrage comedy, *Bridget's Sisters,* to encourage cross-class alliances among women against the liquor interests and for female enfranchisement.[40] Although Bridget was stereotyped as an Irish washerwoman from whom a saloon-keeper sought payment for her husband's unpaid liquor bill, the message was that women of all classes and ethnicities had a common interest as mothers and home protectors.

As more people perceived woman suffrage as politically necessary and useful, the measure gained political acceptability, although it never garnered a popular majority nationally. Between 1906 and 1910, signs of a revived and strengthened push for political inclusion emerged: in 1908 the *Muller v. Oregon* decision marked the Supreme Court's acknowledgment of women's right both to earn and to receive protections as mothers.

A Crack in Modern Patriarchy: *Muller v. Oregon*

Most suffragists found much to celebrate in the Supreme Court's 1908 decision to legalize protective legislation in *Muller v. Oregon.* During the early Progressive era, many organized interests struggled to protect and preserve women's traditional primary role as mothers. Justice David J. Brewer, author of the opinion of the court in *Muller v. Oregon,* endorsed their arguments for protective legislation: the state could order reduced hours and regulate the conditions for women's labor to protect women's reproductive capacities. Undeniably, this decision allowed those who thought of women's reproductive capacities as marks of physical weakness to discriminate against women when hiring.[41] But Brewer's intention fulfilled many Progressives' aims to enable women to earn and to mother at the same time.

Muller was a major victory for Progressives, and woman suffragists soon reaped some benefits from the conversion of powerful men such as Brewer. In 1909 Brewer published an article in support of votes for women in *Ladies' World* that Alice Stone Blackwell later reprinted in the *Woman's Journal.* In this article Brewer asked, "Is not mother's love one of the strongest forces in a man's life?" He suggested that "woman's gentle touch" could do much to reform the administration of criminal law. Praising women's contribution to the settlement movement, he asked, "What man is doing more, if as much, for human betterment than Miss Jane Addams of Chicago?" Brewer both opposed military service as a qualification for suffrage and denied that the home barred women from working for their financial security. He asserted that "choice or necessity has driven [woman] into varied pursuits"; that the quality of children mattered more than the quantity; and that Adam and Eve, who were guilty of "mutual sin," were models for the work of men and women by "united labors."[42] Perhaps in gratitude to Brewer, suffragists appropriated his egalitarian image of Adam and Eve: an illustration that depicted this image, "Suffrage Means Success," later appeared in the *Woman's Journal.*[43]

By endorsing limited time at work for middle-class white women and thereby "protecting" their time at home, *Muller* eased the way for a suffrage victory. When challenged for threatening the home, suffragists could now argue that the Supreme Court had endorsed women's standing as both earners and mothers.[44] Although this decision is still controversial,[45] Theda Skocpol observes that at the time *Muller* helped open the door to maternalist social policies and illustrated how women could be considered both politically included and different from men.[46]

The Supreme Court's endorsement of protective legislation countered the antis' rigid views of women's roles with a more flexible vision. It also enhanced opportunities for professional and working-class women to unite with suffragists. Early on, suffragist nativism and racism had stood in the way of any such mass movement. But the opposition of Addams and Kelley to Shaw's nativism fostered multiethnic and cross-class mobilization. And in addition to the child labor question, another issue of protection for women united suffragists across region and ideology: prostitution, which white elite women labeled "white slavery."

"White Slavery" and Woman Suffrage Reform

Some social historians interpret the "white slavery scare" of the early twentieth century as an overreaction to the celebration of sexual freedom, particularly on the part of women, and to the passing of the more staid Victorian codes.[47] Although these scholars illuminate the rigidity of this era's middle-class sexual norms, they overlook how the opposition to prostitution also imposed limits upon what could be demanded of women in both the home and the workplace. Like *Muller,* the white slave scare represented demands for more appropriate protections for women.

Catt's major contribution to the mobilization of opinion against prostitution was her story about Li Po Ton. This story was widely reprinted during the twentieth century, which indicates that it had some power to gain attention for the suffrage cause.[48] Catt rarely raised this issue in public, but in her 1901 NAWSA address she named prostitution as one of three major obstacles to the political inclusion of women.[49]

Although Catt's denunciation of prostitution carried nativist innuendoes, Jane Addams produced *A New Conscience and an Ancient Evil* mainly to raise the awareness necessary to combat the sex trade in Chicago. Unlike Catt, Addams avoided making nativist or racist statements. Referring to prostitution as "commercialized vice" rather than "white slavery," she emphasized how the pervasiveness of the sex trade in Chicago meant that black and immigrant women could not live in the city without fearing it. Addams included accounts of French, Norwegian, and other women's encounters with "procurers," confirmed that young girls were kidnapped frequently, and described the particular vulnerability of "colored women" who recently moved to Chicago.

"Colored families," Addams reported, could not find housing in areas of the city other than those closest to the neighborhoods filled with "commercialized vice." Thus, colored girls found themselves assigned "in the capacity of domestic servants by unscrupulous employment agencies who would not venture to thus treat a white girl. The community forces the very people who have confessedly the shortest history of social restraint, into a dangerous proximity with the vice districts of the city. This results, as might easily be predicted, in a very large number of colored girls entering a disreputable life."[50] Addams did not urge a return to some pristine past. Instead she identified the obstacles that native-born black families faced in their struggle for freedom and denounced the toleration of commercialized vice, especially the luring of girls with false promises of well-paying, steady jobs.

She believed that once enfranchised, women would stop the worst abuses in these trades. Echoing Willard, Addams asserted, "If political rights were once given to women, if the situation were theirs to deal with as a matter of civic responsibility, one cannot imagine that the existence of the social evil would remain unchallenged in its semi-legal protection."[51]

Addams also reported that the United States had fallen behind other countries in the reform of commercialized vice. Norwegian women had obtained for every illegitimate child the right to inherit the father's name and property and had secured care for the mother. The age of consent was raised to eighteen in states where women had the vote, but only eight other states set the age of consent as high. Admitting that there was little hope for the complete eradication of prostitution, Addams insisted that enfranchised women would "offer some protection to the white slaves themselves" from arbitrary arrest and police examination without the presence of a matron.[52]

Jane Addams's account warned that the sex trade threatened all women and children, but her rhetoric lacked the negative stereotyping that Catt had used. Addams's call for the control of vice became a universal call for women to see themselves as equals across ethnic divides, equals as victims and as potential reformers of the political system's weak protections.

Black suffragists and southern white suffragists also vigorously opposed commercialized vice. Mary Church Terrell excoriated southern white women for "publicly proclaiming their coloured sister's immorality to the world in both the newspapers and leading periodicals of the North, while they gloat in ghoulish glee over her shame."[53] In a 1915 *Crisis* article "Black Women and Reform," N. H. Burroughs asserted, "The Negro woman is the white woman's as well as the white race's most needed ally in preserving an unmixed race . . . She needs the ballot to reckon with men who place no value upon her virtue, and to mold healthy public sentiment in favor of her own protection."[54]

Southern white suffragists viewed prostitution as a bulwark of gender inequality that required a change in attitudes about sexuality: "When men gave up the notion that women were created principally for their pleasure and need, when women outgrew this idea, when men and women received equal pay and achieved legal equality—only then, concluded one suffragist, would the question of the social evil be solved."[55] And if Jacquelyn Dowd Hall correctly interprets lynching as a system that reminded white women of their subordinate position and terrorized black men but preserved white men's sexual access to black women, it is difficult to imagine that southern white suffragists' opposition to prostitution wasn't a protest against this white male hypocrisy.[56]

Taken together, the liquor interests' power, political corruption, child labor, and "white slavery" proved to the suffragists that men neither protected women in the home nor protected society from dangerous evils. Following Willard, they judged men guilty of allowing the proliferation of vice. Of course the reformers pictured the votes of respectable women as a means for cleansing the political system of its worst negligence. Numerous cartoons published in the *Woman's Journal* between 1912 and 1914 display "white slavery" or the "white slaver" as an enemy to the suffrage cause[57] (see Figures 10 and 11).

These cartoons and their arguments strongly refuted antisuffragists' claims that votes for women represented an effort to destabilize society. But by calling prostitution "white slavery" and depicting only white women as its victims, reformers preserved their racial identities and, except for Addams, forgot that many black women also were prostitutes.

The appeals to stop postponing woman's suffrage emphasized that women celebrated their sexual difference from men but refused to accept their political powerlessness. In Michigan, suffragists answered claims that voting would threaten the family by arguing that the "radical change" in "American domestic conditions did not affect the natural instincts of woman. She was still the woman with the selfsame powers, capabilities and desires. The only difference was that today these functions found their expression under different conditions and under different auspices."[58] The suffragists even produced films to counter the negative stereotypes of women in Hollywood's silent films, which featured "man-hating suffragists, bumbling husbands, and confused children." The reformers' films, in contrast, encouraged audiences to think that enfranchised women would address the needs of "working women, tenement dwellers, and neglected children" by challenging political corruption but remaining thoroughly feminine. They promoted women as morally superior to men and dedicated primarily to marriage and family. Although these images reinforced gender stereotypes by portraying the reformers as publicly active women, they also fused women's traditional roles with new ones—of voting and making political policy.[59]

Suffragists did not hesitate to display the illogic of their opponents' formulations. For example, Tennessee reformers isolated antisuffragists' contradictory reasons for opposing the vote:

Because no woman will leave her domestic duties to vote.
Because no woman who votes will attend to her domestic duties.
Because it will make dissension between husband and wife.
Because every wife will vote exactly as her husband does.

In the oral presentation "Why We Oppose Women Traveling in Railway Trains," the suffragists knocked the antis' arguments with hilarious results: "Because traveling in trains is not a natural right. Because our great-grandmothers never asked to travel in trains. Because woman's place is in the home and not the train." Another presentation mocked both the exaggerations and underestimation of the vote: "The ballot is greatly over estimated. It has never done anything for anybody. Lots of men tell me this. And the corresponding argument is—the ballot is what makes man man. It is what gives him all his dignity and all of his superiority to woman. Therefore, if we allow women to share this privilege, how could a woman look up to her own husband?"[60]

After 1910 most national leaders avoided sharp, embarrassing clashes over white supremacy and immigrant-dominated urban political machines by focusing more intently on how women voters could advance social policies. Maternalistic reformers may not have needed the suffragists, but Kelley and Addams demonstrated that the suffragists needed the maternalists. Suffragists promoted legislation against child labor and prostitution as well as mothers' pensions, protective legislation for women in the workplace, and compulsory education. Socialist suffragists applauded this approach—after all, they had encouraged it in the first place—and they helped to secure legislative gains in Massachusetts and Wisconsin. They mobilized popular support for constitutional amendments in California, Montana, Oregon, Nevada, and New York. Only in New York did the socialist suffragists organize and recruit separately from the mainstream reformers.[61]

In Washington, which in 1910 became the first state to pass the measure since the Idaho victory in 1894, the Protestant clergy, State Federation of Labor, the Grange, and the Farmers' Union endorsed it. They used multiple arguments for woman suffrage, including republican maternalistic assertions that "fortunate women" are obliged to try to better conditions for "the many women who have no leisure and few comforts"; the nativist sentiment that enfranchised women would increase the "proportion of native-born electors"; the moralistic view that women would be sober when voting; and the more egalitarian, liberal view that "one sex should not undertake to make all the laws for another sex."[62]

The 1911 and 1914 campaigns in Montana were led by college-educated women such as the state's own first congresswoman, Jeannette Rankin. Montana suffragists promoted the vote as a means for women "to develop themselves" and gain "a stronger sense of social justice." Like the Massachusetts leaders, Montana reformers made alliances with labor unions and farmers. In this way, they promoted changes in economic and social policies such as "adequate labor standards," pure foods, public health regulations, peace, and the transformation of "a state orphan asylum into an experimental child care center." The nativist sentiments expressed by the reformers took on the character of Catt's view of comparative injustice: a Seattle suffragist told audiences of workers that she deserved "as much voice in the government . . . as does my Chinese laundryman who has been in this country only a few years." Montana reformers also publicized the collusion between antisuffragists and the liquor interests. Some eastern suffragists such as Irish laundry worker Margaret Hinchey traveled to Montana to mobilize popular support for the reform, which passed in November 1914.[63]

Ronald Schaffer argues that Progressive era woman suffragists began to win campaigns because male reformers and elected officials perceived them as potential aides in the passage of social policy reforms. By promoting social policy reforms, suffragists also enhanced the perception that women's political participation was necessary for good government. In Montana, women voters delivered on their promises, at least in the short run. In 1915 "the state legislature passed a workmen's compensation act, provided financial aid to dependent orphans, and set up a retirement fund for public school teachers. The following year a prohibition referendum was passed, and in 1917, the legislators established an eight-hour day for women workers and created penalties for men who did not support their families."[64]

In his study of thirty-seven women who led woman suffrage campaigns in California between 1897 and 1911, Schaffer identifies a mix of first- and second-generation suffragists who justified the reform as an equal rights aim, as a "social feminist"[65] measure that would increase the power of mothers in the family as well as in the public sphere, and as a "personal feminist" goal to assure women's "dignity and independence." California suffragists then tailored their appeals to suit the priorities of their audiences: rural women heard plays on the fear of urban corruption seeping into the countryside, and urban working women heard that with the vote they could obtain better labor standards. Because they had to win support from a heavily Catholic population, California suffragists "were also careful to screen out ideas that might upset certain ethnic and religious groups or alienate any large bloc of voters."[66] Like suffragists in other states, these leaders maintained strong ties with the state WCTU, and "the California Equal Suffrage Association set up committees on peace, child labor, education, and the white slave trade."[67]

In Kansas, Jane Addams spoke in favor of suffrage prior to the 1912 victory. A referendum campaign had failed there in 1894 largely because, as voters in municipal elections, Kansas women had partisan leanings and so were unable to conduct a nonpartisan campaign. By 1912 Kansas suffragists had made extra efforts to keep the campaign nonpartisan and to obscure the participation of their strongly prosuffrage state WCTU. Although she does not provide details of specific social policy reforms that Kansas suffragists promoted, Wilda M. Smith argues that the measure passed "because the voters had either been convinced of the justness of it as a part of the progressive reform sweeping the nation or they realized the granting of suffrage was the least the women would settle for."[68]

Steven M. Buechler appraises the Illinois suffragists' promotion of social policy reforms as a consequence of cross-class mobilization in general and Jane Addams's efforts in particular. By 1910 the Illinois suffragists had enrolled members from three subgroups: "the traditionally conservative club movement, working-class and immigrant women, and the urban-based, upper-class club movement." Each group "had its own reasons for wanting suffrage"; as a result, the campaigns for women's votes became fragmented.[69]

Despite their differences, the Illinois suffragists subsequently cooperated enough to win a legislative majority in favor of woman suffrage in presidential elections. Suffragists had identified a partial enfranchisement option under article 2, section 2 of the U.S. Constitution: "Each state shall appoint, in such Manner as the Legislature thereof may direct, a Number of Electors, equal to the whole number of Senators and Representatives to which the State may be entitled in the Congress." Eleanor Flexner argues that in 1913 Grace Wilbur Trout and Elizabeth Booth led a "carefully organized campaign" that was aided by prosuffrage Progressive Party legislators who held "the balance of power" and passed the measure. The Illinois victory added considerable momentum to the revived federal amendment campaign.[70]

Second-generation suffragists in Ohio established many local organizations between 1902 and 1906, and the state WCTU actively participated in organizing suffrage conventions. Between 1900 and 1910 Ohio reformers passed resolutions favoring legislative reform regarding "child labor, 'taxation without representation,' rights of labor, the 'social evil,' suppression of the 'white slave traffic,' nonpartisanship in politics, and abolition of the death penalty."[71] Karolena Fox argues that the passage of much protective legislation in Michigan under pressure from women but without their votes made female enfranchisement seem unnecessary; still, women won the vote in Michigan in 1918 and in Ohio in 1919.[72] In Wisconsin and Indiana women teachers revitalized the reform effort and tied women's votes to educational issues.[73]

In Connecticut, Wisconsin, and New Jersey, suffragists appealed to labor, farm groups, church societies, students, and women's clubs.[74] New Jersey suffragists argued that reforms such as the Eight Hour Law for working women, anti–child labor legislation, mothers' pensions, laws requiring equal pay for equal work, and laws that raised the age of consent for girls were more likely to be instituted in states where women voted.[75] In Connecticut, Katharine Houghton Hepburn and Katherine Beach Day introduced suffrage in Hartford by prodding local women "to abolish the white slave trade and prostitution in the city." Connecticut reformers established strong ties with organized labor, and they tied votes for women to "a wide range of issues, including child labor, prostitution, political corruption, and fair work standards."[76]

A powerful organization and vigorous leadership did not win women the vote in the state of New York in 1915. Schaffer argues that the effort was premature: the reformers had failed "to manufacture" enough supportive public opinion. The 1917 effort, however, which came on the tails of the U.S. entry into World War I, did succeed.[77] Historians believe that parades, protests, and jawboning about the war were crucial for the passage; the votes of an extraordinary number of eastern European Jewish men who valued equal voice for their wives also played a decisive role.[78]

In 1917, blatant nativist appeals to ensure that voters were "naturalized citizens" appear to have helped suffragists win the vote in South Dakota, a state with a large German-American population.[79] The South Dakota campaign was unusual in that it spotlighted nativist issues; Anne and Andrew Scott observe that the loss of six previous campaigns was due to "a mobilization of the alien vote by American-born political manipulators."[80]

Southern suffragists decided after 1910 to downplay white supremacy as a reason for the political inclusion of women. Despite many suffragists' loyalty to white supremacy, Marjorie Spruill Wheeler argues that many southern suffragists decided to rely on "the Progressive Movement rather than the disfranchisement movement." Southern white suffragists accused their opponents of using race to "trump up" charges against them when the suffragists supported votes for black women or revived efforts to enforce the Fourteenth and Fifteenth Amendments. Some of these woman suffrage leaders—Mary Johnston and Lila Valentine in Virginia, Pattie Rufner Jacobs in Alabama, and Sue White in Tennessee—actually did oppose the disenfranchisement measures and the denial of voting rights to qualified blacks, but they kept silent in public. Not unlike some southern blacks, they followed "Booker T. Washington's 'Atlanta Compromise,'" in which the "advocacy of the health and welfare of Southern blacks was tolerated" but the "advocacy of their rights was not."[81]

Aileen Kraditor persuasively argues that the southern reformers' enthusiasm for the states' rights strategy reveals their predominantly racist motives because the secretaries of most state organizations admitted in a 1916 NAWSA survey that "the Negro problem" impeded victories. But Wheeler makes an equally compelling case that the states' rights strategy was pursued because some white leaders considered it their most appropriate path. They wanted to show the nation that they could persuade "the men of their states to enfranchise them and thereby formally recognize female equality, individuality, and desirability as voters—a situation they considered infinitely preferable to being enfranchised through federal coercion."[82]

In her study of the campaigns in Alabama, Mary Martha Thomas confirms that reformers did not let their defense of white supremacy overwhelm their efforts after 1910. Nellie Kimball Murdock, an officer in the Birmingham association, also chaired the Alabama Child Labor Committee, which pushed suffragists to promote their cause as a means to fight child labor. The state convention in 1914 "adopted resolutions favoring other women's issues: paying women equally with men for equal work, establishing an eight-hour day and minimum wage for women, making mothers co-guardians with fathers, and raising the age of consent from twelve years to twenty-one years." Jane Addams attended an executive meeting shortly thereafter and encouraged Alabama suffragists "to work for suffrage in order to abolish child labor."[83]

Massachusetts reformers also adapted British suffragists' militant tactics, relied on organized labor, and applied Catt's precinct method of organization to Boston. Although they failed to pass a suffrage amendment, these reformers achieved what the first generation had been unable to do: in 1914 and 1915 they managed to obtain the support of two successive legislatures. This success constituted crucial groundwork for the Nineteenth Amendment, which was ratified by a large margin in Massachusetts in 1919.[84]

Tennessee suffragists concentrated on social policy reforms supported by women as well as on winning endorsements from labor unions and professional associations such as the state bar association. In 1915 reformers also persuaded both houses of the state legislature to pass a state constitutional amendment for woman suffrage. Tennessee's rules for passing a state constitutional amendment were the same as in Massachusetts. The amendment was defeated in 1916, but the effort served as an important warm-up for the 1919 ratification of the Nineteenth Amendment.[85]

Most of the state amendment campaigns failed. But the successes between 1910 and 1917 indicate that victories depended on two accomplishments: building hierarchical but open organizations, and making alliances with organized interests such as labor and farm lobbies and social policy reformers. By focusing on the vote as their primary aim but portraying women voters as supporters of multiple policy objectives, the suffragists won an adequate base of native-born, educated, elite white male support. Their imitation of party machine structures also helped the suffragists to win party officials' support or to beat them at their own games.

Numerous campaign failures revealed how strong popular resistance to the idea of women voting still was. Joseph F. Mahoney's statistical study of the failed referendum campaign in New Jersey in 1915 indicates that immigrant voters were no more likely to oppose or support the measure than were native-born American voters. For example, votes for women won 47.1 percent of the vote in Passaic, a city that "had the highest percentage of naturalized voters and which ranked third in immigrant-related voters."[86]

Thus, numerous white male voters opposed the political inclusion of women just as they had opposed the enfranchisement of black men during

Reconstruction. That opposition led the suffragists to concentrate on winning a federal amendment and to hope that elected representatives would show more tolerance and dedication to their liberal aims than the voters at large. After 1917, armed with 339 electoral votes from "female suffrage states," the reformers made their final successful drive for the vote.

The Federal Amendment Campaign, 1910–1920

Eileen McDonagh suggests that reformers' linking of suffrage to social policy instead of to the superior qualifications of educated, native-born white women reaped success: between 1911 and 1915 victories for suffrage in popular votes in the West, Midwest, and East correlated with "educational commitment" and prohibition.[87] Before reformers could persuade elected federal representatives to support votes for women, they needed a core constituency from states that already had passed the measure as well as realistic possibilities for passing the measure in Congress. Such opportunities evaporated after the Republicans gained control of Congress in 1894; not until after the challenge from the Progressive Party in 1912 and the disintegration of Speaker Joseph G. Cannon's power base in the House did the factional disputes within both political parties improve access to legislative leadership and intensify competition for agenda setting.[88]

The revolt against Cannon removed from the Speaker of the House the power to appoint or extend tenure on committees beyond one year: "The new rules provided that all members of the standing committees, including their chairmen, would be elected by the House, at the commencement of each Congress." The separation of "party" from the position of Speaker was followed by each party's election of a caucus chair, a floor leader, and party whips. These reforms weakened the boss system within Congress and gave organized interests new electoral opportunities to set the federal policy agenda.[89] Woman suffragists also gained much when Champ Clark, a Democrat from Missouri and future supporter of woman suffrage, was elected Speaker of the House.

The Senate was also an arena of reform in 1911 when Nelson Aldrich, the most powerful member of the Senate, retired: "With the departure of . . . dynamic leaders from the Chamber, power was fragmented within the parties. It became common for both Republicans and Democrats to elect a different floor leader in each session, and the floor leadership did not necessarily correspond with the caucus chairmanship. Under these conditions, party unity was hard to maintain."[90] Subsequently, issue-based, bipartisan congressional coalitions legislated the income tax, direct election of senators, prohibition, the Clayton Anti-Trust Act, the Federal Reserve and Federal Trade Commission Acts, and woman suffrage.

The American woman suffragists' federal amendment victory was predicated upon these reforms in Congress, but the suffragists did not take immediate advantage of them. From 1910 to 1915 they continued to concentrate on winning state victories. There were eight successive state victories between 1910 and 1915 as well as fifteen additional successes between 1915 and 1919.

Multiple Ideologies in the Federal Amendment Campaign

Among second-generation NAWSA leaders, Carrie Chapman Catt stood out as the major proponent of the federal amendment over the state-by-state method for female enfranchisement. In 1900, before a Senate committee, she presented a speech entitled "Why We Ask for the Submission of an Amendment." In this speech she identified "custom" as the main impediment to woman suffrage but singled out liberal aims as its impetus. Changes in women's lives, she argued, "have not come because women wished for them or men welcomed them. A liberal board of trustees, a faculty willing to grant a trial, an employer willing to experiment, a broad-minded church willing to hear a woman preach, a few liberal souls in a community willing to hear a woman speak—these have been the influences which have brought the changes." She regretted, however, that "the interest of party" and "personal ambition for place" often barred approval of controversial issues by "men of higher standing and more liberal opinion." For this reason, she urged NAWSA to campaign mainly for a federal amendment.[91]

Between 1908 and the formal launching of the federal amendment campaign in 1914, NAWSA reformers disagreed about its importance. Southern suffragists, for example, resisted this method until many realized that in most southern states they had little hope of winning the reform.[92] Despite these disagreements, and before she became president of NAWSA for a second time, Catt laid the groundwork for a renewed national federal amendment campaign.

Catt's first public step to rebuild this campaign consisted of a speech to the U.S. Senate in 1910. At the time of the Constitution's passage and ratification, she observed, religious qualification was dropped to facilitate the inclusion of "Catholic Maryland," "Quaker Pennsylvania," and "Congregational Massachusetts" in a single nation. In addition to their passing an inclusive naturalization law in 1790, she suggested that the founders shared an understanding that "citizenship should carry with it the right to vote." Immigrant men found advocates in "political parties and statesmen," and "their enfranchisement was made easy by state constitutional action." But woman suffragists were forced to prove themselves worthy of the vote. "Ordinary fair play," she maintained, "should compel every believer in democracy and individual liberty, no matter what are his views on woman suffrage, to grant to women the easiest process of enfranchisement and that is the submission of Federal Amendment."[93]

In a 1915 appeal to the Senate, Catt reiterated these points. To become enfranchised, no group of men had had to sustain a long-term struggle. Women, by comparison, had held innumerable meetings, circulated thousands of pamphlets, raised much money, and spent many hours at the polls. Their latest referendum campaign in New York State, Catt asserted, was defeated by their opponents, who had been "aided and abetted by the weak-minded and illiterate," including "the male inmates of the almshouse and rescue home" as well as male drunkards. Because many states required a voter referendum for the ratification of amendments to state constitutions, Catt added a plea that the reformers not be forced to win support from majorities of the masses of male voters. Catt stated, "Even the Federal Amendment is difficult enough, with ratification of 36 Legislatures required, but we may at least appeal to a higher class of men."[94]

In these appeals Catt ignored the disenfranchisement of both black and native-born white men in most southern states. She overlooked the fears that propertyless white men had of disenfranchisement during the Jacksonian era. And she sidestepped the fact that ethnic party machines, especially in big cities, had emerged as a kind of reform movement from within led by politically included but economically and socially excluded men as their way of obtaining and protecting civil rights. Catt's call for a federal amendment banked upon the likelihood that most elected representatives in Congress and the state legislatures were native-born, Protestant white males who already considered themselves culturally superior to Catholics, Jews, and immigrants. The applause and regard that Catt achieved during the final stage of the suffrage movement confirm that she correctly appraised the kind of appeals that would win over her audience of senators.

Catt's description of her hopes for the Woman Suffrage Party previewed the single-minded commitment that distinguished her leadership and her "Winning Plan." Catt promoted her design, which imitated the political party machine's structure and demands for loyalty, as the "plan of work . . . which men have evolved after a century of political experience as the best one for campaign purposes." She asked, in highly republican language (quite a change from her more nativistic personal development appeals), whether men and women would

> overlook the non-essentials in their loyalty to the one essential—a united whole; will they sink personality in service to the great cause? These things time must tell us. Is it possible for a "machine" to remain operative which has no "bosses," no "graft," no personal rewards to offer, and whose sole motor power is self-sacrificing, conscientious service to a noble cause? Time must answer. I believe the appointed time has come for New York women, and I believe they will take their places and nobly do their duty by this great cause.[95]

Catt's efforts to sustain reformers' primary interest in winning the vote distinguish her as the central leader of what had become feminist entrepreneurial tactics. Beginning with Harriot Stanton Blatch's endeavors in New York City in 1910, suffragists had pressured candidates before elections in order to create alliances with men who responded affirmatively and put pressure on those who expressed ambivalence or opposition. Blatch urged suffragists to ask each party leader and voter the simple question: Do you support woman suffrage? In 1914 Alice Paul's Congressional Union, later renamed The Woman's Party, formally announced its efforts to oppose candidates whose parties, such as the Democrats, refused to endorse woman suffrage. Paul's organization collaborated with a massive petition campaign to force the Anthony amendment onto Congress's agenda. Even though the amendment failed, both the Senate and the House of Representatives brought the issue to their floors in 1914. Suffragists kept track of their congressional supporters and opponents; they passed this information back to local suffrage organizations.[96]

Feminist entrepreneurship involved advancing woman suffrage onto the national government agenda. Some of its methods, however, clashed with egalitarian ideals. The protests Alice Paul organized against President Wilson's campaign for "democracy in the world"—on the grounds that women lacked "democracy at home"—sustained egalitarian themes. Less egalitarian was the 1916 NAWSA convention members' silent pleading for President Wilson to endorse votes for women.[97] Both delivered the message that women wanted the vote, but the methods of conveying it had become more important than the implications of the message itself.

Although the more cautious NAWSA did not endorse Paul's strident tactics, its leaders imitated their methods between 1915 and 1919. They prepared their "front door" lobbyists—"front door" distinguished woman suffragists from prostitutes used by "backdoor" lobbies—to cultivate and monitor support for the federal amendment in Congress. The approach was public, strictly nonpartisan, and geared to keep the issue alive: lobbyists were to learn the biographies of representatives, how each member stood on the issue, and the name of his secretary, and to listen politely when approaching him on the issue. Moreover, the lobbyists were not to take notes in the offices or halls, not *ever* to lose one's temper and most important of all, to "hold each interview confidential."

Behind this appearance of deference to the representative, however, lobbyists were told to monitor closely each representative's response. The "Directions for Lobbyists" included the following: "Be sure to keep his *party* constantly in mind while talking with him . . . Do find opportunity to make notes on one interview before starting another. If necessary, step into the 'Ladies' dressing room to do this." In addition, the lobbyists skillfully approached each and every congressman and senator, usually with a suffragist from his region, if not his district. Meanwhile, the coordinators tabulated the lobbyists' information precisely; the lobby's ability to increase pressure and support thereby improved. Although southern legislators represented the region most opposed to the measure, Maud Wood Park credits the southern suffragists for demonstrating lobbying tactics that subdued the opposition.[98]

In Congress, NAWSA lobbying began in the House of Representatives. Eventually, the suffragists were able to coordinate actions by the speaker, party floor leaders, and whips. A cue group was established in "the house: the seventeen 'members . . . counted as . . . most active friends' agreed to insure that the promised voters for the suffrage committee, were all in the House at critical moments. An Ohio Republican, for example, had charge of Republican votes . . . in his own and a neighboring state; and a Colorado Democrat looked after our Democratic votes in three states."[99]

In 1917 the NAWSA lobby expanded the "cue" group into an informal steering committee for the amendment within the House. Confident that such a body would be of inestimable assistance, the lobbyists' hopes were ultimately vindicated: "It proved to be the one group in our Congressional experience in which members of both parties worked harmoniously for the interests of woman suffrage and in which we never found an instance of politics played for personal or party advantage."[100]

More divisive party politics in the Senate precluded the formation of an informal steering committee among its members. Faced with coordination across party lines, the lobbyists set up their own steering committee by selecting party representatives from among themselves.[101]

Despite these extensive networks, the suffragists could not control the bill in the Senate when it reached the point of debate and vote. The issue was repeatedly subordinated to party competition, with Republicans claiming to be more supportive of the measure than Democrats. Even though President Woodrow Wilson urged Democrats to support votes for women, southern Democrats managed to keep the reform at bay from 1916 to late 1918, the year when the Democrats lost control of Congress. As David Morgan observes, the suffragists' mobilization against northern Democrats as payment for the southern wing's opposition to woman suffrage contributed notably to the new Republican majorities. At a special session of Congress called in May 1919, the Republicans proudly flaunted a "moral victory" in light of the southern Democratic senators' refusal to make woman suffrage an indisputably bipartisan measure. Both the House and the Senate easily passed the measure and sent it to the state legislatures on June 4, 1919.[102]

For its success, the suffragists' "front door lobby" depended upon and exacted support from state and local suffrage organizations. Without grassroots reformers to send letters and delegations and to pressure state representatives to intervene with national representatives, the lobby would not have been taken seriously. Park explained this dependence: "The function of a lobby such as ours is many-sided. It must translate public opinion to legislators in terms that they will understand. Then it must report to workers in the legislative districts the advisable next step to get or to hold a favorable vote. Most important of all, the lobby must discover friends in public office who will work actively for the success of the cause and keep those friends on the job without annoying them by too much prodding."[103]

Certainly the lobby succeeded largely because positions such as the Speaker of the House and Majority Leader of the Senate had become weakened. The NAWSA lobby in Congress consolidated a vanguard of supporters in the House that shepherded the amendment from committee to the floor and from house to house until it passed. They also used this federally structured grassroots organization to ensure the amendment's ratification. In 1929, E. Pendleton Herring remarked that twentieth-century suffragists "blazed the way for the lobbying organizations in the capital."[104]

Conclusion:
A Liberal Feminist Legacy

*A*FTER THE Nineteenth Amendment had been secured, Carrie Chapman Catt celebrated liberal principles in a speech that blamed the founders' toleration of slavery for both the failure of many southern states to endorse votes for women and the struggle's long duration. Catt excoriated the founders of the American republic for their lack of courage, particularly their unwillingness to condemn slavery in the Declaration of Independence—a mistake that also flawed the Constitution of the United States. Defending "the Negro" as "the innocent victim who has been wronged at every turn," Catt exploded in anger at the continued repudiation of "social equality" by both the North and the South. In self-congratulation for having overruled southerners' use of "the mask of states' rights" to prevent national progress, Catt exclaimed, "I thank God that there was a *federal* way of extending political liberalism to the splendid glorious women of the South."[1] And she encouraged the suffragists to preserve their shared commitments to solve "great problems" despite their many differences:

> Let us, daughters of North and South, East and West, take a vow today that as we have labored understandably together with confidence in each other, so will we aim together to meet the great problems of our day when they are due in order that ours may be a nation loyally honored by every man and woman in it. We may vote different tickets, indeed we may support many parties; but if we are true to this idea: 'never allow a real problem to be neglected,' we shall not be far apart.[2]

By calling on women to be sentinels for liberal principles that American men had not lived up to, Catt idealistically envisioned women voters as a moral check on men's political proclivities to evade "real problems." She recognized, however, that real "differences" among women, based on party and regional loyalties, would compete with women's political identities as women. The slogan "never allow a real problem to be neglected" reminded women of slavery and their own political exclusion. Civil rights goals, Catt implied, ought to unite women despite other political differences.

Catt's bold statement of contempt for American traditions of political exclusion, particularly the toleration of slavery, departed sharply from her single-issue focus on winning the vote, particularly for educated, native-born white women. Participation in the suffrage movement transformed Catt, and her later comments indicate that she regretted using exclusionary tactics such as ethnically disparaging remarks, racial segregation, and elitist sentiments. Many immigrants and blacks probably did not find Catt's argument redeeming.

Still Catt struck an egalitarian theme in this speech, one that echoed Jane Addams's, Harriot Stanton Blatch's, and Florence Kelley's appeals for the vote for women. In their view, woman suffrage was needed both to invest women's unique resources in the public sphere and to protect their ability to maintain home and family. To win the vote, these leaders had relied on expedient tactics. In addition to racial segregation, nativism, and the exploitation of woman suffragists in unions, the reform leaders had accepted that most men could not be persuaded to consider women as equals. By just arguing that women should have the right to vote, the suffragists avoided considering whether and how winning the vote would enable women to overcome the most debilitating aspects of second-class citizenship.

Scholars have long debated the political significance of the Nineteenth Amendment. Anne Firor Scott and Andrew MacKay Scott interpret the amendment as an entitlement that women should have as citizens in a democracy: "If one accepts the central democratic principle, consent of the governed, then women should have the vote and participate in the decisions of the government under which they live. All other arguments are secondary."[3] Seeing the lack of change generated by the Nineteenth Amendment, however, William O'Neill and Judith Shklar make striking criticisms of the measure. O'Neill argues that women's lack of attention to a postsuffrage reform agenda made the victory hollow: "If the ballot had not meant so much to suffragists, if they had truly cared more about the social ends which the vote was supposed to facilitate, they would not have let themselves become so carried away by momentary passions."[4] Shklar observes, "The real irony was that because women had adopted the dominant attitudes of their time and place so completely, their final victory led to no noticeable political change at all."[5]

Truth is on both sides of this debate. As residents of a nominally democratic nation, all politically excluded groups had strong incentives to seek the vote. That educated, native-born, white women—taught to see their race and class as superior—felt compelled to put winning the vote ahead of social policy reform or fundamental economic change is not surprising. But dwelling on suffragists' toleration of political inequality and the movement's failure to generate "noticeable change" overshadows less noticeable but important strides, such as the development of women's political confidence, the formulation of alternative conceptions of citizenship, and most importantly, women's victory over the tyrannical majority opinion.

Few people agreed with the radical egalitarian premise that, despite sex differences, women and men were naturally equal and thus required political equality. Many continued to believe that sex differences were marks of a natural inequality that provided a foundation for political inequality. The middle and most popular concept confounded the suffragists: the genders were naturally equal despite sex differences (for example, most members of religious denominations considered men and women equal as God's creatures), but this natural equality did not justify political equality. According to this viewpoint, sex differences gave men and women different abilities for maintaining the social order: women were best able to nurture and preserve order in the home, whereas men were best suited for protecting and preserving the public order. The inclination of most political theorists and citizens to adopt such complex and nuanced premises as these was the biggest hurdle for woman suffragists. Clarion calls to support political equality for women could not erase the fact of biological sex differences, a historic division of life's labors, or knowledge about how to perform tasks that had been defined by gender.

To win votes for women, reform leaders had to participate in a double struggle familiar to leaders of most interest groups: first, to learn leadership skills and to recruit and keep active a core of suffragists across the nation; and second, to persuade skeptical audiences that women both deserved and were qualified to vote. To recruit members who would stay, woman suffragists had to envision how the vote would improve women's lives. But to make headway on a legislative agenda and convert male voters, woman suffrage leaders had to calm fears of unexpected change and promote votes for women as unthreatening, simple justice.

Because resistance to the idea that women could be politically equal to men was so strong, social reformers such as Frances Willard and Jane Addams were more effective mobilizers of popular support for woman suffrage than were the woman suffragists. By drawing attention to the cruelties many women suffered at the hands of drunken men, Frances Willard overcame the limitations of her predecessors and portrayed the vote as a means for women to achieve power and protection. Building upon her view that God had graced women with the moral authority that grew out of mother-love, Willard fashioned a radical vision of women leading a social and political revolution that would integrate women into the political arena and men into the home. Willard's feminism of fear produced expectations that good mothers ought to be full citizens and that as full citizens women would set a new standard for good citizenship.

By 1910 Blatch, Addams, and Kelley had mobilized a mass base of supporters, and it was less necessary to envision the changes women needed and could achieve through voting. Because the final decade of struggle was devoted almost exclusively to winning a place for woman suffrage on legislative agendas and passing the measure, leaders such as Catt used the safest political tactics: a single-issue focus, nonpartisan and patriotic appeals, one-on-one lobbying, and organized parades.

O'Neill follows Aileen Kraditor in making overdrawn distinctions about the implications of these reformers' use of expediency during the latter stage of the suffragist movement (as opposed to its early phase, when principle and moral reform prevailed). From the start of the woman's rights movement, both justice and expediency mattered and sometimes leaders made difficult trade-offs between them. But none of these elements was ever fully sacrificed for any of the others. Some leaders such as Catt may have been less than "good persons" at times, but successful political reform often requires exactly that.[6]

These overdrawn distinctions have generated false dichotomies obscuring the ideological change and complex conflicts that occurred among second-generation reformers. The ideological change was the most prominent feature: most second-generation leaders who put suffrage first developed a new basis for consensus—not for congruent consciousnesses—in order to respond to members' overlapping interests in suffrage. For example, personal development mattered to the post-Willard WCTU leaders, but they promoted educational qualifications for the vote that leaders such as Harriot Stanton Blatch opposed. Jane Addams resisted making the vote's exclusive purpose personal development, but she defended the vote as necessary for the practice of republican motherhood in new, intensively interdependent urban communities. By arguing that women's support for compulsory education, protective legislation, and other "maternalist" social welfare reforms would cultivate suffrage allies among working-class male voters, Florence Kelley bridged urban republican motherhood and the feminism of personal development.

Rather than distinguish woman suffrage reformers' arguments and strategies as principled versus expedient, it makes more sense to identify the appeals targeted to win approval from different audiences. Garrison's blend of the liberalism of equal rights with images of republican mothers performing public service drew egalitarian-minded women into abolitionist efforts and helped to engender the feminism of equal rights. The feminism of equal rights nourished Stanton, Anthony, Stone, Blackwell, as well as a number of socialist and liberal feminists who campaigned for suffrage during the twentieth century. This ideology also grabbed the attention of radical Republicans, who constituted a minority of suffrage supporters in Congress and the state legislatures after Reconstruction.

Willard's blend of a feminism of fear with symbols of republican motherhood and Americanist ideas of true civilization mobilized hundreds of thousands of women for temperance reform and diminished fears women had about political participation in general and the vote in particular. In the Colorado woman suffrage campaign of 1893, reformers used Willard's pointed questions about women's need for self-protection and worth as mothers to win support.

Each mobilization effort for the political inclusion of women reveals the short distance between principle and expediency in a political reform movement. Garrison defended woman's rights as much for women's participation in his movement as for his belief in equal rights. Stanton's desire to recruit female supporters prompted her effort to convert temperance reformers to woman's rights with nativist symbolism in the early 1850s. Stanton failed, but Frances Willard's sophisticated ideological trickery mobilized vast numbers of women for temperance reform and moderated the opposition to the idea of women voting.

Through her story about Li Po Ton, which blended the feminism of fear with the feminism of personal development, Carrie Chapman Catt aimed to unite women across class, region, and ethnicity. Drawing on Willard's ideology but attaching it to urban problems, Jane Addams cast a model for urban republican mothers as activists rather than spectators or men's advisors. None of these leaders appears to have ever given serious thought to the exclusive use of principle to achieve political reform. Instead, each invoked principle carefully as a powerful means to achieve concrete collective action gains: recruitment, agenda setting, or popular support.

Until they won the federal amendment, women depended upon men for every legislative advance of their cause. It is difficult to imagine just how powerless women were without the vote. No elected official had to listen to *any* woman's suggestion for legislative reform. Woman suffragists learned that it was politically unwise to rely on a single group of men, even if the men were dedicated to egalitarian goals.

The alliances that Colorado woman suffragists forged between the WCTU, the Farmers' Alliance, the Knights of Labor, and the Colorado People's Party established a coalition powerful enough to obtain votes for women. But some Colorado suffragists subsequently hastened the coalition's disintegration through their participation in the Republican Party. Thus, suffragists used the Populists' egalitarian rhetoric to achieve short-term electoral aims. They had to cooperate with organized interests and political parties at least until they achieved necessary legislative gains.

The short-term character of suffrage coalitions continued into the twentieth century partly because of women's multiple political identifications: women saw themselves as belonging to the Socialists, Republicans, Democrats, Prohibitionists, or Progressives as much as to the suffrage movement. Many clearly identified themselves as members of the white middle or upper class even more than as women. But these multiple identifications grew in importance largely because suffrage leaders in the twentieth century calculated that women could not win the vote unless they exploited their ties to and indirect memberships in political parties and other organized interests that could legislate suffrage.

The resistance to the idea of men sharing political power with women led Catt and other organized suffrage leaders to manipulate institutional structures of power and act expediently. If they had not done so, and had stubbornly insisted upon converting a large majority of citizens to considering women as men's equals, women might still lack voting rights. The eleventh-hour defeat of the most recent equal rights amendment campaign revealed that deep institutionalized opposition still works against the conception of women as men's political equals.[7]

The liberal feminist ideologies of equal rights, fear, and personal development enabled woman's rights and woman suffrage leaders to mobilize different groups at different times. With the feminism of equal rights, Garrisonian women established woman's rights and woman suffrage as critical goals for liberal reformers who wanted to overcome the subordination of women in the home, workplace, school, and church. With the feminism of fear, Frances Willard awakened many women's consciousnesses about the usefulness of suffrage to protect themselves, their children, and families from the cruelties caused by drunken men. With the feminisms of personal development, Catt, Addams, and other leaders justified women's multiple agendas and affirmed multifaceted political aims without imposing one model of citizenship or policy platform on women. By insisting that the personal development and protection of each depended on guaranteed rights for the personal development and protection of all, reformers such as Addams, Florence Kelley, and a host of American socialists fashioned an egalitarian blend of the feminisms of fear and personal development. These leaders reintroduced egalitarian principles into their arguments: guarantees such as the right to vote, the eight-hour day, and anti–child labor laws were necessary to ensure the personal development of all citizens. This was a weaker egalitarian argument than the Garrisonians' vision of inclusive equality, but it also was compatible with the illiberal but securely established traditions of meritocracy, republican motherhood, and racial segregation.

Despite their use of conservative tactics, many suffragists—particularly those converted to the cause by Addams, Willard, Kelley, and the socialists—would have perceived the Nineteenth Amendment as egalitarian. They would have celebrated the transfer of electoral power into women's hands also as a victory for women: women won the vote without relinquishing their political identities as morally conscientious citizens who needed and deserved special protections for their unique motherly contributions. To these women, the Nineteenth Amendment, like the Fourteenth and Fifteenth Amendments, provided a Constitutional foundation for potentially radical change.

Such change was elusive in 1920, owing to the formidable ideological and organizational opposition to the political inclusion of women. When the federal amendment passed, only thirteen states had passed a constitutional amendment for woman suffrage, and thirteen more state legislatures had instituted laws that allowed women to vote only in presidential elections.[8] Eleanor Flexner implied that the movement's success owed much to the exceptional leadership acumen of Carrie Chapman Catt. But two suffrage organizations had been rapidly established in the 1870s by women who possessed strong leadership skills. Local suffrage organizations continued to emerge throughout the nation; many suffragists made hundreds of legislative appeals that were blocked or defeated.

The suffragists lacked neither organization nor leadership. They lost many more legislative efforts than they won because of the deep opposition to their cause and the formidable barriers to putting such a controversial liberal reform issue on any government agenda in the United States. Catt admitted that the advantage of a federal amendment campaign was that it allowed reformers to bypass voter referenda: she realized that men elected to office were more disposed than male voters at large to support political inclusion for women. When women won the vote, they gained the right to use it as self-interested citizens to achieve their goals. But they still faced the task of persuading men that they should listen to women's concerns.

The peculiarities of agenda-setting procedures—especially the criteria for legislative passage and the conflicts within and between political parties over agenda priorities—shaped the timing of gains for woman suffrage reform. As John Kingdon explains, the high hurdles of widespread acceptability and partisan expediency must be overcome before any reform issue reaches a government agenda.

Proponents of woman suffrage found it difficult to overcome these obstacles. In 1893, the efforts of the third-party Populists to hold on to power gave Colorado suffragists the opportunity to win a voter referendum. By 1920 woman suffragists had won as many state victories for presidential suffrage as constitutional amendments because the former reform required only the endorsement of state legislatures, not the approval of a majority of voters in a statewide referendum.

These hurdles to agenda setting forced woman suffragists to deradicalize their demands and promises. Just before the 1893 victory in Colorado, suffragists warned against overly moralistic rhetoric or inflated promises and urged reformers to "just be women" seeking a measure of justice. Maud Wood Park reported that suffrage lobbyists in Congress avoided confrontations with opponents that would elicit public statements against the reform. Catt's guidelines for mobilizing voter support in New York City avoided appeals for women's political freedom and urged reformers to concentrate voters' attention on women's contributions to the community. These careful, conservative tactics were designed to thwart or deter victory by antisuffragists. Such tactics should not, however, obscure the radical character or potential of the transformation of women from a politically excluded to an included group. Woman suffragists did what was necessary to put their issue on government agendas; they did not ignore purposeful uses women would make of their votes.

The determination of both opponents of woman suffrage and supporters recruited by Willard and Addams to emphasize the differences between women and men explains why it was easier for women to make political gains by calling for protection or by offering their unique talents to politics than by demanding equality. From the 1920s to the late 1960s, proponents of protective legislation made headway much faster than supporters of the equal rights amendment. Protective legislation recognized gender differences and affirmed women's right to participate in the workforce without exploitation. But in 1920 supporters of equality for women by protection of difference could not see that by itself the right to vote would not provide women with the kind of equal protection they hoped for.

Although many voters, along with the southern "states' rights" suffragists, perceived the victory of the Nineteenth Amendment as a radical step forward, many Americans probably did not share this sentiment. For instance, most men in elective office knew that they could deter women from candidacy for elective office. It would not have been difficult to use the logic that Chief Justice Morrison Waite used in *Minor v. Happersett* to distinguish citizenship from voting. If women could be citizens but lack the right to vote, then women could win the right to vote but still lack full citizenship, which includes equal access to candidacy for office, equal rights to work, and equal respect for personal choice and political participation. The logic of *Minor* could and has continued to be used to enforce women's second-class citizenship.[9]

The shift of woman suffragists' focus away from equality and toward meritocratic aims strikes many as the transformation of a potentially radical reform movement into a cause of narrow self-interest. But to perceive women's struggle for the vote as a sellout by a privileged group is to forget that until 1920 most women in the United States, from the richest to the poorest, lacked an independent political voice. To transform women from a politically excluded group into an included group, reform leaders had to make careful distinctions between their purpose (which always had radical potential) and the more conservative strategies and tactics they designed to achieve it. By winning support with meritocratic arguments, nativist sentiments, and upper-class chauvinism, many Progressive era suffragists revealed the limits of their commitment to equality. Their limitations, however, do not alter the fact that the Nineteenth Amendment gave all women the right to vote and hold office. This victory set the stage for potential uses of electoral power by women, most of which still remain to be seen.

True, woman suffrage was deradicalized as a reform aim. The allegiance of its first promoters to the practice and principles of inclusive equality within the Garrisonian abolitionist movement tied the idea of votes for women to one of the most ambitious agendas for liberal democratic social reform ever seen in the United States. After the Civil War, this group's utopian strategies for change through conscience faded away; their consensus that Constitutional amendments had become a more appropriate means for achieving political inclusion signaled a conservative turn toward institutional deference. Stanton's derogatory remarks about the easy enfranchisement of new male immigrants and former male slaves, along with Henry Blackwell's pandering to southern racism, introduced a middle-class voice of self-righteous condescension into the suffrage movement. Such arguments portrayed votes for women as the cause of fearful, excluded intellectuals who considered themselves superior and who lacked commitment to political equality beyond proving that the "qualified" deserved the vote as much as did the "unqualified."

Woman suffrage depended much on the reformers' manipulation of illiberal values, particularly those regarding perceptions of women. Opponents of woman's rights and woman suffrage trumpeted expectations that if women became voters the family would disintegrate; femininity would be lost; God's will would be subverted; and the best, most reliable models of goodness would vanish. When they tolerated white supremacy, advocated educational qualifications for the vote, spoke derisively about immigrants, and imposed elite republican ideals of personal achievement, woman suffragist leaders revealed the limits of their commitment to inclusive equal rights. The consensus between reform leaders and their opponents that native-born whites should govern the United States delimits how far even the most liberal reformers stood from a consistent application of their ideals.

The sovereignty of the U.S. Constitution made the Nineteenth Amendment a sterling victory, but it also imposed women's equal citizenship on those who opposed this reform. It is worth remembering that suffragists won only eleven state constitutional amendments. In the thirteen states where they won presidential suffrage and the two that gave women the vote for primary elections, the reformers won the support of state legislators, not endorsements from majorities of male voters. Woman suffrage represented, therefore, a reform created mainly by political elites. The Nineteenth Amendment encouraged but by no means guaranteed women political equality in their precincts, political parties, and local or state governments.

After 1920, women could vote. They had earned their membership. But the struggle for full political inclusion had just begun. Still unfinished was the struggle of women for political office, for respect of women and children's rights in policy making, for equal participation in decision-making even after they won office, and for power to set political and governmental agendas. These struggles, most of which still remain unfinished, constitute the legacy of suffragists' liberal visions.

Notes

Index

Notes

Abbreviations

Archives, UC, Boulder   Archives, University of Colorado at Boulder Libraries, Boulder, Colorado

Blackwell MSS   *The Blackwell Family Papers* (papers of Henry Blackwell, Lucy Stone, and Alice Stone Blackwell). Manuscripts Division, Library of Congress

Catt MSS   *The Papers of Carrie Chapman Catt,* New York Public Library

CTB   *Colorado Temperance Bulletin*, Western Historical Collection, University of Colorado at Boulder

DN   *The Denver News*

DR   *The Denver Republican*

DT   *The Denver Times*

FWML   Woman's Christian Temperance Union Papers, Frances Willard Memorial Library, WCTU, Evanston, Illinois

HWS   *The History of Woman Suffrage,* 6 vols. Vols. 1–3 ed. by Elizabeth Cady Stanton, Susan Anthony, and Mathilda Joslyn Gage (vols. 1 and 2, Rochester, N.Y., 1881; vol. 3, 1886). Vol. 4 ed. by Susan B. Anthony and Ida Husted Harper (Rochester, N.Y., 1902). Vols. 5 and 6 ed. by Ida Husted Harper (New York, 1922).

HWUS   *The History of Women in the United States: Historical Articles on Women's Lives and Activities,* ed. and with an introduction by Nancy F. Cott (Munich; reprint New York: K. G. Saur, 1992). Includes a two-part volume (19) on woman suffrage.

LC   Library of Congress, Manuscripts Division

Meredith MSS   *The Ellis Meredith Papers,* The Colorado Historical Society, Denver, Colorado

NAW   *Notable American Women, 1607–1950: A Biographical Dictionary,* ed. Edward T. James, Janet Wilson James, and Paul S. Boyer (Cambridge, Mass., 1971)

NYPL   New York Public Library, Manuscripts Division

NYT   *The New York Times*

RMDN   *The Rocky Mountain Daily News*

RMN   *The Rocky Mountain News*

WJ   *The Woman's Journal* (Boston, 1870–1893). Schlesinger Library, Radcliffe College, Microfilm

WSC, DPL   Woman Suffrage Collection, Department of Western History, Denver Public Library, Denver, Colorado

Introduction

1. Rogers Smith defines this concept in his article "'One United People': Second Class Female Citizenship and the American Quest for Community," *Yale Journal of Law and the Humanities* 1 (1989): 229–293.

2. Chilton Williamson, *American Suffrage: From Property to Democracy, 1760–1860* (Princeton, N.J.: Princeton University Press, 1960), pp. 158–241, 260–280.

3. Ellen Carol DuBois, "The Radicalism of the Woman Suffrage Movement: Notes toward the Reconstruction of Nineteenth-Century Feminism," *Feminist Studies* 3 (1975): 63–71; Carl Degler, *At Odds: Women and the Family in America from the Revolution to the Present* (New York: Oxford University Press, 1980), pp. 328–361.

4. Aileen Kraditor, *The Ideas of the Woman Suffrage Movement, 1890–1920* (Garden City, N.Y.: Anchor, 1971), pp. 64–184; William O'Neill, *Everyone Was Brave: A History of Feminism in America* (Garden City, N.Y.: Quadrangle, 1971), pp. 30–76, 349–359; Judith Shklar, *American Citizenship: The Quest for Inclusion* (Cambridge, Mass.: Harvard University Press, 1991), pp. 59–62.

5. Nineteenth-century feminists identified their aims as *woman's* rights and *woman* suffrage. I will respect this usage but refer to the reformers themselves as "women."

6. Kraditor, *Ideas of the Woman Suffrage Movement,* pp. 105–189; O'Neill, *Everyone Was Brave,* pp. 30–76, 349–359.

7. Kristi Anderson, "Generation, Partisan Shift, and Realignment: A Glance Back to the New Deal," in Norman H. Nie, Sidney Verba, and John R. Petrocik, eds., *The Changing American Voter* (Cambridge, Mass.: Harvard University Press, 1976), pp. 74–77, 85–91.

8. On the importance of confidence and self-respect among reform leaders see Lawrence Goodwyn, *The Populist Moment: A Short History of the Agrarian Revolt in America* (New York: Oxford University Press, 1978), pp. xix–xx; for biographical background on woman suffrage founders, see Miriam Gurko, *The Ladies of Seneca Falls: The Birth of the Woman's Rights Movement* (New York: Schocken, 1976), pp. 30–81, 108–140; Kathleen Barry, *Susan B. Anthony: A Biography of a Singular Feminist* (New York: Ballantine, 1988); Elisabeth Griffith, *In Her Own Right: The Life of Elizabeth Cady Stanton* (New York: Oxford University Press, 1984); and Andrea Moore Kerr, *Lucy Stone: Speaking Out for Equality* (New Brunswick, N.J.: Rutgers University Press, 1992).

9. Smith, "'One United People,'" p. 232.

10. This typology of liberal feminisms is an extension and adaptation of Judith Shklar's typology of three liberalisms. See Judith Shklar, "The Liberalism of Fear," in Nancy Rosenblum, ed., *Liberalism and the Moral Life* (Cambridge, Mass.: Harvard University Press, 1989), pp. 23–28.

11. Shklar, *American Citizenship,* pp. 57–62; and Helen L. Sumner-Woodbury, *Equal Suffrage* (New York: Harper & Brothers, 1909), pp. 211–213. Sumner-Woodbury's book, written during the last phase of the woman suffrage campaigns, presented much evidence to suggest that the enfranchisement of women would generate little change in the structure of government or the family. Sumner-Woodbury emphasized instead that women who took clear stands on social policy issues would find voting useful.

12. Alice Rossi, *The Feminist Papers* (New York: Bantam, 1974), pp. 3–6.

13. The phrase is from Sheila Rothman, *Woman's Proper Place: A History of Changing Ideals and Practices, 1870 to the Present* (New York: Basic, 1978).

14. Thomas Hobbes, *The Leviathan* (1651), ed. C. B. MacPherson (Baltimore, Md.: Penguin, 1971), pp. 187, 196, 211, 253–257, 285. John Locke, *Two Treatises of Government,* ed. Peter Laslett (Cambridge: Cambridge University Press, 1988), pp. 158–161, 172–174, 186–187, 303–321.

15. Carole Pateman, *The Sexual Contract* (Stanford, Calif.: Stanford University Press, 1988), pp. 39–57, 97–99, 168–172.

16. Ibid., pp. 64–66, 143–153, 208–209.

17. My conceptions of the elitist republican tradition and the Americanist tradition draw considerably on Rogers Smith's definitions of the "multiple traditions" in American politics: liberal, republican, and Americanist. See Rogers M. Smith, "Beyond Tocqueville, Myrdal, and Hartz: The Multiple Traditions in America," *American Political Science Review* 84 (1993): 549–566; and "The 'American Creed' and American Identity: The Limits of Liberal Citizenship in the United States," *Western Political Quarterly* 41 (1988): 225–251. Smith elaborates on the distinctions made between women's natural rights and political rights in "'One United People,'" pp. 233–250.

18. Smith, "'One United People,'" p. 239.

19. Ibid., p. 240.

20. Linda Kerber, *Women of the Republic: Intellect and Ideology in Revolutionary America* (Chapel Hill: University of North Carolina Press, 1980), pp. 235–237, 269–288. Sara Evans found additional evidence to support Kerber's argument. See her *Born for Liberty: A History of Women in America* (New York: Free Press, 1989), pp. 53–66, 70–81.

21. Shklar, *American Citizenship,* pp. 6–8.

22. Ann Douglas, *The Feminization of American Culture* (New York: Doubleday and Anchor Press, 1988).

23. Gurko, *Ladies of Seneca Falls,* pp. 31–46; Evans, *Born for Liberty,* pp. 70–81; and Lori Ginzberg, *Women and the Work of Benevolence: Morality, Politics, and Class in the Nineteenth-Century United States* (New Haven, Conn.: Yale University Press, 1990), pp. 67–97.

24. Rossi, *Feminist Papers,* pp. 16–117.

25. Smith, "'One United People,'" pp. 257–258; Shklar, *American Citizenship,* pp. 59–62.

26. Janet Giele, *Two Paths to Equality: Temperance, Suffrage, and the Origins of Modern Feminism* (New York: Twayne, 1995), pp. 64–73, 81–84.

27. Suzanne M. Marilley, "Frances Willard and the Feminism of Fear," *Feminist Studies* 19 (1993): pp. 123–146.

28. William Link, *The Paradox of Southern Progressivism, 1880–1930* (Chapel Hill: University of North Carolina Press, 1992), pp. 43–45.

29. Ruth Bordin, *Frances Willard: A Biography* (Chapel Hill: University of North Carolina Press, 1986), p. 112; Ruth Bordin, *Woman and Temperance: The Quest for Power and Liberty, 1873–1900* (Philadelphia: Temple University Press, 1981), pp. 3–4.

30. Marjorie Spruill Wheeler, *New Women of the New South: The Leaders of the Woman Suffrage Movement in the Southern States* (New York: Oxford University Press, 1993).

31. Shklar, *American Citizenship,* pp. 6–8.

32. John Kingdon, *Agendas, Alternatives and Public Policies* (Boston: Little, Brown, 1984), pp. 48–57, 75–94, 173–204.

33. The following studies helped me analyze the relationships between leadership, ideology, and the processes of obtaining and keeping members: Clifford Geertz, "Ideology as a Cultural System," in Clifford Geertz, ed., *The Interpretation of Cultures* (New York: Basic, 1973), pp. 193–233; Goodwyn, *The Populist Moment,* pp. vii–xxiv; James Q. Wilson, *Political Organizations* (New York: Basic, 1973), pp. 195–234; and Robert H. Salisbury, "An Exchange Theory of Interest Groups," *Midwest Journal of Political Science* 13, no. 1 (1969): 1–32.

34. Carole Pateman introduces the concept of modern patriarchy in her book *The Sexual Contract,* pp. 23–25, 77–82. Although Pateman's concept means that male rule is rooted in men's sexual domination of women in civil society, I observe that political equality among men in democratic governments cannot be taken for granted.

35. Shklar, "The Liberalism of Fear," p. 37. Shklar observes that without "multiple centers of power" that are open, accessible, and in demand by a host of active groups, political "freedom is but a hope." Thus, "liberalism is monogamously, faithfully, and permanently married to democracy—but it is a marriage of convenience."

36. Ellen Carol DuBois, *Feminism and Suffrage: The Emergence of an Independent Women's Movement in America, 1848–1869* (Ithaca, N.Y.: Cornell University Press, 1978), pp. 21–52.

37. My interpretation differs from that of Ellen C. DuBois. See her *Feminism and Suffrage,* pp. 21–52.

38. Kingdon, *Agendas,* pp. 46–47.

39. This interpretation contrasts with Aileen Kraditor's view that the suffragists' nativism and racism betrayed their egalitarian heritage. See Kraditor, *Ideas of the Woman Suffrage Movement,* pp. 105–184.

1. The Feminism of Equal Rights

1. Lori D. Ginzberg, *Women and the Work of Benevolence* (New Haven, Conn.: Yale University Press, 1990), pp. 11–35.

2. Nathan Hatch, *The Democratization of American Christianity* (New Haven, Conn.: Yale University Press, 1989). Hatch mentions several women who became "powerful preachers" in this movement (pp. 78–79). For a more extensive view of how the Second Great Awakening raised women's consciousness, see Barbara Leslie Epstein, *The Politics of Domesticity: Women, Evangelism and Temperance in Nineteenth Century America* (Middletown, Conn.: Wesleyan University Press, 1981), pp. 47–48, 55–65, 80–85. Ann Douglas interprets the consequences of the Second Great Awakening on forming a popular culture based on mass consumption in *The Feminization of American Culture* (New York: Anchor, 1988).

3. Epstein, *Politics of Domesticity,* pp. 45–65. On Quakers, see Margaret Hope Bacon, *The Quiet Rebels: The Story of the Quakers in America* (Philadelphia: New Society Publishers, 1985), pp. 84–93. The Hicksites integrated the Scriptures into their services and practice of faith; the orthodox wing retained allegiance to the "Inner Light" and skepticism about the Scriptures.

4. Paula Baker, "Domestication of Politics: Women and American Political Society, 1780–1920" in Ellen Carol DuBois and Vicki L. Ruiz, eds., *Unequal Sisters* (New York: Routledge, 1990), pp. 71–73.

5. *The Federalist [Papers],* ed. Jacob E. Cooke (Middletown, Conn.: Wesleyan University Press, 1961); see esp. no. 7, pp. 36–43, no. 10, pp. 56–65, and no. 23–26, pp. 146–171. The antifederalists also made defense of the territory a high priority, but they supported only defensive war and distrusted Hamilton's esteem of national purposes as an unnecessary and dangerous exaggeration. This further avoidance of responsibility for social welfare policies opened doors for women's participation as public-service volunteers. See Herbert Storing, *What the Anti-Federalists Were For* (Chicago: University of Chicago Press, 1981), pp. 30–32.

6. Baker, "Domestication of Politics," pp. 67–71; Theda Skocpol, *Protecting Soldiers and Mothers: The Political Origins of Social Policy in the United States* (Cambridge, Mass.: Harvard University Press, 1992), pp. 41–62, esp. pp. 54–60, 72–74, 80–81, 92–96.

7. Baker, "Domestication of Politics," pp. 66–91.

8. Barbara Berg, *Remembered Gate: Origins of American Feminism* (Oxford: Oxford University Press, 1978); Sara Evans, *Born for Liberty* (New York: Free Press, 1989), pp. 65–66, 70–75, 83–92; Baker, "Domestication of Politics," pp. 66–91; Ginzberg, *Women and the Work of Benevolence,* pp. 48–53, 60–66. Evans observes that Native American Indian women lost much power in this period, and wives of slave owners who called for reform were exceptional. Ginzberg argues that even though they could not vote,

female benevolent reformers obtained corporate charters for their associations.

9. Ginzberg, *Women and the Work of Benevolence,* pp. 51–53.

10. Joel H. Silbey, *The Transformation of American Politics* (Englewood Cliffs, N.J.: Prentice-Hall, 1967), p. 7.

11. Martin Shefter, "Party, Bureaucracy, and Political Change in the United States," in Louis Maisel and Joseph Cooper, eds., *Political Parties: Development and Decay* (Beverly Hills: Sage, 1978), pp. 214–18; and Skocpol, *Protecting Soldiers and Mothers,* pp. 71–76.

12. Skocpol, *Protecting Soldiers and Mothers,* pp. 80–81.

13. Stanley Elkins, *Slavery: A Problem in American Institutional and Intellectual Life,* 2d ed. (Chicago: University of Chicago Press, 1968), pp. 27–80.

14. Louis Hartz, *The Liberal Tradition in America* (New York: Harcourt, Brace & World, 1955), p. 176.

15. William Lloyd Garrison, "Harsh Language—Retarding the Cause," in *Selections from the Writings and Speeches of William Lloyd Garrison* (1852; New York: Negro Universities Press, 1968), p. 127.

16. Garrison, "The Dangers of the Nation," "Harsh Language—Retarding the Cause," and "Words of Encouragement to the Oppressed," in *Selections,* pp. 44–61, 121–133, 163–173.

17. Judith Shklar, "The Liberalism of Fear," in Nancy Rosenblum, ed., *Liberalism and the Moral Life* (Cambridge, Mass.: Harvard University Press, 1989), pp. 26–27.

18. Garrison, "The Dangers of the Nation," *Selections,* pp. 50–53, esp. p. 50.

19. Aileen S. Kraditor, *Means and Ends in American Abolitionism: Garrison and His Critics on Strategy and Tactics, 1834–1850* (New York: Pantheon, 1969), pp. 214–215.

20. Nancy A. Hewitt, "Feminist Friends: Agrarian Quakers and the Emergence of Woman's Rights in America," *Feminist Studies* 12 (1986): 27–49.

21. Kraditor, *Means and Ends,* pp. 52–62; Margaret Bacon, *Valiant Friend: The Life of Lucretia Mott* (New York: Wueher and Co., 1980), p. 54.

22. Walter Merrill, *Against Wind and Tide: A Biography of* Wm. *Lloyd Garrison* (Cambridge, Mass.: Harvard University Press, 1963), pp. 26–31; Kraditor, *Means and Ends,* pp. 78–117, 36, n. 34.

23. Free blacks helped with Garrison's financial expenses. Garrison to Messrs. S. Snowden et al., 4 April 1833 and Garrison to Isaac Knapp, 11 April 1833, in *The Letters of William Lloyd Garrison, Volume I: I Will Be Heard!* ed. Walter M. Merrill (Cambridge, Mass.: Harvard University Press, 1971), pp. 216–218, 221–222.

24. Eleanor Flexner, *Century of Struggle: The Woman's Rights Movement in the United States,* rev. ed. (Cambridge, Mass.: Harvard University Press, 1975), pp. 41–61; Ellen Carol DuBois, *Feminism and Suffrage: The Emergence of an Independent Women's Movement in America, 1848–1869* (Ithaca, N.Y.: Cornell University Press, 1978), pp. 15–52; Keith Melder,

The Beginnings of Sisterhood: The American Woman's Rights Movement (New York: Schocken, 1977), pp. 62–112; Alma Lutz, *Crusade for Freedom: Women of the Antislavery Movement* (Boston: Beacon, 1968) pp. 21–23, 152–158, 164–173; Blanche Glassman Hersh, *The Slavery of Sex: Female Abolitionists in America* (Ann Arbor: University of Michigan Press, 1993), pp. 10–16, 25–35.

25. Kraditor, *Means and Ends*, pp. 4–10.

26. Garrison, "The Dangers of the Nation," *Selections*, pp. 60–61.

27. Ginzberg, *Women and the Work of Benevolence*, p. 17.

28. Melder, *Beginnings of Sisterhood*, pp. 57–61. Melder provides the best historical account of the origins of woman's rights in the antislavery movement.

29. Ginzberg, *Women and the Work of Benevolence*, pp. 69–74.

30. Garrison to Sarah M. Douglas, 5 March 1832, in Merrill, *Letters*, pp. 143–145. A number of "female literary associations" emerged in 1832 among African-American women. In a letter to Isaac Knapp dated 11 April 1833, Garrison wrote that he received travel contributions of six dollars from the "colored 'Female Literary Society'" and four dollars from the "colored 'Female Tract Society'" (pp. 221–222).

31. Ibid., pp. 143–145.

32. Garrison to Plummer, 4 March 1833, ibid., pp. 208–209.

33. Garrison to Benson, 18 January 1834, ibid., p. 280.

34. Kraditor, *Means and Ends*, pp. 40–41, 55–62.

35. Evans, *Born for Liberty*, pp. 74–76, and Berg, *Remembered Gate*, pp. 178–90.

36. Garrison to Benson, 18 February 1834, in Merrill, *Letters*, pp. 283–284. Merrill remarks that Garrison "gave a good deal of publicity of the First Annual Report of the Executive Committee of the New York Magdalen Society" but encountered indignance from editors who did not share Garrison's view that slave masters' sexual exploitation of female slaves was similar to the deplorable condition of "ten thousand" prostitutes in New York City. See Merrill, *Against Wind and Tide*, pp. 49–50.

37. Keith Melder argues that antislavery reformers' focus on cruelty to women slaves, particularly rape and other forms of sexual violence in addition to prostitution, became a source of identification among women across the races. See Melder, *Beginnings of Sisterhood*, pp. 58–59.

38. Eleanor Flexner, "Maria W. Miller Stewart" in *NAW*, pp. 377–378; see also Marilyn Richardson, ed., *Maria W. Stewart: America's First Black Woman Political Writer* (Bloomington: Indiana University Press, 1987), pp. xiv, 9.

39. Maria W. Miller Stewart, "Religion and the Pure Principles of Morality, The Sure Foundation on Which We Must Build," in Richardson, *Maria W. Stewart*, pp. 29, 30–31.

40. Ibid., p. 35.

41. Stewart, "An Address Delivered Before the Afric-American Female Intelligence Society of America," in Richardson, *Maria W. Stewart*, pp. 50, 53, 55.

42. Larry Ceplair, ed., *The Public Years of Sarah and Angelina Grimké: Se-*

lected Writings, 1835–1839 (New York: Columbia University Press, 1989), p. 37.

43. Ibid., pp. 58–59. Emphasis in text.
44. Ibid., p. 60. Emphasis in text.
45. Ibid., pp. 60–62.
46. Ibid., p. 66. Emphasis in text.
47. Melder, *Beginnings of Sisterhood,* p. 60. See also Catherine Clinton, *The Other Civil War: American Women in the Nineteenth Century* (New York: Hill and Wang, 1984), pp. 67–71.
48. Ginzberg, *Women and the Work of Benevolence,* pp. 63–64.
49. Melder, *Beginnings of Sisterhood,* p. 75.
50. Bacon, *Valiant Friend,* p. 56.
51. Melder, *Beginnings of Sisterhood,* p. 64.
52. Flexner, *Century of Struggle,* p. 51.
53. Ibid., pp. 41, 46–47.
54. Ibid., p. 50.
55. Ibid., pp. 50–52.
56. Ibid.
57. Ibid., p. 51.
58. Merrill, *Against Wind and Tide,* pp. 154–155.
59. Flexner, *Century of Struggle,* p. 51.
60. Kraditor, *Means and Ends,* pp. 52–62.
61. Ibid., pp. 25–30, 54–62, 236–240.
62. Merrill, *Against Wind and Tide,* pp. 149, 154.
63. Ginzberg, *Women and the Work of Benevolence,* pp. 28–32.
64. Stewart, "Religion and the Pure Principles," pp. 28–41, quote on p. 38.
65. Ibid., p. 40. Emphasis in text.
66. Angelina Grimké, "Appeal to the Christian Women of the South," in Ceplair, *Public Years of Sarah and Angelina Grimké,* p. 62.
67. Richardson, *Maria W. Stewart,* pp. 57, 68, 70.
68. Linda K. Kerber, *Women of the Republic: Intellect and Ideology in Revolutionary America* (Chapel Hill: University of North Carolina Press, 1980), pp. 104–111.
69. In addition to antislavery, Stewart addresses many issues and problems facing free African Americans in her community. She was a civil rights reformer as well as an abolitionist.
70. The criticisms of European American finery and luxury leveled by Stewart and perhaps by other free African Americans affected Garrison. In planning their wedding, Garrison told Helen Benson that the celebration would be simple, not grand: "The ceremony," according to biographer Walter Merrill, "must not be marred by the presence of wine nor even, he hoped, by a wedding cake." See Merrill, *Against Wind and Tide,* p. 94.
71. Gerda Lerner, *The Grimké Sisters from South Carolina: Rebels against Slavery* (Boston: Houghton Mifflin, 1967), pp. 129–30, 133; Bacon, *Valiant*

Friend, pp. 59–60; Nancie Caraway, *Segregated Sisterhood: Racism and the Politics of American Feminism* (Knoxville: University of Tennessee Press, 1991), pp. 136–138.

72. Lerner, *Grimké Sisters,* p. 132–134.
73. Bacon, *Valiant Friend,* p. 77.
74. Ibid.
75. Flexner, *Century of Struggle,* pp. 45–46.
76. Aileen Kraditor, *Up from the Pedestal: Selected Writings in the History of American Feminism* (New York: Quadrangle, 1968), p. 51.
77. Flexner, *Century of Struggle,* p. 47.
78. Melder, *Beginnings of Sisterhood,* p. 75. Original source is *Proceedings of the Anti-Slavery Convention of American Women, New York, 1837* (New York, 1837), pp. 8–9; Minutes of the Philadelphia Female Anti-Slavery Society, September 14, 1837, Historical Society of Pennsylvania, Philadelphia. For a brief account of the women's antislavery convention in 1837, see *HWS,* 1:39.
79. Sarah Grimké, "Letters on the Equality of the Sexes," in Alice Rossi, ed., *The Feminist Papers* (New York: Bantam, 1973), p. 308.
80. Ibid., p. 309.
81. Flexner, *Century of Struggle,* p. 97, and Kraditor, *Up from the Pedestal,* pp. 45–52, show the opposition's statements and responses.
82. Flexner, *Century of Struggle,* pp. 46–47.
83. Paula Giddings, *When and Where I Enter: The Impact of Black Women on Race and Sex in America* (New York: Morrow, 1984), pp. 50–53.
84. Flexner, *Century of Struggle,* p. 46.
85. Ginzberg, *Women and the Work of Benevolence,* pp. 17–35, 63–65; see also Berg, *Remembered Gate,* pp. 145–175.
86. Melder, *Beginnings of Sisterhood,* p. 95.
87. Ibid., pp. 98–112; see also Kraditor, *Means and Ends,* pp. 39–77.
88. Melder, *Beginnings of Sisterhood,* p. 83.
89. Kraditor, *Means and Ends,* pp. 52–53.
90. Ibid., pp. 52–53.
91. Ibid., pp. 52–58. See also Andrew Sinclair, *The Emancipation of the American Woman* (New York: Harper & Row, 1965), p. 42, and Melder, *Beginnings of Sisterhood,* p. 90.
92. Kraditor, *Means and Ends,* pp. 95–108, esp. p. 100.
93. Ibid., pp. 52–62.
94. Ginzberg, *Women and the Work of Benevolence,* pp. 86–97.
95. Melder, *Beginnings of Sisterhood,* pp. 105–107.
96. Kraditor, *Means and Ends,* pp. 42–62, provides an in-depth discussion of this development.
97. Bacon, *Valiant Friend,* p. 80.
98. Ibid., pp. 81, 93.
99. Kraditor, *Means and Ends,* pp. 55–58, 235–239.
100. Merrill, *Against Wind and Tide,* pp. 141–160.

101. Flexner, *Century of Struggle,* pp. 71, 361.
102. Melder, *Beginnings of Sisterhood,* pp. 98–103, 109–112. This observation lends support to Abraham Zaleznik's view of sharp differences between the styles of leaders motivated by commitments to principle and those in positions of power because they need personal attachments. See Abraham Zaleznik, "Charismatic and Consensus Leaders: A Psychological Comparison," in Manfred Kets de Vries, ed., *The Irrational Executive: Psychoanalytic Explorations in Management* (New York: International Universities Press, 1984), pp. 126–129.
103. Ginzberg, *Women and the Work of Benevolence,* p. 116.

2. "Liberal Feminisms" and Political Autonomy

1. On married woman's property reform, see Norma Basch, *In the Eyes of the Law: Women, Marriage, and Property in Nineteenth-Century New York* (Ithaca, N.Y.: Cornell University Press, 1982), pp. 113–161; on temperance reform see Ruth Bordin, *Woman and Temperance: The Quest for Power and Liberty, 1873–1900* (Philadelphia: Temple University Press, 1981), pp. 4–5; on Mott and the Senecas, see Margaret Hope Bacon, *Valiant Friend: The Life of Lucretia Mott* (New York: Walker and Co., 1980), pp. 124–125; on Frederick Douglass and women, see *Frederick Douglass: On Women's Rights,* ed. Philip S. Foner (Westport, Conn.: Greenwood, 1976), pp. 12–16, 49–52.
2. Sara Evans, *Born for Liberty: A History of Women in America* (New York: Free Press, 1989), pp. 76–77, 94. See also Basch, *In the Eyes of the Law,* pp. 70–128.
3. Quoted in Basch, *Eyes of the Law,* p. 151, n. 36 (emphasis added). Original source: *Journal of the New York State Convention,* 2:1264–65.
4. Ellen Carol DuBois, *Feminism and Suffrage: The Emergence of an Independent Women's Movement in America, 1848–1869* (Ithaca, N.Y.: Cornell University Press, 1978), pp. 95–104.
5. Ibid., p. 51.
6. *HWS,* 1:50–88, 1:101–406, 1:456–752.
7. Sara M. Evans and Harry C. Boyte, *Free Spaces: The Sources of Democratic Change in America* (New York: Harper & Row, 1986), pp. 17–18 and 81–85.
8. *HWS,* 1:63–87, 1:101–170, 1:201–406, 1:456–752.
9. Ibid., pp. 540–541. Nancy F. Cott explains why these women trusted so much in each other in *The Bonds of Womanhood: "Woman's Sphere" in New England, 1780–1835* (New Haven, Conn.: Yale University Press, 1977), pp. 160–206.
10. *HWS,* 1:541.
11. Ibid., p. 542.

12. Ibid.
13. "The Declaration of Sentiments," in *HWS*, 1:70–73.
14. Ibid.
15. Carole Pateman, *The Sexual Contract* (Stanford, Calif.: Stanford University Press, 1988), pp. 90–91.
16. "The Declaration of Sentiments," p. 71.
17. Elisabeth Griffith, *In Her Own Right: The Life of Elizabeth Cady Stanton* (New York: Oxford University Press, 1984), pp. 45–46.
18. Zilliah R. Eisenstein, *The Radical Future of Liberal Feminism* (Boston: Northeastern University Press, 1993), pp. 162–167.
19. *HWS*, 1:72.
20. "Declaration of Sentiments," p. 72.
21. Ibid. See also Rogers Smith's "The 'American Creed' and American Identity: The Limits of Liberal Citizenship in the United States," *The Western Political Quarterly* 41(1988): 245; and "'One United People': Second-Class Female Citizenship and the American Quest for Community," *Yale Journal of Law and the Humanities* 1 (1989): 263–265.
22. *HWS*, 1:482.
23. Ibid., p. 565.
24. Kathleen Barry, *Susan B. Anthony: A Biography of a Singular Feminist* (New York: Ballantine, 1988), p. 93.
25. Judith Shklar, "The Liberalism of Fear," in Nancy L. Rosenblum, ed., *Liberalism and the Moral Life* (Cambridge, Mass.: Harvard University Press, 1989), pp. 26, 37.
26. "The Declaration of Sentiments," pp. 72–73.
27. Douglass, *On Woman's Rights*, p. 51.
28. Dexter Chamberlain Bloomer, *Life and Writings of Amelia Bloomer* (New York: Schocken, 1975), p. 64.
29. Ibid., p. 59.
30. Ann Douglas, *The Feminization of American Culture* (New York: Anchor, 1988), pp. 44–117.
31. Ibid., pp. 44–60, 72–76.
32. Keith Melder, *The Beginnings of Sisterhood: The American Woman's Rights Movement, 1800–1850* (New York: Schocken, 1977), p. 142.
33. Douglas, *Feminization of American Culture*, p. 78.
34. "Declaration of Sentiments," p. 72.
35. Bloomer, *Life and Writings of Amelia Bloomer*, pp. 55–64, 84–89.
36. Ibid., p. 59.
37. Bordin, *Woman and Temperance*, pp. 118–123.
38. Harriet Taylor, "The Enfranchisement of Women," *The Westminster Review*, 55 (1851): 289–311.
39. Ibid., p. 289.
40. Ibid., p. 293. Emphasis added.
41. *HWS*, 1:825.

42. Ibid.

43. Ibid.

44. Judith N. Shklar, *American Citizenship: The Quest for Inclusion* (Cambridge, Mass.: Harvard University Press, 1991), pp. 7–8, 12–16, 25–62.

45. "Resolutions of the Second Worcester Convention, 1851," *HWS*, 1:826.

46. Ellen DuBois interprets the reformers' description of the vote as the "cornerstone" of the movement as evidence that they made suffrage their "preeminent" goal. Because the reformers carefully disavowed any effort to "undervalue" other methods and selected this metaphor to prove they were not seeking equality, "cornerstone" more properly signifies connection than predominance. See DuBois, *Feminism and Suffrage,* p. 46.

47. Glenda Riley, *Divorce: An American Tradition* (New York: Oxford University Press, 1991), pp. 45–47.

48. Elizabeth Cady Stanton, "Divorce," *The Lily,* 1 April 1850, p. 31. Emphasis in text.

49. "Women's Temperance Convention," *The Lily* 4 (May 1852): 35. See also *HWS,* 1:480–483.

50. *HWS,* 1:496.

51. Blackwell was Antoinette Brown in 1853; she did not marry until 24 January 1856. See Barbara M. Solomon, "Antoinette Louisa Brown Blackwell," in *NAW,* pp. 158–161.

52. *HWS,* 1:723–729.

53. Ibid., pp. 732–37.

54. "Summary and Minutes of the Mob Convention in New York," September 6 and 7, 1853, *HWS,* 1:546.

55. Ibid., p. 549. Emphasis in text.

56. Ibid., p. 549.

57. Ibid., pp. 552–555.

58. Ibid., pp. 552, 554.

59. Ibid., p. 560.

60. Ibid.

61. Ibid., pp. 560–61.

62. Ibid., p. 561.

63. Ibid., p. 561.

64. Ibid., pp. 553, 573.

65. Ibid., p. 568. Sojourner Truth first subdued such hecklers with her famous speech, "Ain't I a Woman," at an 1851 woman's rights convention in Akron, Ohio. See Eleanor Flexner, *Century of Struggle: The Woman's Rights Movement in the United States,* rev. ed. (Cambridge, Mass.: Harvard University Press, 1975), pp. 90–92.

66. "Minutes of the 1853 National Woman's Rights Convention" (Cleveland National Convention), *HWS,* 1:124.

67. Ibid., p. 125.

68. See "Summary of Massachusetts Woman's Rights Movement," *HWS,* 1:246–

259, for a chronicle of the campaigns for woman suffrage in Massachusetts during the 1850s. The Massachusetts legislature intensely resisted this pressure, responding at one point that whereas "50,000 women . . . petitioned for a law to repress the sale of intoxicating liquor, only two thousand petition for the right to vote!" *HWS*, 1:254. Woman's rights reformers in New York State promoted suffrage as well as married woman's property rights. Between 1853 and 1854, thirteen thousand signatures were gathered on equal rights petitions in thirty of New York's sixty counties. See "Minutes of 1853 Woman's Rights State Convention" (New York State), *HWS*, 1:588–589.

69. Lucy Stone to Antoinette Brown, 11 July 1855, in Carol Lasser and Marlene Deahl Merrill, eds., *Friends and Sisters; Letters between Lucy Stone and Antoinette Brown Blackwell, 1846–93* (Urbana: University of Illinois Press, 1987), pp. 143–145.

70. "Mrs. Stanton's Reply," Stanton to Gerrit Smith, 21 December 1855, *HWS*, 1:840.

71. Barry, *Susan B. Anthony*, pp. 78–86, 97–104, esp. p. 98.

72. Griffith, *In Her Own Right*, pp. 83–85, 86–107.

73. Barry, *Susan B. Anthony*, pp. 110–111.

74. *HWS*, 1:133–140, 227–228.

75. "Minutes of 1854 National Woman's Rights Convention" (National Convention in Philadelphia), *HWS*, 1:382–383.

76. Ibid., p. 383.

77. "Minutes of the 1858 National Woman's Rights Convention" (Mozart Hall), *HWS*, 1:671.

78. Ibid. Oliver Johnson added to Parker Pillsbury's message by naming several churches that recognized woman's rights, including one, "Progressive Friends," that had been recently formed.

79. Ibid., pp. 647–648.

80. Ibid., p. 650.

81. "Minutes of the 1860 Woman's Rights Convention" (Tenth National Woman's Rights Convention), *HWS*, 1:700–701.

82. Ibid., p. 712.

83. Ibid., pp. 712–714. Longfellow also elaborated a vision on transforming woman's "separate sphere." First, the "ideas and customs"—"this *vis inertiae*"—sustaining it would need to be overcome. Second, men should spend more time at home. Third, "no woman attends to [household affairs] utterly," and "there is no one sphere fitted for all men, any more than for all women."

84. Ibid., pp. 688–752.

85. Miriam Gurko, *The Ladies of Seneca Falls: The Birth of the Woman's Rights Movement* (New York: Schocken, 1976), pp. 156–206; Flexner, *Century of Struggle*, pp. 83–91; and DuBois, *Feminism and Suffrage*, pp. 24–31, 40–52.

86. DuBois, *Feminism and Suffrage*, p. 51.

87. The women's rights reformers adopted an informal structure that Jane J.

Mansbridge sees as one organizational means to maintain "unitary" democracy—shared rule by like-minded participants in a small group. Large groups usually cannot survive with such informal structures, but the federalist National Organization for Women (NOW) maintains a relatively informal hierarchical structure and much autonomy for local associations. See Jane J. Mansbridge's *Beyond Adversary Democracy* (New York: Basic, 1980), pp. 278, 281–289, and "Feminism and the Forms of Freedom," in Frank Fischer and Carmen Sirranni, eds., *Critical Studies in Organization and Bureaucracy* (Philadelphia: Temple University Press, 1984), pp. 472–481. On NOW's organizational structure, see Joyce Gelb and Marian Lief Palley, *Women and Public Policies,* rev. ed. (Princeton, N.J.: Princeton University Press, 1987), pp. 13–26.

88. "Appeal to the Women of New York," *HSW,* 1:744.
89. "History of Woman's Rights in New York State," *HWS,* 1:745, 1:747–748.
90. Ibid., pp. 747–52.

3. Putting Suffrage First

1. On Reconstruction from the perspective of radical Republicans, see Michael Les Benedict, *A Compromise of Principle: Congressional Republicans and Reconstruction, 1863–1869* (New York: W. W. Norton, 1974), and Joseph James, *The Framing of the Fourteenth Amendment,* Illinois Studies in the Social Sciences 37 (Urbana: University of Illinois Press, 1956). W. E. B. Du Bois comprehensively recounts the role blacks played in his *Black Reconstruction in America: An Essay toward a History of the Part which Black Folk Played in the Attempt to Reconstruct Democracy in America, 1860–1880* (New York: Atheneum, 1979). Ellen Carol DuBois studies in depth how Reconstruction affected the woman's rights movement in *Feminism and Suffrage: The Emergence of an Independent Women's Movement in America, 1848–1869* (Ithaca, N.Y.: Cornell University Press, 1978); see also Eleanor Flexner, *Century of Struggle: The Woman's Rights Movement in the United States,* rev. ed. (Cambridge, Mass.: Harvard University Press, 1975), pp. 145–158; Miriam Gurko, *The Ladies of Seneca Falls: The Birth of the Woman's Rights Movement* (New York: Schocken, 1976), pp. 208–256; and Andrew Sinclair, *Emancipation of the American Woman* (New York: Harper and Row, 1945), pp. 177–196. Catherine Clinton details women's participation in the Civil War, and she explains how woman's rights reformers perceived Reconstruction reform as a setback in *The Other Civil War: American Women in the Nineteenth Century* (New York: Hill and Wang, 1984), pp. 80–96.

2. Alice Stone Blackwell, "Charles Sumner and Women," *WJ,* 31 December 1892, p. 424. Paul Kleppner thoroughly demonstrates the importance of public opinion during Reconstruction in his book, *The Third Electoral Sys-*

tem, 1853–1892 (Chapel Hill: University of North Carolina Press, 1979). On the challenge that Republicans faced in winning support for black male suffrage, see pp. 90–96.

3. Ellen DuBois contends that from the "perspective of the growth of feminism rather than achievement of the vote," these upheavals "advanced the movement." See her *Feminism and Suffrage,* pp. 200–201.

4. *Laws and Joint Resolutions of the Last Session of the Confederate Congress (November 7, 1864–March 18, 1865) Together with the Secret Acts of Previous Congresses,* ed. Charles W. Ramsdell (Durham, N.C.: Duke University Press, 1941), pp. 118–119. President Davis approved the enlistment of male slaves for military service on March 13, 1865. See Shelby Foote, *The Civil War: A Narrative; Red River to Appomattox* (New York: Random House, 1974), pp. 859–861. The Union army enlisted (sometimes by decree) the service of former slaves by 1862, and not with promises of equal treatment; see Geoffrey C. Ward with Ric Burns and Ken Burns, *The Civil War: An Illustrated History* (New York: Alfred A. Knopf, 1990), pp. 246–253. General Sherman opposed the enlistment of "Negroes" because he thought Negro families should have their male protectors at home; see M. A. DeWolfe Howe, ed., *Home Letters of General Sherman* (New York: Charles Scribner's Sons, 1909), pp. 249–253, 327–330; and Lloyd Lewis, *Sherman: Fighting Prophet* (New York: Harcourt, Brace and Company, 1932), pp. 243–246. I am grateful to Alasdair MacIntyre for bringing to my attention the differential treatment of African-American male slaves by the Union and Confederate armies. Brian Burchett informed me about Sherman's views on the Union Army's enlistment policy for slaves.

5. Rogers M. Smith, "'One United People': Second-Class Female Citizenship and the American Quest for Community," *Yale Journal of Law & the Humanities* 1 (1989): 229–293.

6. Du Bois, *Black Reconstruction,* pp. 66–81.

7. Ibid., pp. 82, 94–100.

8. Ibid., pp. 106–126, 153–157. Emphasis added. According to Du Bois, the presence in Louisiana of a black community that possessed a modicum of economic power, unity, and self-respect made their dissent more likely to succeed than that of other communities. He states: "If this experiment in Reconstruction had been attempted anywhere but in Louisiana, it is possible that the whole question of Negro suffrage would not have been raised then or perhaps for many years after." See also pp. 154–157.

9. Ibid., p. 104.

10. Ibid., pp. 104–112.

11. Ibid., p. 112, as quoted in turn by Issac Hill, *A Sketch of the 29th Regiment of Connecticut Colored Troops* (Baltimore, Md.: Daugherty, Maguire & Co., 1867), microfilm, p. 27.

12. Du Bois, *Black Reconstruction,* pp. 158–159.

13. Ibid., p. 162.

14. Judith N. Shklar, *American Citizenship: The Quest for Community* (Cambridge, Mass.: Harvard University Press, 1991), pp. 43–47.

15. Nancy C. M. Hartstock, "Masculinity, Citizenship, and the Making of War," *PS* 17 (1984): 198–202; Carole Pateman, "Equality, Difference, Subordination: The Politics of Motherhood and Women's Citizenship," in Gisela Bock and Susan James, eds., *Beyond Equality and Difference: Citizenship, Feminist Politics and Female Subjectivity* (New York: Routledge, 1992), pp. 23–24. Judith Shklar considers this problem part of the late-nineteenth-century political culture; see her *American Citizenship,* p. 59.

16. Du Bois, *Black Reconstruction,* pp. 165–167, 247–261.

17. DuBois, *Feminism and Suffrage,* pp. 55–78; Flexner, *Century of Struggle,* pp. 145–152.

18. Du Bois, *Black Reconstruction,* p. 266.

19. James, *The Framing of the Fourteenth Amendment,* p. 130.

20. Sumner to the Duchess Argyll, 3 April 1866. Sumner explained, "But after most careful consideration I see no substantial protection for the freedman except in the franchise. He must have this—(1) For his own protection; (2) For the protection of the white Unionist; and (3) For the peace of the country. We put the musket in his hands because it was necessary; for the same reason we must give him the franchise." Sumner added that the Unionists in the South also needed freedman's votes. See Sumner to Duchess Argyll, in Edward L. Pierce, ed., *Memoir and Letters of Charles Sumner, Vol. IV, 1860–1874* (Boston: Roberts Brothers, 1893), p. 275. "Charles Sumner and Women," *WJ,* 31 December 1892, p. 424. If Stone Blackwell's statement is true, then there is little reason to believe that the framers of the Fourteenth Amendment objected philosophically to the political inclusion of women. They inserted the word "male" for the sake of expediency.

21. "Charles Sumner and Women," p. 424.

22. *HWS,* 2:154.

23. Ibid., p. 174.

24. Stone to Abby Kelley Foster, 24 January 1867, in Leslie Wheeler, ed., *Loving Warriors: Selected Letters of Lucy Stone and Henry B. Blackwell, 1853 to 1893* (New York: Dial, 1981), pp. 215–217. Emphasis in text.

25. Benedict, *A Compromise of Principle,* p. 115.

26. Du Bois, *Black Reconstruction,* p. 341.

27. *HWS,* 2:215–216.

28. Ibid., p. 216.

29. Ibid., pp. 220, 214–216.

30. Ibid., p. 221.

31. Ibid., p. 222.

32. Ibid., pp. 223–224.

33. Ibid., p. 209.

34. DuBois, *Feminism and Suffrage,* pp. 92–104.

35. Ibid., p. 100; see also *HWS,* 2:382.

36. *HWS*, 2:312.
37. Benedict, *A Compromise of Principle*, p. 328.
38. William Gillette, *The Right to Vote: Politics and the Passage of the Fifteenth Amendment* (Baltimore, Md.: The Johns Hopkins University Press, 1982), pp. 31–45.
39. Benedict, *A Compromise of Principle*, p. 331.
40. Ibid., pp. 331–336.
41. Clinton, *The Other Civil War*, pp. 93–96.
42. Elisabeth Griffith, *In Her Own Right: The Life of Elizabeth Cady Stanton* (New York: Oxford University Press, 1984), p. 127.
43. Wheeler, *Loving Warriors*, p. 225.
44. DuBois, *Feminism and Suffrage*, pp. 60–78, 162–202.
45. Ibid., 164–169.
46. *HWS*, 2:382.
47. Ibid., p. 383.
48. Ibid., p. 397.
49. Flexner, *Century of Struggle*, pp. 154–155.
50. DuBois, *Feminism and Suffrage*, pp. 92–125.
51. Flexner, *Century of Struggle*, pp. 154–158.
52. Walter Merrill, *Against Wind and Tide: A Biography of Wm. Lloyd Garrison* (Cambridge, Mass.: Harvard University Press, 1963), p. 321; James Brewer Stewart, *Wendell Phillips, Liberty's Hero* (Baton Rouge: Louisiana State University Press, 1986), pp. 281–285.
53. Shklar, *American Citizenship*, pp. 58–61.
54. Flexner, *Century of Struggle*, pp. 169–171.
55. *HWS*, 2:756–760. The AWSA's first "Call" appealed for the creation of a national suffrage organization that would be "at once more comprehensive and more widely representative" than any of the existing associations.
56. Ibid., p. 764.
57. Ibid., pp. 804–809. At the 1870 AWSA convention the Union Woman Suffrage Society petitioned to merge with the AWSA—Frederick Douglass, Isabella Beecher Hooker, Samuel May, and Theodore Tilton named themselves petitioners. A resolution to plan a merger of the two associations was voted down, but Henry Blackwell proposed that all associations that were willing to put votes for women first were welcome in the AWSA. Blackwell's resolution passed unanimously.
58. Ibid., pp. 756–757, 803–804.
59. DuBois, *Feminism and Suffrage*, p. 100; Henry B. Blackwell, "What the South Can Do," in *Up from the Pedestal: Selected Writings in the History of American Feminism*, ed. Aileen S. Kraditor (New York: Quadrangle, 1968), pp. 253–257. See also *HWS*, 2:382.
60. *HWS*, 2:384.
61. Ibid., p. 311.
62. Ibid., p. 353.

63. Ibid., pp. 352, 353.
64. Judith Shklar, "The Liberalism of Fear," *Liberalism and the Moral Life,* ed. Nancy L. Rosenblum (Cambridge, Mass.: Harvard University Press, 1989), pp. 26–28.
65. *HWS,* 2:348–355.
66. Stone to Stanton, 19 October 1869, in Wheeler, *Loving Warriors,* p. 229. Emphasis in text.
67. DuBois, *Feminism and Suffrage,* pp. 199–201; Stone to Campbell, 19 July 1876, pp. 254–255; Stone to Stanton, 30 August 1876, p. 257, both in Wheeler, *Loving Warriors.*
68. Flexner, *Century of Struggle,* p. 226.
69. Smith, "'One United People,'" pp. 260–263.
70. Carrie Chapman Catt, *Woman Suffrage and Politics* (New York: Scribner's, 1923), pp. 109–110.
71. Albina Washburn, "Woman Voting in Colorado," *WJ,* 12 June 1875, p. 189.
72. Ibid.
73. Ibid.
74. Ibid. In an interview conducted during the 1930s, Albina Washburn's daughter, Winona Washburn Taylor, states that the Washburns were among the first settlers in Colorado when they moved there in 1860 from Freeport, Illinois. According to Taylor, Albina was the first teacher in the Big Thompson area, "before a district was organized." See *1930s Interviews,* Civil Works Administration, Interviews, unpub. typescript, 1933–1934, Colorado Historical Society, Denver, Colo. [hereafter *1930s Interviews*], p. 282.
75. Billie Barnes Jensen, "The Woman Suffrage Movement in Colorado" (master's thesis, University of Colorado at Boulder, 1959), pp. 27–28. Jensen cites a few incidents of women voting in the territory in the 1860s and 1870s. Apparently women voted in the election for the Greeley postmaster in 1871 as well as for an Arapahoe County school board election in 1872. Jensen noted that the *Rocky Mountain News* responded to the school election incident with a query about whether women "would now pay the poll tax"; see p. 28.
76. Stone to Campbell, Blackwell MSS, 7 August 1875.
77. Lucy Stone, "The Constitution for Colorado," *WJ,* 25 December 1875, p. 412. Emphasis added.
78. Ibid.
79. Ibid.
80. Campbell to Blackwell, Blackwell MSS, 15 December 1875.
81. R. G. Dill, *The Political Campaigns of Colorado* (Denver: Arapahoe, 1895), p. 5.
82. LeRoy Hafen, *Colorado and Its People* (New York: Lewis Historical, 1948), p. 343.
83. Ibid. See also Dill, *Political Campaigns,* pp. 6–7.

84. Hafen, *Colorado and Its People,* p. 344.
85. Campbell to Blackwell, Blackwell MSS, 15 December 1875.
86. Campbell to Stone and Blackwell, Blackwell MSS, 20 December 1875. Campbell wrote to Stone in reference to the loss of the Washburns that she "was so disappointed in the help I had expected from them that I nearly lost all hope."
87. David B. Truman, *The Governmental Process: Political Interests and Public Opinion,* 2d ed. (New York: Alfred A. Knopf, 1971), pp. 157–167. This switch shows that multiple identifications do not stop people from setting political priorities.
88. Campbell to Stone, Blackwell MSS, 20 December 1875.
89. Ibid.
90. Ibid.
91. Ibid.
92. "Suffrage Convention in Colorado," *WJ,* 22 January 1876, p. 29.
93. Ibid., pp. 28–29.
94. Ibid., p. 29.
95. Ibid.
96. Martin Shefter, "Party Organization, Electoral Mobilization, and Regional Variations in Reform Success," Paper delivered at the 1978 Annual Meeting of the American Political Science Association, New York City, pp. 5–6. See also Martin Shefter, *Political Parties and the State: The American Historical Experience* (Princeton, N.J.: Princeton University Press, 1994), pp. 167–190. Shefter argues that reform movements have tended to succeed in the West where "broad-based mass parties" are absent. Until Illinois gave women presidential suffrage in 1913, only western states had enfranchised women.
97. "Bromwell, Hon. Henry P. H., Biography," *Denver Tribune,* suppl. 14 February 1876, p. 1. A transcript of this article can be found in the biographical collections of the Colorado Historical Society. On 24 February 1866, Representative Bromwell made a speech in support of the radical Republicans' plan for Reconstruction. See "Speech of Hon. H. P. H. Bromwell of Illinois on Reconstruction" (Washington, D.C.: Congressional Globe Office, 1866).
98. "Woman Suffrage Hearing in Colorado," *WJ,* 5 February 1876, p. 45.
99. Ibid.
100. Ibid.
101. *Proceedings of the Constitutional Convention,* p. 267. The *Woman's Journal* published the full text of Bromwell and Vigil's minority report; see "Woman Suffrage in Colorado," *WJ,* 19 February 1876, p. 60.
102. *Proceedings of the Constitutional Convention,* pp. 267, 268.
103. Ibid., p. 270.
104. Ibid., pp. 270–271.
105. Ibid., pp. 268–269.
106. Ibid., pp. 268–269.

107. Ibid., pp. 269–270.

108. Ibid., p. 730.

109. Joseph G. Brown, *The History of Equal Suffrage in Colorado: 1868–1898* (Denver: News Job Printing, 1898), pp. 9–10.

110. *Proceedings of the Constitutional Convention,* p. 733.

111. "Annual Meeting, American Woman Suffrage Association," *WJ,* 7 October 1876, pp. 325, 328.

112. "The Colorado Campaign," *WJ,* 20 January 1877, p. 24.

113. Ibid.

114. Ibid. Avery noted that since 12 March 1876, the Woman Suffrage Society "entered into possession of 'The Woman's Column' in the *Rocky Mountain News.*"

115. Ibid.

116. Brown, *Equal Suffrage in Colorado,* pp. 11–12.

117. Dill, *Political Campaigns of Colorado,* pp. 5–6, and "Interview with John L. Routt," Bancroft Collection, University of Colorado at Boulder.

118. U.S. Department of Commerce, Bureau of the Census, "Population of Colorado," in *Report of the Population of the U.S., 1880,* vol. 1 (Washington, D.C.: Government Printing Office, 1883), pp. 560–561.

119. Duane A. Smith, *Rocky Mountain Mining Camps: The Urban Frontier* (Lincoln: University of Nebraska Press, 1967), pp. 227–234.

120. Ibid., 227–241, and Lyle W. Dorsett, *The Queen City: A History of Denver* (Boulder: Bruett Publishing Company, 1977), pp. 107–110.

121. *HWS,* 3:720n.

122. "Mrs. Shields in Colorado," *WJ,* 14 April 1877, p. 117.

123. S. Jennie Griffin, "Woman Suffrage in Colorado," *WJ,* 19 May 1877, p. 160.

124. "The Question of Suffrage," *The Pueblo Chieftain,* 24 January 1877.

125. Griffin, "Woman Suffrage in Colorado," p. 160.

126. Campbell to Stone, Blackwell MSS, 8 July 1877.

127. Margaret Campbell, "The Situation in Colorado," *WJ,* 27 October 1877, p. 344.

128. "The Suffrage Vote in Colorado," *WJ,* 1 December 1877, p. 380.

129. Ibid.

130. Henry Blackwell, "The Lesson of Colorado," *WJ,* 20 October 1877, p. 332.

131. Henry Blackwell, "Victory Deferred in Colorado," *WJ,* 13 October 1877, p. 324.

132. Campbell, "The Situation in Colorado," p. 344.

133. Ibid.

134. Blackwell, "Victory Deferred," p. 324.

135. Ibid.

136. Campbell, "The Situation in Colorado," p. 344.

137. Ibid.

138. "Colorado Opponents of Woman Suffrage," *WJ,* 3 November 1877, p. 352.

139. Blackwell, "The Lesson," p. 332.

17. For an elaboration of this argument, see Frances Willard, "Woman in the Pulpit" in Carolyn De Swarte Gifford, ed., *The Defense of Women's Rights to Ordination in the Methodist Episcopal Church* (New York: Garland, 1987).

18. Willard, "Home Protection," p. 354.

19. Ibid., pp. 354–355, 358.

20. Ibid.

21. Epstein, *Politics of Domesticity*, pp. 45–65. For the most complete account of how women's roles as moral authorities both liberated and inhibited their collective action as women, see Nancy Cott, *The Bonds of Womanhood* (New Haven, Conn.: Yale University Press, 1977).

22. Barrington Moore, Jr., *Injustice: The Social Bases of Obedience and Revolt* (White Plains, N.Y.: M. E. Sharpe, 1978), p. 91. Moore defines moral inventiveness as "the capacity to fashion from existing cultural traditions historically new standards of condemnation for what exists."

23. Abraham Zaleznik and David Moment, *The Dynamics of Interpersonal Behavior* (New York: John Wiley and Sons, 1964), pp. 461–462.

24. This new fusion of authority for the political inclusion of women appears as early as 1874 in her organizational plan, *Hints and Helps*.

25. Willard, "Home Protection," p. 355.

26. Ibid.

27. Ibid., pp. 354–355. Bordin contends that Willard exaggerated her feelings of sadness and unfairness about this experience when she transferred it from her diaries to her autobiography, *Glimpses of Fifty Years*. See Bordin, *Frances Willard*, p. 22.

28. "Frances Willard: Extracts from her 4th of July Speech," *WJ*, 24 January 1880, p. 30.

29. Willard, "Home Protection," p. 355.

30. Special attention has been given to Willard's racism and ethnocentrism by Bordin in *Frances Willard*, pp. 221–223; and by Sara Evans in her *Born for Liberty: A History of Women in America* (New York: Free Press, 1989), pp. 129–130.

31. Shklar, *Ordinary Vices*, p. 37.

32. Willard, "Home Protection."

33. Frances Willard, "Miss Willard's Annual Address," *WJ*, 23 November 1889; see also Frances Willard, "Miss Willard's Address," *WJ*, 21 November 1891. For an extended discussion of how the Americanist tradition perpetuated sexism, see Smith, "'One United People,'" pp. 229–293.

34. Ellen Carol DuBois, *Feminism and Suffrage: The Emergence of an Independent Women's Movement in America, 1848–1869* (Ithaca, N.Y.: Cornell University Press, 1978), pp. 95–96, 174–178. Willard's refusal to endorse and promote the antilynching campaign led by Ida B. Wells contradicts her commitment to stop physical cruelty. See Bordin, *Frances Willard*, pp. 216–218.

35. Willard, "Home Protection," pp. 354–358.

36. "Extracts from the 4th of July Speech," p. 30.
37. "Miss Willard on Woman," *WJ*, 10 November 1888, pp. 355, 362.
38. Ibid. Reverend Richard Heber Newton was an Episcopal minister whom Joseph Cullen Ayer characterizes as "the foremost liberal preacher in his denomination" during the late nineteenth century. See Joseph Cullen Ayer, "Richard Heber Newton," in *The Dictionary of American Biography,* vol. 7, s.v. "Richard Heber Newton." Newton published many books, including *Womanhood: Lectures on Woman's Work in the World* (New York: Putnam, 1881).
39. Willard praised Edward Bellamy's novel *Looking Backward* for its portrait of the state transformed from a war machine into a provider of necessary services. See Bordin, *Frances Willard,* pp. 145–149.
40. "Letter from Frances Willard," *WJ*, 26 April 1884, pp. 136–137. Strong resonances can be found between Willard's reference "to play mother" and Sara Ruddick's contention that primary child care providers be called mothers. See Sara Ruddick, *Maternal Thinking: Toward a Politics of Peace* (New York: Ballantine, 1989), pp. 28–57.
41. "Frances Willard's Work," *New York Times,* 17 November 1894. Barbara Epstein observes that Willard linked workers' struggles for an eight-hour day and better wages with the struggle for family integrity, especially increased time for fathers to spend with children. See Epstein, *Politics of Domesticity,* pp. 140–142.
42. "Miss Willard on Suffrage," *WJ*, 2 May 1885, p. 139.
43. Willard, *Glimpses of Fifty Years* (New York: Source Book Press, 1970), pp. 392, 394–395.
44. "Miss Willard's Annual Address" (1889), p. 370; and Willard, *Glimpses of Fifty Years,* pp. 604–615.
45. "Miss Willard's Annual Address" (1889), p. 370.
46. Epstein, *Politics of Domesticity,* p. 132.
47. Willard, *Glimpses of Fifty Years,* p. 614.
48. Ibid., pp. 420–421, 463, 612. See also "Miss Willard's Annual Address" (1889). Willard's promotion of honest answers to children's questions about sexuality undermines Epstein's claim that Willard promoted sexual repression. See Willard, *Glimpses of Fifty Years,* pp. 83–84.
49. Carol Gilligan, *In a Different Voice: Psychological Theory and Women's Development* (Cambridge, Mass.: Harvard University Press, 1982), pp. 24–63, 128–129. Gilligan restricts her discussion of early woman's rights struggles to contributions made by Stanton and Anthony. In my view, Willard's contributions support her argument better.
50. Willard, *Glimpses of Fifty Years,* pp. 426–27.
51. Rogers Smith, *Liberalism and American Constitutional Law* (Cambridge, Mass.: Harvard University Press, 1990), pp. 36–59. See also his "One United People," pp. 229–231, 263–268.
52. Louise A. Tilly and Joan W. Scott, *Women, Work, and Family* (New York:

Holt, Rinehart, and Winston, 1978), pp. 227–230. Tilly and Scott argue that similar ideas and associations provided the bridge between the preindustrial world and the industrialized one for women in Britain and France.

53. Ross Evans Paulson, *Women's Suffrage and Prohibition: A Comparative Study of Equality and Social Control* (Glenview, Ill.: Scott, Foresman, 1973), pp. 113–116.

54. Suzanne M. Marilley, *Why the Vote? Woman Suffrage and the Politics of Democratic Development in the United States, 1820–1893* (Ann Arbor, Mich.: University Microfilms International, 1986), pp. 324–326, 327–344, 384–389, 406–414.

55. "The Grangers on Woman Suffrage," *WJ*, 1 September 1877.

56. Ibid.

57. Ibid.

58. Bordin, *Woman and Temperance*, pp. 6–7, 12.

59. *Minutes of the Woman's National Christian Temperance Union, 1881–1885 and 1887–1894.* Except for 1884, this data appears in the *Appendices of Annual Reports,* Archives, National Women's Christian Temperance Union, FWML. The data for 1884 appears under "Western States," p. cxxxi.

60. *Tenth Annual WCTU Convention, 1889* (Denver, Colo.: John Dove Press, 1889), Archives, UC, Boulder, p. 27.

61. Bordin, *Woman and Temperance*, p. 8.

62. Ibid., pp. 8–9.

63. "Notes," *WJ*, 13 April 1878.

64. *Tenth Annual WCTU Convention*, 1889, p. 27.

65. Ibid. See "List of Delegates." Washburn is listed as a delegate from Loveland. The name "Big Thompson" was changed to "Loveland" during the 1880s.

66. Ibid., p. 26. Shields died in 1885.

67. *Colorado WCTU Annual Report, 1884* (Colorado Springs, Colo.: Daily State Republican Printing House, 1884), Archives, UC, Boulder, pp. 12–16.

68. *Colorado WCTU Annual Report, 1882* (Colorado Springs, Colo.: The Gazette Publishing Co., 1882), Archives, UC, Boulder, p. 15.

69. Ibid., p. 15. See also Bordin, *Woman and Temperance*, pp. 91–116.

70. M. F. Gray-Pitman, "B, Response," *Colorado WCTU Annual Report, 1882,* pp. 9–10.

71. Ibid.

72. "Annual Address of the President," *Colorado WCTU Annual Report, 1884,* pp. 14–15.

73. *Colorado WCTU Annual Report, 1884,* p. 12.

74. "Annual Address of the President," *Colorado WCTU Annual Report, 1888* (Denver, Colo.: Challenge Publishing Co., 1888), Archives, UC, Boulder, p. 24.

75. Bordin, *Woman and Temperance*, pp. 117–125.

76. *Colorado WCTU Annual Report, 1888,* pp. 24, 28.

77. "Suffrage League in Colorado Springs," *WJ*, 11 July 1885.

78. *Colorado WCTU Annual Report, 1888,* pp. 50–51.
79. *Colorado WCTU Annual Report, 1889* (Denver, Colo.: John Dove, 1889), Archives, UC, Boulder, p. 60.
80. *Colorado WCTU Annual Report, 1888,* p. 51.
81. *Colorado WCTU Annual Report, 1889,* p. 60.
82. Ibid., p. 61.
83. *Colorado WCTU Annual Report, 1891* (Colorado Springs, Colo.: Republic Publishing Co., 1892), Archives, UC, Boulder.
84. *Colorado WCTU Annual Report, 1892* (La Veta, Colo.: Frank Staplin, Printer), Archives, UC, Boulder, p. 85.
85. *Colorado WCTU Annual Report, 1890* (Pueblo, Colo.: W. J. Jackson Publishing, 1890), Archives, UC, Boulder, p. 65.

5. An Exceptional Victory

1. Eleanor Flexner, *Century of Struggle: The Woman's Rights Movement in the United States,* rev. ed. (Cambridge, Mass.: Harvard University Press, 1975), p. 228; Alan Grimes, *The Puritan Ethic and Woman Suffrage* (New York: Oxford University Press, 1967), p. 22.
2. John Kingdon, *Agendas, Alternatives, and Public Policies* (Boston: Little, Brown, 1984), pp. 1–4, 138, 157–160, 167–170, 173–204.
3. James Edward Wright, *Politics of Populism: Dissent in Colorado* (New Haven, Conn.: Yale University Press, 1974), pp. 136–138.
4. "To the Women of Colorado: The Record of Parties on the Equal Suffrage Amendment," November 1893, p. 3, *The Populist Party of Colorado* (n.p.), Denver Public Library. The data on partisan distribution in the 1893 Colorado Assembly can be found in Wright, *Politics of Populism,* p. 163.
5. Wright, *Politics of Populism,* pp. 143–144.
6. Norman Pollack, "Introduction," in Norman Pollack, ed., *The Populist Mind* (Indianapolis, Ind.: Bobbs-Merrill, 1967), p. xix.
7. Kingdon, *Agendas,* pp. 189–191.
8. Ruth Bordin, *Frances Willard: A Biography* (Chapel Hill: University of North Carolina Press, 1986), pp. 142–144.
9. Frances Willard, *Glimpses of Fifty Years: The Autobiography of an American Woman* (Chicago: Woman's Temperance Publication Association, 1889), pp. 412–413.
10. Ibid., pp. 413–415. Emphasis in text.
11. David Thomas Brundage, *The Making of Working-Class Radicalism in the Mountain West: Denver, Colorado, 1880–1903* (Ann Arbor: University Microfilms International, 1982), pp. 102–103. Brundage implies that the low attendance of women caused the message of shared purpose to "fall on deaf ears." But traditional women, such as WCTU members, probably avoided evening meetings that mixed the sexes.

12. Emma Ghent Curtis, "The Forces that Carried Colorado," *WJ,* 2 December 1893, p. 380.

13. Leslie Wheeler, *Loving Warriors: A Revealing Portrait of an Unprecedented Marriage* (New York: Dial, 1981), p. 350.

14. Brundage, *Making of Working-Class Radicalism,* pp. 106–109.

15. Mari Jo Buhle, *Women and American Socialism, 1870–1920* (Urbana: University of Illinois Press, 1981), pp. 83–89.

16. Ibid., p. 88. Original source: *Farmer's Wife,* January 1892.

17. *Minutes of the National Woman's Christian Temperance Union with Addresses, Reports, and Constitution,* 19th Annual Meeting, Denver, Colo., 28 October to 2 November 1892 (Chicago: Woman's Temperance Publishing Association, 1892), pp. 113–114, FWML.

18. "To Protect Homes," *RMDN,* 29 October 1892; and Ellis Meredith, "Women's World: What Does It Mean?" *RMDN* (Denver), 30 October 1892.

19. "All Along the Line," *WJ,* 26 November 1892, p. 382.

20. Ibid., pp. 90–91; see also Bordin, *Frances Willard,* pp. 176–189.

21. Ibid., pp. 151–152.

22. "Defense of the Home," *RMDN,* 15 October 1891, p. 3.

23. "Daily Object Lessons on Silver," *RMDN,* 11 September 1892, p. 1.

24. Ibid.

25. "General J. B. Weaver," *RMDN,* 12 September 1892. Weaver used the idea of home protection when he criticized the growth of corporate power. See Pollack, *Populist Mind,* pp. 127, 145, 147, 149–150, 155–156.

26. "General J. B. Weaver," *RMDN,* 12 September 1892.

27. Sharon Hartman Strom, "Leadership and Tactics in the American Woman Suffrage Movement: A New Perspective from Massachusetts," *HWUS,* p. 176.

28. Ibid.

29. "Colorado," *HWS,* 4:513, and Meredith to Anthony, Meredith MSS, 7 August 1893.

30. "Women's Congress," *RMN,* 9 October 1889.

31. Ibid., and "Female Suffrage," *DN,* 11 October 1889.

32. "Female Suffrage," *DN,* 11 October 1889.

33. *HWS,* 4:509.

34. *Colorado WCTU Annual Reports,* 1891 and 1892, WHC.

35. "Colorado," *HWS,* 4:509, 4:513.

36. Tyler was the state organizer in Rhode Island and Massachusetts for three years under the auspices of the NWSA. See "Woman Recognized," *RMDN,* 1 January 1894.

37. *HWS,* 4:511.

38. Billie Barnes Jensen, "The Woman Suffrage Movement in Colorado" (master's thesis, University of Colorado at Boulder, 1959), pp. 66–70.

39. *HWS,* 4:512.

40. Flexner, *Century of Struggle,* p. 228.
41. Wright, *Politics of Populism,* p. 166.
42. Jensen, "Woman Suffrage in Colorado," p. 71.
43. Nelson O. McClees, "Colorado General Election," *WJ,* 19 August 1893, p. 260.
44. *HWS,* 4:512–513.
45. Ibid., p. 512.
46. Wright, *Politics of Populism,* pp. 163–166.
47. Albina Washburn, "Colorado Suffrage Items," *WJ,* 27 August 1892, p. 276.
48. Julie Roy Jeffrey, "Women in the Southern Farmers' Alliance: A Reconstruction of the Role and Status of Women in the Late Nineteenth-Century South," *Feminist Studies* 3 (1975): 72–91. Jeffrey found that southern women also were encouraged to participate in the Alliance and Populist parties.
49. Pollack, *The Populist Mind,* p. 63.
50. Helen M. Reynolds, "Good News from Colorado," *WJ,* 30 September 1893, p. 306; "Colorado Items," *WJ,* 21 October 1893, p. 332.
51. Curtis, "Forces," *WJ,* 2 December 1893, p. 380.
52. Joseph G. Brown, *Equal Suffrage in Colorado, 1868–1898* (Denver, Colo.: News Job Printing, 1898), p. 18.
53. Ibid., p. 19. See also *HWS,* 4:513–518.
54. *HWS,* 4:513. Ellis Meredith is also "Mrs. Stansbury." Meredith was in the midst of a divorce during the campaign.
55. Jensen, "Woman Suffrage in Colorado," pp. 74–75.
56. "Editorial Notes," *WJ,* 15 April 1893, p. 113.
57. "Editorial Notes," *WJ,* 21 April 1893, p. 121.
58. *HWS,* 4:513–14. In a letter to her husband, Henry Blackwell, Stone lamented, "They have no money, only one small society. &c. . . . Colorado seems to me to be a hopeless case, but we are to confer once more with the Colorado woman." See Stone to Blackwell, 21 May 1893, in Wheeler, *Loving Warriors,* p. 351.
59. Stone and Anthony considered Kansas a better opportunity because women in that state had municipal suffrage whereas Colorado women had only school suffrage. See "Editorial Notes," *WJ,* 27 May 1893, p. 161; Chapman to Meredith, Meredith MSS, 23 June 1893.
60. Blackwell to Stone, 19 May 1893, in Wheeler, *Loving Warriors,* p. 350, emphasis in text. Blackwell may have learned of the opportunities in Colorado's state politics at the National Republican Convention that he had just attended; as a chief editor of the *Woman's Journal,* he also was well informed of strides made in mobilization for woman suffrage in the states.
61. Chapman to Meredith, Meredith MSS, 23 June 1893.
62. See the following letters: Stone to Meredith, 12 June 1893 and 27 June 1893; Chapman to Meredith, 23 June 1893; Meredith to Chapman, 30 June 1893; Chapman to Meredith, 5 July 1893; Chapman to Meredith, 16 July 1893, all in Meredith MSS.

63. See Douglas Rae, *The Political Consequences of Electoral Laws* (New Haven, Conn.: Yale University Press, 1971), pp. 25–28.
64. Meredith to Anthony, Meredith MSS, 14 June 1893.
65. Meredith to Chapman, Meredith MSS, 30 June 1893. The postcard survey consisted of two questions: (1) Will you advocate suffrage? and (2) Will you use suffrage matter if furnished?
66. Ibid.
67. Ibid. See also Chapman to Meredith, Meredith MSS, 5 July 1893.
68. Chapman to Meredith, Meredith MSS, 23 June 1893, emphasis in text. She wrote, "Men are so largely governed by party commands that until parties will ratify an amendment in their platform, we cannot poll the full vote of those who are friendly."
69. Ibid.
70. "Corresponding Secretary's Report," *Minutes of the National WCTU* (1892), FWML.
71. "Suffrage News from Colorado," 19 August 1893, p. 261.
72. Meredith to Chapman, 30 June 1893; Anthony to Meredith, 16 July 1893, both in Meredith MSS. According to Meredith, the WCTU had already been contacted; the state WCTU leaders "promised to make suffrage the dominant issue," but opted "to work by themselves," and they would not donate money to the state suffrage organization. Anthony told Meredith: "Both Mrs. Chapman and I think you should *hold no big meeting* in Denver or any of the large cities, until *after* you have held *ward* meetings, made a house to house canvass to get the names of men and women in favor and those against. Do all you can in the wards of the counties—all through September, say, and then in October—take the cities with big and rousing meetings." Emphasis in text.
73. Meredith to Chapman, Meredith MSS, 30 June 1893.
74. Anthony to Meredith, Meredith MSS, 16 July 1893.
75. Ibid. Emphasis in text.
76. Meredith to Anthony, Meredith MSS, 7 August 1893.
77. Chapman to Meredith, Meredith MSS, 5 July 1893. Ida H. Harper, *The Life and Work of Susan B. Anthony,* vol. 2 (Indianapolis, Ind.: Hollenbeck, 1898), pp. 780–798.
78. Many letters were exchanged about finances. See Meredith to Anthony, Meredith MSS, 14 June 1893. Meredith reported that funds promised even by prominent men such as the state's attorney general had not appeared. She implied that although the state association would fund some travel expenses, the Colorado leaders needed "speakers who can organize and raise money sufficient to pay their way, and next floods of literature." See also Stone to Meredith, 27 June 1893; Chapman to Meredith, 23 June 1893 and 5 July 1893, Meredith MSS.
79. Chapman to Meredith, Meredith MSS, 5 July 1893.
80. Chapman to Meredith, Meredith MSS, 16 July 1893.

81. "The World's Suffrage Congress," *WJ*, 19 August 1893, p. 261. Blackwell mentioned his success for the Colorado cause in two letters to Lucy Stone: Blackwell to Stone, 11 August 1893; and Blackwell to Stone, 15 August 1893, both in Blackwell MSS.

82. Helen Reynolds, "How Colorado Was Carried," *WJ*, 18 November 1893, p. 364.

83. Aileen S. Kraditor, *The Ideas of the Woman Suffrage Movement, 1890–1920* (Garden City, N.Y.: Anchor, 1971), pp. 38–57.

84. Anthony to Meredith, Meredith MSS, 11 August 1893.

85. *CTB,* vol. 3, no. 13. A letter from Frances Belford, Superintendent of the Legislative Department, reported that two legislators were promoting the cause, "petitions were pouring in," and the house was giving the measure inadequate attention. "Editorial Notes," *WJ*, 26 August 1893, p. 265.

86. "Prohibition Department," *CTB,* vol. 3, no. 9, 1 February 1893, WHC.

87. Albina Washburn, "Public Sentiment in Colorado," *WJ*, 8 July 1893, p. 212.

88. "Mrs. Weaver on Politics," *WJ*, 12 August 1893, p. 250.

89. "Good News from Colorado," *WJ*, 30 September 1893, p. 305.

90. "Suffrage News from Colorado," *WJ*, 19 August 1893, p. 261.

91. The article "Colorado Women Moving" (*WJ*, 2 September 1893, p. 276) reported that a mass meeting of women was organized at the August 12 convocation of the CESA. Moreover, the Canon City branch of the organization followed Blackwell's advice and conducted "a house to house canvass" to "see every voter in Fremont County." In another article, "Woman's Column Valued in Colorado," Durango reformer Lillian Hartman Johnson requested that the *Woman's Journal* send "the enrollment books" that Blackwell had offered for door-to-door campaigning. Sixty of the 125 state newspapers were also reported to "have offered space for suffrage matter each week." Nebraska suffrage reformers announced their plans to "send a speaker, whose expenses they will defray, who will help us for one month." The organization of a suffrage association in Coal Creek by the Canon City suffragists also was reported.

92. "Mrs. Chapman in Colorado," *WJ*, 16 September 1893, p. 292.

93. "The Situation in Colorado," *WJ*, 23 September 1893, p. 300.

94. Ibid.

95. Ibid.

96. Reynolds, "How Colorado Was Carried," pp. 361, 364–365.

97. Van Voris, *Carrie Chapman Catt*, pp. 36–37.

98. "Equal Suffrage: To the Women of Colorado, Greeting," *CTB,* vol. 3, no. 20, 1 June 1893.

99. "An Appeal for Colorado," *WJ*, 3 June 1893, p. 172.

100. "Suffrage News from Colorado," *WJ*, 19 August 1893, p. 261.

101. "Excellent Advice," *WJ*, 23 September 1893, p. 300.

102. The New English Bible, Oxford Study Edition (New York: Oxford University Press, 1976), p. 2. In his critique of Robert Filmer's *Patriarica,* John Locke

also referred to this passage as evidence against the idea that rulers must be fathers. See *John Locke, Two Treatises of Government,* ed. Peter Laslett (Cambridge: Cambridge University Press, 1988), pp. 152–153, 161–163.

103. Kraditor, *Ideas,* pp. 43–57.

104. "A Few Leading Questions," CESA, Denver, Colo., 1893, WSC, DPL, leaflet 7.

105. "To the Women of Colorado," (CESA), WSC, DPL, leaflet 3.

106. Ibid.

107. "An Appeal to the Voters of Colorado" (CESA), WSC, DPL, leaflet 4.

108. Ibid.

109. Bordin, *Woman and Temperance,* pp. 90–98, 110–116. The *Colorado Temperance Bulletins* contain much such rhetoric. See Archives, UC, Boulder.

110. "For Better or Worse?" *DR,* 19 October 1893.

111. Washburn, "Public Sentiment in Colorado." Washburn stated that his speech "was simply a splendid argument, mostly from the Bible standpoint, for equal 'dominion' for women and men over all things."

112. "For Equal Rights," *DR,* 6 November 1893, WSC, DPL. Reverend O'Ryan referred to the blessings of life that were given to Mary; women's occupation during apostolic times of "the highest positions in the ministrations of the church as shown by the order of deaconesses"; and the regular extension of woman's jurisdiction beyond "the domestic limits" by the church, whose leaders "coveted" their advice "in spiritual matters." He also confidently asserted that women "would purify politics."

113. "Plea for Fair Play," *RMDN* (Denver), 16 October 1893. Reed argued that just as the "Negro" and the laborer relied on the vote to protect their rights, working women also needed the vote to exert control over their working conditions. He suggested that middle-class women and those who were wealthier would benefit from the franchise by the extinction of "offensive condescension." Reed defined "offensive condescension" as male chivalry— "the habit of bowing and scraping before women as if they were mentally taller." Reed stated that this "old habit of patronizing and condescending to women has come down and lingers, and will linger as long as there is recognized inequality." Women are not asking for a gift in the ballot, he explained, "they ask for equal freedom."

114. *HWS,* 4:518; and "It Was over 6,000," *DT,* 2 December 1893. The *Denver Times* misreported the total votes against woman suffrage as 29,451 instead of 29,551.

115. "It Was over 6,000."

116. U.S. Department of Commerce, Bureau of the Census, *Statistical Abstract of the United States, 1890* (Washington), pp. 14–15.

117. "The Boston Tea Party . . . ," *WJ,* 23 December 1893, p. 404.

118. "To the Women of Colorado: The Record of the Parties on the Equal Suffrage Amendment; To What Party Are the Women Indebted for the Privilege of the Ballot?" (The Colorado Populist Party, November 1893), pp. 2–3; see also ibid., p. 3.

119. Without a more detailed analysis of the campaign—especially in the southern counties—to explain the constituencies and activist leaders of the opposition, the Populists' evaluation remains suggestive but inconclusive.

120. Henry B. Blackwell, "Victory in Colorado," *WJ*, 11 November 1893, p. 356.

121. Reynolds, "How Colorado Was Carried," p. 361. Reynolds credited the "easy success" of the reform to Populists and organized labor in Colorado, who voted for woman suffrage "almost *en masse*" because these organizations espoused "'equal rights' as a life-long principle."

122. "Equal Suffrage Approved" (CESA), WSC, DPL.

123. Reynolds, "The Colorado Campaign," *The Woman's Tribune*, 18 November 1893.

124. "The Boston Tea Party . . . ," p. 404. Chapman's testimony about the opposition of the liquor interests casts further doubt on Flexner's assumption that they "were napping."

125. Martha Pease, "A Retrospective Glance at the Campaign Last Fall," *The Woman Voter*, vol. 1, no. 24, 29 June 1894, p. 8.

126. Curtis, "Forces," p. 380.

127. Ibid. According to Curtis, Lake's influence in the mining camps was "very great."

128. Ella Beecher Giddings, "The Temperance Movement in Colorado," *WJ*, 20 January 1894, p. 20.

129. "Honor Due the Colorado W.C.T.U.," letter from Julia A. Sabine, *WJ*, 3 February 1894, p. 40.

130. Thomas R. Dye, *Who's Running America? The Carter Years*, 2d ed. (Englewood Cliffs, N.J.: Prentice-Hall, 1979), pp. 143–164.

131. I compiled these statistics by identifying the counties where the vote for woman suffrage met or exceeded 51 percent. After identifying the counties that listed a local WCTU in 1893, I used the following atlas compendium to identify the counties that the local WCTU came from: William Thorndale and William Dollarhide, *Map Guide to the U.S. Federal Censuses, 1790–1920* (Baltimore, Md.: Genealogical Publishing, 1987). I am grateful to Dave Leege for suggesting how to frame this data analysis and to Timothy J. Kenny for the map reference.

132. "To the Women of Colorado," p. 3.

133. After the suffrage victory, Colorado's parties either formed women's organizations or the women who were already affiliated with a political party formed conjunctive women's associations. See *HWS*, 4:520–21.

134. Wright, *Politics of Populism*, pp. 198–199.

135. Ibid., pp. 194–204. Wright notes that the statistics do not uphold Waite's view that women voted against him more than did his other expected constituencies.

136. Brown, *Equal Suffrage in Colorado*, p. 37.

137. Ibid., 37–38.

138. Ibid., 37–42.

139. "Suffrage in Denver: Women's Vote Has Achieved a Great Reform, Says Mrs. Suffren," *NYT*, 25 June 1912, p. 10, col. 7. See also "Concerning Women," *WJ*, 19 March 1910, p. 45.

140. Edward Taylor, "Equal Suffrage in Colorado," *Congressional Record, Reprint*, 24 April 1912 (Washington, 1912); also in Archives, Colorado Historical Society, Denver, Colo., pp. 5–11.

141. Chief Justice David Brewer commented in an article written for *Ladies' World* and reprinted by the *Woman's Journal* that Colorado women deserved credit for Lindsey's election when he ran on an independent ticket after being "denied a renomination by each of the great political parties." See "Justice Brewer for Woman Suffrage," *WJ*, 27 November 1909, p. 192; "Judge Lindsey on Equal Suffrage," *WJ*, 9 March 1906, p. 36; and "The Latest Word from Judge Lindsey," *WJ*, 2 April 1910, p. 55.

142. "Our 'Fighting Machine,'" *WJ*, 19 February 1910, p. 32; as well as "Denver Housewives for Reform" and "A Tribute to Women," *WJ*, 4 June 1910, p. 90.

143. Sumner, *Equal Suffrage*, p. 104.

144. Ibid., pp. 20, 22.

145. *HWS*, 4:646 and Harper, *Susan B. Anthony*, 3:780–798. Walter T. K. Nugent explains how Kansas Republicans connived to displace Kansas Populists in the 1894 elections by opposing votes for women in "How the Populists Lost in 1894," *Kansas Historical Quarterly* 31 (autumn 1965), pp. 245–255.

146. *HWS*, 4:646.

6. Airs of Respectability

1. Aileen Kraditor, *The Ideas of the Woman Suffrage Movement, 1890–1920* (Garden City, N.Y.: Anchor, 1971), pp. 43–45, 51–55, 86–91; William O'Neill, *Everyone Was Brave: A History of Feminism in America* (Garden City, N.Y.: Quadrangle, 1971), pp. 49–76; Judith Shklar, *American Citizenship: The Quest for Inclusion* (Cambridge, Mass.: Harvard University Press, 1991), pp. 57–62; Nancie Caraway, *Segregated Sisterhood: Racism and the Politics of American Feminism* (Knoxville: University of Tennessee Press, 1991), pp. 142–157; Rogers M. Smith, "'One United People': Second Class Female Citizenship and the American Quest for Community," *Yale Journal of Law and the Humanities* 1 (1989): 229–293.

2. *HWS*, 4:14–30, 4:56–84, 4:112–123; Ruth Bordin, *Frances Willard: A Biography* (Chapel Hill: University of North Carolina Press, 1986), pp. 97–111.

3. Elisabeth Griffith, *In Her Own Right: The Life of Elizabeth Cady Stanton* (New York: Oxford University Press, 1984), p. 178. For a fuller account of the conflicts over reunification of the AWSA with the NWSA, see Kathleen Barry, *Susan B. Anthony: A Biography of a Singular Feminist* (New York: Ballantine, 1988), pp. 283–300.

4. Barry, *Susan B. Anthony,* pp. 297–299. The full text of Stanton's speech is published in Ellen Carol DuBois, ed., *Elizabeth Cady Stanton / Susan B. Anthony: Correspondence, Writings, Speeches* (New York: Schocken, 1981), pp. 222–227.

5. Judith Shklar, *American Citizenship: The Quest for Inclusion* (Cambridge, Mass.: Harvard University Press, 1991), p. 60.

6. Caraway, *Segregated Sisterhood,* pp. 148–163; Anna Julia Cooper, "Woman versus the Indian," in Anna Julia Cooper, ed.; *A Voice from the South* (1892; New York: Oxford University Press, 1988), pp. 80–127; and Rosalyn Terborg-Penn, "Discontented Black Feminists: Prelude and Postscript to the Passage of the Nineteenth Amendment," in Darlene Clark Hine, ed., *Black Women in United States History,* vol. 4, bk. 8 (Brooklyn, N.Y.: Carlson Publishing, 1990), pp. 1159–76.

7. Caraway, *Segregated Sisterhood,* pp. 157–167; Glenda Elizabeth Gilmore, "Gender and Jim Crow: Women and the Politics of White Supremacy in North Carolina, 1896–1920" (Ph.D. diss., University of North Carolina, 1992), pp. 438–480; Paula Giddings, *When and Where I Enter: The Impact of Black Women on Race and Sex in America* (New York: William Morrow, 1984), pp. 119–131; and Evelyn Brooks Higginbotham, *Righteous Discontent: The Women's Movement in the Black Baptist Church, 1880–1920* (Cambridge, Mass.: Harvard University Press, 1993), pp. 88–119.

8. In 1891 J. P. H. Russ introduced the idea of votes for white women in Arkansas. The measure received three readings but only four affirmative votes (*HWS,* 4:476). In 1890 several measures were introduced in the Mississippi legislature to give property-owning married white women the vote. All were defeated (*HWS,* 4:786).

9. Marjorie Spruill Wheeler, *New Women of the New South: The Leaders of the Woman Suffrage Movement in the Southern States* (New York: Oxford University Press, 1993), p. 108.

10. Ellen Carol DuBois, "Working Women, Class Relations, and Suffrage Militance: Harriot Stanton Blatch and the New York Woman Suffrage Movement, 1894–1909," in Ellen Carol DuBois and Vicki L. Ruiz, eds., *Unequal Sisters: A Multi-Cultural Reader in U.S. Women's History* (New York: Routledge, 1990), p. 180.

11. "Editorial Notes," *WJ,* 20 November 1909, p. 185.

12. Henry B. Blackwell, "What the South Can Do (1867)" in Aileen S. Kraditor, ed., *Up from the Pedestal: Selected Writings in the History of American Feminism* (New York: Quadrangle, 1968), p. 255. Emphasis added.

13. Wheeler, *New Women,* pp. 113–116.

14. Blackwell, "What the South Can Do," pp. 254–255.

15. C. Van Woodward, *Origins of the New South, 1877–1913* (Baton Rouge: Louisiana State University Press, 1971), pp. 51–74; Jacqueline Jones, *Labor of Love, Labor of Sorrow: Black Women, Work, and the Family from Slavery to the Present* (New York: Basic, 1985), pp. 44–151. J. Morgan

Kousser argues that electoral laws shrunk the electorate and altered the political system in ways white violence did not in *The Shaping of Southern Politics: Suffrage, Restriction and the Establishment of the One-Party South, 1880–1910* (New Haven, Conn.: Yale University Press, 1974), pp. 1–9, 18–21.

16. Blackwell, "What the South Can Do," p. 256.

17. Wheeler, *New Women,* pp. 89, 108. Jacqueline Dowd Hall explains how Jesse Daniel Ames, a southern white woman, led a women's movement against lynching in Hall's *Revolt against Chivalry: Jesse Daniel Ames and the Women's Campaign against Lynching* (New York: Columbia University Press, 1993). Although Glenda Gilmore observes that most white women tacitly accepted lynching against blacks as well as whites' armed siege of city governments (such as that of Wilmington, North Carolina, in 1898), she also argues that by competing to achieve high voter turnouts, southern white voters and black women voters in North Carolina deflected threats of violence. See Gilmore, "Gender and Jim Crow," pp. 215–226, 445–447.

18. Henry Brown Blackwell, "Woman Suffrage Proposed in Louisiana," *WJ,* 3 December 1904, p. 388. One of the "convicts elected to office" was James Michael Curley, future mayor of Boston. He was put in prison for taking a civil service test under a false name. See Jack Beatty, *The Rascal King: The Life and Times of James Michael Curley, 1874–1958* (Reading, Mass.: Addison-Wesley, 1992), pp. 77–82.

19. John Stuart Mill, *Considerations on Representative Government* (Indianapolis, Ind.: Bobbs-Merrill, 1958), pp. 154–171, esp. pp. 161–164.

20. Jacqueline Van Voris, *Carrie Chapman Catt: A Public Life* (New York: Feminist Press, 1987), pp. 16–17.

21. Ibid., pp. 55–113.

22. Eleanor Flexner, *Century of Struggle: The Woman's Rights Movement in the United States,* rev. ed. (Cambridge, Mass.: Harvard University Press, 1975), pp. 287–292.

23. Robert Booth Fowler, *Carrie Catt: Feminist Politician* (Boston: Northeastern University Press, 1986), pp. 71–76.

24. Van Voris, *Carrie Chapman Catt,* pp. 30–31.

25. Ibid., pp. 29–32, quotation on p. 32.

26. "Subject and Sovereign," Catt MSS, c. 1888. Catt exaggerated the benefits given to Native American Indians, including the franchise. See Sharon L. O'Brien, *American Indian Tribal Governments* (Norman: University of Oklahoma Press, 1989), pp. 68–70, 80, 146–151.

27. "The American Sovereign," Catt MSS, c. 1896. This speech was mistakenly dated as written in or around 1888. Parts of it could not have been written until after the first part of the 1890 census was published in 1895.

28. "4th of July, 1889, Rockford, Illinois," Catt MSS. Unpublished speech.

29. Sinclair, *Emancipation of American Woman,* pp. 293–298.

30. Wheeler, *New Women,* pp. 115–118.

31. William A. Link, *The Paradox of Southern Progressivism, 1880–1930* (Chapel Hill: University of North Carolina Press, 1992), pp. 301–304.

32. J. Morgan Kousser argues that the introduction of the Australian ballot into the southern states added fuel to the disenfranchisement process because it swept away the mode of voting that many illiterate white southern male voters knew and had favored. Educated elite southern women, however, probably perceived this reform as an opportunity to demand the vote. See Kousser, *Shaping of Southern Politics,* pp. 52–60.

33. For the story of how Charlotte Hawkins Brown financed The Palmer School by appealing for white support, see Gilmore, "Gender and Jim Crow," pp. 379–400; and Hall, *Revolt against Chivalry,* pp. 59–128.

34. Wheeler, *New Women of the New South,* p. 114.

35. *HWS,* 4:184.

36. Ibid., p. 177.

37. Ibid., p. 178.

38. "Why Southern Women Desire the Ballot," *WJ,* 26 January 1895, pp. 26–32, and 2 February 1895, p. 34.

39. Gilmore, "Gender and Jim Crow," pp. 188–195.

40. Mary Gray Peck, *Carrie Chapman Catt* (New York: H. W. Wilson, 1944), p. 83.

41. Sinclair, *Emancipation of American Woman,* p. 225.

42. Sharon Hartman Strom, "Leadership and Tactics in the American Woman Suffrage Movement: A New Perspective from Massachusetts," *Journal of American History,* vol. 62, no. 2 (1975): 298.

43. Maud Wood Park, *The Front Door Lobby* (Boston: Beacon, 1960), pp. 26–28.

44. Kousser, *Shaping of Southern Politics,* pp. 39–62, 257–265.

45. Link, *Paradox of Southern Progressivism,* p. 299.

46. Anne F. Scott, "Women, Religion, and Social Change in the South, 1830–1930," in Samuel S. Hill, Jr., ed., *Religion and the Solid South* (Nashville: Abingdon, 1972), pp. 92–121.

47. Anne F. Scott, *The Southern Lady: From Pedestal to Politics, 1830–1930* (Chicago: University of Chicago Press, 1970), pp. 144–150.

48. Ibid., pp. 164–184.

49. Wheeler, *New Women,* pp. 40–45, 74–75. Anne Firor Scott observes that the son of Elizabeth Avery Meriwether reported "that shortly after the war when her husband was engaged in organizing a local Ku Klux Klan, Mrs. Meriwether had suggested giving the vote to white women as an alternative to terrorizing Negro men." See Scott, *Southern Lady,* p. 173.

50. Ira Katznelson, *City Trenches: Urban Politics and the Patterning of Class in the United States* (New York: Pantheon, 1981), pp. 45–58, 65–72; Robert Wiebe, *The Search for Order* (New York: Hill and Wang, 1967), pp. 30–43; Martin Shefter, *Political Crisis/Fiscal Crisis: The Collapse and Revival of New York City* (New York: Basic, 1985), pp. 13–28.

51. "The National American Convention of 1903," *HWS*, 5:74–75.
52. Ibid., p. 83.
53. *HWS*, 5:37.
54. "The National American Convention of 1903," p. 60, n. 1.
55. Wheeler, *New Women of the New South*, pp. 74–99.
56. Scott, *Southern Lady*, p. 183, n. 33.
57. Wheeler, *New Women of the New South*, pp. 79–82.
58. Scott, *Southern Lady*, p. 168. Scott summarized the main arguments made by the opposition. Her assertions have been demonstrated by the following sample of scholars: Elna C. Green, "Those Opposed: The Anti-Suffragists in North Carolina, 1900–1920," *The North Carolina Historical Review*, vol. 67, no. 3 (1990): 315–332; Link, *Paradox of Southern Progressivism*, pp. 296–304; and Wheeler, *New Women*, pp. 25–37, 127–128, 174–178.
59. Hall, *Revolt against Chivalry*, pp. 137–145. Elna Green found that North Carolina legislators claimed that they would not be able to bar black women from voting. See Green, "Those Opposed," pp. 318–319.
60. Green, "Those Opposed," p. 318.
61. Hall, *Revolt against Chivalry*, pp. 107–191.
62. Wheeler, *New Women of the New South*, pp. 120–125.
63. *HWS*, 5:105–106. Ida Husted Harper described Mary Church Terrell as follows: "Mrs. Mary Church Terrell (D.C.), a highly educated woman, showing little trace of [N]egro blood."
64. Mary Church Terrell, "A Plea for the White South by a Colored Woman," in *Black Women in United States History*, ed. Darlene C. Hine, vol. 13, *Quest for Equality: The Life and Writings of Mary Eliza Church Terrell, 1863–1954*, ed. Beverly W. Jones (Brooklyn: Carlson, 1990), pp. 239–254.
65. Wheeler, *New Women*, pp. 119–125.
66. Shaw quoted in Wheeler, *New Women*, p. 121. Original source is Anna Howard Shaw to Laura Clay, The Laura Clay Papers, 15 November 1906, Special Collections and Archives, Margaret I. King Library, University of Kentucky, Lexington, Ky.
67. Wheeler, *New Women*, pp. 122–123.
68. Henry B. Blackwell, "The Chain Gang in Georgia," *WJ*, 13 August 1904, p. 263.
69. Wheeler, *New Women*, pp. 133–171.
70. Cynthia Neverdon-Morton, *Afro-American Women of the South and the Advancement of the Race, 1895–1925* (Knoxville: University of Tennessee Press, 1989), p. 204. In 1919, according to Neverdon-Morton, "when NACW [the National Association of Colored Women] requested membership in NAWSA, Ida Husted Harper, NAWSA publicist, through Mary Church Terrell, asked NACW to hold its application until after the Senate vote. The black women agreed to do so."
71. Mary Martha Thomas, *The New Woman in Alabama: Social Reforms and Suffrage, 1890–1920* (Tuscaloosa: University of Alabama Press, 1992), p. 84.

72. David Levering Lewis, *W. E. B. Du Bois: Biography of a Race, 1868–1919* (New York: Henry Holt, 1993), pp. 417–418.

73. Mary Church Terrell, "The Justice of Woman Suffrage" (1912) in *Black Women in United States History,* ed. Darlene Clark Hine, vol. 13, *Quest for Equality: The Life and Writings of Mary Eliza Church Terrell, 1863–1954,* ed. Beverly W. Jones (Brooklyn: Carlson, 1990), p. 308.

74. Flexner, *Century of Struggle,* pp. 317–318.

75. Barry, *Susan B. Anthony,* pp. 296–299. The organization remained active under Gage until her death in 1898.

76. "International Council of Women—Hearing of 1888," *HWS,* 4:130, 4:132.

77. "Miss Shaw's Address," *WJ,* 17 February 1906, pp. 26–28.

78. *HWS,* 4:1079.

79. Flexner, *Century of Struggle,* pp. 280, 309.

80. "Woman Suffrage," *America,* 17 April 1909, p. 4; "Woman Suffrage," *America,* 1 May 1909, p. 58; "What the Pope Did Not Say," *America,* 8 May 1909, p. 102; "Topics of Interest: Genesis of Woman Suffrage," *America,* 16 October 1915, p. 5; "Votes for Women," *America,* 13 November 1915, pp. 110–111; and Edward F. Murphy, "What Women Wanted," *America,* 20 November 1915, pp. 128–130.

81. Alice Stone Blackwell, "The Pope and Woman Suffrage," *WJ,* 1 May 1909, p. 70.

82. Barbara Hilkert Andolsen, *"Daughters of Jefferson; Daughters of Bootblacks": Racism and American Feminism* (Macon, Ga.: Mercer University Press, 1986), pp. 39–40.

83. Van Voris, *Carrie Chapman Catt,* p. 222, n. 2.

84. Carrie Lane Chapman, "A True Story," *WJ,* 19 September 1891, p. 304. Although it is hard to believe that even a man of little wealth with some social standing in China would have sold his granddaughter into the sex trade just because he disliked women, historian Lucie Cheng Hirata documented a similar type of transaction. Lucie Cheng Hirata, "Chinese Immigrant Women in Nineteenth-Century California," in Carol Ruth Berkin and Mary Beth Norton, eds., *Women of America: A History* (Boston: Houghton Mifflin, 1979), p. 230. There is also some dispute about whether a parent would deliberately initiate such a sale. According to Chinese feminist scholar Koh Tai Ann, a locally prestigious Chinese grandfather would stand to gain much more from the arrangement of a financially advantageous marriage; the sale of a young girl would make sense only if he faced an enormous financial crisis. I am grateful to Koh Tai Ann, dean of the School of Art, Nanyang Technological University, for her view that this act would have been exceptional in China.

85. Paul C. P. Siu, *The Chinese Laundryman: A Study of Social Isolation* (New York: New York University Press, 1987), pp. 8–22.

86. Chapman, "A True Story," p. 304.

87. Hirata, "Chinese Immigrant Women," pp. 229–232.

88. Chapman, "A True Story," p. 304.
89. Hirata, "Chinese Immigrant Women," p. 230.

7. The Feminism of Personal Development

1. *HWS,* 4:158–161.
2. "The National American Convention and Hearings of 1892," *HWS,* 4:194–195.
3. Elizabeth Cady Stanton, "The Solitude of Self," in Ellen C. DuBois, ed., *Elizabeth Cady Stanton / Susan B. Anthony: Correspondence, Writings, Speeches* (New York: Schocken, 1981), pp. 246–254.
4. Rogers M. Smith, "Beyond Tocqueville, Myrdal, and Hartz: The Multiple Traditions in America," *American Political Science Review* 87 (1993): 561–562.
5. Sharon Hartman Strom, "Leadership and Tactics in the American Woman Suffrage Movement: A New Perspective from Massachusetts," *HWUS,* vol. 19, pt. 1, pp. 174–176.
6. See Meredith Tax, *The Rising of the Women: Feminist Solidarity and Class Conflict, 1880–1917* (New York: Monthly Review Press, 1980); and Nancy Schrom Dye, *As Equals & as Sisters: Feminism, Unionism, and Women's Trade Union League of New York* (Columbia: University of Missouri Press, 1980).
7. Harriot Stanton Blatch, "An Open Letter to Mrs. Stanton," *WJ,* 22 December 1894, p. 402.
8. Mari Jo Buhle and Paul Buhle, eds., *The Concise History of Woman Suffrage: Selections from the Classic Work of Stanton, Anthony, Gage, and Harper* (Urbana: University of Illinois Press, 1978), p. 366.
9. Ellen Carol DuBois, "Working Women, Class Relations, and Suffrage Militance: Harriot Stanton Blatch and the New York Woman Suffrage Movement, 1894–1909," in Ellen Carol DuBois and Vicki L. Ruiz, eds., *Unequal Sisters: A Multi-Cultural Reader in U.S. Women's History* (New York: Routledge, Chapman & Hall, 1990), p. 190.
10. Harriot Stanton Blatch, "Respects Her Foewomen: But Mrs. Blatch Believes They Put the Cart before the Horse," *NYT,* 2 June 1912.
11. DuBois, "Working Women," pp. 184–191.
12. On parades, lobbying, and criticism of the press, see ibid. and Blatch, "Respects Her Foewomen"; on blame of political conservatism see "Mrs. Blatch on Mrs. Ward," *WJ,* 25 July 1908, p. 120; and on electoral opposition strategies see "Question the Candidates," *WJ,* 15 January 1910, p. 11.
13. "The National American Convention of 1898," *HWS,* 4:312–313.
14. "The National American Convention of 1904," *HWS,* 5:95–98.
15. Mari Jo Buhle, *Women and American Socialism, 1870–1920* (Urbana: University of Illinois Press, 1981), pp. 214–245.

16. "Florence Kelley's Address," *WJ*, 3 March 1906, pp. 33–35.

17. Addams did not conceive "Americanizing" as a process of assimilation that caused deference to Americanist ideas of superiority. She meant that in efforts to stop health-threatening practices such as the slaughter of animals in basements, women would be more effective than men. See Jane Addams, "The Modern City and the Municipal Franchise for Women," *WJ*, 7 April 1906, p. 55.

18. Theda Skocpol, *Protecting Soldiers and Mothers: The Political Origins of Social Policy in the United States* (Cambridge, Mass.: Harvard University Press, 1992), pp. 318–319.

19. Eleanor Flexner, *Century of Struggle: The Woman's Rights Movement in the United States*, rev. ed. (Cambridge, Mass.: Harvard University Press, 1975), p. 266, and William O'Neill, *Everyone Was Brave: A History of Feminism in America* (New York: Quadrangle, 1971), p. 122.

20. *HWS*, 5:27.

21. Ibid., p. 30.

22. "International Suffrage Alliance," *WJ*, 10 March 1906, p. 38.

23. "Mrs. Catt's International Address," *WJ*, 27 June 1908.

24. Quoted by Jacqueline Van Voris in *Carrie Chapman Catt: A Public Life* (New York: Feminist Press, 1987), p. 105.

25. "Do a Majority of Women . . . Want the Ballot?" statement of Mr. Franklin W. Collins of Nebraska before the Senate Woman Suffrage Committee in April 1912 in Anne Firor Scott and Andrew MacKay Scott, *One Half the People: The Fight for Woman Suffrage* (Urbana: University of Illinois Press, 1982), pp. 106–111.

26. William A. Link, *The Paradox of Southern Progressivism, 1880–1930* (Chapel Hill: University of North Carolina Press, 1992), pp. 299–304.

27. Carl Degler, *At Odds: Women and the Family in America from the Revolution to the Present* (New York: Oxford University Press, 1980), p. 356.

28. Rogers M. Smith, "'One United People': Second-Class Female Citizenship and the American Quest for Community," *Yale Journal of Law and the Humanities* 1 (1989): 269–282.

29. Stephen Skowronek, *Building a New American State: The Expansion of National Administrative Capacities, 1877–1920* (Cambridge: Cambridge University Press, 1982), pp. 59–82, 165–176.

30. Sara Evans and Harry Boyte, *Free Spaces: The Sources of Democratic Change in America* (New York: Harper & Row, 1986), pp. vii–x, 17–25.

31. John D. Buenker, "The Urban Political Machine and Woman Suffrage: A Study in Political Adaptability," *The Historian*, vol. 33, no. 2 (1971): 161, 264–265.

32. "To Get a Man's Vote, Sit on His Doorstep," *NYT*, 6 March 1909.

33. Carrie Chapman Catt, "The New York Party," *WJ*, 19 February 1910, pp. 29–30; Ronald Schaffer, "The New York City Woman Suffrage Party, 1909–1919," in *HWUS*, vol. 19, pt. 2, pp. 453–471.

34. Schaffer, "The New York City Woman Suffrage Party, 1909–1919," p. 464.

35. Sidney R. Bland, "Fighting the Odds: Militant Suffragists in South Carolina," in *HWUS,* vol. 19, pt. 2, pp. 586–597.

36. "State Correspondence: New York," *WJ,* 5 February 1910.

37. DuBois, "Working Women," pp. 185–191.

38. "Chinese Suffrage Meeting," *NYT,* 11 April 1912.

39. "Chinese Women to Parade for Woman Suffrage," *NYT,* 14 April 1912.

40. Alice Stone Blackwell, *"Bridget's Sisters:* A Humorous Play, Founded on Fact," *WJ,* 20 January 1912.

41. Judith A. Baer, *The Chains of Protection: Judicial Response to the Women's Labor Legislation* (Westport, Conn.: Greenwood, 1978), pp. 31–41, 61–67, 167–169; Smith, "'One United People,'" pp. 271–273.

42. Alice Stone Blackwell, "Justice Brewer for Woman Suffrage," *WJ,* 27 November 1909.

43. "Suffrage Means Success," *WJ,* 28 September 1912.

44. Carl Degler also considers the *Muller* decision a stride forward for suffrage. See Degler, *At Odds,* pp. 358–359.

45. Kristin Luker, *Abortion and the Politics of Motherhood* (Berkeley: University of California, 1984), pp. 113–118. For an assessment of the "difference concept" in protective legislation, see Deborah C. Rhode, "Definitions of Difference," in *Theoretical Perspectives on Sexual Difference* (New Haven, Conn.: Yale University Press, 1990), pp. 197–212.

46. Skocpol, *Protecting Soldiers and Mothers,* pp. 369–372.

47. Peter G. Filene, *Him/Her/Self: Sex Roles in Modern America,* 2d ed. (Baltimore, Md.: The Johns Hopkins University Press, 1986), pp. 19–93; John D'Emilio and Estelle B. Freedman, *Intimate Matters: A History of Sexuality in America* (New York: Harper & Row, 1988), pp. 203–221.

48. According to Van Voris, the story was reprinted in *WJ,* 16 March 1901, p. 87, and again 25 January 1913, p. 26. "Another True Story," written in the same vein, was in *The Woman Voter,* January 1914. See Van Voris, *Carrie Chapman Catt,* p. 222, n. 2.

49. "The National American Convention of 1901," in *HWS,* 5:6.

50. Jane Addams, *A New Conscience and an Ancient Evil* (New York: Arno Press & the *New York Times,* 1972), p. 119.

51. Ibid., p. 192.

52. Ibid., pp. 193–194.

53. Mary Church Terrell, "A Plea for the White South by a Colored Woman," in *Black Women in United States History,* ed. Darlene C. Hine, vol. 13, *Quest for Equality: The Life and Writings of Mary Eliza Church Terrell, 1863–1954,* ed. Beverly W. Jones (Brooklyn: Carlson, 1990), p. 253.

54. N. H. Burroughs, "Black Women and Reform," in Hine, *Black Women in the United States,* vol. 5, p. 187.

55. Link, *Paradox of Southern Progressivism,* pp. 119–120.

56. Jacquelyn Dowd Hall, *Revolt against Chivalry: Jesse Daniel Ames and the*

Women's Campaign against Lynching, rev. ed. (New York: Columbia University Press, 1993), pp. 149–157.

57. Alice Sheppard includes Frederikke Palmer's cartoon in her *Cartooning for Suffrage* (Albuquerque: University of New Mexico Press, 1994), p. 134.

58. Karolena M. Fox, "History of the Equal Suffrage Movement in Michigan," *Michigan History Magazine* 2 (1918): 106.

59. Kay Sloan, "Sexual Warfare in the Silent Cinema: Comedies and Melodramas of Woman Suffragism," in *HWUS,* vol. 19, pt. 2, pp. 515–539.

60. A. Elizabeth Taylor, *The Woman Suffrage Movement in Tennessee* (New York: Octagon, 1978), pp. 86–89.

61. Buhle, *Women and American Socialism, 1870–1920,* pp. 229–239; Ronald Schaffer, "The New York City Woman Suffrage Party, 1909–1919," in *HWUS,* vol. 19, pt. 2, pp. 453–471.

62. T. A. Larson, "The Woman Suffrage Movement in Washington," in *HWUS,* vol. 19, pt. 1, p. 348.

63. Ronald Schaffer, "The Montana Woman Suffrage Campaign, 1911–14," in *HWUS,* vol. 19, pt. 1, pp. 352–366.

64. Ibid., p. 365.

65. Naomi Black, *Social Feminism* (Ithaca, N.Y.: Cornell University Press, 1989), pp. 31–39, 53–62.

66. Ronald Schaffer, "The Problem of Consciousness in the Woman Suffrage Movement: A California Perspective," in *HWUS,* vol. 19, pt. 2, pp. 367–391.

67. Ibid., p. 380.

68. Wilda M. Smith, "A Half Century of Struggle: Gaining Woman Suffrage in Kansas," in *HWUS,* vol. 19, pt. 1, p. 142.

69. Steven M. Buechler, *Transformation of the Woman Suffrage Movement: The Case of Illinois, 1850–1892* (New Brunswick, N.J.: Rutgers University Press, 1986), pp. 148–167, 174–182.

70. Flexner, *Century of Struggle,* pp. 269–270.

71. Eileen R. Rausch, "'Let Ohio Women Vote': The Years to Victory, 1900–1920" (Ph.D. diss., University of Notre Dame, October 1984), pp. 35–65, quote on p. 61.

72. Fox, "History of Equal Suffrage," pp. 90–99.

73. Genevieve G. McBride, *On Wisconsin Women: Working for Their Rights from Settlement to Suffrage* (Madison: University of Wisconsin Press, 1993), pp. 189–197; Alene L. Sloan, *Some Aspects of the Woman Suffrage Movement in Indiana* (Ann Arbor: University Microfilms International, 1982), pp. 123, 133.

74. Marilyn Grant, "The 1912 Suffrage Referendum: An Exercise in Political Action," in *HWUS,* vol. 19, pt. 1, pp. 291–315. See esp. pp. 306–309. This is a study of the Wisconsin movement.

75. Felice D. Gordon, *After Winning: The Legacy of the New Jersey Suffragists, 1920–1947* (New Brunswick, NJ: Rutgers University Press, 1986), pp. 18–19.

76. Carole Nichols, *Votes and More for Women: Suffrage and After in Connecti-*

cut (New York: Haworth, 1983), pp. 12–13. On ties with organized labor, see pp. 24–29.

77. Schaffer, "New York City Woman Suffrage Party," p. 466.

78. On the suffragists' alliances with the machines, see John D. Buenker, "The Urban Political Machine and Woman Suffrage: A Study in Political Adaptability," *The Historian* 33 (1971): 264; Buenker, *Urban Liberalism and Progressive Reform* (New York: Norton & Company, 1973), p. 161; and Schaffer, "New York City Woman Suffrage Party," p. 270. On the Eastern European Jews, see Elinor Lerner, "Jewish Involvement in the New York City Woman Suffrage Movement," *American Jewish History,* vol. 70, no. 4 (1981): 442–61.

79. Patricia O'Keefe Easton, "Woman Suffrage in South Dakota: The Final Decade, 1911–1920," in *HWUS,* vol. 19, pt. 2, pp. 617–637.

80. Scott and Scott, *One Half the People,* p. 167.

81. Marjorie Spruill Wheeler, *New Women of the New South: The Leaders of the Woman Suffrage Movement in the Southern States* (New York: Oxford University Press, 1993), pp. 127–131.

82. Aileen S. Kraditor, "Tactical Problems of the Woman-Suffrage Movement in the South," in *HWUS,* vol. 19, pt. 1, pp. 272–290, esp. pp. 277–278, 288. Wheeler, *New Women,* p. 171.

83. Mary Martha Thomas, *The New Woman in Alabama: Social Reforms and Suffrage, 1890–1920* (Tuscaloosa: University of Alabama Press, 1992), pp. 154–155.

84. Strom, "Leadership and Tactics," pp. 172–191.

85. Taylor, *Woman Suffrage Movement in Tennessee,* pp. 70–74, 91–95.

86. Joseph F. Mahoney, "Woman Suffrage and the Urban Masses," in *HWUS,* vol. 19, pt. 2, pp. 413–436, quote on p. 429.

87. Eileen L. McDonagh and H. Douglas Price, "Woman Suffrage in the Progressive Era: Patterns of Opposition and Support in Referenda Voting, 1910–1918," *American Political Science Review* 79 (1985): 431.

88. David Morgan, *Suffragists and Democrats* (Lansing: Michigan State University Press, 1972).

89. *Congressional Quarterly's Guide to Congress,* 4th ed. (Washington: Congressional Quarterly, 1991), pp. 50–51.

90. Ibid., p. 19.

91. "The National American Convention of 1900," *HWS,* 4:370.

92. Wheeler, *New Women,* pp. 133–171.

93. "Statement by Mrs. Carrie Chapman Catt at Senate Hearing in 1910," *HWS,* 5:745–746.

94. "Address of Mrs. Carrie Chapman Catt at Senate Hearing, Dec. 15, 1915" *HWS,* 5:752–753.

95. Carrie Chapman Catt, "The New York Party," pp. 29–30.

96. Flexner, *Century of Struggle,* pp. 275–279.

97. Ibid., p. 289.

98. Maud Wood Park, *The Front Door Lobby* (Boston: Beacon, 1960), pp. 26–28, 38–39, 66. The persuasion tactics were carefully and elaborately worked out: delegations were instructed to write and call on the representatives as *individuals* rather than merely as a group member. Moreover, delegations were asked "to choose, if possible, women whose families have political influence in the man's own party and who are representative of the different sections of his district." Finally the NAWSA emphasized the importance of "work by men in the home Districts" (p. 66, emphasis in text).

99. Ibid., p. 108.

100. Ibid., pp. 128–129.

101. Ibid., pp. 128–131.

102. Morgan, *Suffragists and Democrats,* pp. 129–144.

103. Park, *Front Door Lobby,* p. 269.

104. Edward Pendleton Herring, *Group Representation before Congress* (Baltimore, Md.: The Johns Hopkins University Press, 1929), pp. 194–95.

Conclusion

1. Carrie Chapman Catt, "Why the Southeastern States of the U.S. Refused Suffrage to Women" (1920). Unpublished notes. Catt MSS. Emphasis added.

2. Ibid.

3. Anne Firor Scott and Andrew MacKay Scott, *One Half the People: The Fight for Woman Suffrage* (Urbana: University of Illinois Press, 1982), p. 47.

4. William O'Neill, *Everyone Was Brave: A History of Feminism in America* (New York: Quadrangle, 1971), p. 75.

5. Judith N. Shklar, *American Citizenship: The Quest for Inclusion* (Cambridge, Mass.: Harvard University Press, 1991), p. 60.

6. Ibid., pp. 5–9.

7. Jane Mansbridge, *Why We Lost the ERA* (Chicago: University of Chicago Press, 1986), pp. 23–28, 38–39, 173–186.

8. Scott and Scott, *One Half the People,* pp. 166–168.

9. Rogers Smith, "'One United People': Second Class Female Citizenship and the American Quest for Community," *Yale Journal of Law and the Humanities* 1 (1989): 282–293. Smith will provide a comprehensive account of dilemmas of liberal egalitarianism in his forthcoming book, *Civic Ideals: Conflicting Visions of Citizenship in American Law* (New Haven, Conn.: Yale University Press, 1996).

Index